PhD

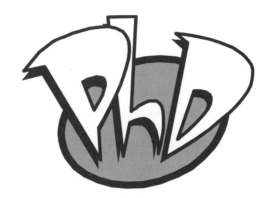

Other books by Jorge Cham:

"Life is Tough and then You Graduate: The Second Piled Higher and Deeper Comic Strip Collection"

"Scooped! The Third Piled Higher and Deeper Comic Strip Collection"

"Academic Stimulus Package: The Fourth Piled Higher and Deeper Comic Strip Collection"

Piled Higher and Deeper

A Graduate Student
Comic Strip Collection

by

Jorge Cham

Piled Higher and Deeper Publishing
www.phdcomics.com

"Piled Higher and Deeper" the comic strip originally appeared in The Stanford Daily Newspaper at Stanford University.

Cover Design: Carmen Cham
Publishers: Jorge Cham and Lucinda Shih
Editorial Advice: Kim Lewis Brown
Legal Consultation: Matthew David Brozik

www.phdcomics.com

Printed in Canada
Ninth Printing, October 2011

ISBN-10: 0-9721695-0-4
ISBN-13: 978-0972169509

Library of Congress Control Number: 2002107808

For Suelika

Foreword

It is 4am in the morning, and I am procrastinating. There is a group meeting in a few hours and a guest lecture later in the afternoon that I need to prepare for. Camera-ready copies of two papers I am first-author in are due in a few days. I am supposed to defend my thesis in two months, but I haven't written a single chapter yet. And yet, I find myself working day and night to get this comic strip collection to print. Perhaps this has something to do with the fact that my advisor is on sabbatical in Europe.

Piled Higher and Deeper the comic strip started in a conversation over dinner with my brother (who I will always argue is the better cartoonist). Between stuffed chicken wings and pad thai, he was complaining about how college comic strips are limited by the silly problems that undergrads face, and didn't they know that grad school is where true pain really begins? Now, at this point, I had never really drawn a comic strip (not counting, of course, the few pages of "ShazHam, the mild-mannered pig-turned-thunder god" or "Guppy-man, who wields his fan-tastic yo-yo to fight crime" that I drew in the sixth grade), but I had just recently read the 25-year Doonesbury retrospective and I was inspired.

Five years later, with Chapter 1 of my thesis "almost started" and with the prospect of becoming a professor myself, I am thankful to the people who have encouraged me to express my anxieties as cartoons and speech balloons in this comic strip: Suelika, without whom this comic would just be about some bitter old grad student. My labmates and friends, who gave constant inspiration for the characters in the comic: Michael C., Sanjay, Maria, Beth, Michael T., Allison, Chris, Weston, Krista, Sean and Jonathan. My advisor, who was never a model for "Prof. Smith" and who has always been supportive and even a fan of the comic himself. My family, for their love. Finally, I am thankful to the fans, who, despite my lack of effort to advertise this comic strip, have helped spread the comic's website to the point where grad students from over 1000 universities and from around the world (including countries like Brazil, Turkey, India and Egypt) now come to *www.phdcomics.com* for their weekly dose of procrastination.

Back to my present situation, maybe I *am* procrastinating from the things that I "should" be doing. In graduate school, there is always something that we "should" be doing. But the truth of the matter is that I wouldn't want to be doing anything else right now. In addition to being dutiful, rigorous, rational scholars, we all have our secret lives. Some of us draw comic strips, others make blown-glass art, play the jazz oboe, or even practice competitive roller-skate dancing. Graduate school is as much about discovering truth in science and culture as it is about discovering truth in ourselves.

So get out there and procrastinate. Procrastinate with purpose and with pride.

Jorge Cham
Stanford University, May 2002

www.phdcomics.com

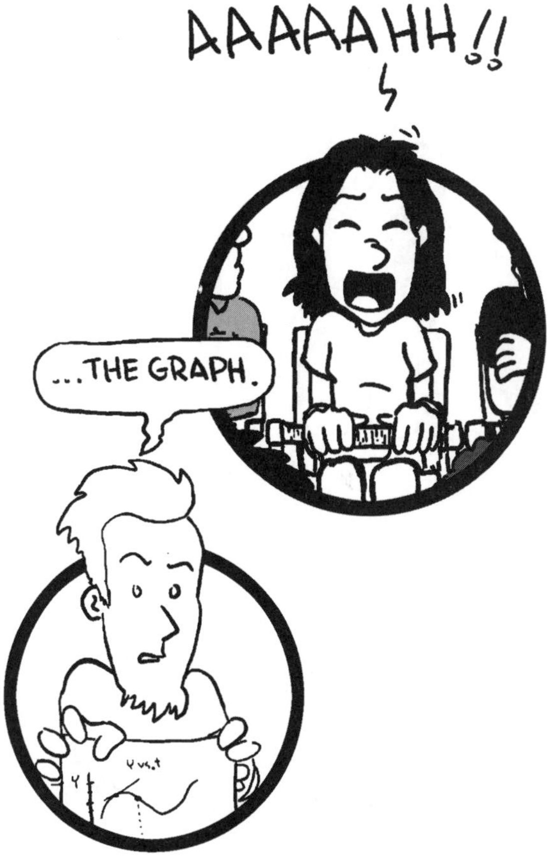
AAAAAHH!!
...THE GRAPH.

YEAR ONE

1997-1998

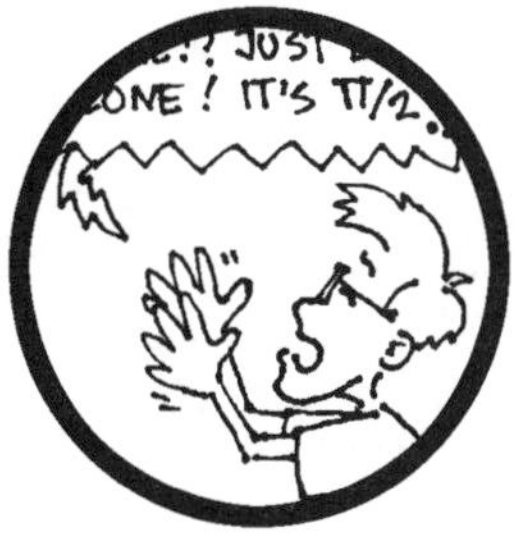

MY FIRST CLASS AT STANFORD...
SO THESE ARE MY FELLOW GRAD STUDENTS. THEY LOOK PRETTY NORMAL...
THEY'RE NOT THAT INTIMIDATING. THEY'RE JUST...
copyright © 1997 jorge cham
...VERY CLOSE.

HI MOM... SORRY I HAVEN'T CALLED IN A WHILE, I...
GRAD SCHOOL'S BEEN HARD, EVERYBODY'S SO SMART HERE... AND THE LOANS... I THINK I...
WHAT?
copyright © 1997 jorge cham
NO, MOM, I HAVEN'T SEEN HER OR ANYBODY FAMOUS ON CAMPUS YET.

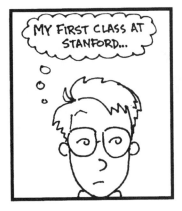

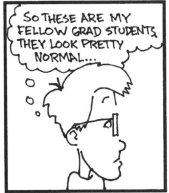

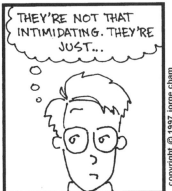

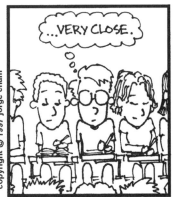

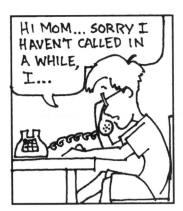

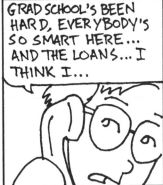

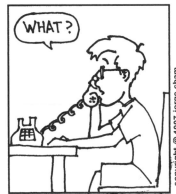

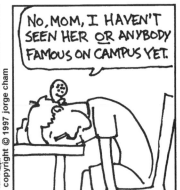

4 A.M.- HOMEWORK SET #4...
WHY ARE WE DOING THIS?
YOU MEAN, WHY ARE WE SUBMITTING OURSELVES TO GRAD SCHOOL INSTEAD OF WORKING OUT THERE, GETTING RICH, GETTING ENOUGH SLEEP AND ACTUALLY ENJOYING LIFE?
I DON'T KNOW, MY FRIEND. I DON'T KNOW...
NO, I MEAN WHY ARE WE DOING THE PROBLEMS FROM THE WRONG CHAPTER.
copyright © 1997 jorge cham

HI, WELCOME TO E80's PROBLEM SESSION. I'M YOUR T.A.
I'M NOT GOING TO GIVE YOU ANY ANSWERS TO THE HOMEWORK, JUST HELP YOU GET STARTED. ANY QUESTIONS?
CAN WE ASSUME THAT $\omega_n = \sqrt{\frac{k}{m}}$?
BUT WHY!?
WHY IS IT IMPORTANT?
I DON'T GET IT.
copyright © 1997 jorge cham
π/2!! THE ANSWER IS π/2! WHAT DO YOU WANT FROM ME!? JUST LEAVE ME ALONE! IT'S π/2!!

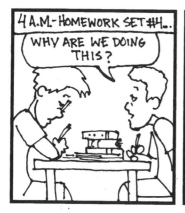

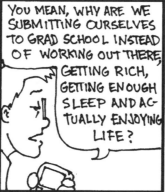

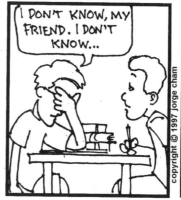

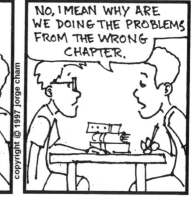

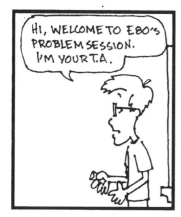

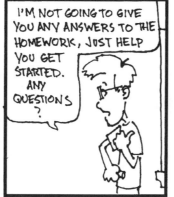

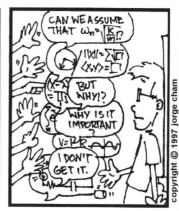

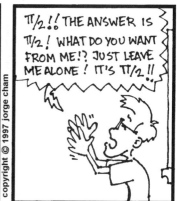

HERE ARE THE HOMEWORKS FOR YOU TO GRADE.
I WANT THE GRADES TO HAVE A GAUSSIAN DISTRIBUTION WITH AN 81.079 MEAN AND A 5.742 STANDARD DEVIATION.
ALSO, MAKE EACH QUESTION WORTH 10 POINTS AND GIVE PARTIAL CREDIT.
copyright © 1997 jorge cham
THEY'RE TRUE/FALSE QUESTIONS, SIR.
CAN YOU DO IT OVER THE WEEKEND?

TRICK OR TREAT!!
HOW CUTE!
HERE YOU GO...
DON'T YOU HAVE ANY CASH?
NO...
THAT'S OK. WE TAKE VISA AND ATM.
copyright © 1997 jorge cham

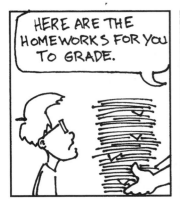

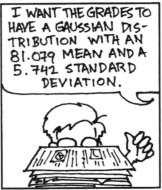

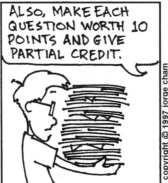

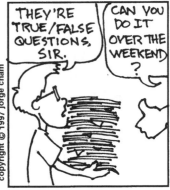

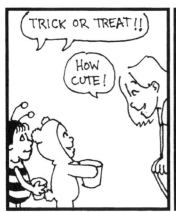

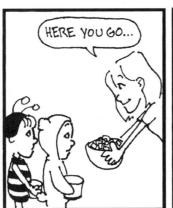

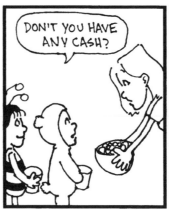

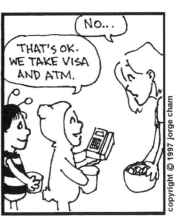

HEY! A FAMILIAR FACE! HOW ARE YOU
PRETTY GOOD, HOW IS STANFORD TREATING YA?
NOT TOO BAD. I THINK I'M GETTING THE HANG OF I...
POW!
copyright © 1997 jorge cham
WHAT HAPPENED ...?
IT'S THE QUARTER SYSTEM. BETTER GET USED TO IT. HERE COMES WINTER QUARTER ...

YOU'VE GOT TO ADMIT, THOUGH, BEING A WOMAN IN ENGINEERING...
THE DATING ODDS ARE IN YOUR FAVOR
YEAH...
THE ODDS ARE GOOD...
copyright © 1997 jorge cham
BUT THE GOODS ARE ODD.
SNIFF SNIFF!

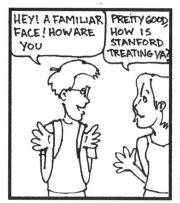

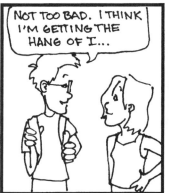

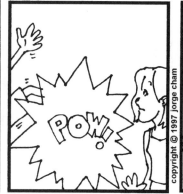

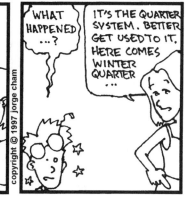

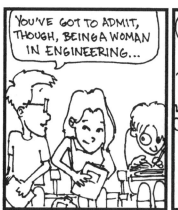

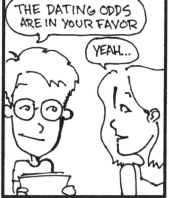

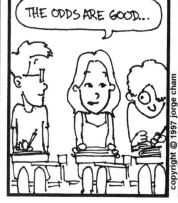

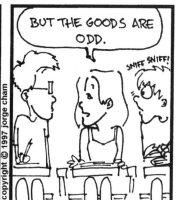

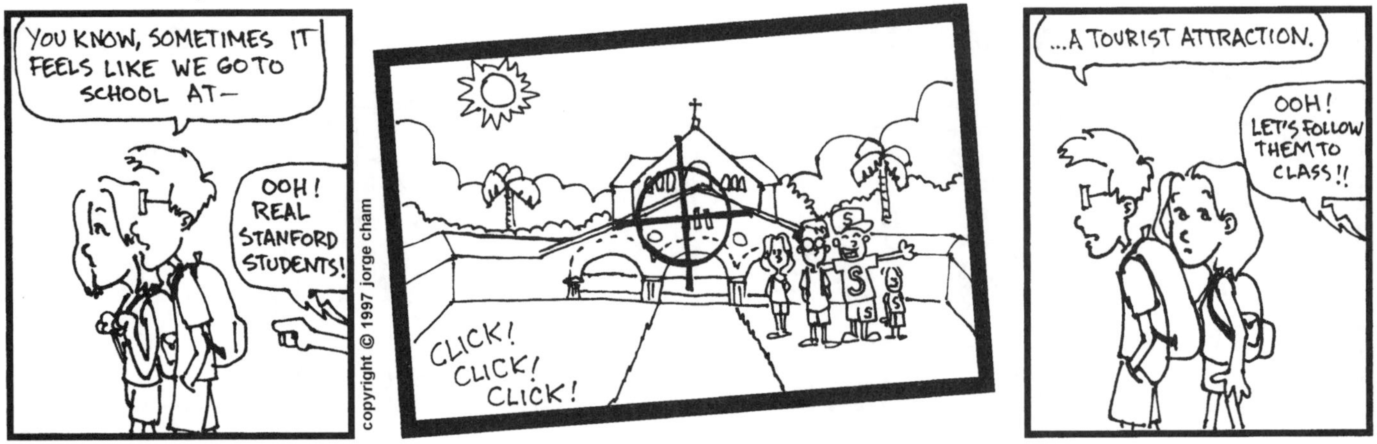
YOU KNOW, SOMETIMES IT FEELS LIKE WE GO TO SCHOOL AT—
OOH! REAL STANFORD STUDENTS!
copyright © 1997 jorge cham
CLICK! CLICK! CLICK!
...A TOURIST ATTRACTION.
OOH! LET'S FOLLOW THEM TO CLASS!!

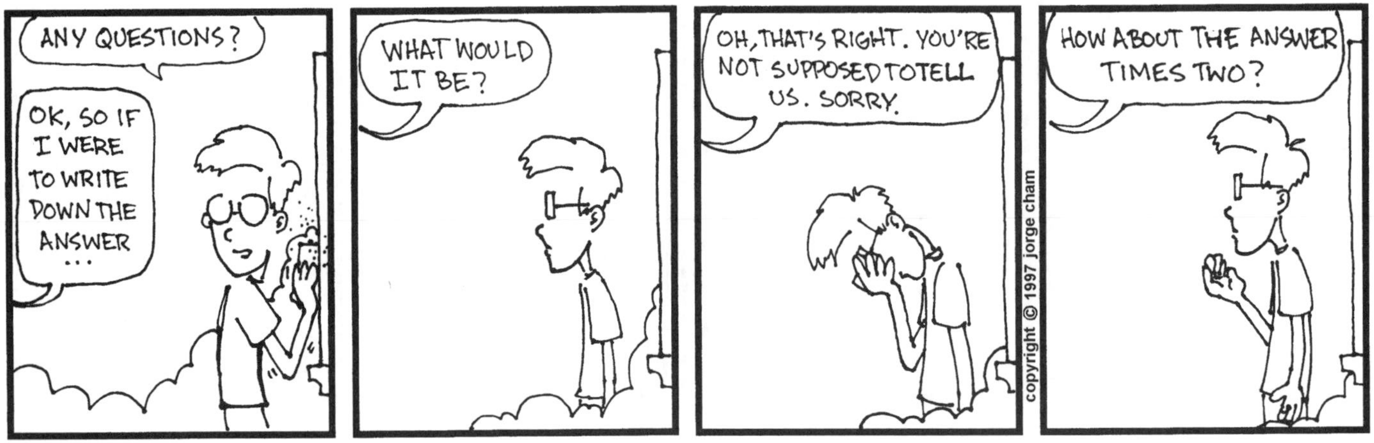
ANY QUESTIONS?
OK, SO IF I WERE TO WRITE DOWN THE ANSWER ...
WHAT WOULD IT BE?
OH, THAT'S RIGHT. YOU'RE NOT SUPPOSED TO TELL US. SORRY.
copyright © 1997 jorge cham
HOW ABOUT THE ANSWER TIMES TWO?

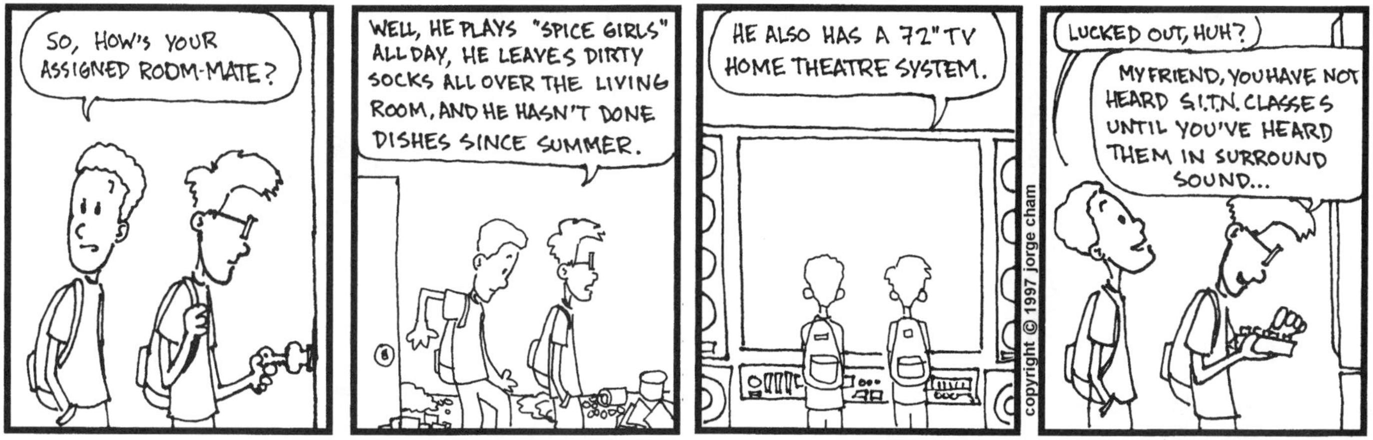
SO, HOW'S YOUR ASSIGNED ROOM-MATE?
WELL, HE PLAYS "SPICE GIRLS" ALL DAY, HE LEAVES DIRTY SOCKS ALL OVER THE LIVING ROOM, AND HE HASN'T DONE DISHES SINCE SUMMER.
HE ALSO HAS A 72" TV HOME THEATRE SYSTEM.
copyright © 1997 jorge cham
LUCKED OUT, HUH?
MY FRIEND, YOU HAVE NOT HEARD S.I.T.N. CLASSES UNTIL YOU'VE HEARD THEM IN SURROUND SOUND...

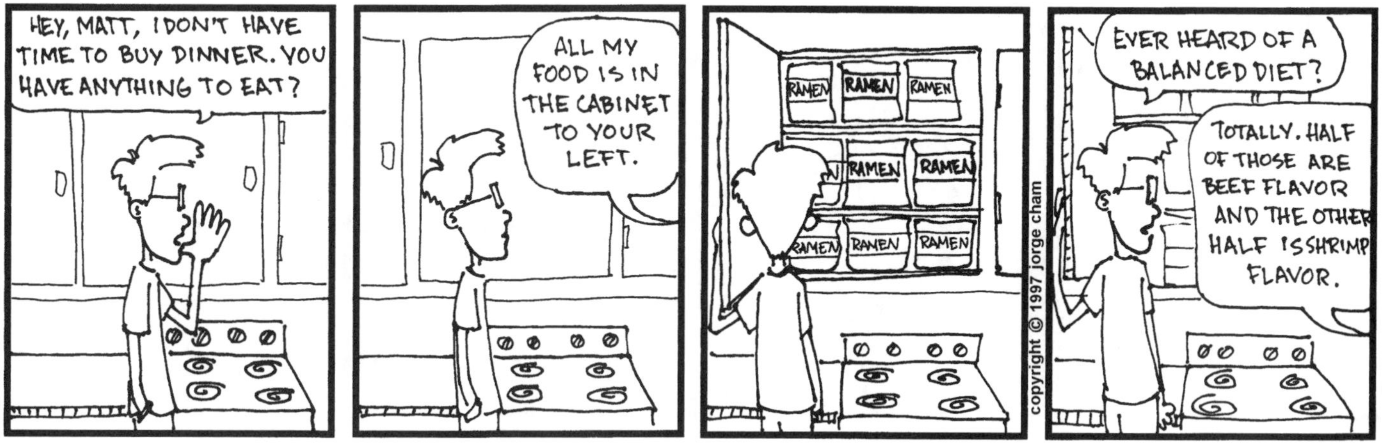
HEY, MATT, I DON'T HAVE TIME TO BUY DINNER. YOU HAVE ANYTHING TO EAT?
ALL MY FOOD IS IN THE CABINET TO YOUR LEFT.
RAMEN
copyright © 1997 jorge cham
EVER HEARD OF A BALANCED DIET?
TOTALLY. HALF OF THOSE ARE BEEF FLAVOR AND THE OTHER HALF IS SHRIMP FLAVOR.

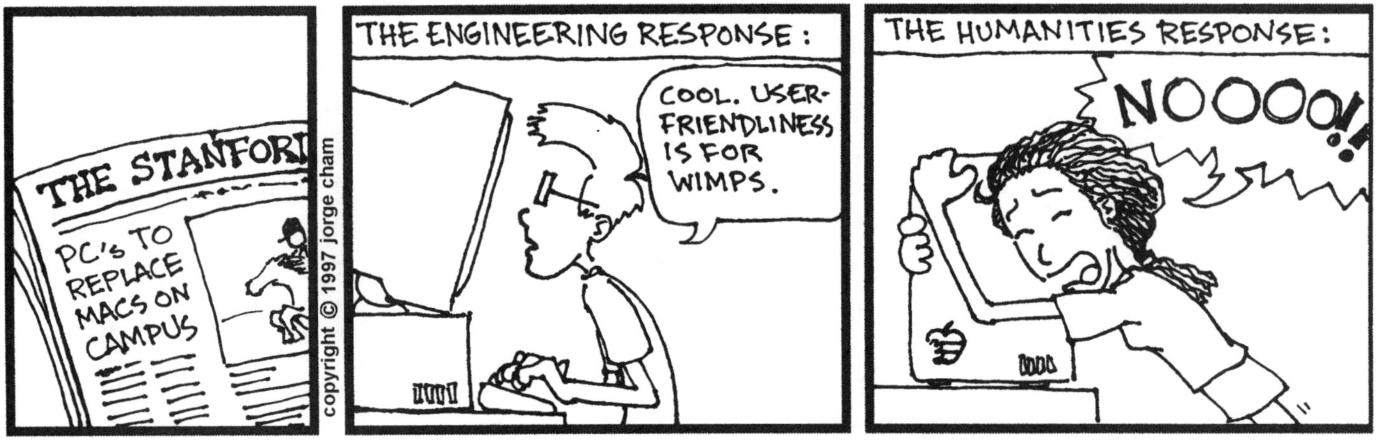
THE STANFORD
PC's TO REPLACE MACS ON CAMPUS
copyright © 1997 jorge cham
THE ENGINEERING RESPONSE:
COOL. USER-FRIENDLINESS IS FOR WIMPS.
THE HUMANITIES RESPONSE:
NOOOO!!

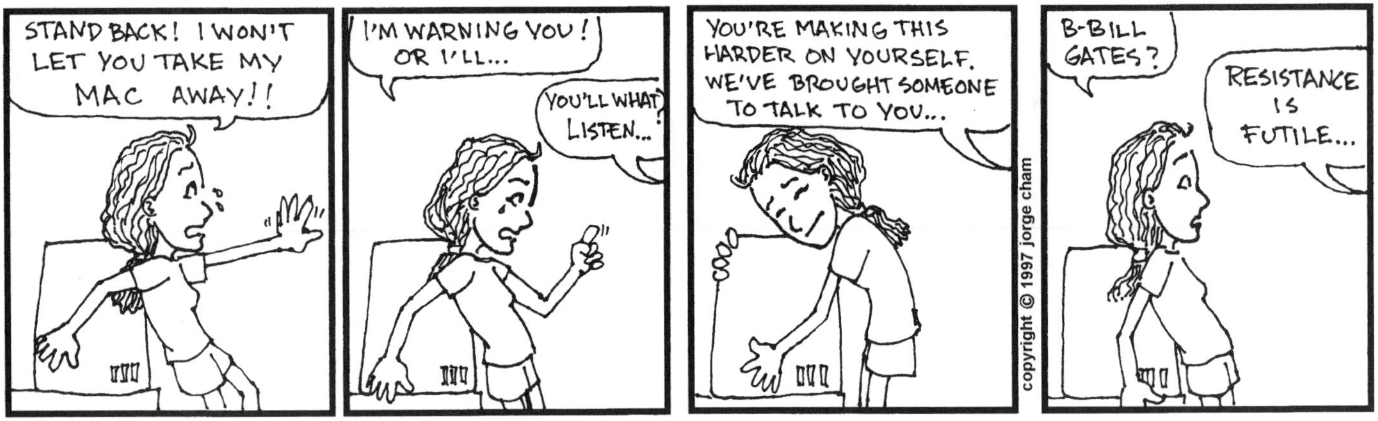
STAND BACK! I WON'T LET YOU TAKE MY MAC AWAY!!
I'M WARNING YOU! OR I'LL...
YOU'LL WHAT? LISTEN...
YOU'RE MAKING THIS HARDER ON YOURSELF. WE'VE BROUGHT SOMEONE TO TALK TO YOU...
copyright © 1997 jorge cham
B-BILL GATES?
RESISTANCE IS FUTILE...

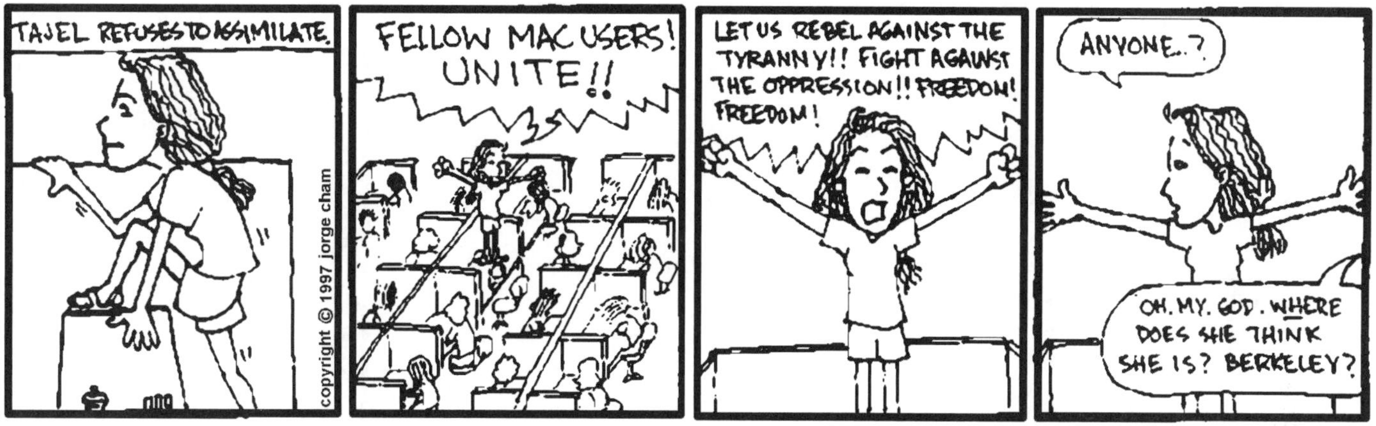
TAJEL REFUSES TO ASSIMILATE.
copyright © 1997 jorge cham
FELLOW MAC USERS! UNITE!!
LET US REBEL AGAINST THE TYRANNY!! FIGHT AGAINST THE OPPRESSION!! FREEDOM! FREEDOM!
ANYONE..?
OH. MY. GOD. WHERE DOES SHE THINK SHE IS? BERKELEY?

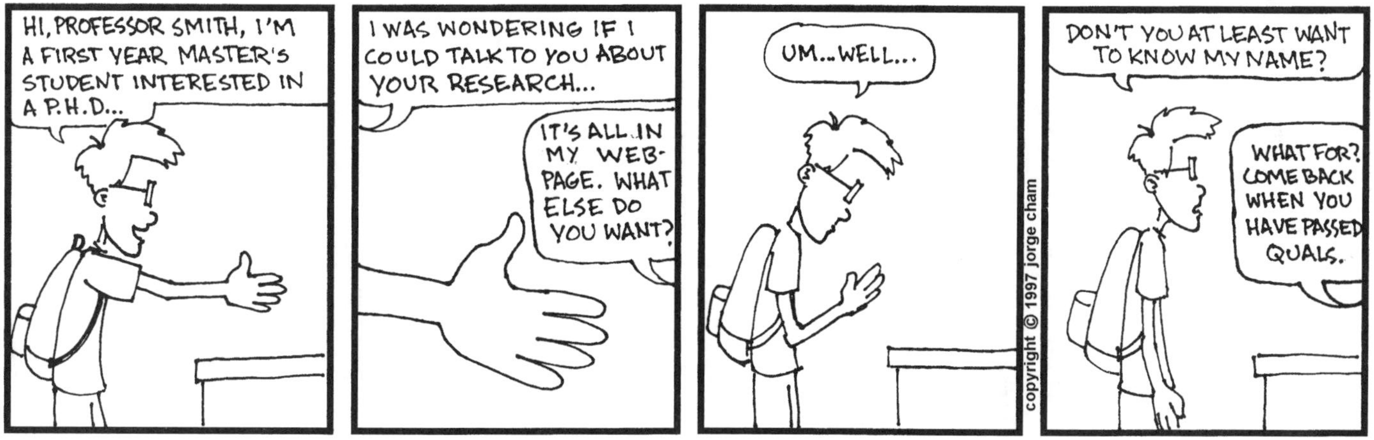
HI, PROFESSOR SMITH, I'M A FIRST YEAR MASTER'S STUDENT INTERESTED IN A P.H.D...
I WAS WONDERING IF I COULD TALK TO YOU ABOUT YOUR RESEARCH...
IT'S ALL IN MY WEB-PAGE. WHAT ELSE DO YOU WANT?
UM...WELL...
copyright © 1997 jorge cham
DON'T YOU AT LEAST WANT TO KNOW MY NAME?
WHAT FOR? COME BACK WHEN YOU HAVE PASSED QUALS.

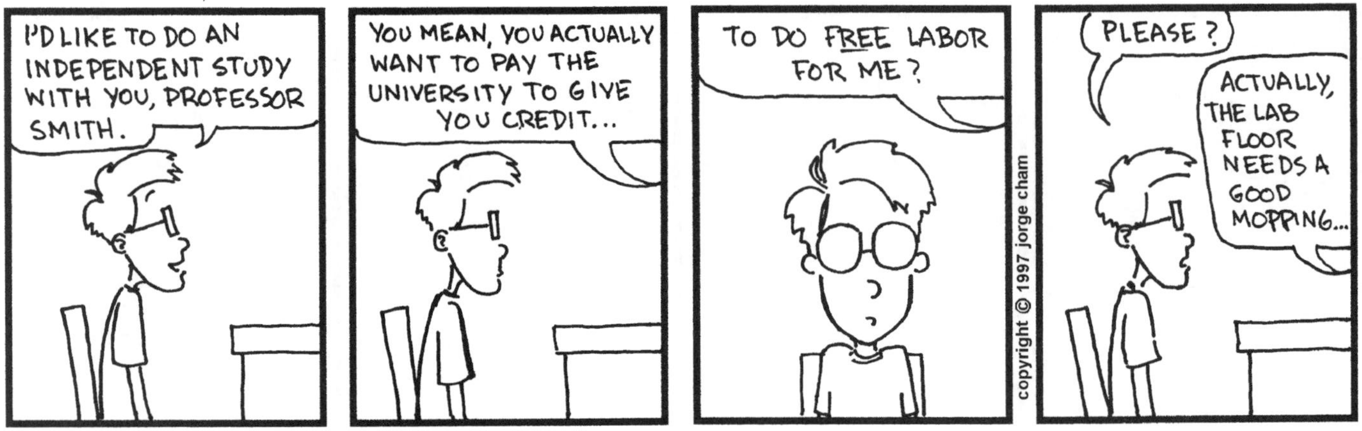
I'D LIKE TO DO AN INDEPENDENT STUDY WITH YOU, PROFESSOR SMITH.
YOU MEAN, YOU ACTUALLY WANT TO PAY THE UNIVERSITY TO GIVE YOU CREDIT...
TO DO FREE LABOR FOR ME?
copyright © 1997 jorge cham
PLEASE?
ACTUALLY, THE LAB FLOOR NEEDS A GOOD MOPPING...

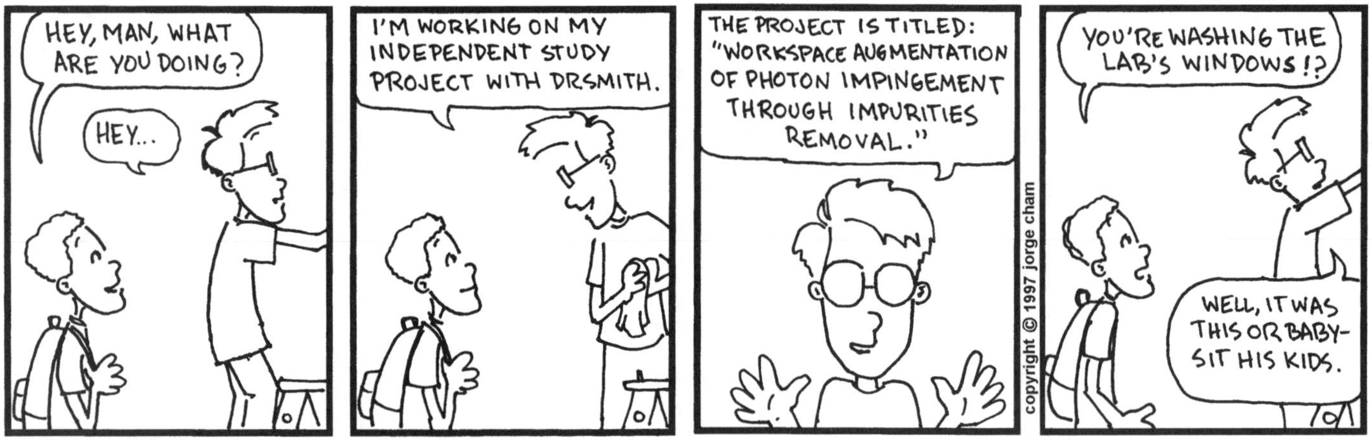
HEY, MAN, WHAT ARE YOU DOING?
HEY...
I'M WORKING ON MY INDEPENDENT STUDY PROJECT WITH DR SMITH.
THE PROJECT IS TITLED: "WORKSPACE AUGMENTATION OF PHOTON IMPINGEMENT THROUGH IMPURITIES REMOVAL."
copyright © 1997 jorge cham
YOU'RE WASHING THE LAB'S WINDOWS!?
WELL, IT WAS THIS OR BABY-SIT HIS KIDS.

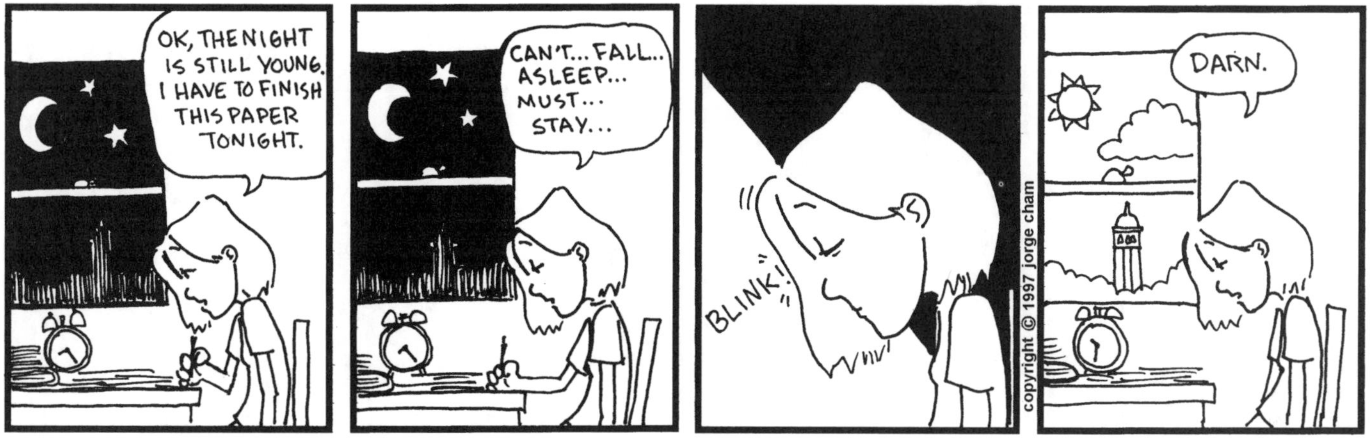
OK, THE NIGHT IS STILL YOUNG. I HAVE TO FINISH THIS PAPER TONIGHT.
CAN'T... FALL... ASLEEP... MUST... STAY...
BLINK!
copyright © 1997 jorge cham
DARN.

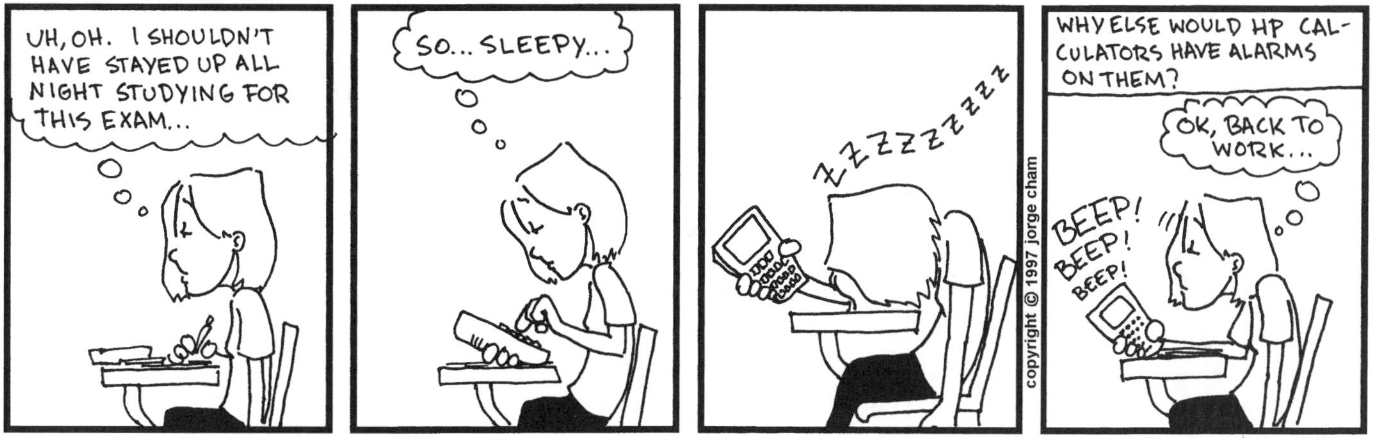
UH, OH. I SHOULDN'T HAVE STAYED UP ALL NIGHT STUDYING FOR THIS EXAM...
SO... SLEEPY...
ZZZZZZZZZZ
copyright © 1997 jorge cham
WHY ELSE WOULD HP CALCULATORS HAVE ALARMS ON THEM?
BEEP! BEEP! BEEP!
OK, BACK TO WORK...

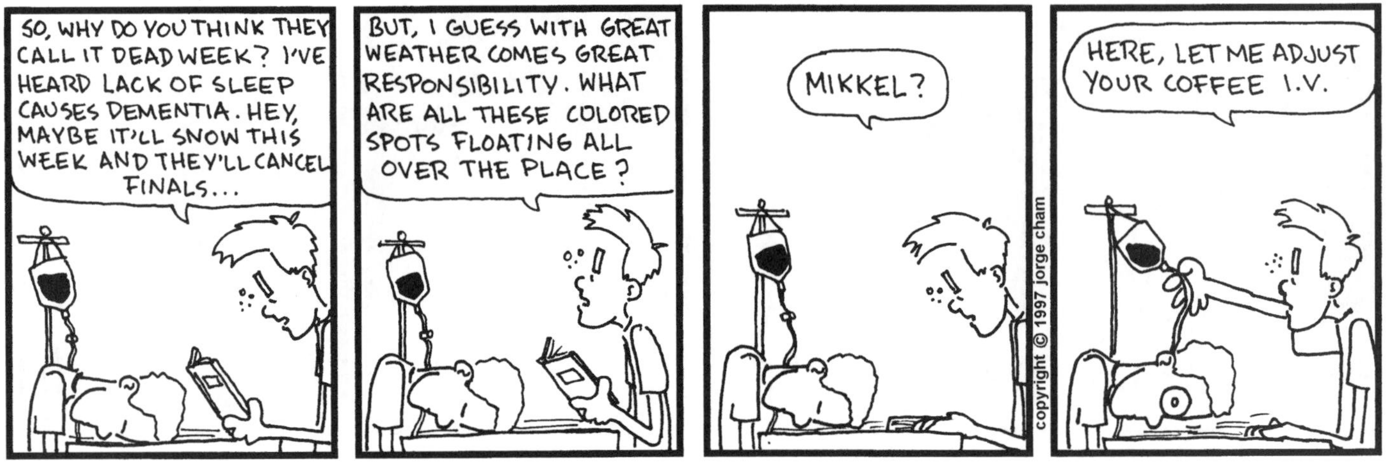
SO, WHY DO YOU THINK THEY CALL IT DEAD WEEK? I'VE HEARD LACK OF SLEEP CAUSES DEMENTIA. HEY, MAYBE IT'LL SNOW THIS WEEK AND THEY'LL CANCEL FINALS...
BUT, I GUESS WITH GREAT WEATHER COMES GREAT RESPONSIBILITY. WHAT ARE ALL THESE COLORED SPOTS FLOATING ALL OVER THE PLACE?
MIKKEL?
copyright © 1997 jorge cham
HERE, LET ME ADJUST YOUR COFFEE I.V.

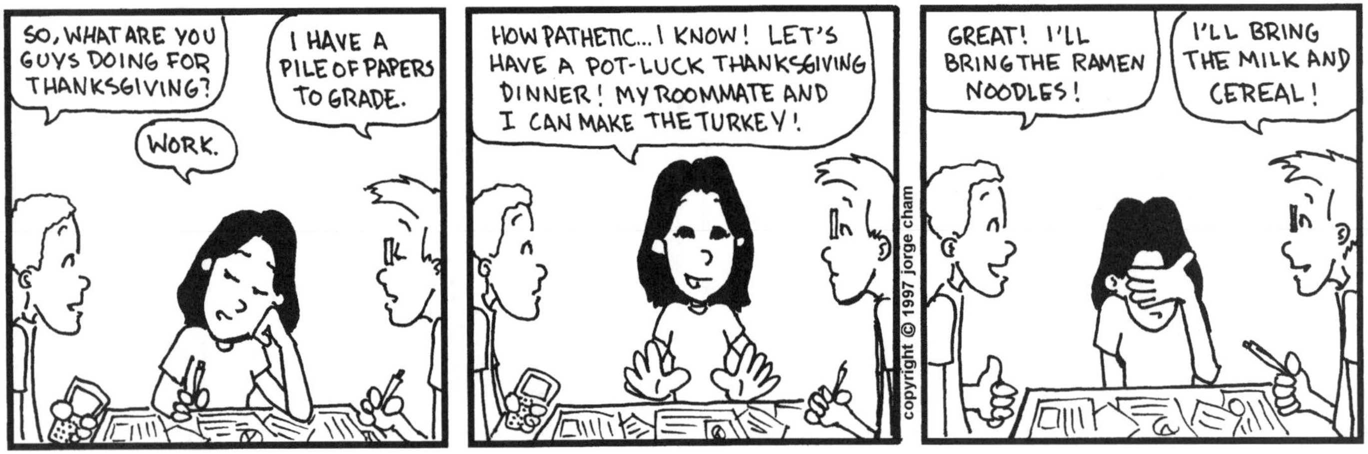
SO, WHAT ARE YOU GUYS DOING FOR THANKSGIVING?
WORK.
I HAVE A PILE OF PAPERS TO GRADE.
HOW PATHETIC... I KNOW! LET'S HAVE A POT-LUCK THANKSGIVING DINNER! MY ROOMMATE AND I CAN MAKE THE TURKEY!
copyright © 1997 jorge cham
GREAT! I'LL BRING THE RAMEN NOODLES!
I'LL BRING THE MILK AND CEREAL!

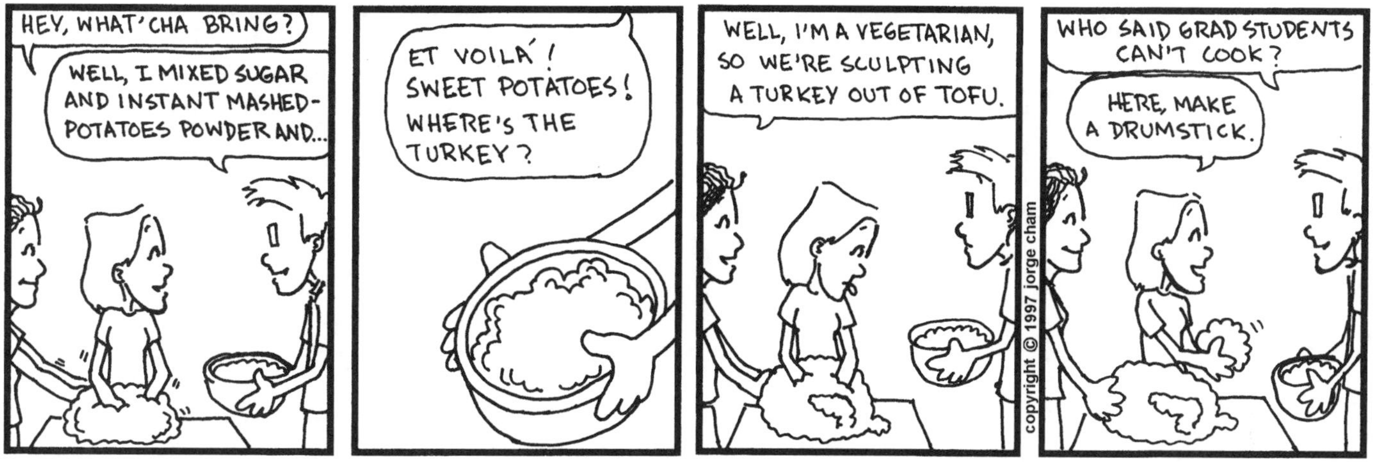
HEY, WHAT'CHA BRING?
WELL, I MIXED SUGAR AND INSTANT MASHED-POTATOES POWDER AND...
ET VOILÀ! SWEET POTATOES! WHERE'S THE TURKEY?
WELL, I'M A VEGETARIAN, SO WE'RE SCULPTING A TURKEY OUT OF TOFU.
copyright © 1997 jorge cham
WHO SAID GRAD STUDENTS CAN'T COOK?
HERE, MAKE A DRUMSTICK.

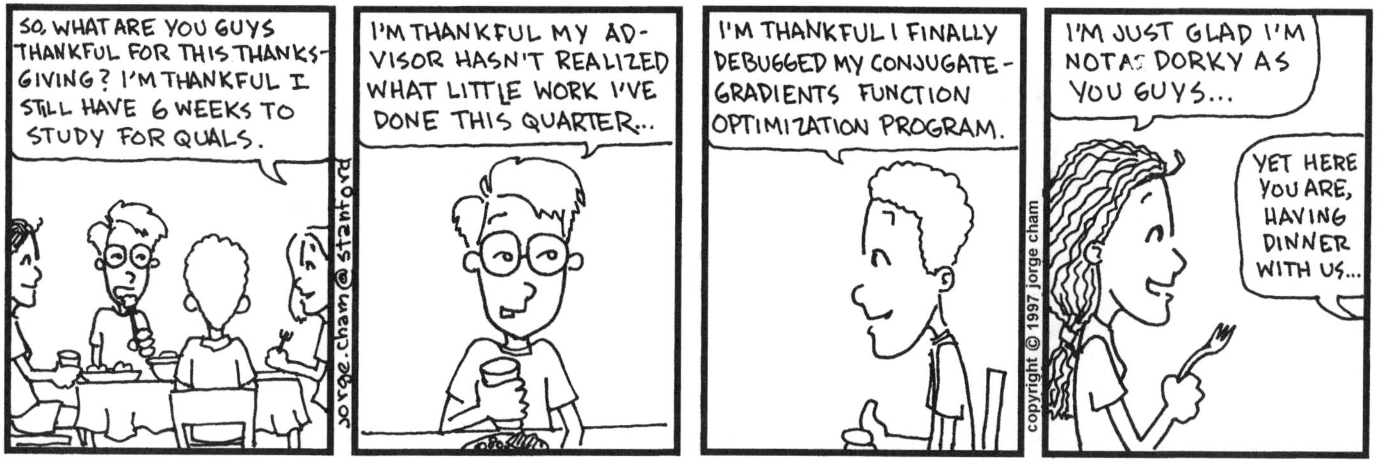
SO, WHAT ARE YOU GUYS THANKFUL FOR THIS THANKS-GIVING? I'M THANKFUL I STILL HAVE 6 WEEKS TO STUDY FOR QUALS.
jorge.cham@stanford
I'M THANKFUL MY AD-VISOR HASN'T REALIZED WHAT LITTLE WORK I'VE DONE THIS QUARTER...
I'M THANKFUL I FINALLY DEBUGGED MY CONJUGATE-GRADIENTS FUNCTION OPTIMIZATION PROGRAM.
copyright © 1997 jorge cham
I'M JUST GLAD I'M NOT AS DORKY AS YOU GUYS...
YET HERE YOU ARE, HAVING DINNER WITH US...

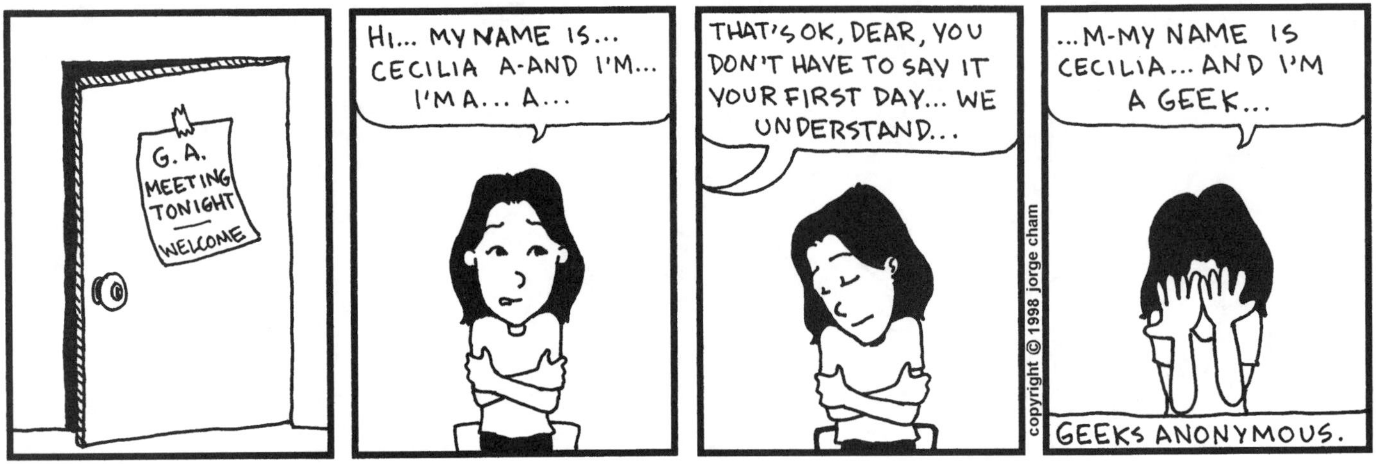
G. A. MEETING TONIGHT
WELCOME
HI... MY NAME IS... CECILIA A-AND I'M... I'M A... A...
THAT'S OK, DEAR, YOU DON'T HAVE TO SAY IT YOUR FIRST DAY... WE UNDERSTAND...
copyright © 1998 jorge cham
...M-MY NAME IS CECILIA... AND I'M A GEEK...
GEEKS ANONYMOUS.

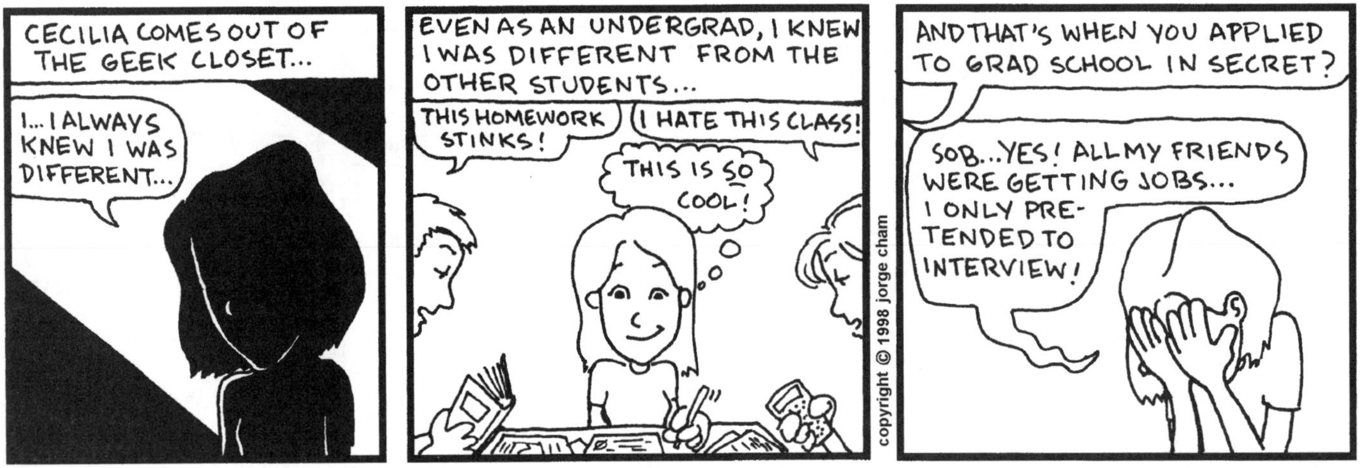
CECILIA COMES OUT OF THE GEEK CLOSET...
I... I ALWAYS KNEW I WAS DIFFERENT...
EVEN AS AN UNDERGRAD, I KNEW I WAS DIFFERENT FROM THE OTHER STUDENTS...
THIS HOMEWORK STINKS!
I HATE THIS CLASS!
THIS IS SO COOL!
copyright © 1998 jorge cham
AND THAT'S WHEN YOU APPLIED TO GRAD SCHOOL IN SECRET?
SOB... YES! ALL MY FRIENDS WERE GETTING JOBS... I ONLY PRE-TENDED TO INTERVIEW!

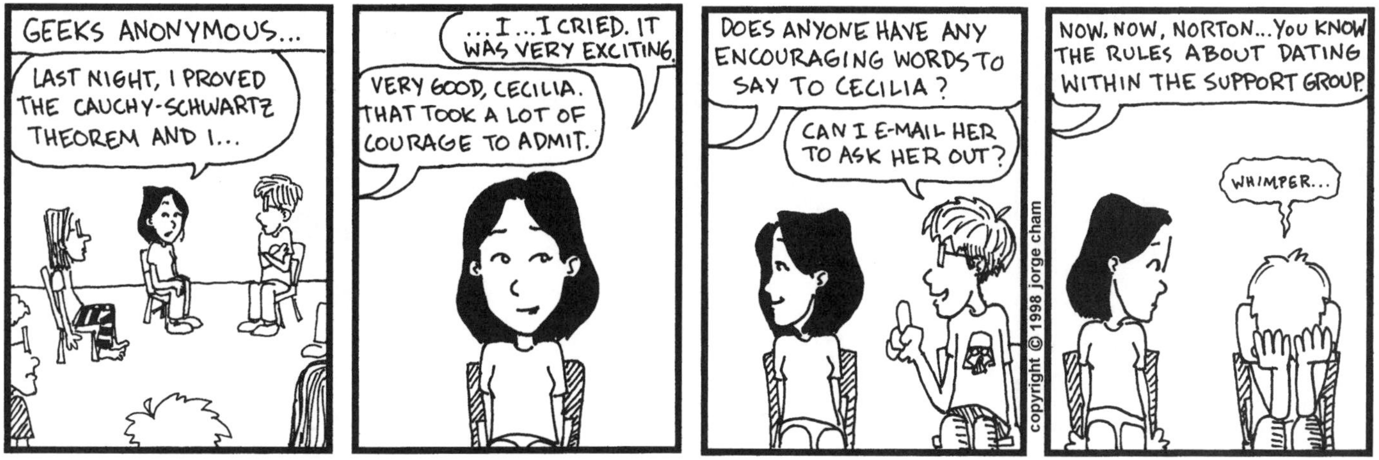
GEEKS ANONYMOUS...
LAST NIGHT, I PROVED THE CAUCHY-SCHWARTZ THEOREM AND I...
...I...I CRIED. IT WAS VERY EXCITING.
VERY GOOD, CECILIA. THAT TOOK A LOT OF COURAGE TO ADMIT.
DOES ANYONE HAVE ANY ENCOURAGING WORDS TO SAY TO CECILIA?
CAN I E-MAIL HER TO ASK HER OUT?
copyright © 1998 jorge cham
NOW, NOW, NORTON...YOU KNOW THE RULES ABOUT DATING WITHIN THE SUPPORT GROUP.
WHIMPER...

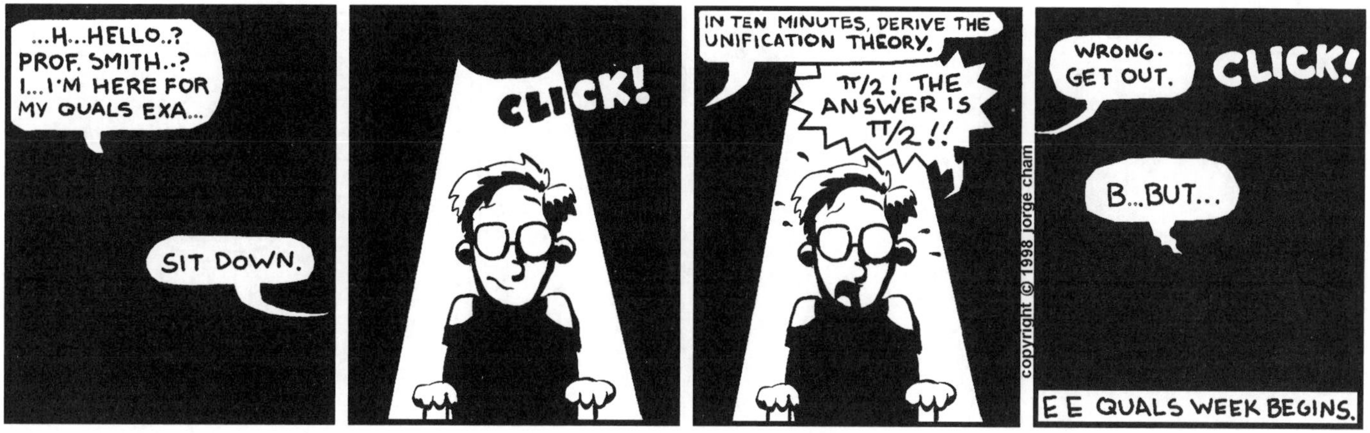
...H...HELLO..? PROF. SMITH..? I...I'M HERE FOR MY QUALS EXA...
SIT DOWN.
CLICK!
IN TEN MINUTES, DERIVE THE UNIFICATION THEORY.
π/2! THE ANSWER IS π/2!!
copyright © 1998 jorge cham
WRONG. GET OUT.
CLICK!
B...BUT...
E E QUALS WEEK BEGINS.

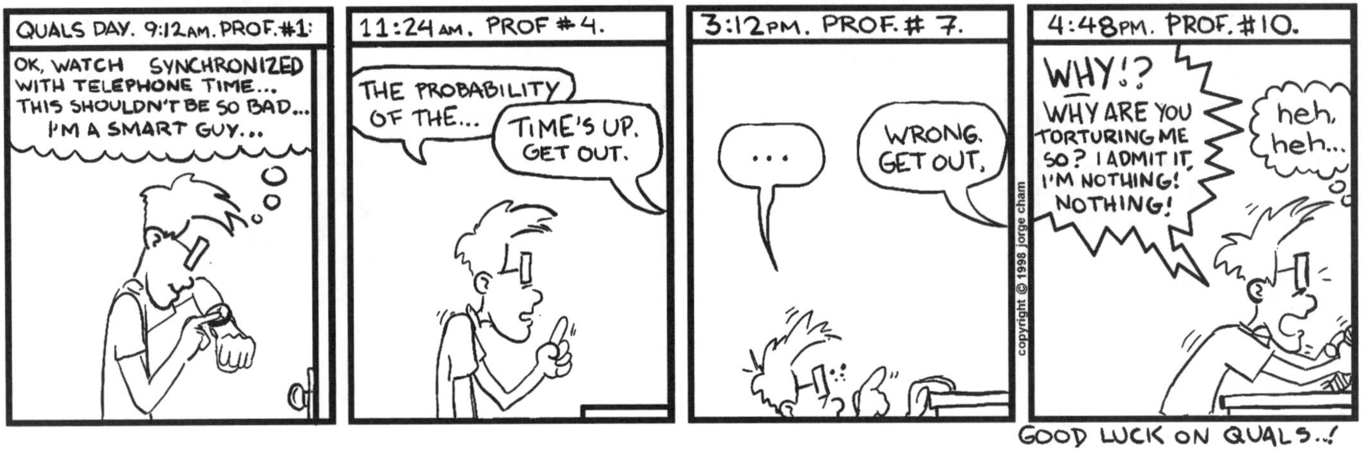
QUALS DAY. 9:12AM. PROF. #1:
OK, WATCH SYNCHRONIZED WITH TELEPHONE TIME... THIS SHOULDN'T BE SO BAD... I'M A SMART GUY...
11:24AM. PROF #4.
THE PROBABILITY OF THE...
TIME'S UP. GET OUT.
3:12PM. PROF. # 7.
...
WRONG. GET OUT.
copyright © 1998 jorge cham
4:48PM. PROF. #10.
WHY!?
WHY ARE YOU TORTURING ME SO? I ADMIT IT, I'M NOTHING! NOTHING!
heh, heh...
GOOD LUCK ON QUALS..!

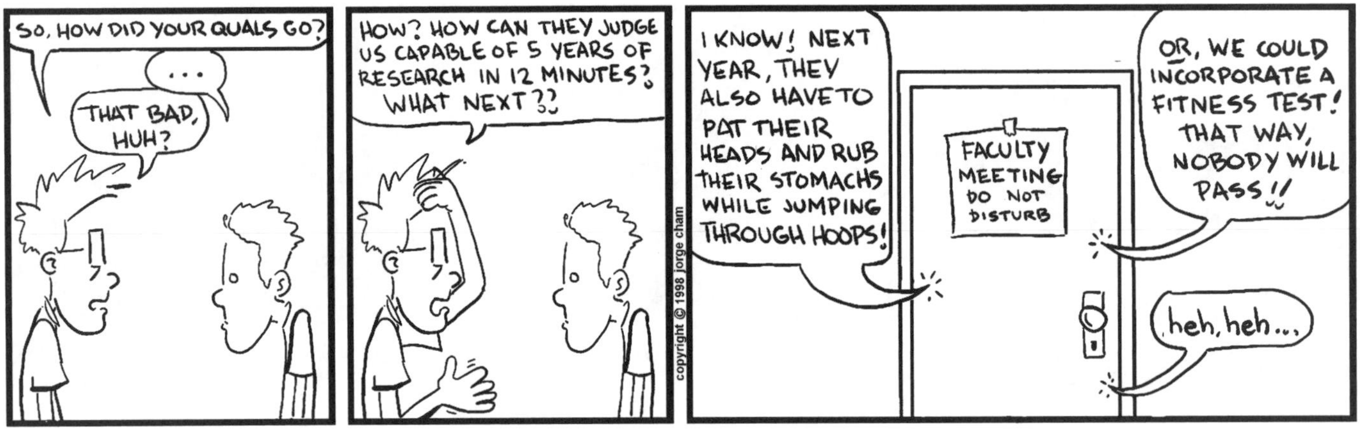
SO, HOW DID YOUR QUALS GO?
...
THAT BAD, HUH?
HOW? HOW CAN THEY JUDGE US CAPABLE OF 5 YEARS OF RESEARCH IN 12 MINUTES? WHAT NEXT??
copyright © 1998 jorge cham
I KNOW! NEXT YEAR, THEY ALSO HAVE TO PAT THEIR HEADS AND RUB THEIR STOMACHS WHILE JUMPING THROUGH HOOPS!
FACULTY MEETING DO NOT DISTURB
OR, WE COULD INCORPORATE A FITNESS TEST! THAT WAY, NOBODY WILL PASS!!
heh, heh...

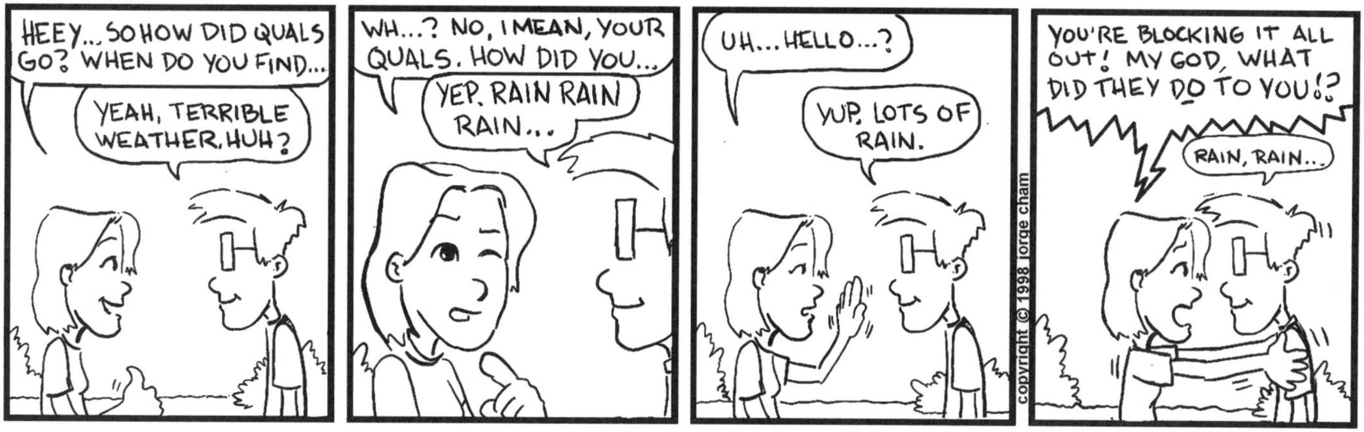
HEEY... SO HOW DID QUALS GO? WHEN DO YOU FIND...
YEAH, TERRIBLE WEATHER, HUH?
WH...? NO, I MEAN, YOUR QUALS. HOW DID YOU...
YEP. RAIN RAIN RAIN...
UH... HELLO...?
YUP. LOTS OF RAIN.
copyright © 1998 jorge cham
YOU'RE BLOCKING IT ALL OUT! MY GOD, WHAT DID THEY DO TO YOU!?
RAIN, RAIN...

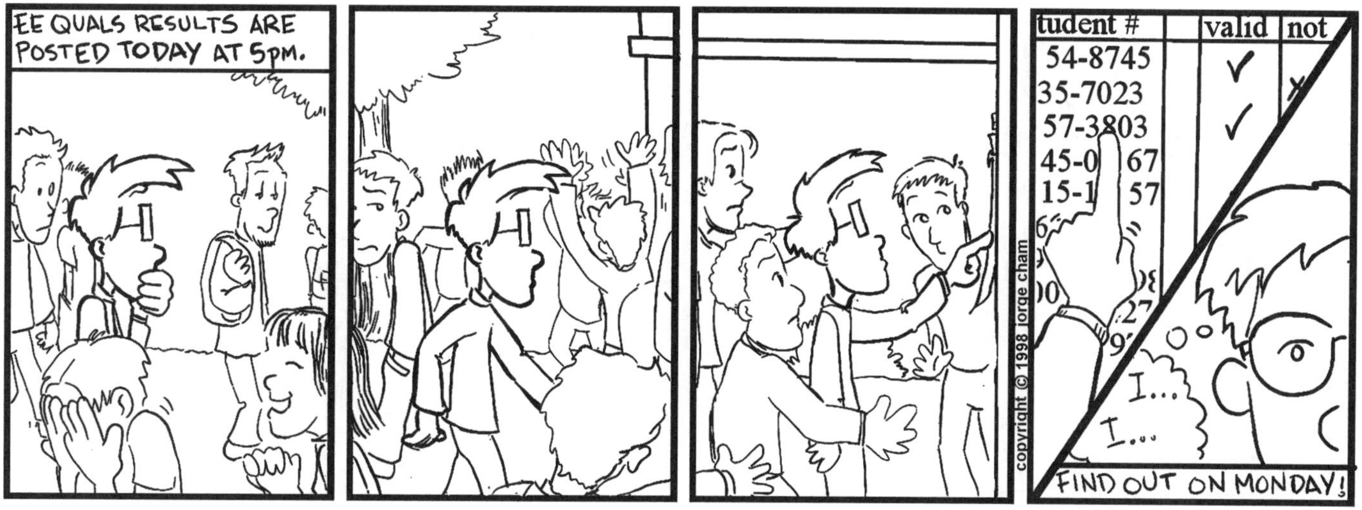
EE QUALS RESULTS ARE POSTED TODAY AT 5pm.
copyright © 1998 jorge cham
tudent #
valid
not
54-8745
35-7023
57-3803
I...
I...
FIND OUT ON MONDAY!

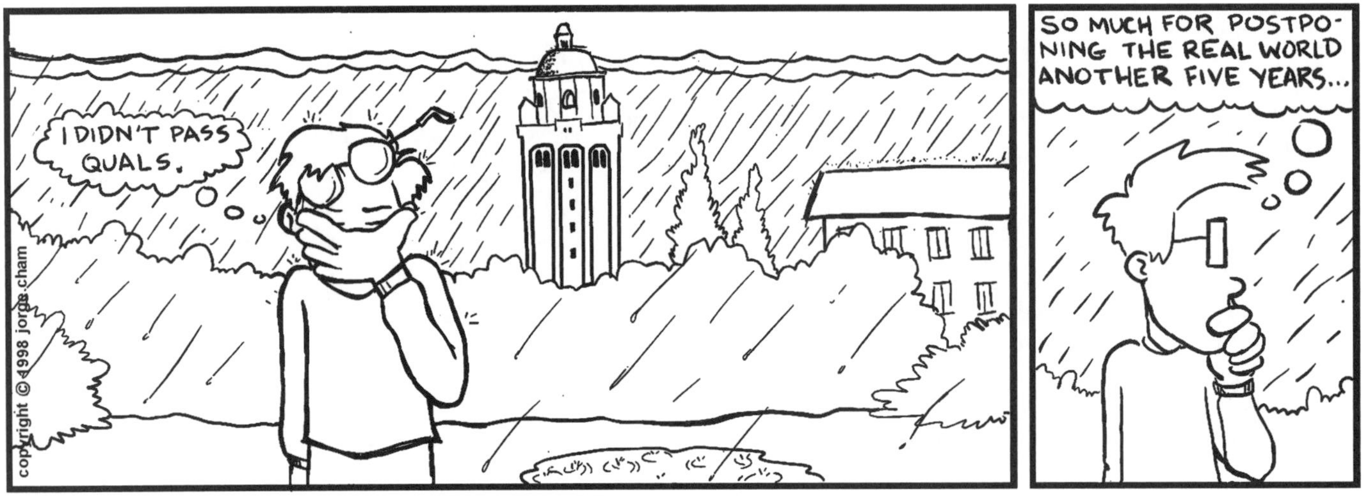
I DIDN'T PASS QUALS.
SO MUCH FOR POSTPONING THE REAL WORLD ANOTHER FIVE YEARS...
copyright © 1998 jorge cham

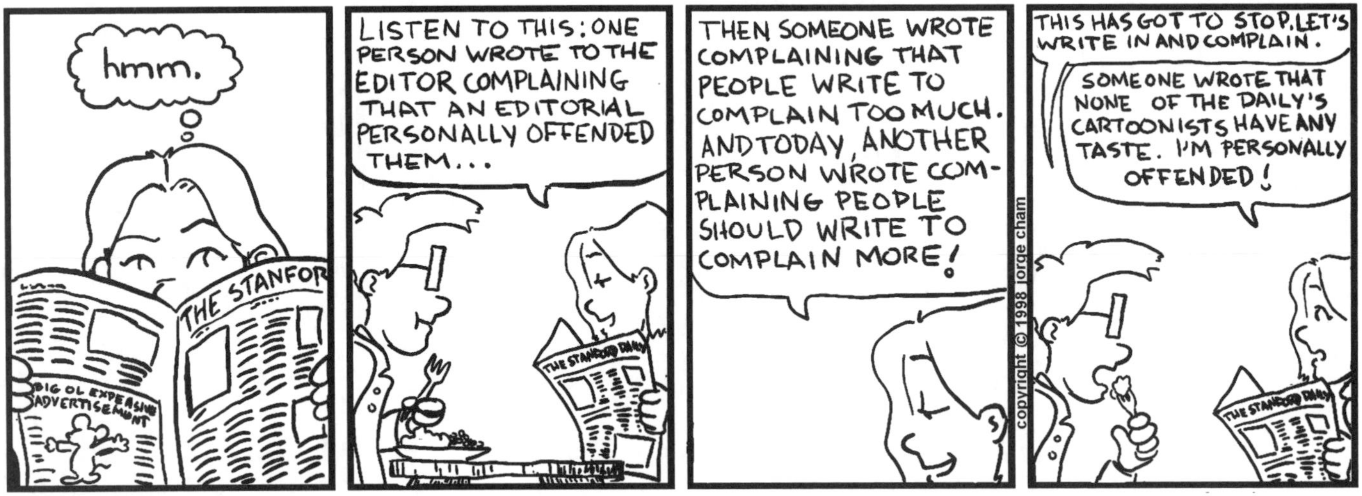
hmm.
THE STANFOR
LISTEN TO THIS: ONE PERSON WROTE TO THE EDITOR COMPLAINING THAT AN EDITORIAL PERSONALLY OFFENDED THEM...
THEN SOMEONE WROTE COMPLAINING THAT PEOPLE WRITE TO COMPLAIN TOO MUCH. AND TODAY, ANOTHER PERSON WROTE COMPLAINING PEOPLE SHOULD WRITE TO COMPLAIN MORE!
copyright © 1998 jorge cham
THIS HAS GOT TO STOP. LET'S WRITE IN AND COMPLAIN.
SOMEONE WROTE THAT NONE OF THE DAILY'S CARTOONISTS HAVE ANY TASTE. I'M PERSONALLY OFFENDED!

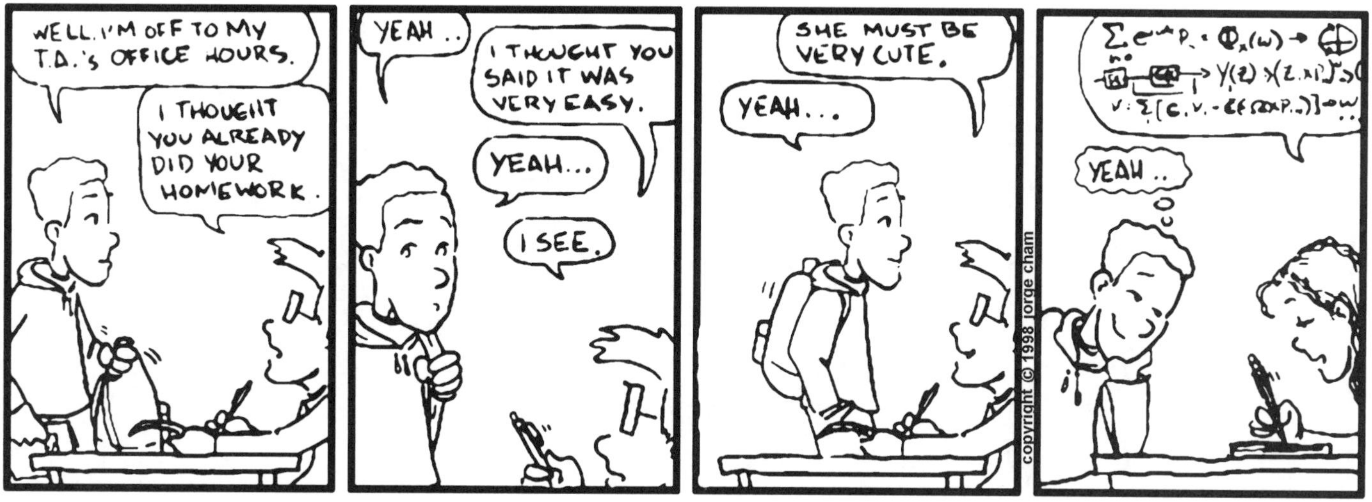
WELL, I'M OFF TO MY T.A.'S OFFICE HOURS.
I THOUGHT YOU ALREADY DID YOUR HOMEWORK.
YEAH..
I THOUGHT YOU SAID IT WAS VERY EASY.
YEAH...
I SEE.
SHE MUST BE VERY CUTE.
YEAH...
copyright © 1998 jorge cham
YEAH..

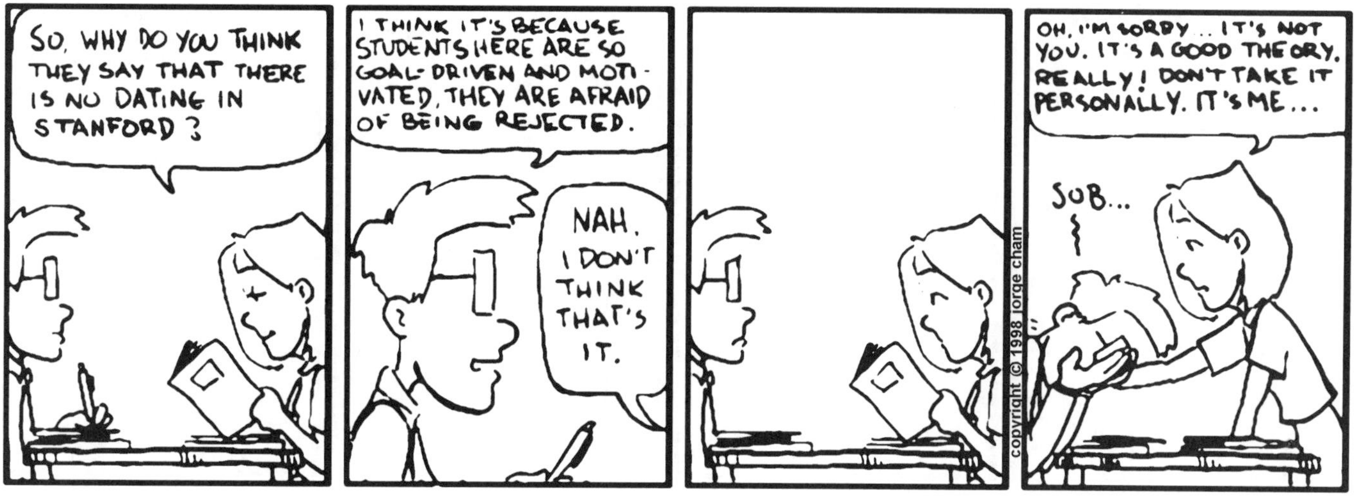
SO, WHY DO YOU THINK THEY SAY THAT THERE IS NO DATING IN STANFORD?
I THINK IT'S BECAUSE STUDENTS HERE ARE SO GOAL-DRIVEN AND MOTI-VATED, THEY ARE AFRAID OF BEING REJECTED.
NAH. I DON'T THINK THAT'S IT.
copyright © 1998 jorge cham
OH, I'M SORRY... IT'S NOT YOU. IT'S A GOOD THEORY. REALLY! I DON'T TAKE IT PERSONALLY. IT'S ME...
SOB...

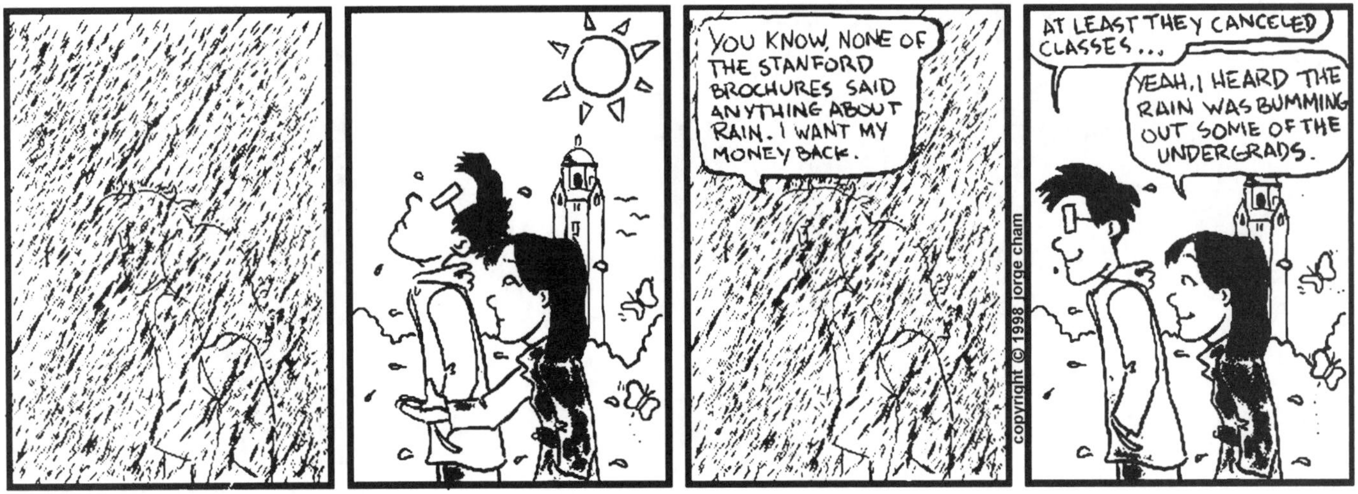
YOU KNOW, NONE OF THE STANFORD BROCHURES SAID ANYTHING ABOUT RAIN. I WANT MY MONEY BACK.
AT LEAST THEY CANCELED CLASSES...
YEAH, I HEARD THE RAIN WAS BUMMING OUT SOME OF THE UNDERGRADS.
copyright © 1998 jorge cham

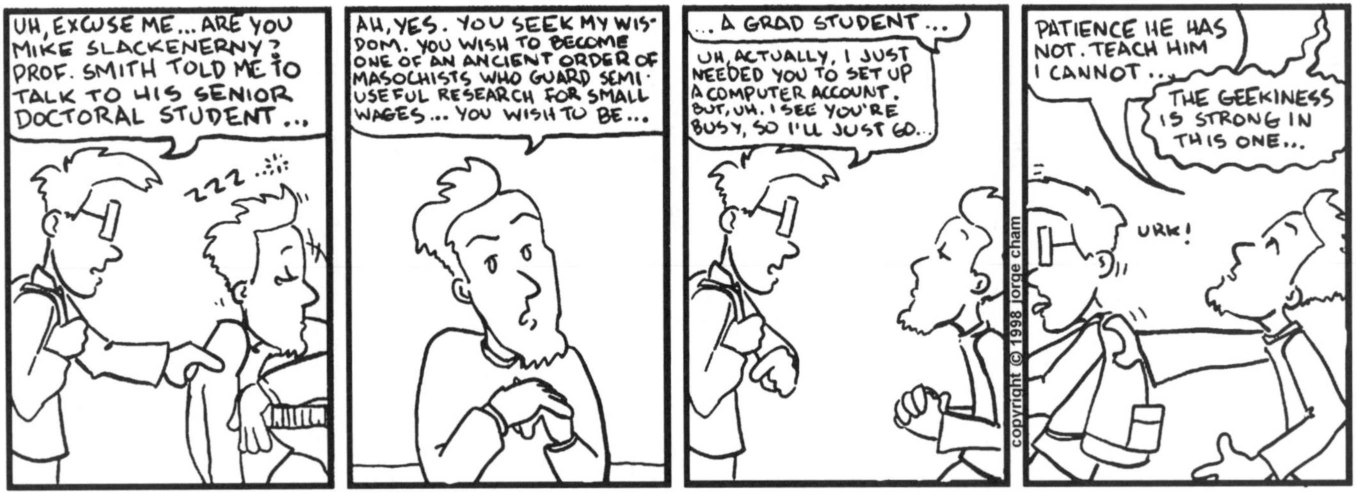
UH, EXCUSE ME... ARE YOU MIKE SLACKENERNY? PROF. SMITH TOLD ME TO TALK TO HIS SENIOR DOCTORAL STUDENT...
ZZZ
AH, YES. YOU SEEK MY WISDOM. YOU WISH TO BECOME ONE OF AN ANCIENT ORDER OF MASOCHISTS WHO GUARD SEMI-USEFUL RESEARCH FOR SMALL WAGES... YOU WISH TO BE...
...A GRAD STUDENT...
UH, ACTUALLY, I JUST NEEDED YOU TO SET UP A COMPUTER ACCOUNT. BUT, UH, I SEE YOU'RE BUSY, SO I'LL JUST GO...
PATIENCE HE HAS NOT. TEACH HIM I CANNOT...
THE GEEKINESS IS STRONG IN THIS ONE...
URK!
copyright © 1998 jorge cham

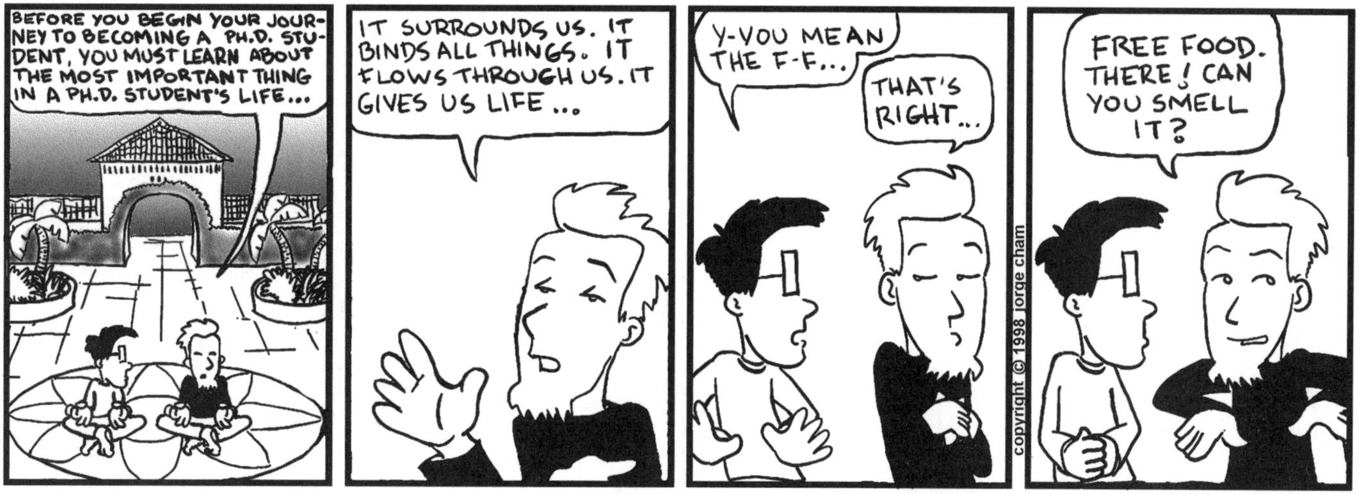
BEFORE YOU BEGIN YOUR JOURNEY TO BECOMING A PH.D. STUDENT, YOU MUST LEARN ABOUT THE MOST IMPORTANT THING IN A PH.D. STUDENT'S LIFE...
IT SURROUNDS US. IT BINDS ALL THINGS. IT FLOWS THROUGH US. IT GIVES US LIFE...
Y-YOU MEAN THE F-F...
THAT'S RIGHT...
FREE FOOD. THERE! CAN YOU SMELL IT?
copyright © 1998 jorge cham

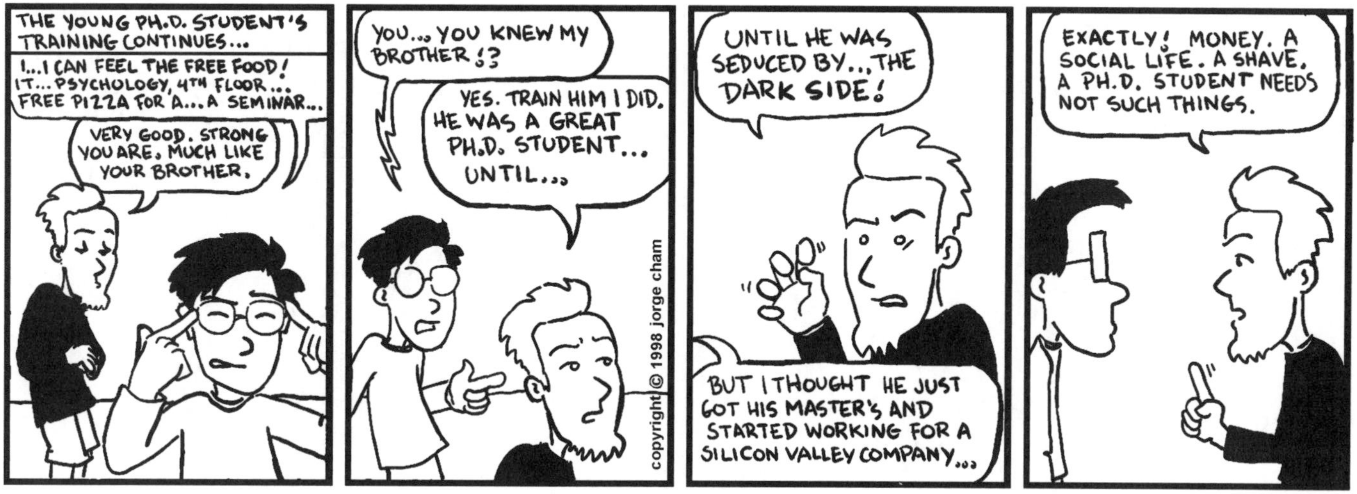
THE YOUNG PH.D. STUDENT'S TRAINING CONTINUES...
I...I CAN FEEL THE FREE FOOD! IT... PSYCHOLOGY, 4TH FLOOR... FREE PIZZA FOR A... A SEMINAR...
VERY GOOD. STRONG YOU ARE, MUCH LIKE YOUR BROTHER.
YOU... YOU KNEW MY BROTHER!?
YES. TRAIN HIM I DID. HE WAS A GREAT PH.D. STUDENT... UNTIL...
copyright © 1998 jorge cham
UNTIL HE WAS SEDUCED BY... THE DARK SIDE!
BUT I THOUGHT HE JUST GOT HIS MASTER'S AND STARTED WORKING FOR A SILICON VALLEY COMPANY...
EXACTLY! MONEY. A SOCIAL LIFE. A SHAVE. A PH.D. STUDENT NEEDS NOT SUCH THINGS.

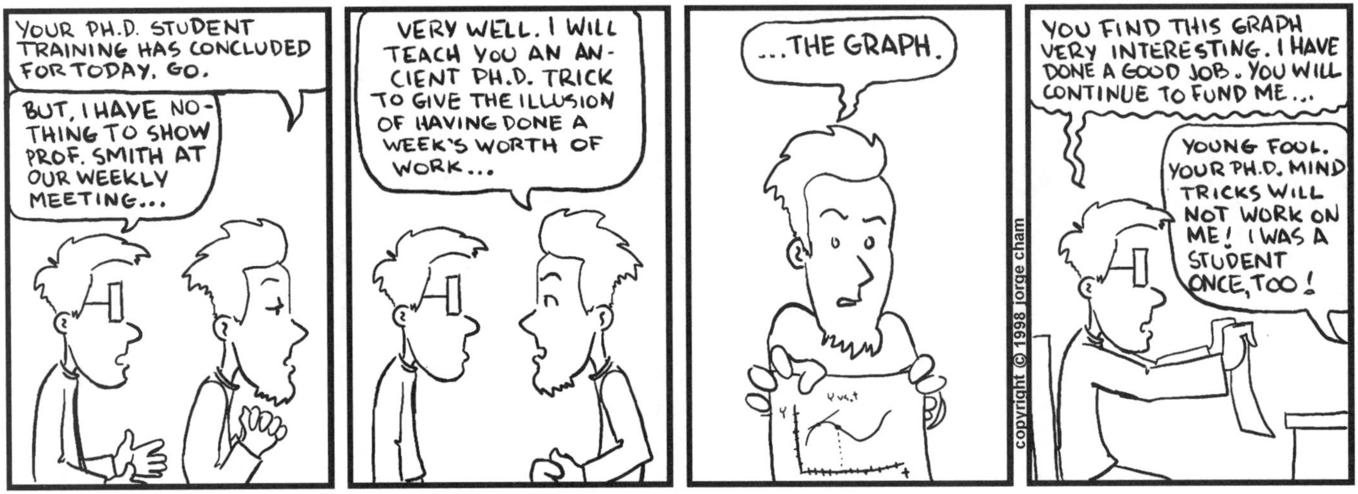
YOUR PH.D. STUDENT TRAINING HAS CONCLUDED FOR TODAY. GO.
BUT, I HAVE NOTHING TO SHOW PROF. SMITH AT OUR WEEKLY MEETING...
VERY WELL. I WILL TEACH YOU AN ANCIENT PH.D. TRICK TO GIVE THE ILLUSION OF HAVING DONE A WEEK'S WORTH OF WORK...
...THE GRAPH.
copyright © 1998 jorge cham
YOU FIND THIS GRAPH VERY INTERESTING. I HAVE DONE A GOOD JOB. YOU WILL CONTINUE TO FUND ME...
YOUNG FOOL. YOUR PH.D. MIND TRICKS WILL NOT WORK ON ME! I WAS A STUDENT ONCE, TOO!

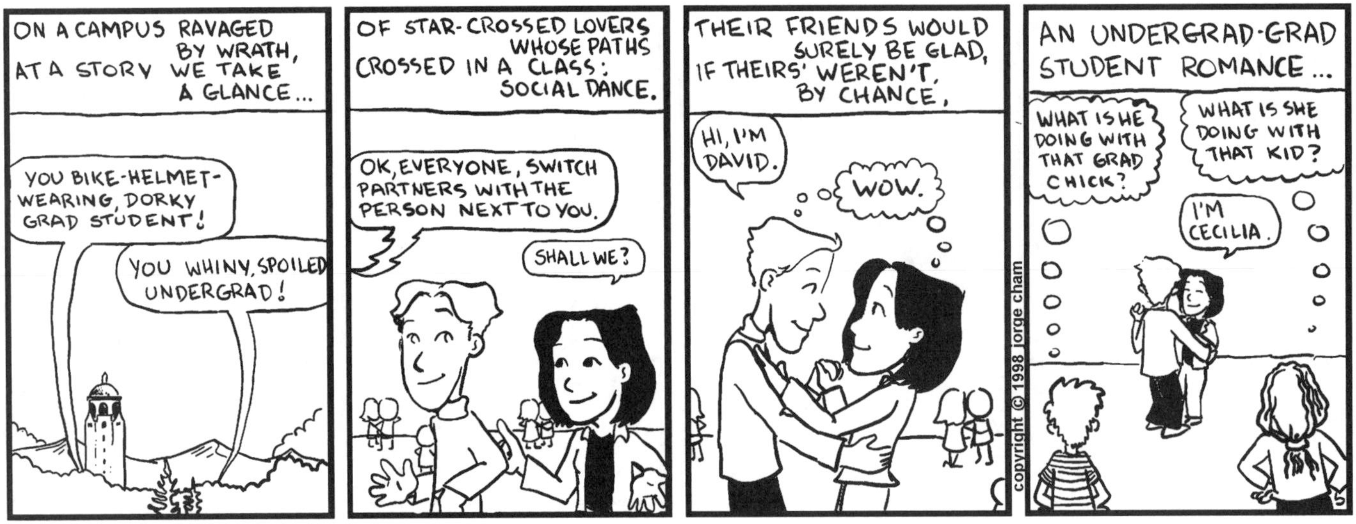
ON A CAMPUS RAVAGED BY WRATH, AT A STORY WE TAKE A GLANCE...
YOU BIKE-HELMET-WEARING, DORKY GRAD STUDENT!
YOU WHINY, SPOILED UNDERGRAD!
OF STAR-CROSSED LOVERS WHOSE PATHS CROSSED IN A CLASS: SOCIAL DANCE.
OK, EVERYONE, SWITCH PARTNERS WITH THE PERSON NEXT TO YOU.
SHALL WE?
THEIR FRIENDS WOULD SURELY BE GLAD, IF THEIRS' WEREN'T, BY CHANCE,
HI, I'M DAVID.
WOW.
copyright © 1998 jorge cham
AN UNDERGRAD-GRAD STUDENT ROMANCE...
WHAT IS HE DOING WITH THAT GRAD CHICK?
WHAT IS SHE DOING WITH THAT KID?
I'M CECILIA.

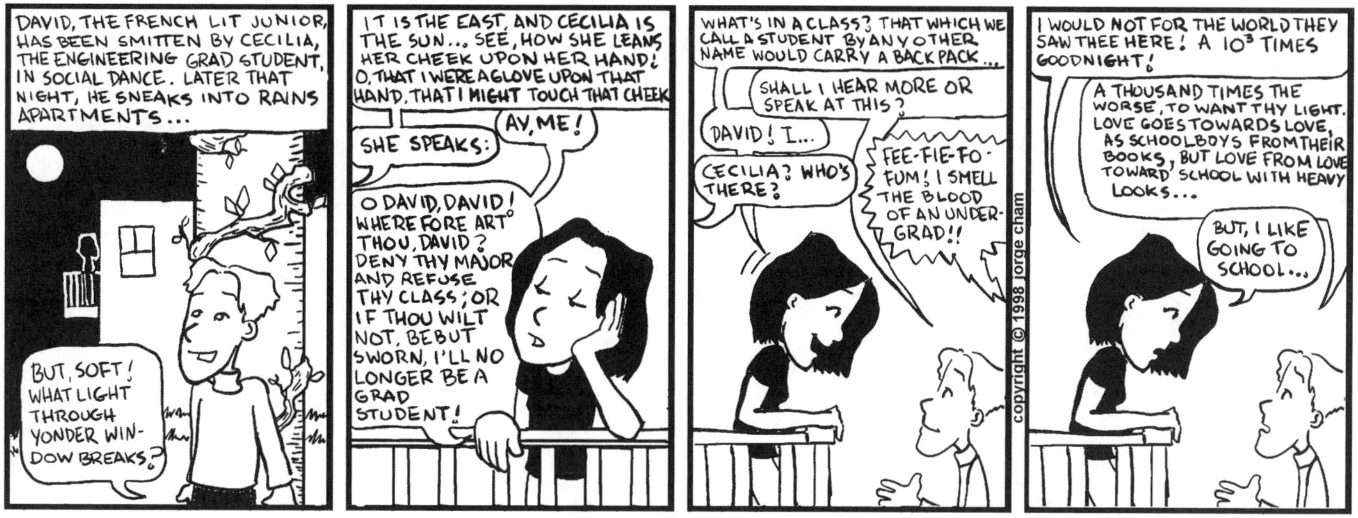
DAVID, THE FRENCH LIT JUNIOR, HAS BEEN SMITTEN BY CECILIA, THE ENGINEERING GRAD STUDENT, IN SOCIAL DANCE. LATER THAT NIGHT, HE SNEAKS INTO RAINS APARTMENTS...
BUT, SOFT! WHAT LIGHT THROUGH YONDER WINDOW BREAKS?
IT IS THE EAST, AND CECILIA IS THE SUN... SEE, HOW SHE LEANS HER CHEEK UPON HER HAND! O, THAT I WERE A GLOVE UPON THAT HAND, THAT I MIGHT TOUCH THAT CHEEK
SHE SPEAKS:
AY, ME!
O DAVID, DAVID! WHEREFORE ART THOU, DAVID? DENY THY MAJOR AND REFUSE THY CLASS; OR IF THOU WILT NOT, BE BUT SWORN, I'LL NO LONGER BE A GRAD STUDENT!
WHAT'S IN A CLASS? THAT WHICH WE CALL A STUDENT BY ANY OTHER NAME WOULD CARRY A BACKPACK...
SHALL I HEAR MORE OR SPEAK AT THIS?
DAVID! I...
CECILIA? WHO'S THERE?
FEE-FIE-FO-FUM! I SMELL THE BLOOD OF AN UNDER-GRAD!!
copyright © 1998 jorge cham
I WOULD NOT FOR THE WORLD THEY SAW THEE HERE! A 10^3 TIMES GOODNIGHT!
A THOUSAND TIMES THE WORSE, TO WANT THY LIGHT. LOVE GOES TOWARDS LOVE, AS SCHOOLBOYS FROM THEIR BOOKS, BUT LOVE FROM LOVE TOWARD SCHOOL WITH HEAVY LOOKS...
BUT, I LIKE GOING TO SCHOOL...

with apologies to william shakespeare...

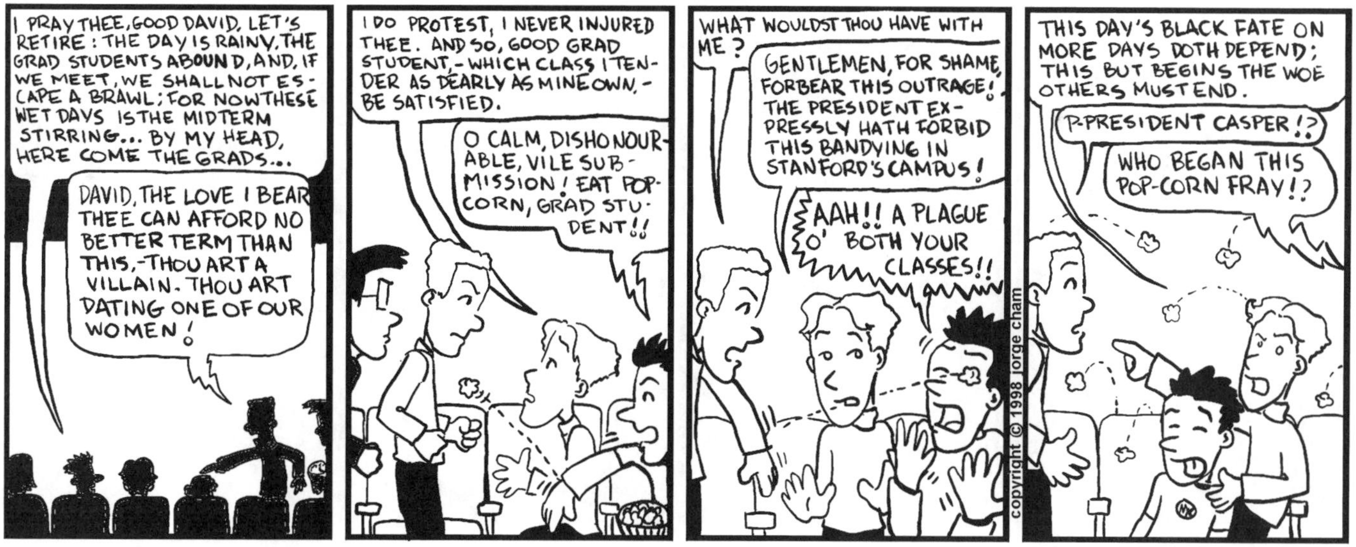
I PRAY THEE, GOOD DAVID, LET'S RETIRE: THE DAY IS RAINY, THE GRAD STUDENTS ABOUND, AND, IF WE MEET, WE SHALL NOT ESCAPE A BRAWL; FOR NOW THESE WET DAYS IS THE MIDTERM STIRRING... BY MY HEAD, HERE COME THE GRADS...
DAVID, THE LOVE I BEAR THEE CAN AFFORD NO BETTER TERM THAN THIS,-THOU ART A VILLAIN. THOU ART DATING ONE OF OUR WOMEN!
I DO PROTEST, I NEVER INJURED THEE. AND SO, GOOD GRAD STUDENT,- WHICH CLASS I TENDER AS DEARLY AS MINE OWN,- BE SATISFIED.
O CALM, DISHONOURABLE, VILE SUBMISSION! EAT POPCORN, GRAD STUDENT!!
WHAT WOULDST THOU HAVE WITH ME?
GENTLEMEN, FOR SHAME, FORBEAR THIS OUTRAGE! THE PRESIDENT EXPRESSLY HATH FORBID THIS BANDYING IN STANFORD'S CAMPUS!
AAH!! A PLAGUE O' BOTH YOUR CLASSES!!
copyright © 1998 jorge cham
THIS DAY'S BLACK FATE ON MORE DAYS DOTH DEPEND; THIS BUT BEGINS THE WOE OTHERS MUST END.
P-PRESIDENT CASPER!?
WHO BEGAN THIS POP-CORN FRAY!?

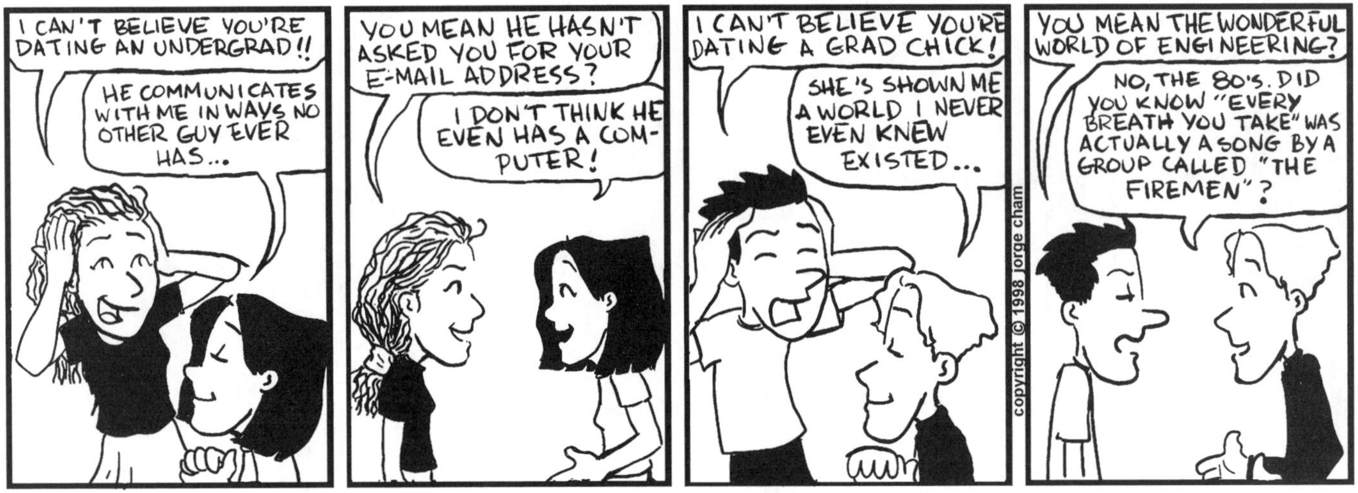
I CAN'T BELIEVE YOU'RE DATING AN UNDERGRAD!!
HE COMMUNICATES WITH ME IN WAYS NO OTHER GUY EVER HAS...
YOU MEAN HE HASN'T ASKED YOU FOR YOUR E-MAIL ADDRESS?
I DON'T THINK HE EVEN HAS A COMPUTER!
I CAN'T BELIEVE YOU'RE DATING A GRAD CHICK!
SHE'S SHOWN ME A WORLD I NEVER EVEN KNEW EXISTED...
copyright © 1998 jorge cham
YOU MEAN THE WONDERFUL WORLD OF ENGINEERING?
NO, THE 80'S. DID YOU KNOW "EVERY BREATH YOU TAKE" WAS ACTUALLY A SONG BY A GROUP CALLED "THE FIREMEN"?

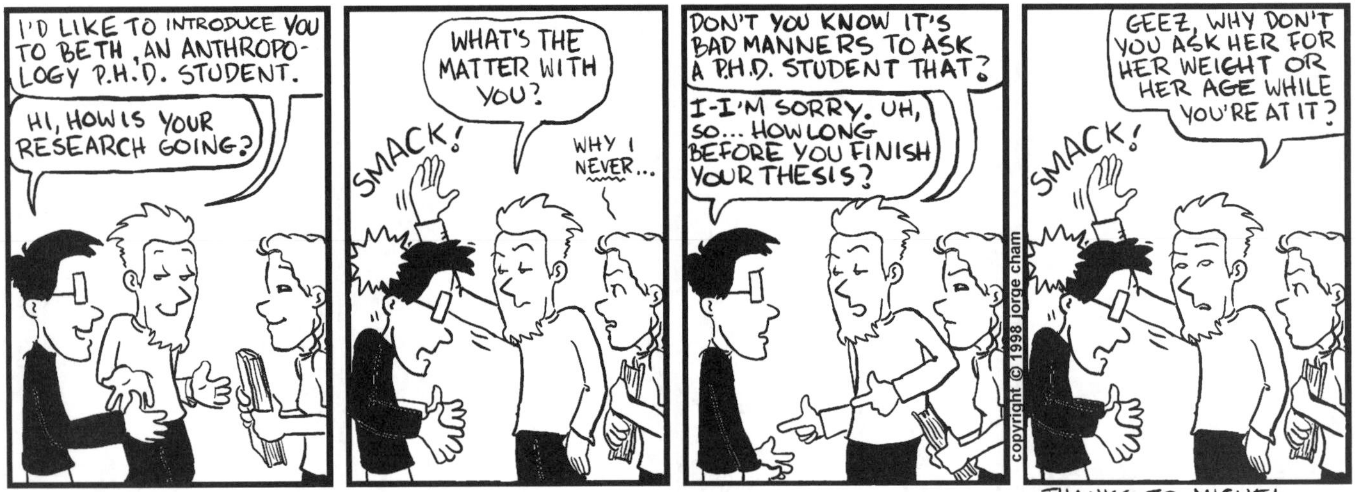
I'D LIKE TO INTRODUCE YOU TO BETH, AN ANTHROPOLOGY P.H.D. STUDENT.
HI, HOW IS YOUR RESEARCH GOING?
SMACK!
WHAT'S THE MATTER WITH YOU?
WHY I NEVER...
DON'T YOU KNOW IT'S BAD MANNERS TO ASK A P.H.D. STUDENT THAT?
I-I'M SORRY. UH, SO... HOW LONG BEFORE YOU FINISH YOUR THESIS?
copyright © 1998 jorge cham
SMACK!
GEEZ, WHY DON'T YOU ASK HER FOR HER WEIGHT OR HER AGE WHILE YOU'RE AT IT?

THANKS TO MIGUEL...

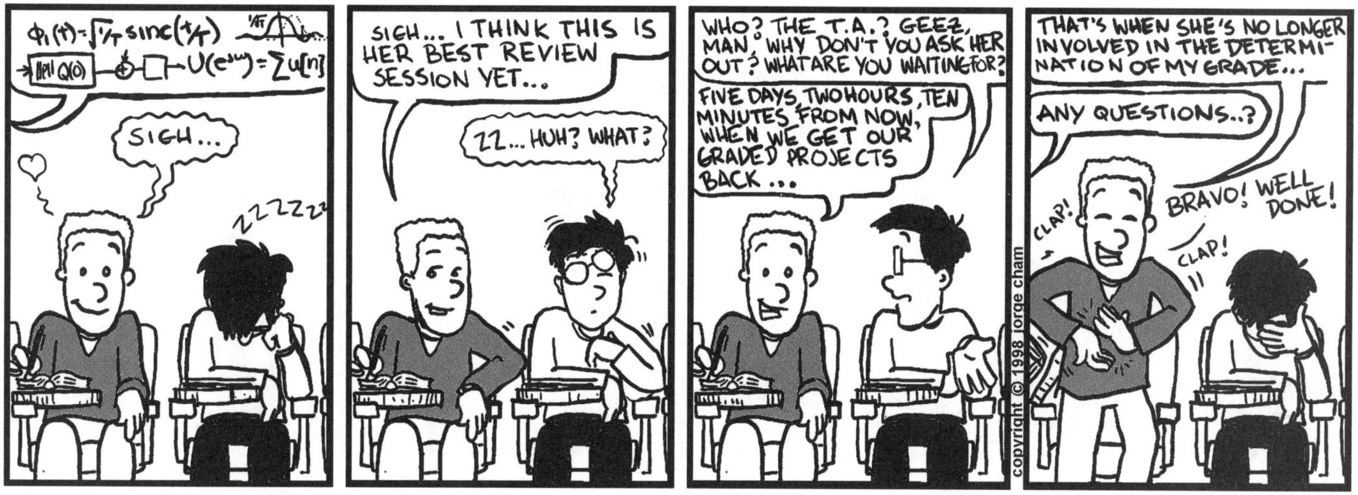
SIGH...
ZZZZZZZ
SIGH... I THINK THIS IS HER BEST REVIEW SESSION YET...
ZZ... HUH? WHAT?
WHO? THE T.A.? GEEZ, MAN, WHY DON'T YOU ASK HER OUT? WHAT ARE YOU WAITING FOR?
FIVE DAYS, TWO HOURS, TEN MINUTES FROM NOW, WHEN WE GET OUR GRADED PROJECTS BACK...
THAT'S WHEN SHE'S NO LONGER INVOLVED IN THE DETERMINATION OF MY GRADE...
ANY QUESTIONS..?
CLAP!
BRAVO! WELL DONE!
CLAP!
copyright © 1998 jorge cham

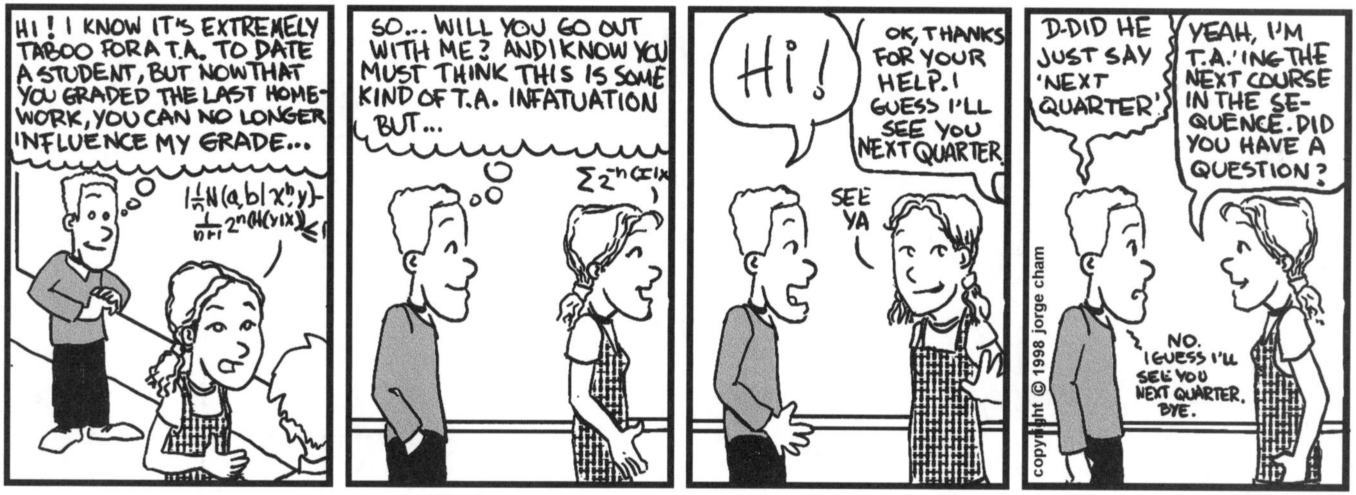
HI! I KNOW IT'S EXTREMELY TABOO FOR A T.A. TO DATE A STUDENT, BUT NOW THAT YOU GRADED THE LAST HOMEWORK, YOU CAN NO LONGER INFLUENCE MY GRADE...
SO... WILL YOU GO OUT WITH ME? AND I KNOW YOU MUST THINK THIS IS SOME KIND OF T.A. INFATUATION BUT...
Hi!
OK, THANKS FOR YOUR HELP. I GUESS I'LL SEE YOU NEXT QUARTER.
SEE YA
D-DID HE JUST SAY 'NEXT QUARTER'?
YEAH, I'M T.A.'ING THE NEXT COURSE IN THE SEQUENCE. DID YOU HAVE A QUESTION?
NO. I GUESS I'LL SEE YOU NEXT QUARTER. BYE.
copyright © 1998 jorge cham

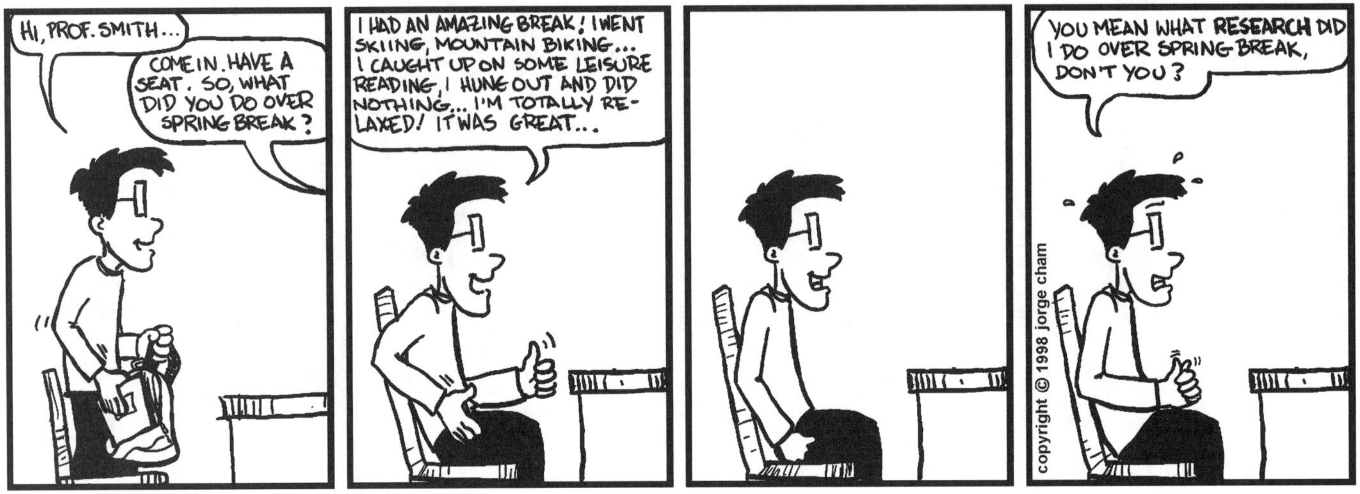
HI, PROF. SMITH...
COME IN. HAVE A SEAT. SO, WHAT DID YOU DO OVER SPRING BREAK?
I HAD AN AMAZING BREAK! I WENT SKIING, MOUNTAIN BIKING... I CAUGHT UP ON SOME LEISURE READING, I HUNG OUT AND DID NOTHING... I'M TOTALLY RE-LAXED! IT WAS GREAT...
YOU MEAN WHAT RESEARCH DID I DO OVER SPRING BREAK, DON'T YOU?
copyright © 1998 jorge cham

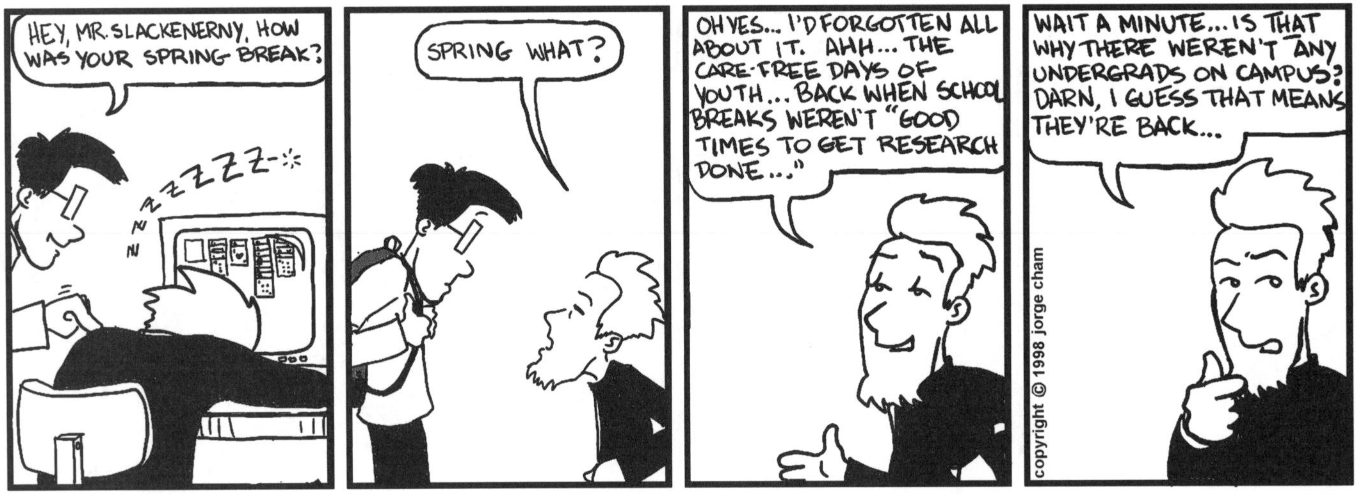
HEY, MR. SLACKENERNY, HOW WAS YOUR SPRING BREAK?
ZZZZZZZ
SPRING WHAT?
OH YES... I'D FORGOTTEN ALL ABOUT IT. AHH... THE CARE-FREE DAYS OF YOUTH... BACK WHEN SCHOOL BREAKS WEREN'T "GOOD TIMES TO GET RESEARCH DONE..."
WAIT A MINUTE... IS THAT WHY THERE WEREN'T ANY UNDERGRADS ON CAMPUS? DARN, I GUESS THAT MEANS THEY'RE BACK...
copyright © 1998 jorge cham

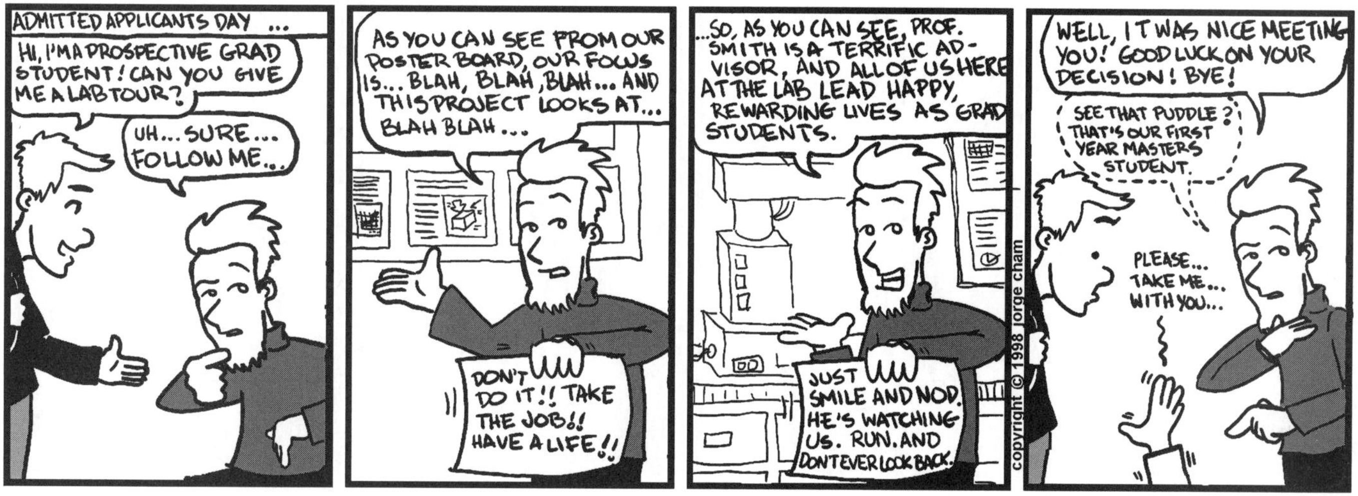
ADMITTED APPLICANTS DAY ...
HI, I'M A PROSPECTIVE GRAD STUDENT! CAN YOU GIVE ME A LAB TOUR?
UH... SURE... FOLLOW ME...
AS YOU CAN SEE FROM OUR POSTER BOARD, OUR FOCUS IS... BLAH, BLAH, BLAH... AND THIS PROJECT LOOKS AT... BLAH BLAH...
DON'T DO IT!! TAKE THE JOB!! HAVE A LIFE!!
...SO, AS YOU CAN SEE, PROF. SMITH IS A TERRIFIC ADVISOR, AND ALL OF US HERE AT THE LAB LEAD HAPPY, REWARDING LIVES AS GRAD STUDENTS.
JUST SMILE AND NOD. HE'S WATCHING US. RUN. AND DON'T EVER LOOK BACK.
copyright © 1998 jorge cham
WELL, IT WAS NICE MEETING YOU! GOOD LUCK ON YOUR DECISION! BYE!
SEE THAT PUDDLE? THAT'S OUR FIRST YEAR MASTERS STUDENT.
PLEASE... TAKE ME... WITH YOU...

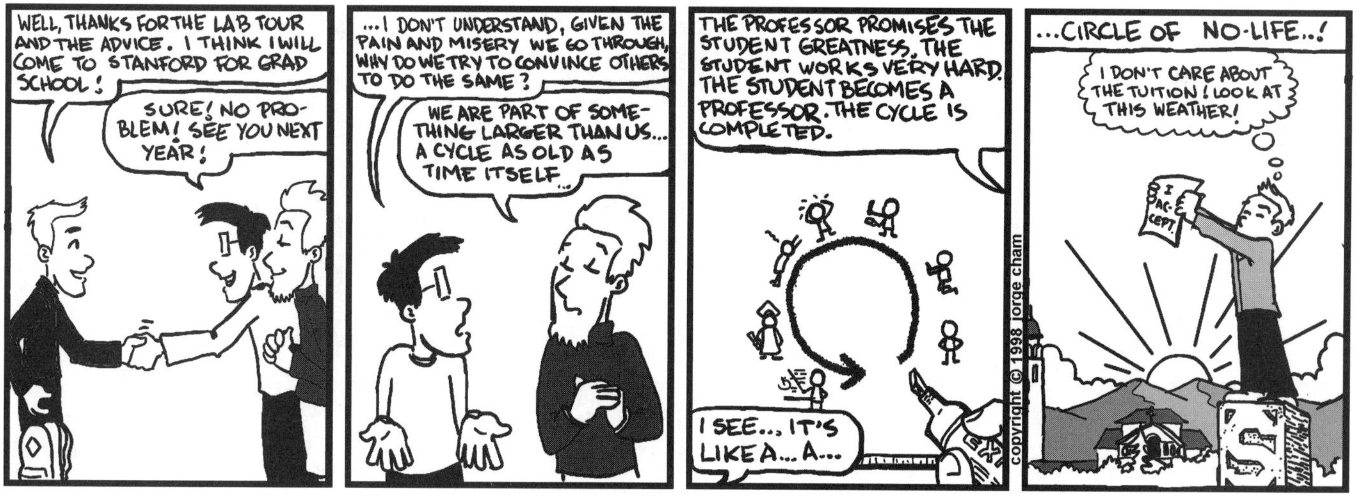
WELL, THANKS FOR THE LAB TOUR AND THE ADVICE. I THINK I WILL COME TO STANFORD FOR GRAD SCHOOL!
SURE! NO PROBLEM! SEE YOU NEXT YEAR!
...I DON'T UNDERSTAND, GIVEN THE PAIN AND MISERY WE GO THROUGH, WHY DO WE TRY TO CONVINCE OTHERS TO DO THE SAME?
WE ARE PART OF SOMETHING LARGER THAN US... A CYCLE AS OLD AS TIME ITSELF...
THE PROFESSOR PROMISES THE STUDENT GREATNESS, THE STUDENT WORKS VERY HARD. THE STUDENT BECOMES A PROFESSOR. THE CYCLE IS COMPLETED.
I SEE..., IT'S LIKE A... A...
copyright © 1998 jorge cham
...CIRCLE OF NO-LIFE..!
I DON'T CARE ABOUT THE TUITION! LOOK AT THIS WEATHER!
I ACCEPT!

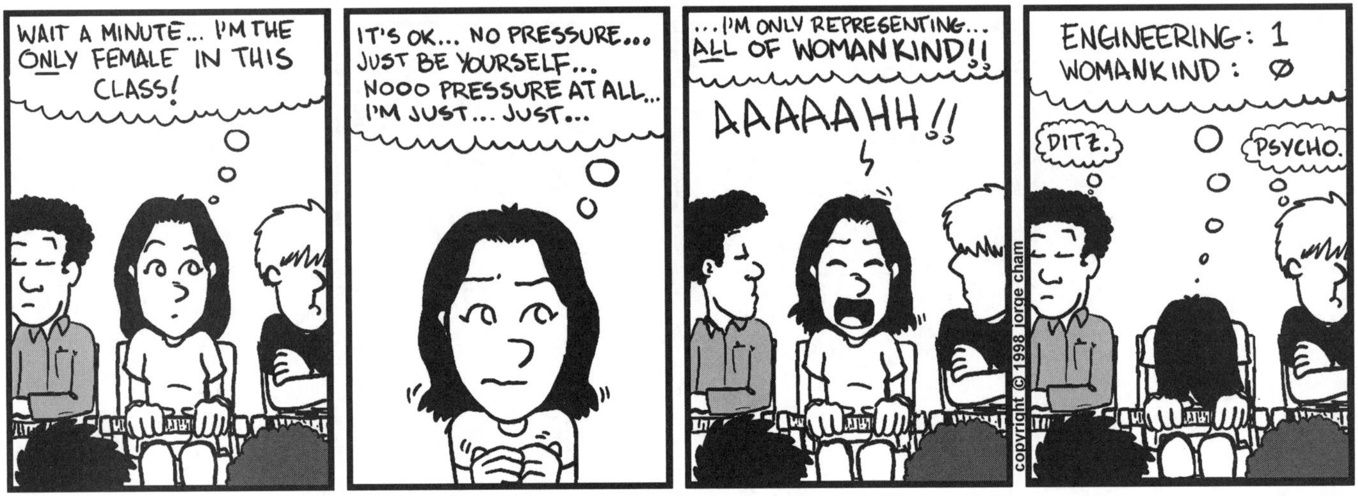
WAIT A MINUTE... I'M THE ONLY FEMALE IN THIS CLASS!
IT'S OK... NO PRESSURE... JUST BE YOURSELF... NOOO PRESSURE AT ALL... I'M JUST... JUST...
...I'M ONLY REPRESENTING... ALL OF WOMANKIND!!
AAAAAHH!!
copyright © 1998 jorge cham
ENGINEERING: 1
WOMANKIND: Ø
DITZ.
PSYCHO.

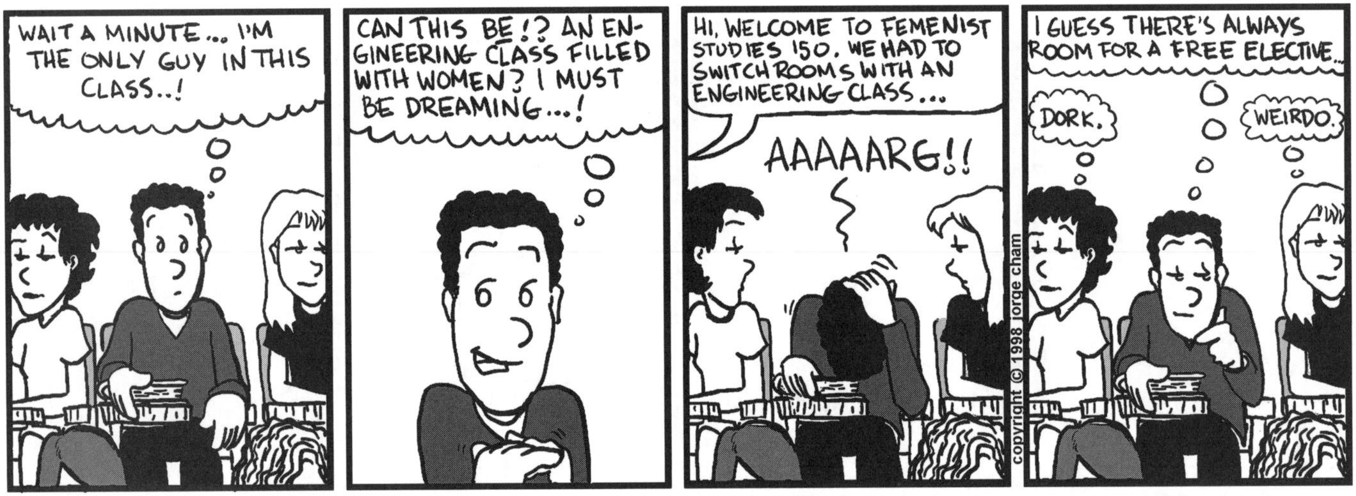
WAIT A MINUTE... I'M THE ONLY GUY IN THIS CLASS...!
CAN THIS BE!? AN ENGINEERING CLASS FILLED WITH WOMEN? I MUST BE DREAMING...!
HI, WELCOME TO FEMENIST STUDIES 150. WE HAD TO SWITCH ROOMS WITH AN ENGINEERING CLASS...
AAAAARG!!
copyright © 1998 jorge cham
I GUESS THERE'S ALWAYS ROOM FOR A FREE ELECTIVE...
DORK.
WEIRDO.

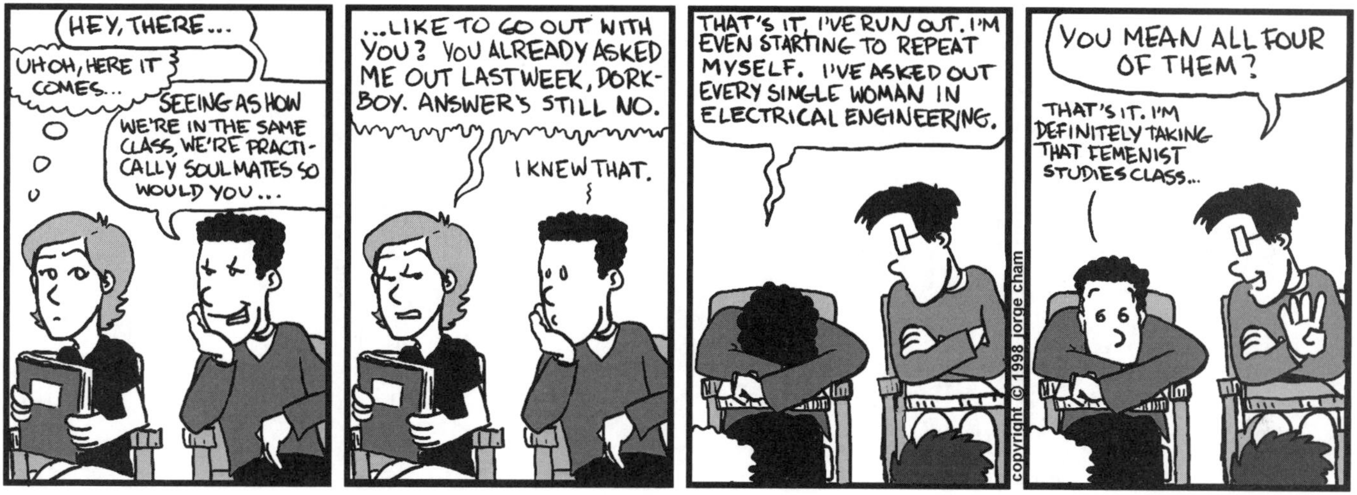
HEY, THERE...
UH OH, HERE IT COMES...
SEEING AS HOW WE'RE IN THE SAME CLASS, WE'RE PRACTI-CALLY SOULMATES SO WOULD YOU...
...LIKE TO GO OUT WITH YOU? YOU ALREADY ASKED ME OUT LAST WEEK, DORK-BOY. ANSWER'S STILL NO.
I KNEW THAT.
THAT'S IT, I'VE RUN OUT. I'M EVEN STARTING TO REPEAT MYSELF. I'VE ASKED OUT EVERY SINGLE WOMAN IN ELECTRICAL ENGINEERING.
copyright © 1998 jorge cham
YOU MEAN ALL FOUR OF THEM?
THAT'S IT. I'M DEFINITELY TAKING THAT FEMENIST STUDIES CLASS...

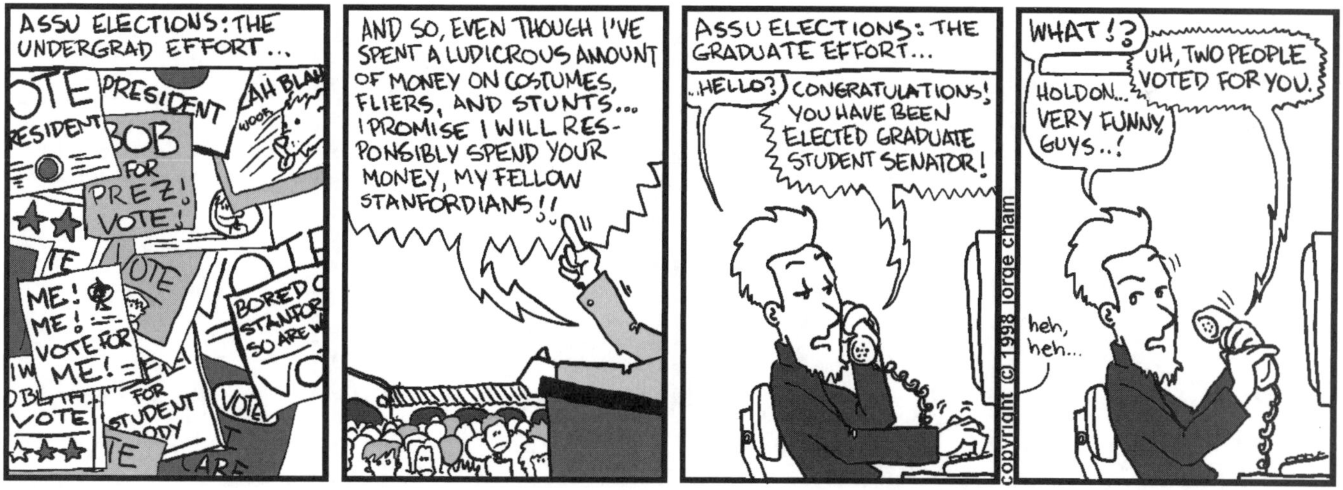
ASSU ELECTIONS: THE UNDERGRAD EFFORT...
PRESIDENT
BOB FOR PREZ! VOTE!
ME! ME! VOTE FOR ME!
FOR STUDENT
AND SO, EVEN THOUGH I'VE SPENT A LUDICROUS AMOUNT OF MONEY ON COSTUMES, FLIERS, AND STUNTS... I PROMISE I WILL RES-PONSIBLY SPEND YOUR MONEY, MY FELLOW STANFORDIANS!!
ASSU ELECTIONS: THE GRADUATE EFFORT...
..HELLO?
CONGRATULATIONS! YOU HAVE BEEN ELECTED GRADUATE STUDENT SENATOR!
copyright © 1998 jorge cham
WHAT!?
UH, TWO PEOPLE VOTED FOR YOU.
HOLD ON.. VERY FUNNY, GUYS..!
heh, heh...

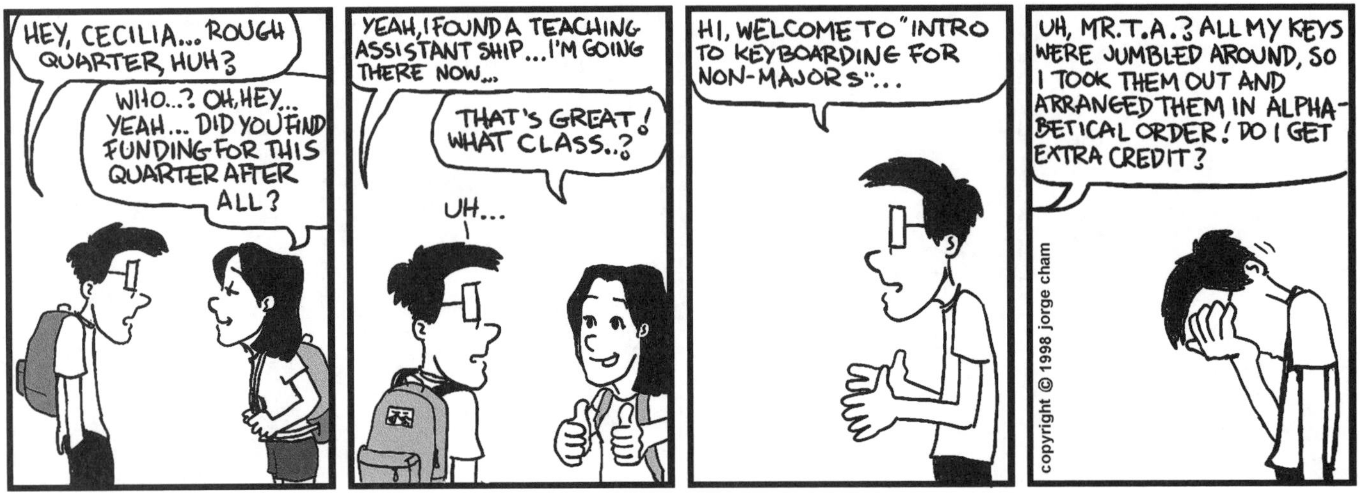
HEY, CECILIA... ROUGH QUARTER, HUH?
WHO..? OH, HEY... YEAH... DID YOU FIND FUNDING FOR THIS QUARTER AFTER ALL?
YEAH, I FOUND A TEACHING ASSISTANT SHIP... I'M GOING THERE NOW...
THAT'S GREAT! WHAT CLASS..?
UH...
HI, WELCOME TO "INTRO TO KEYBOARDING FOR NON-MAJORS"...
UH, MR. T.A.? ALL MY KEYS WERE JUMBLED AROUND, SO I TOOK THEM OUT AND ARRANGED THEM IN ALPHA-BETICAL ORDER! DO I GET EXTRA CREDIT?
copyright © 1998 jorge cham

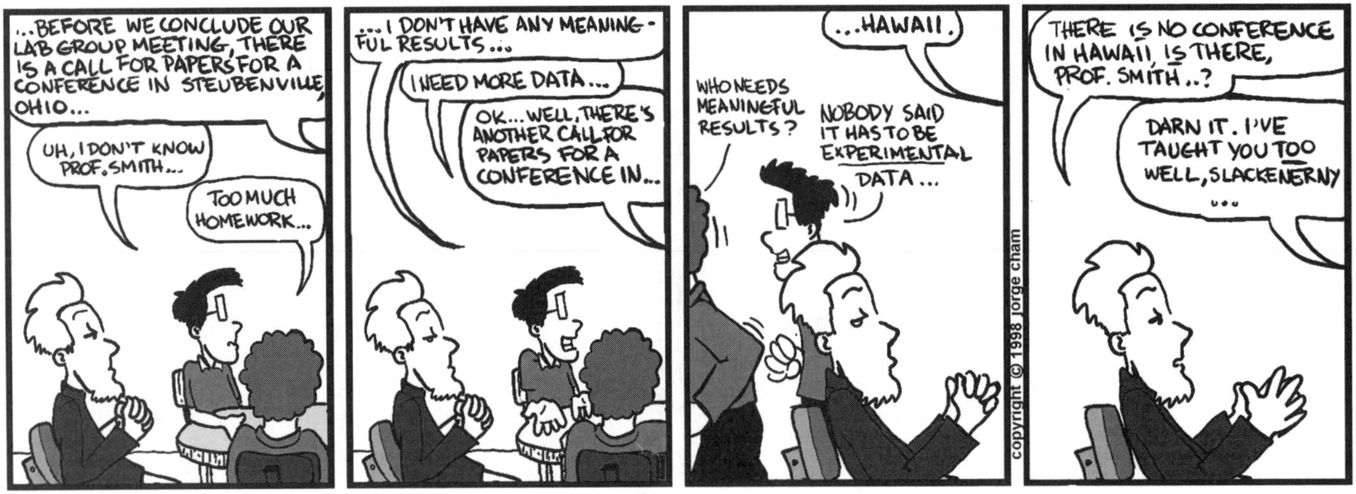
...BEFORE WE CONCLUDE OUR LAB GROUP MEETING, THERE IS A CALL FOR PAPERS FOR A CONFERENCE IN STEUBENVILLE, OHIO...
UH, I DON'T KNOW PROF. SMITH...
TOO MUCH HOMEWORK...
...I DON'T HAVE ANY MEANING-FUL RESULTS...
I NEED MORE DATA...
OK... WELL, THERE'S ANOTHER CALL FOR PAPERS FOR A CONFERENCE IN...
...HAWAII.
WHO NEEDS MEANINGFUL RESULTS?
NOBODY SAID IT HAS TO BE EXPERIMENTAL DATA...
copyright © 1998 jorge cham
THERE IS NO CONFERENCE IN HAWAII, IS THERE, PROF. SMITH..?
DARN IT. I'VE TAUGHT YOU TOO WELL, SLACKENERNY...

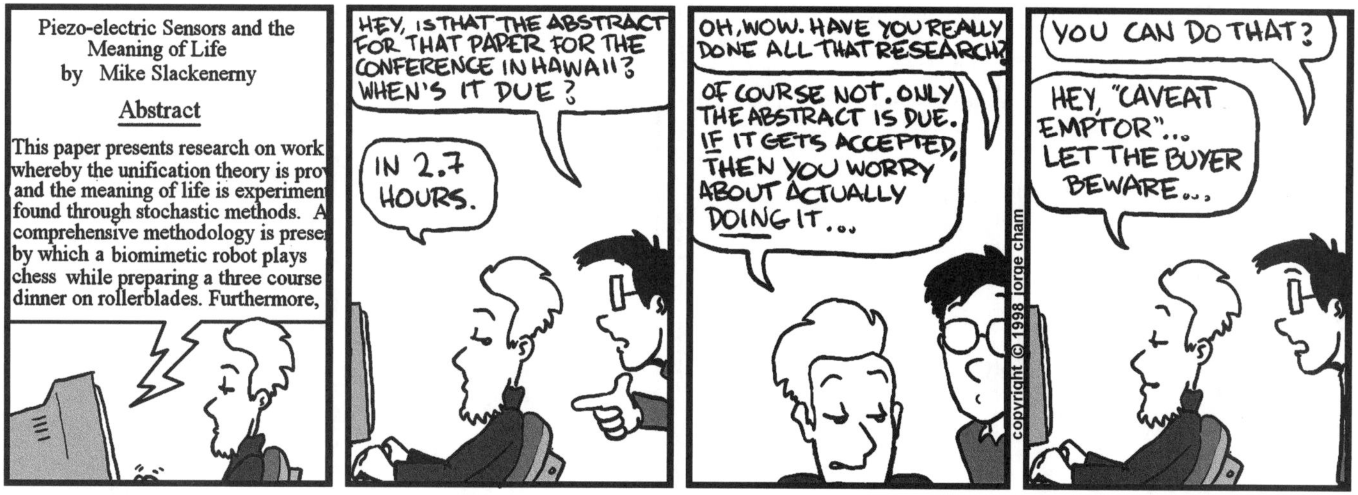
Piezo-electric Sensors and the Meaning of Life
by Mike Slackenerny
Abstract
This paper presents research on work whereby the unification theory is prov and the meaning of life is experimen found through stochastic methods. A comprehensive methodology is prese by which a biomimetic robot plays chess while preparing a three course dinner on rollerblades. Furthermore,
HEY, IS THAT THE ABSTRACT FOR THAT PAPER FOR THE CONFERENCE IN HAWAII? WHEN'S IT DUE?
IN 2.7 HOURS.
OH, WOW. HAVE YOU REALLY DONE ALL THAT RESEARCH?
OF COURSE NOT. ONLY THE ABSTRACT IS DUE. IF IT GETS ACCEPTED, THEN YOU WORRY ABOUT ACTUALLY DOING IT...
copyright © 1998 jorge cham
YOU CAN DO THAT?
HEY, "CAVEAT EMPTOR"... LET THE BUYER BEWARE...

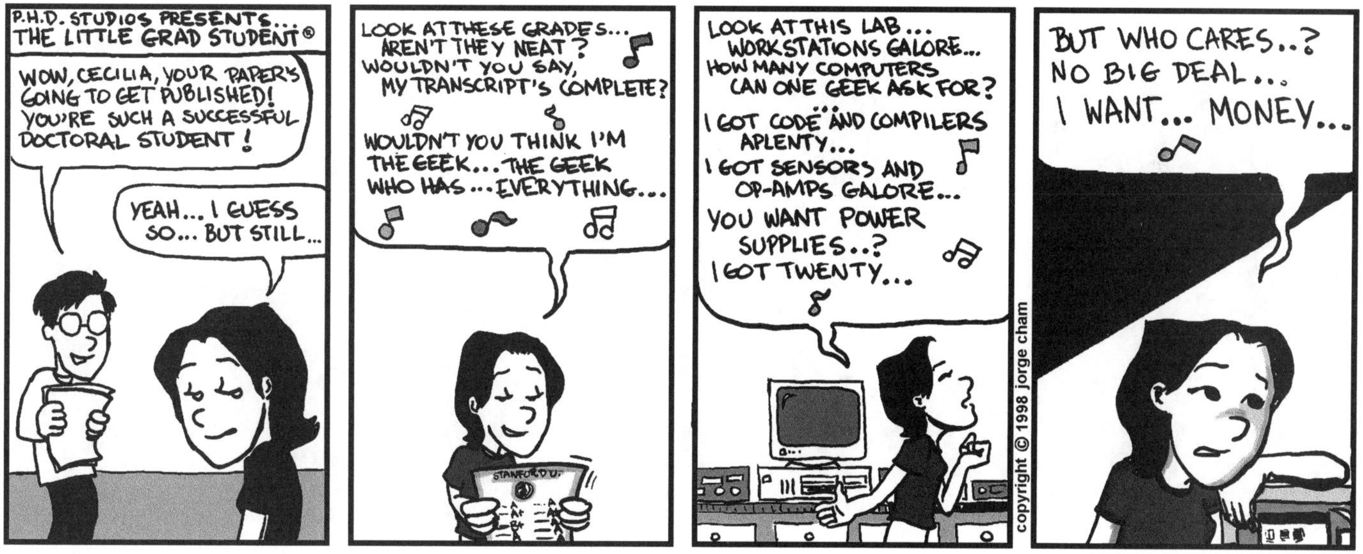
P.H.D. STUDIOS PRESENTS...
THE LITTLE GRAD STUDENT®
WOW, CECILIA, YOUR PAPER'S GOING TO GET PUBLISHED! YOU'RE SUCH A SUCCESSFUL DOCTORAL STUDENT!
YEAH... I GUESS SO... BUT STILL...
LOOK AT THESE GRADES... AREN'T THEY NEAT? WOULDN'T YOU SAY, MY TRANSCRIPT'S COMPLETE? WOULDN'T YOU THINK I'M THE GEEK... THE GEEK WHO HAS... EVERYTHING...
STANFORD U.
LOOK AT THIS LAB... WORKSTATIONS GALORE... HOW MANY COMPUTERS CAN ONE GEEK ASK FOR? I GOT CODE AND COMPILERS APLENTY... I GOT SENSORS AND OP-AMPS GALORE... YOU WANT POWER SUPPLIES..? I GOT TWENTY...
copyright © 1998 jorge cham
BUT WHO CARES..? NO BIG DEAL... I WANT... MONEY...

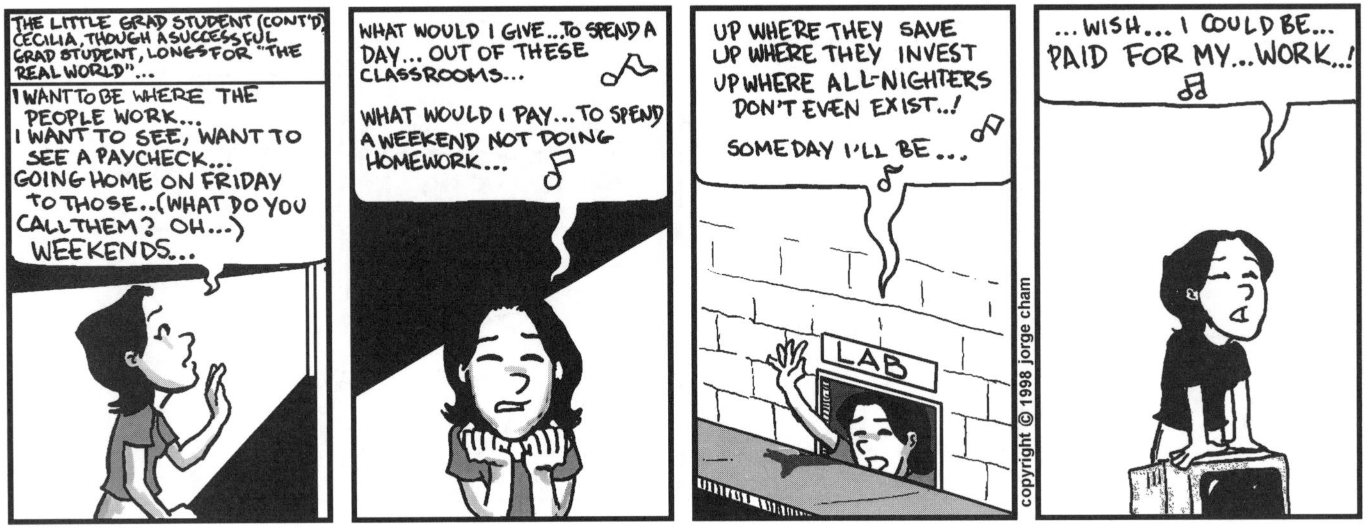
THE LITTLE GRAD STUDENT (CONT'D) CECILIA, THOUGH A SUCCESSFUL GRAD STUDENT, LONGS FOR "THE REAL WORLD"...
I WANT TO BE WHERE THE PEOPLE WORK... I WANT TO SEE, WANT TO SEE A PAYCHECK... GOING HOME ON FRIDAY TO THOSE..(WHAT DO YOU CALL THEM? OH...) WEEKENDS...
WHAT WOULD I GIVE...TO SPEND A DAY... OUT OF THESE CLASSROOMS...
WHAT WOULD I PAY...TO SPEND A WEEKEND NOT DOING HOMEWORK...
UP WHERE THEY SAVE UP WHERE THEY INVEST UP WHERE ALL-NIGHTERS DON'T EVEN EXIST..!
SOMEDAY I'LL BE...
LAB
copyright © 1998 jorge cham
...WISH... I COULD BE... PAID FOR MY...WORK..!

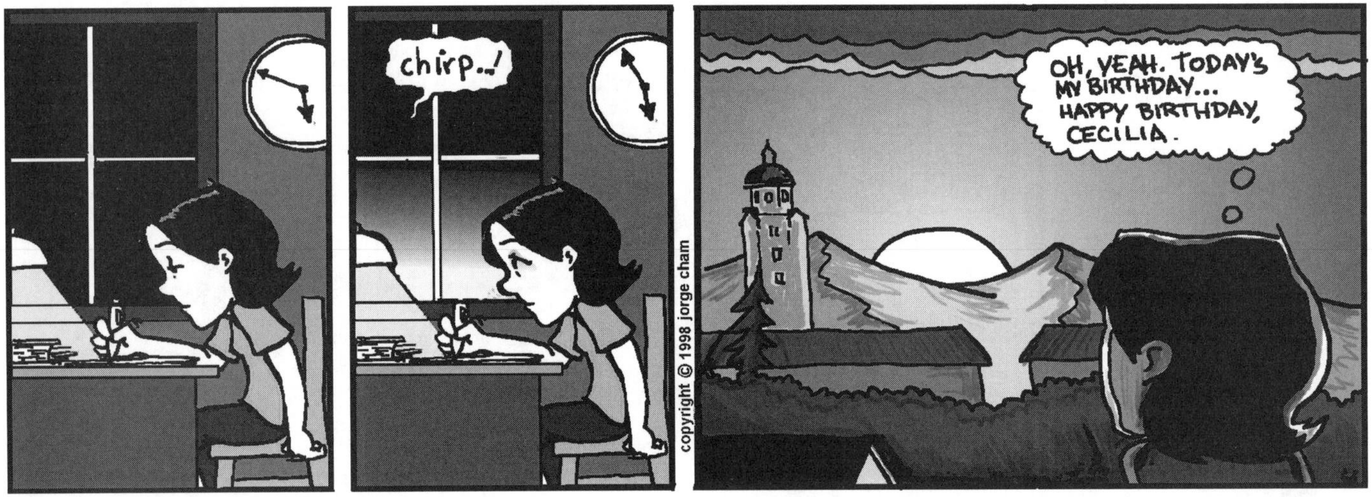
chirp..!
copyright © 1998 jorge cham
OH, YEAH. TODAY'S MY BIRTHDAY... HAPPY BIRTHDAY, CECILIA.

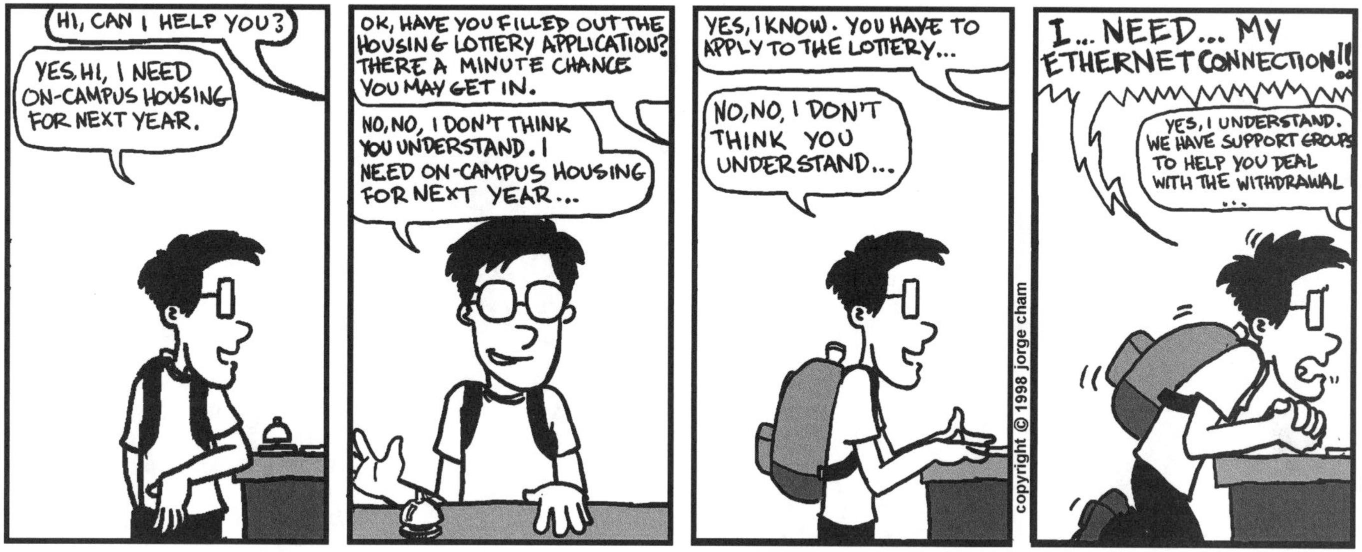
HI, CAN I HELP YOU?
YES, HI, I NEED ON-CAMPUS HOUSING FOR NEXT YEAR.
OK, HAVE YOU FILLED OUT THE HOUSING LOTTERY APPLICATION? THERE A MINUTE CHANCE YOU MAY GET IN.
NO, NO, I DON'T THINK YOU UNDERSTAND. I NEED ON-CAMPUS HOUSING FOR NEXT YEAR...
YES, I KNOW. YOU HAVE TO APPLY TO THE LOTTERY...
NO, NO, I DON'T THINK YOU UNDERSTAND...
copyright © 1998 jorge cham
I... NEED... MY ETHERNET CONNECTION!!
YES, I UNDERSTAND. WE HAVE SUPPORT GROUPS TO HELP YOU DEAL WITH THE WITHDRAWAL...

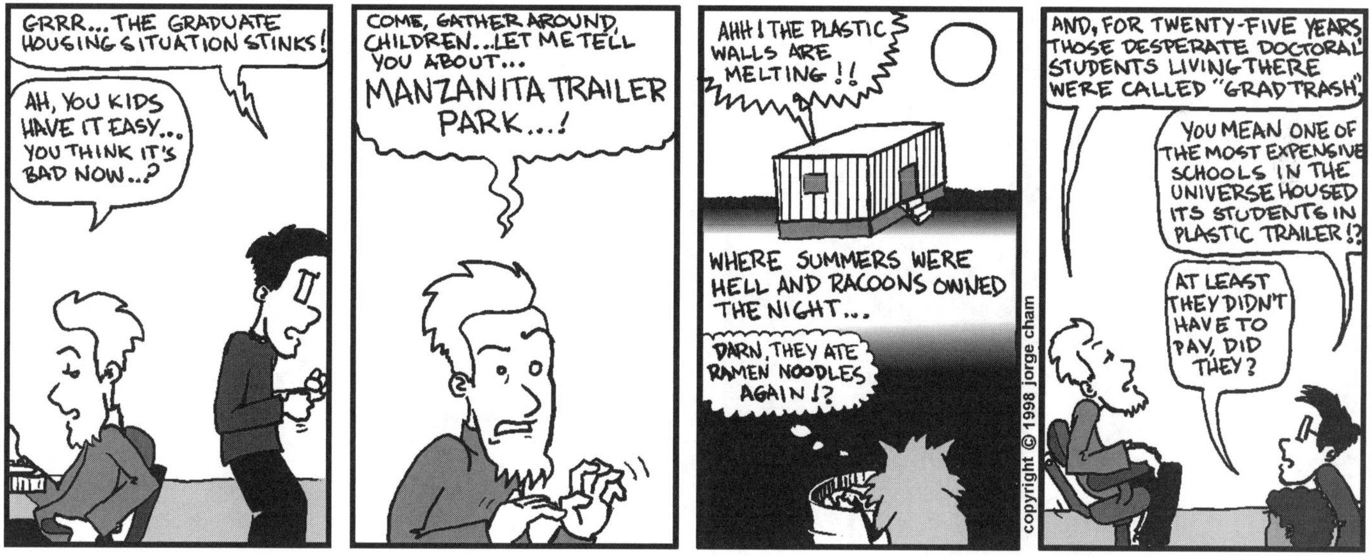
GRRR... THE GRADUATE HOUSING SITUATION STINKS!
AH, YOU KIDS HAVE IT EASY... YOU THINK IT'S BAD NOW...?
COME, GATHER AROUND, CHILDREN... LET ME TELL YOU ABOUT... MANZANITA TRAILER PARK...!
AHH! THE PLASTIC WALLS ARE MELTING!!
WHERE SUMMERS WERE HELL AND RACOONS OWNED THE NIGHT...
DARN, THEY ATE RAMEN NOODLES AGAIN!?
copyright © 1998 jorge cham
AND, FOR TWENTY-FIVE YEARS THOSE DESPERATE DOCTORAL STUDENTS LIVING THERE WERE CALLED "GRADTRASH".
YOU MEAN ONE OF THE MOST EXPENSIVE SCHOOLS IN THE UNIVERSE HOUSED ITS STUDENTS IN PLASTIC TRAILER!?
AT LEAST THEY DIDN'T HAVE TO PAY, DID THEY?

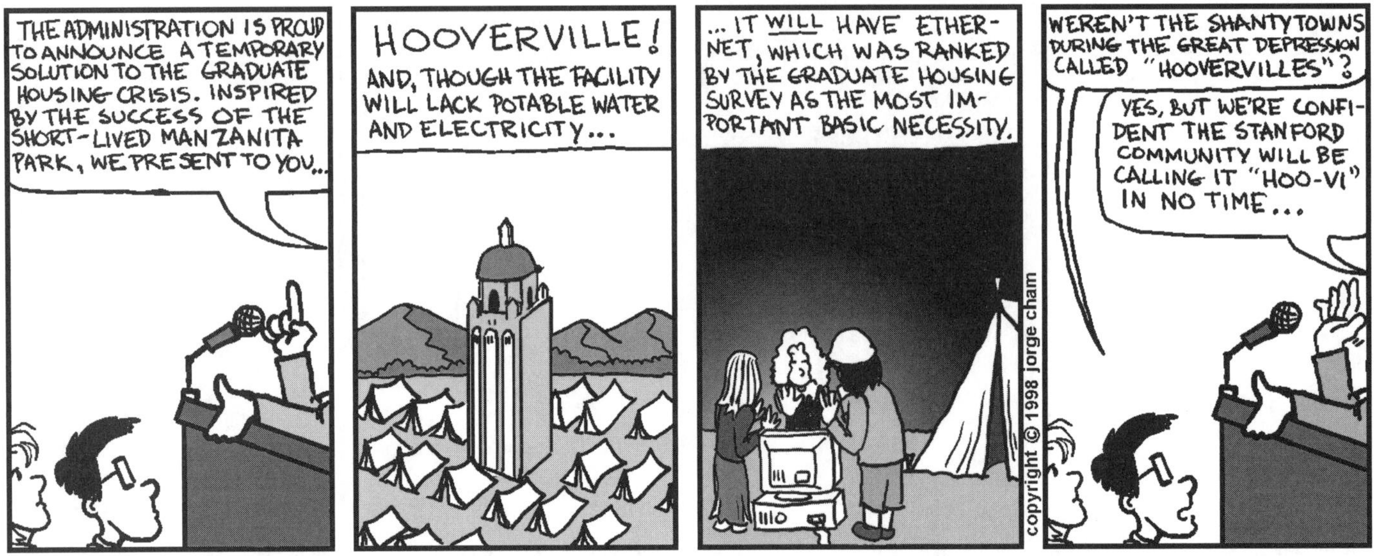
THE ADMINISTRATION IS PROUD TO ANNOUNCE A TEMPORARY SOLUTION TO THE GRADUATE HOUSING CRISIS. INSPIRED BY THE SUCCESS OF THE SHORT-LIVED MANZANITA PARK, WE PRESENT TO YOU...
HOOVERVILLE!
AND, THOUGH THE FACILITY WILL LACK POTABLE WATER AND ELECTRICITY...
... IT WILL HAVE ETHERNET, WHICH WAS RANKED BY THE GRADUATE HOUSING SURVEY AS THE MOST IMPORTANT BASIC NECESSITY.
copyright © 1998 jorge cham
WEREN'T THE SHANTYTOWNS DURING THE GREAT DEPRESSION CALLED "HOOVERVILLES"?
YES, BUT WE'RE CONFIDENT THE STANFORD COMMUNITY WILL BE CALLING IT "HOO-VI" IN NO TIME...

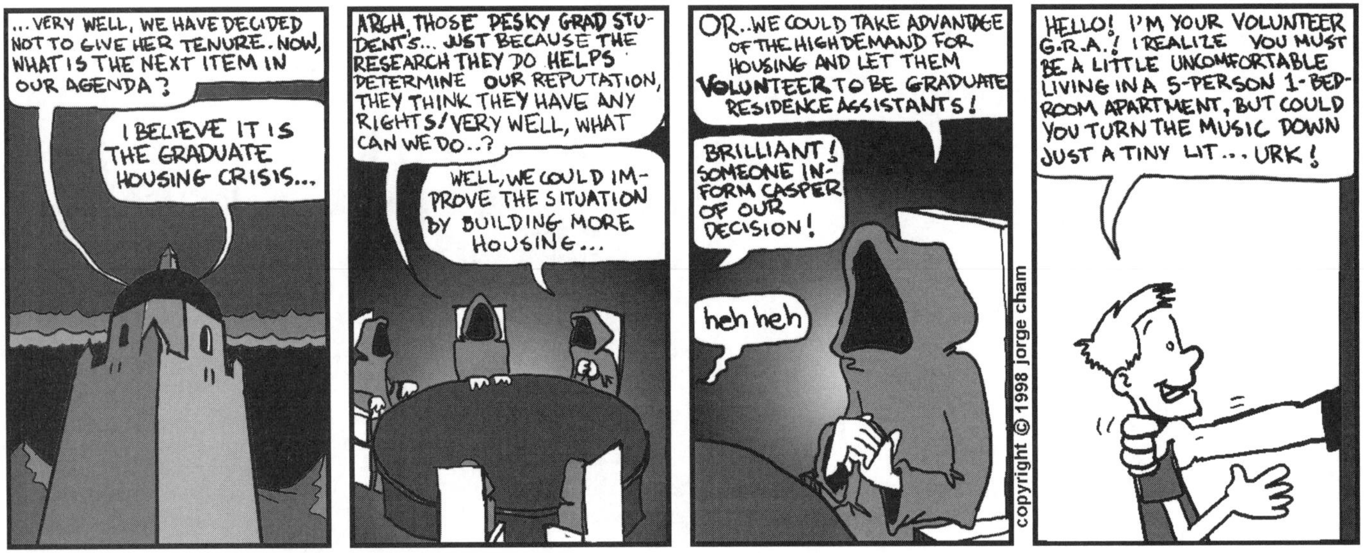
...VERY WELL, WE HAVE DECIDED NOT TO GIVE HER TENURE. NOW, WHAT IS THE NEXT ITEM IN OUR AGENDA?
I BELIEVE IT IS THE GRADUATE HOUSING CRISIS...
ARGH, THOSE PESKY GRAD STUDENT'S... JUST BECAUSE THE RESEARCH THEY DO HELPS DETERMINE OUR REPUTATION, THEY THINK THEY HAVE ANY RIGHTS! VERY WELL, WHAT CAN WE DO..?
WELL, WE COULD IMPROVE THE SITUATION BY BUILDING MORE HOUSING...
OR.. WE COULD TAKE ADVANTAGE OF THE HIGH DEMAND FOR HOUSING AND LET THEM VOLUNTEER TO BE GRADUATE RESIDENCE ASSISTANTS!
BRILLIANT! SOMEONE INFORM CASPER OF OUR DECISION!
heh heh
copyright © 1998 jorge cham
HELLO! I'M YOUR VOLUNTEER G.R.A.! I REALIZE YOU MUST BE A LITTLE UNCOMFORTABLE LIVING IN A 5-PERSON 1-BEDROOM APARTMENT, BUT COULD YOU TURN THE MUSIC DOWN JUST A TINY LIT... URK!

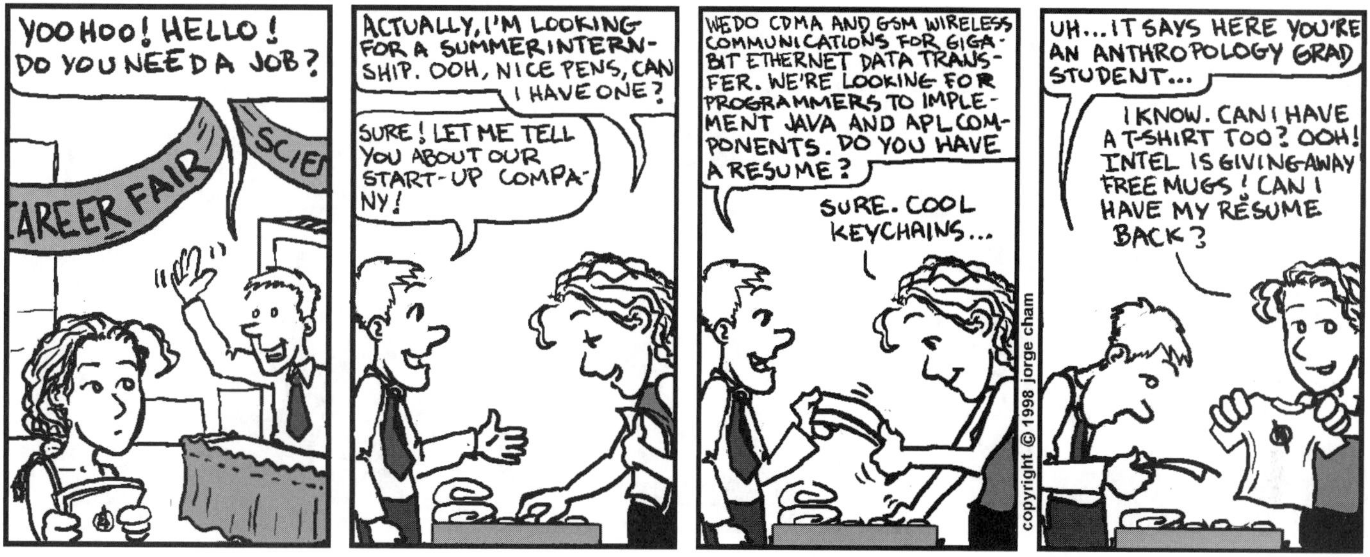
YOO HOO! HELLO! DO YOU NEED A JOB?
CAREER FAIR
ACTUALLY, I'M LOOKING FOR A SUMMER INTERNSHIP. OOH, NICE PENS, CAN I HAVE ONE?
SURE! LET ME TELL YOU ABOUT OUR START-UP COMPANY!
WE DO CDMA AND GSM WIRELESS COMMUNICATIONS FOR GIGABIT ETHERNET DATA TRANSFER. WE'RE LOOKING FOR PROGRAMMERS TO IMPLEMENT JAVA AND APL COMPONENTS. DO YOU HAVE A RESUME?
SURE. COOL KEYCHAINS...
copyright © 1998 jorge cham
UH... IT SAYS HERE YOU'RE AN ANTHROPOLOGY GRAD STUDENT...
I KNOW. CAN I HAVE A T-SHIRT TOO? OOH! INTEL IS GIVING AWAY FREE MUGS! CAN I HAVE MY RESUME BACK?

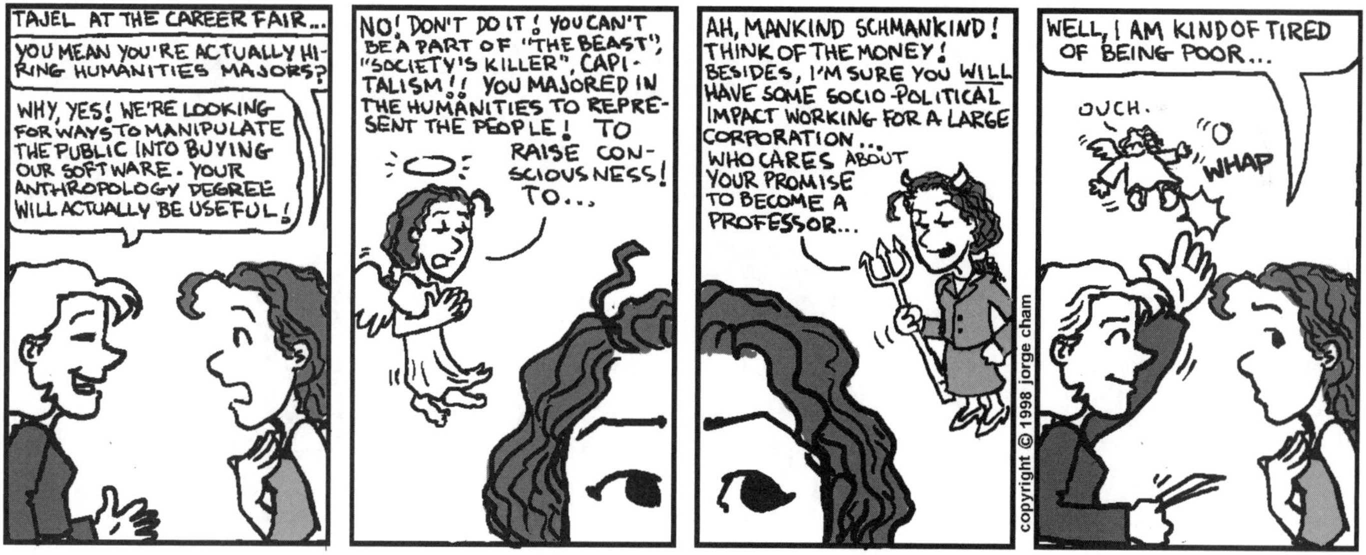
TAJEL AT THE CAREER FAIR...
YOU MEAN YOU'RE ACTUALLY HIRING HUMANITIES MAJORS?
WHY, YES! WE'RE LOOKING FOR WAYS TO MANIPULATE THE PUBLIC INTO BUYING OUR SOFTWARE. YOUR ANTHROPOLOGY DEGREE WILL ACTUALLY BE USEFUL!
NO! DON'T DO IT! YOU CAN'T BE A PART OF "THE BEAST", "SOCIETY'S KILLER", CAPITALISM!! YOU MAJORED IN THE HUMANITIES TO REPRESENT THE PEOPLE! TO RAISE CONSCIOUSNESS! TO...
AH, MANKIND SCHMANKIND! THINK OF THE MONEY! BESIDES, I'M SURE YOU WILL HAVE SOME SOCIO-POLITICAL IMPACT WORKING FOR A LARGE CORPORATION... WHO CARES ABOUT YOUR PROMISE TO BECOME A PROFESSOR...
copyright © 1998 jorge cham
WELL, I AM KIND OF TIRED OF BEING POOR...
OUCH.
WHAP

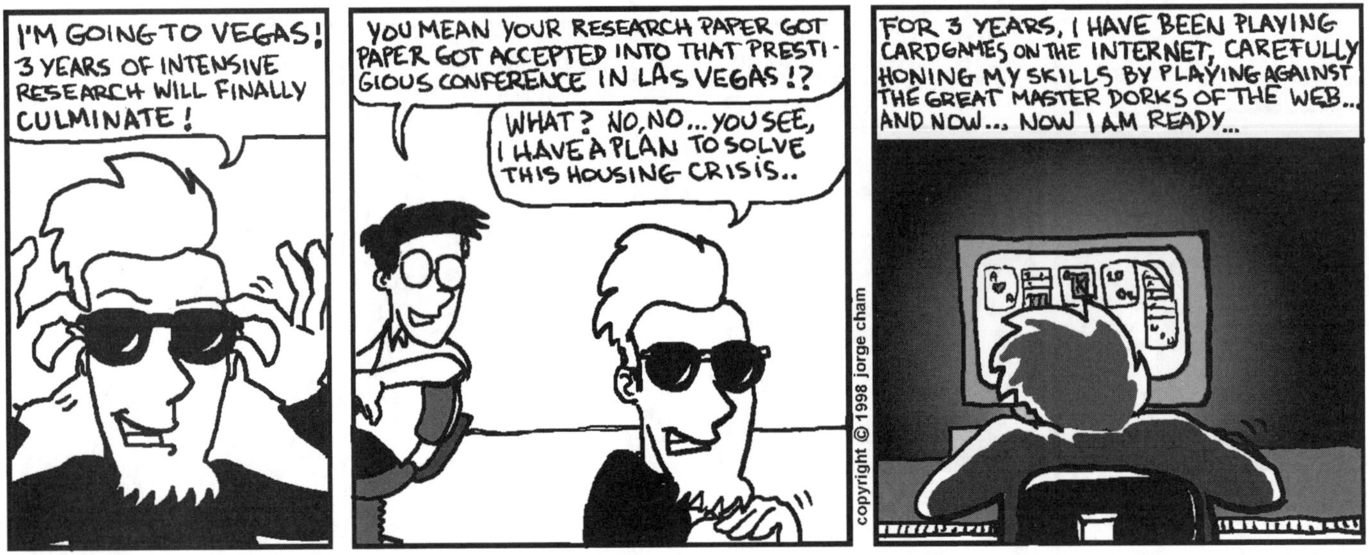
I'M GOING TO VEGAS! 3 YEARS OF INTENSIVE RESEARCH WILL FINALLY CULMINATE!
YOU MEAN YOUR RESEARCH PAPER GOT PAPER GOT ACCEPTED INTO THAT PRESTI-GIOUS CONFERENCE IN LAS VEGAS!?
WHAT? NO, NO... YOU SEE, I HAVE A PLAN TO SOLVE THIS HOUSING CRISIS..
copyright © 1998 jorge cham
FOR 3 YEARS, I HAVE BEEN PLAYING CARDGAMES ON THE INTERNET, CAREFULLY HONING MY SKILLS BY PLAYING AGAINST THE GREAT MASTER DORKS OF THE WEB... AND NOW... NOW I AM READY...

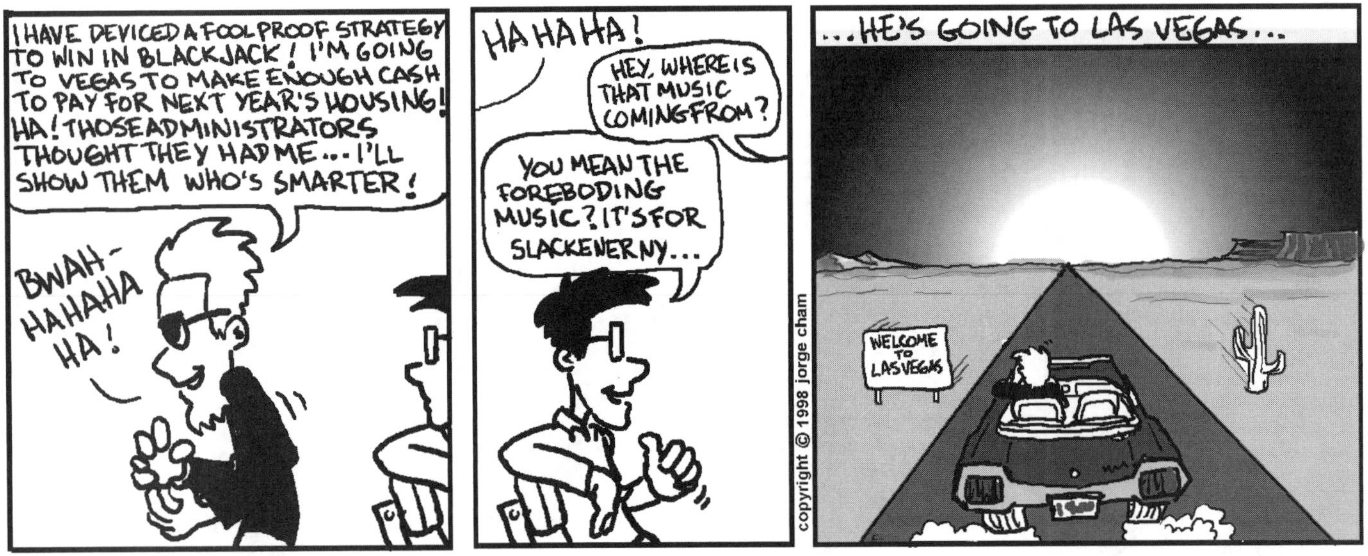
I HAVE DEVICED A FOOL PROOF STRATEGY TO WIN IN BLACKJACK! I'M GOING TO VEGAS TO MAKE ENOUGH CASH TO PAY FOR NEXT YEAR'S HOUSING! HA! THOSE ADMINISTRATORS THOUGHT THEY HAD ME... I'LL SHOW THEM WHO'S SMARTER!
BWAH-HAHAHA HA!
HA HA HA!
HEY, WHERE IS THAT MUSIC COMING FROM?
YOU MEAN THE FOREBODING MUSIC? IT'S FOR SLACKENERNY...
copyright © 1998 jorge cham
...HE'S GOING TO LAS VEGAS...
WELCOME TO LAS VEGAS

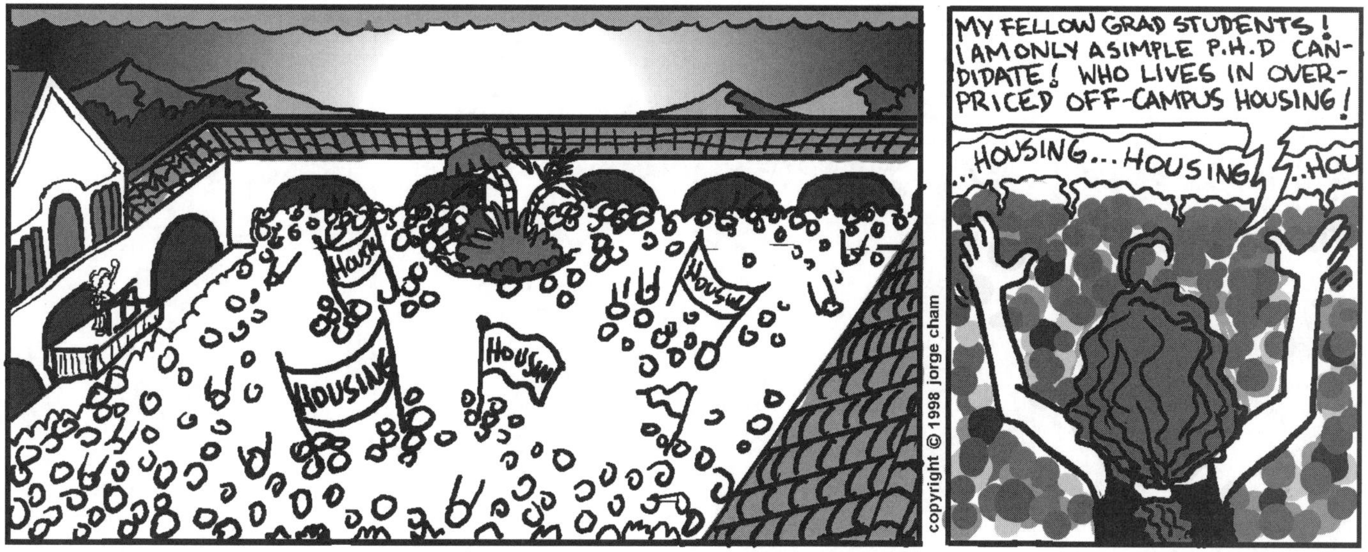
HOUSING
copyright © 1998 jorge cham
MY FELLOW GRAD STUDENTS! I AM ONLY A SIMPLE P.H.D CANDIDATE! WHO LIVES IN OVERPRICED OFF-CAMPUS HOUSING!
...HOUSING... HOUSING
..HOU

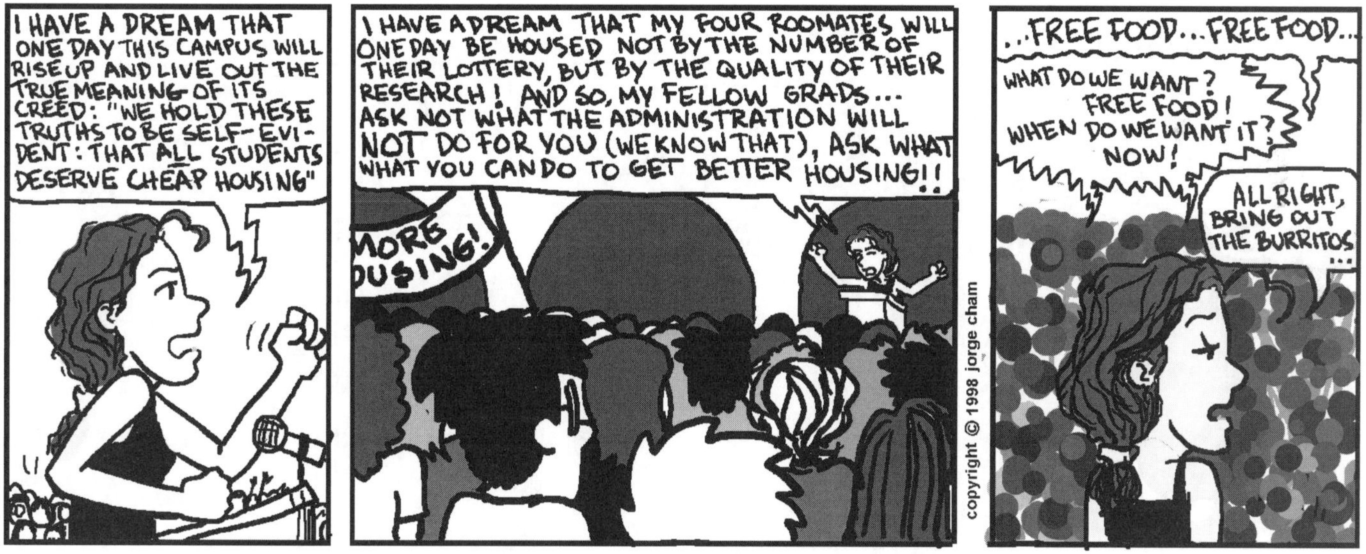
I HAVE A DREAM THAT ONE DAY THIS CAMPUS WILL RISE UP AND LIVE OUT THE TRUE MEANING OF ITS CREED: "WE HOLD THESE TRUTHS TO BE SELF-EVIDENT: THAT ALL STUDENTS DESERVE CHEAP HOUSING"
I HAVE A DREAM THAT MY FOUR ROOMATES WILL ONE DAY BE HOUSED NOT BY THE NUMBER OF THEIR LOTTERY, BUT BY THE QUALITY OF THEIR RESEARCH! AND SO, MY FELLOW GRADS... ASK NOT WHAT THE ADMINISTRATION WILL NOT DO FOR YOU (WE KNOW THAT), ASK WHAT WHAT YOU CAN DO TO GET BETTER HOUSING!!
MORE HOUSING!
copyright © 1998 jorge cham
...FREE FOOD...FREE FOOD...
WHAT DO WE WANT? FREE FOOD! WHEN DO WE WANT IT? NOW!
ALL RIGHT, BRING OUT THE BURRITOS...

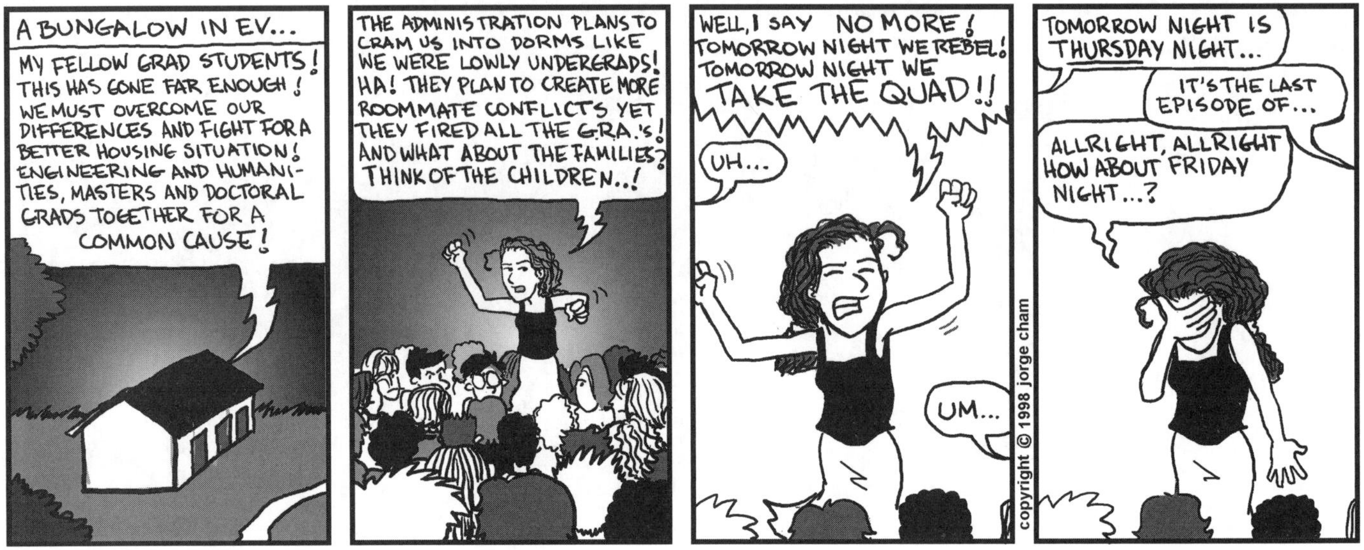
A BUNGALOW IN EV...
MY FELLOW GRAD STUDENTS! THIS HAS GONE FAR ENOUGH! WE MUST OVERCOME OUR DIFFERENCES AND FIGHT FOR A BETTER HOUSING SITUATION! ENGINEERING AND HUMANITIES, MASTERS AND DOCTORAL GRADS TOGETHER FOR A COMMON CAUSE!
THE ADMINISTRATION PLANS TO CRAM US INTO DORMS LIKE WE WERE LOWLY UNDERGRADS! HA! THEY PLAN TO CREATE MORE ROOMMATE CONFLICTS YET THEY FIRED ALL THE G.R.A.'s! AND WHAT ABOUT THE FAMILIES? THINK OF THE CHILDREN..!
WELL, I SAY NO MORE! TOMORROW NIGHT WE REBEL! TOMORROW NIGHT WE TAKE THE QUAD!!
UH...
UM...
copyright © 1998 jorge cham
TOMORROW NIGHT IS THURSDAY NIGHT...
IT'S THE LAST EPISODE OF...
ALLRIGHT, ALLRIGHT HOW ABOUT FRIDAY NIGHT...?

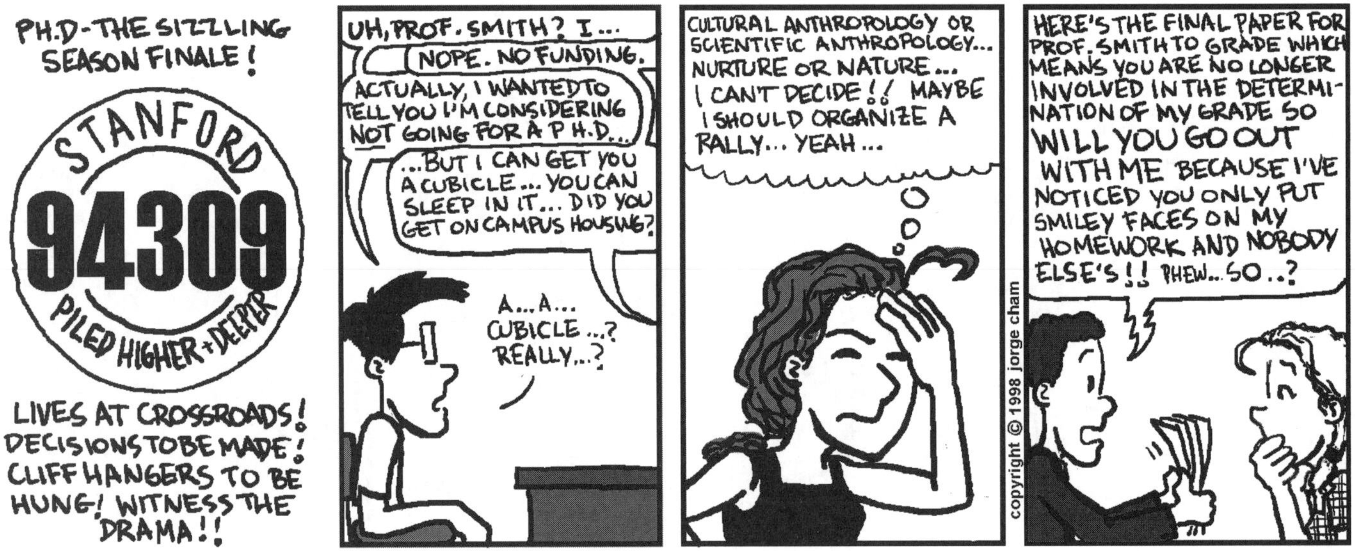
PH.D - THE SIZZLING SEASON FINALE!
STANFORD
94309
PILED HIGHER + DEEPER
LIVES AT CROSSROADS! DECISIONS TO BE MADE! CLIFF HANGERS TO BE HUNG! WITNESS THE DRAMA!!
UH, PROF. SMITH? I...
NOPE. NO FUNDING.
ACTUALLY, I WANTED TO TELL YOU I'M CONSIDERING NOT GOING FOR A PH.D...
...BUT I CAN GET YOU A CUBICLE... YOU CAN SLEEP IN IT... DID YOU GET ON CAMPUS HOUSING?
A... A... CUBICLE...? REALLY...?
CULTURAL ANTHROPOLOGY OR SCIENTIFIC ANTHROPOLOGY... NURTURE OR NATURE... I CAN'T DECIDE!! MAYBE I SHOULD ORGANIZE A RALLY... YEAH...
copyright © 1998 jorge cham
HERE'S THE FINAL PAPER FOR PROF. SMITH TO GRADE WHICH MEANS YOU ARE NO LONGER INVOLVED IN THE DETERMINATION OF MY GRADE SO WILL YOU GO OUT WITH ME BECAUSE I'VE NOTICED YOU ONLY PUT SMILEY FACES ON MY HOMEWORK AND NOBODY ELSE'S!! PHEW... SO..?

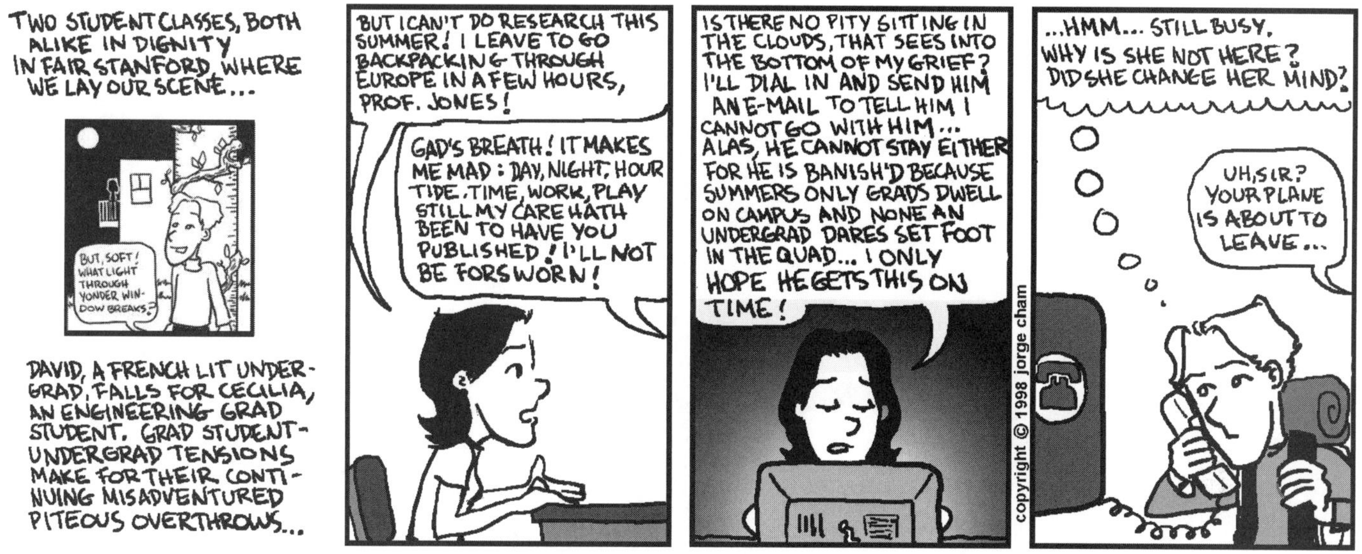
TWO STUDENT CLASSES, BOTH ALIKE IN DIGNITY
IN FAIR STANFORD, WHERE WE LAY OUR SCENE...
BUT, SOFT! WHAT LIGHT THROUGH YONDER WIN-DOW BREAKS?
DAVID, A FRENCH LIT UNDER-GRAD, FALLS FOR CECILIA, AN ENGINEERING GRAD STUDENT. GRAD STUDENT-UNDERGRAD TENSIONS MAKE FOR THEIR CONTI-NUING MISADVENTURED PITEOUS OVERTHROWS...
BUT I CAN'T DO RESEARCH THIS SUMMER! I LEAVE TO GO BACKPACKING THROUGH EUROPE IN A FEW HOURS, PROF. JONES!
GAD'S BREATH! IT MAKES ME MAD: DAY, NIGHT, HOUR TIDE, TIME, WORK, PLAY STILL MY CARE HATH BEEN TO HAVE YOU PUBLISHED! I'LL NOT BE FORSWORN!
IS THERE NO PITY SITTING IN THE CLOUDS, THAT SEES INTO THE BOTTOM OF MY GRIEF? I'LL DIAL IN AND SEND HIM AN E-MAIL TO TELL HIM I CANNOT GO WITH HIM... ALAS, HE CANNOT STAY EITHER FOR HE IS BANISH'D BECAUSE SUMMERS ONLY GRADS DWELL ON CAMPUS AND NONE AN UNDERGRAD DARES SET FOOT IN THE QUAD... I ONLY HOPE HE GETS THIS ON TIME!
copyright © 1998 jorge cham
...HMM... STILL BUSY. WHY IS SHE NOT HERE? DID SHE CHANGE HER MIND?
UH, SIR? YOUR PLANE IS ABOUT TO LEAVE...

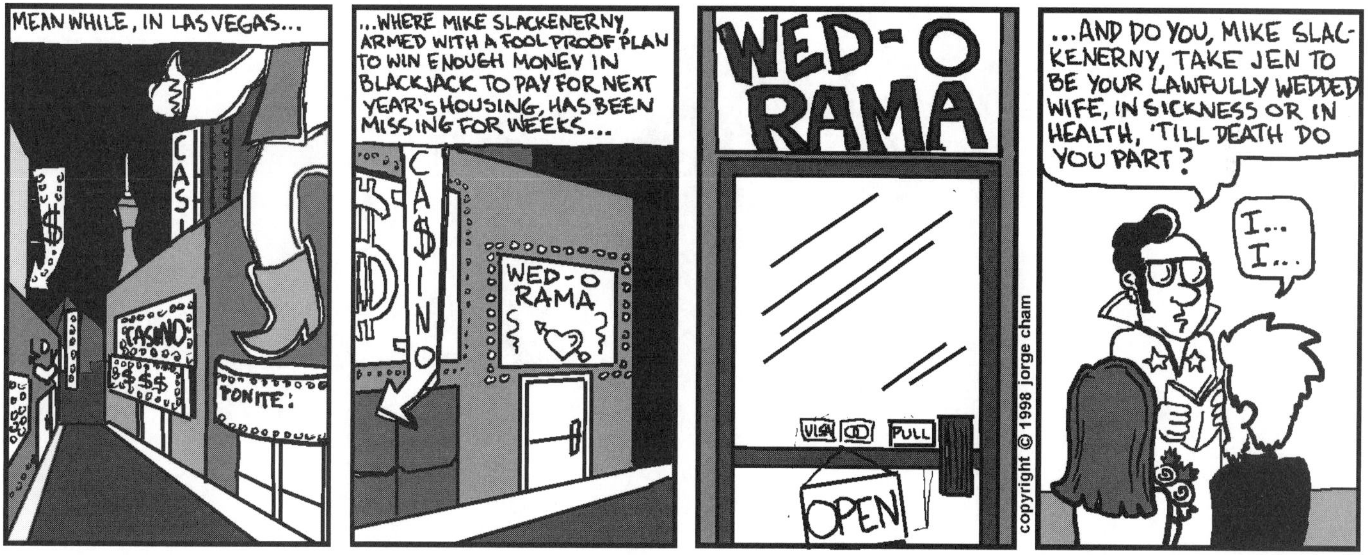
MEANWHILE, IN LAS VEGAS...
CASI
CASINO
TONITE:
...WHERE MIKE SLACKENERNY, ARMED WITH A FOOLPROOF PLAN TO WIN ENOUGH MONEY IN BLACKJACK TO PAY FOR NEXT YEAR'S HOUSING, HAS BEEN MISSING FOR WEEKS...
CASINO
WED-O RAMA
WED-O RAMA
VISA
PULL
OPEN
copyright © 1998 jorge cham
...AND DO YOU, MIKE SLACKENERNY, TAKE JEN TO BE YOUR LAWFULLY WEDDED WIFE, IN SICKNESS OR IN HEALTH, 'TILL DEATH DO YOU PART?
I... I...

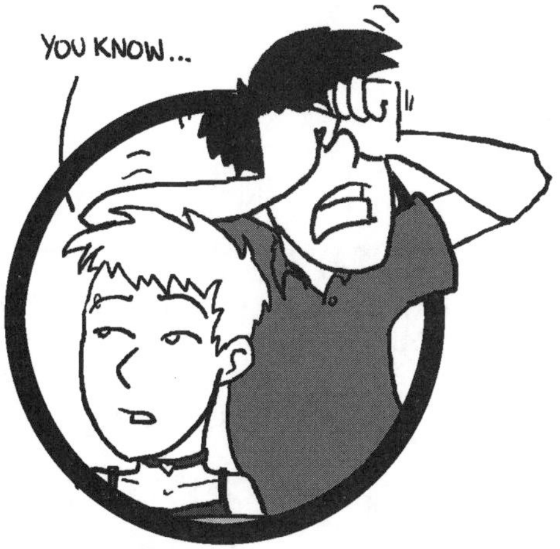
YOU KNOW...

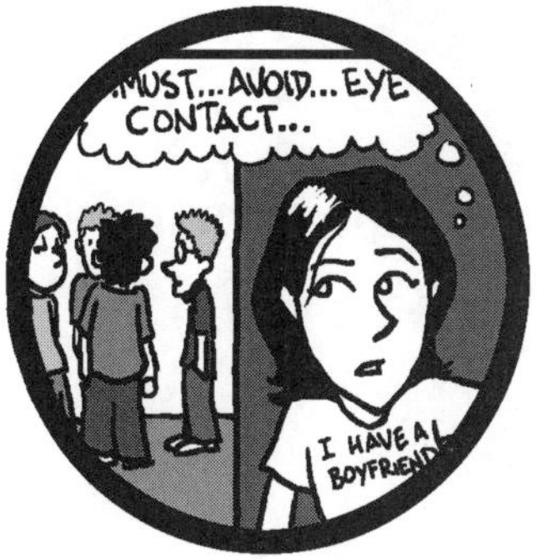
MUST... AVOID... EYE CONTACT...
I HAVE A
BOYFRIEND

YEAR TWO

1998-1999

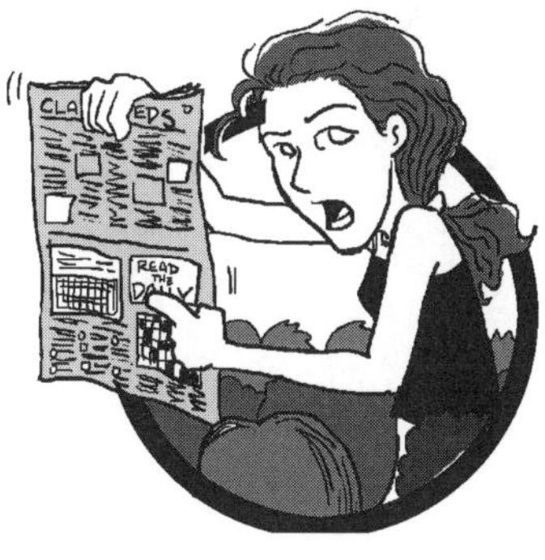

HI! WECOME BACK TO
PILED HIGHER + DEEPER
FOR THOSE OF YOU NEW TO THE CAMPUS, P.H.D. CHRONICLES THE WARM, TOUCHING, COMPLEX EXPERIENCES OF GRADUATE STUDENTS.
HERE'S A SAMPLE OF THE DRAMA YOU CAN EXPECT FROM P.H.D. THIS YEAR:
RESEARCH STINKS.
TAP TAP TAP
DATING STINKS.
CLICK!
QUALS STINK.
LACK OF MONEY STINKS.
copyright © 1998 jorge cham

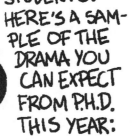

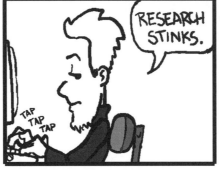

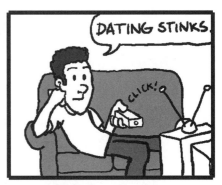

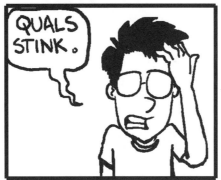

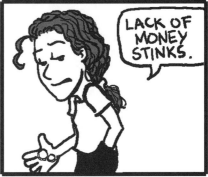

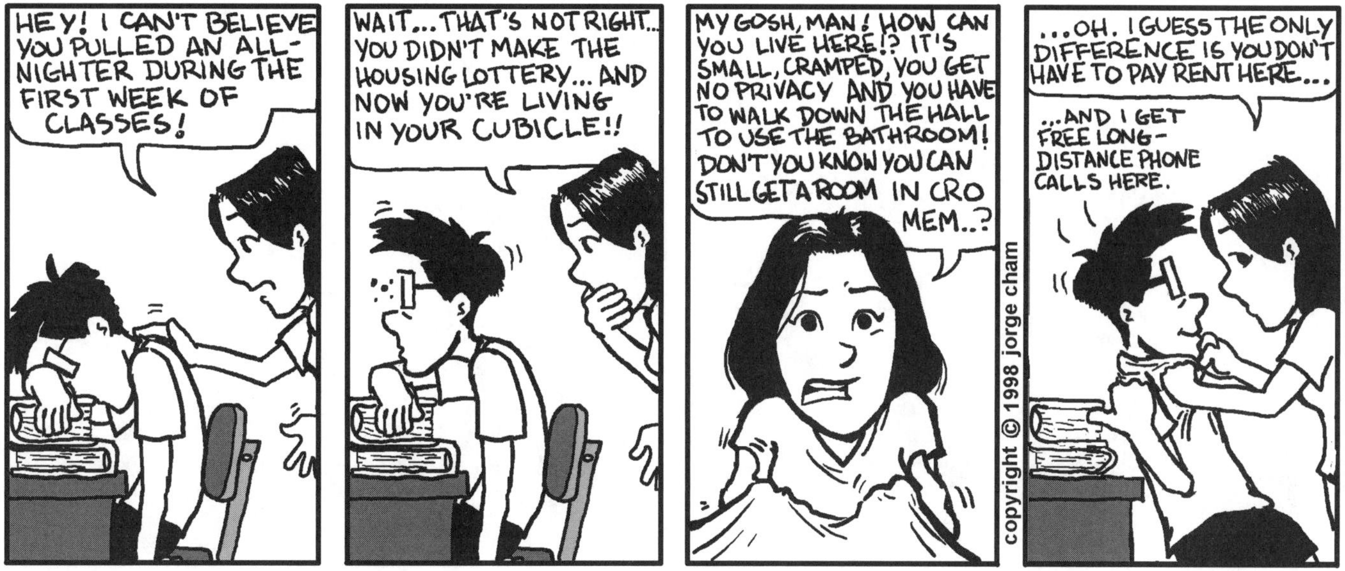
HEY! I CAN'T BELIEVE YOU PULLED AN ALL-NIGHTER DURING THE FIRST WEEK OF CLASSES!
WAIT... THAT'S NOT RIGHT... YOU DIDN'T MAKE THE HOUSING LOTTERY... AND NOW YOU'RE LIVING IN YOUR CUBICLE!!
MY GOSH, MAN! HOW CAN YOU LIVE HERE!? IT'S SMALL, CRAMPED, YOU GET NO PRIVACY AND YOU HAVE TO WALK DOWN THE HALL TO USE THE BATHROOM! DON'T YOU KNOW YOU CAN STILL GET A ROOM IN CRO MEM..?
copyright © 1998 jorge cham
...OH. I GUESS THE ONLY DIFFERENCE IS YOU DON'T HAVE TO PAY RENT HERE...
...AND I GET FREE LONG-DISTANCE PHONE CALLS HERE.

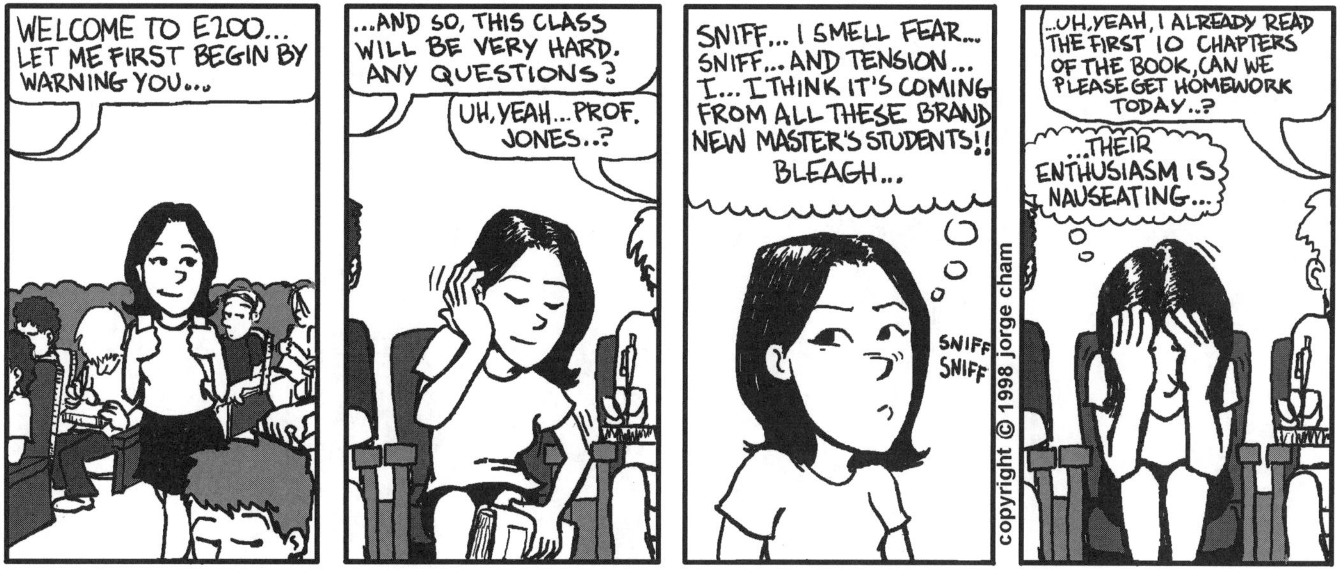
WELCOME TO E200... LET ME FIRST BEGIN BY WARNING YOU...
...AND SO, THIS CLASS WILL BE VERY HARD. ANY QUESTIONS?
UH, YEAH... PROF. JONES..?
SNIFF... I SMELL FEAR... SNIFF... AND TENSION... I... I THINK IT'S COMING FROM ALL THESE BRAND NEW MASTER'S STUDENTS!! BLEAGH...
SNIFF
SNIFF
copyright © 1998 jorge cham
...UH, YEAH, I ALREADY READ THE FIRST 10 CHAPTERS OF THE BOOK, CAN WE PLEASE GET HOMEWORK TODAY..?
...THEIR ENTHUSIASM IS NAUSEATING...

Panel 1: MY FELLOW STUDENTS! ARE WE TO STAND IDLY BY AS RESCOMP HIKES UP THE PRICE FOR IN-ROOM ETHERNET CONNECTION? WHATEVER HAPPENED TO THE PROMISE OF TWO ROUTERS IN EVERY DORM AND A HUB IN EVERY ROOM?

Panel 2: WHY, BACK IN MY UNDER-GRAD UNIVERSITY, STUDENTS HAD 3 BASIC RIGHTS: FREEDOM OF FOOD, THE PURSUIT OF HAPPY HOURS AND CHEAP WEB SURFING! FRANKLY, I'M APPALLED AT...

Panel 3: TAJEL, YOU DON'T EVEN OWN A COMPUTER.

Panel 4: BUT IF I DID, I'D STILL CLAMOR FOR MY RIGHT TO...

TAJEL, YOU DON'T EVEN LIVE ON CAMPUS...

Panel 5:

tudent #
54-8745
35-7023
57-3803
45-0 67
15-1 57
6

Panel 6: AAAAAAAAAA A
AAAAAAAAAAAA
AAAAAAAAAAAAA
AAAAAA AAAAAA
AAAA AA A
AA AA A
A AAA
AA AAAA
A AAAA
A AAAA

Panel 7: SNAP OUT OF IT!!

SMACK!

Panel 8: ARE YOU ALL RIGHT? I ONLY ASKED YOU IF YOU'VE ALREADY STARTED STUDYING FOR **QUALS**...

NOPE, NOT YET.

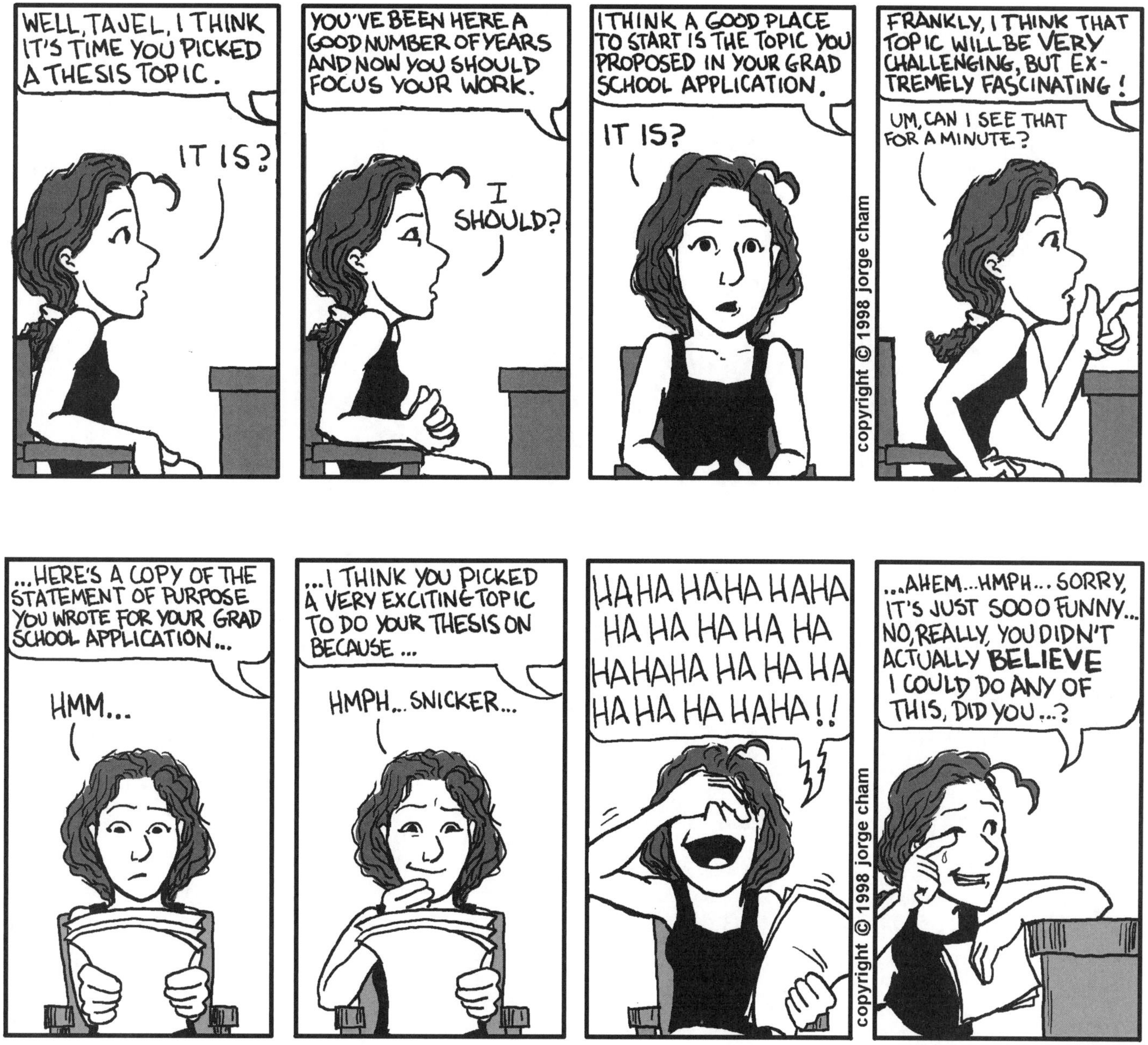
WELL, TAJEL, I THINK IT'S TIME YOU PICKED A THESIS TOPIC.
IT IS?
YOU'VE BEEN HERE A GOOD NUMBER OF YEARS AND NOW YOU SHOULD FOCUS YOUR WORK.
I SHOULD?
I THINK A GOOD PLACE TO START IS THE TOPIC YOU PROPOSED IN YOUR GRAD SCHOOL APPLICATION.
IT IS?
copyright © 1998 jorge cham
FRANKLY, I THINK THAT TOPIC WILL BE VERY CHALLENGING, BUT EXTREMELY FASCINATING!
UM, CAN I SEE THAT FOR A MINUTE?
...HERE'S A COPY OF THE STATEMENT OF PURPOSE YOU WROTE FOR YOUR GRAD SCHOOL APPLICATION...
HMM...
...I THINK YOU PICKED A VERY EXCITING TOPIC TO DO YOUR THESIS ON BECAUSE ...
HMPH... SNICKER...
HAHA HAHA HAHA HA HA HA HA HA HAHAHA HA HA HA HA HA HA HAHA!!
copyright © 1998 jorge cham
...AHEM...HMPH... SORRY, IT'S JUST SOOO FUNNY... NO, REALLY, YOU DIDN'T ACTUALLY **BELIEVE** I COULD DO ANY OF THIS, DID YOU...?

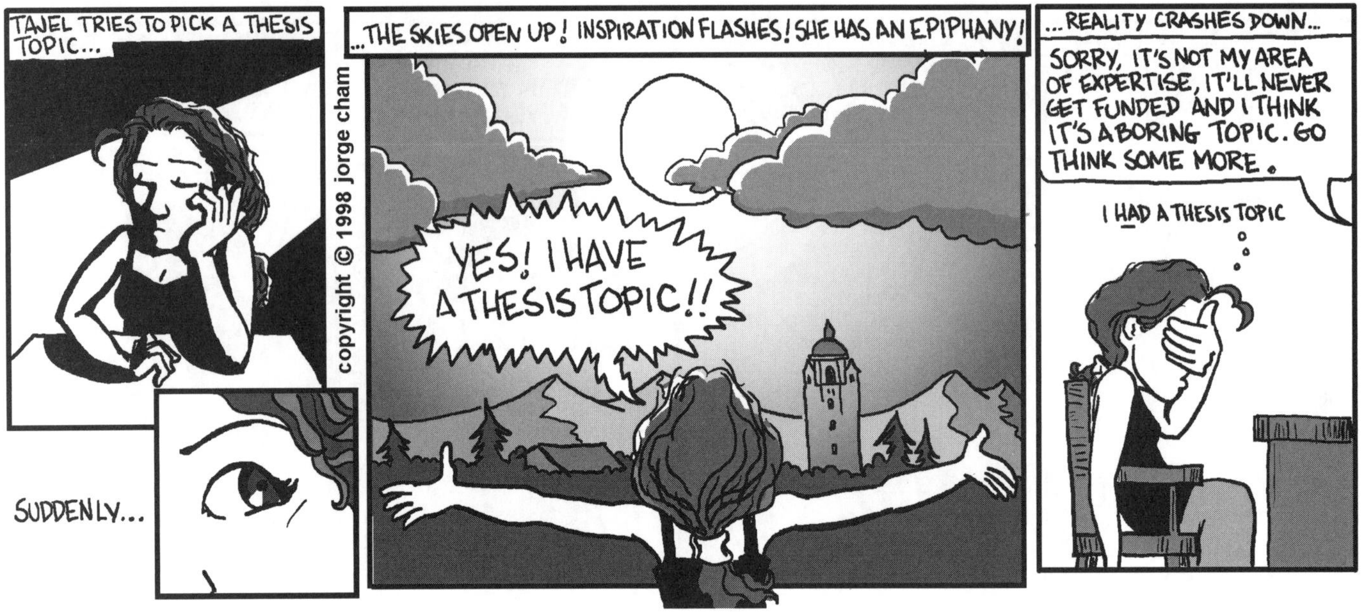
TAJEL TRIES TO PICK A THESIS TOPIC...
SUDDENLY...
...THE SKIES OPEN UP! INSPIRATION FLASHES! SHE HAS AN EPIPHANY!
YES! I HAVE A THESIS TOPIC!!
copyright © 1998 jorge cham
...REALITY CRASHES DOWN...
SORRY, IT'S NOT MY AREA OF EXPERTISE, IT'LL NEVER GET FUNDED AND I THINK IT'S A BORING TOPIC. GO THINK SOME MORE.
I HAD A THESIS TOPIC

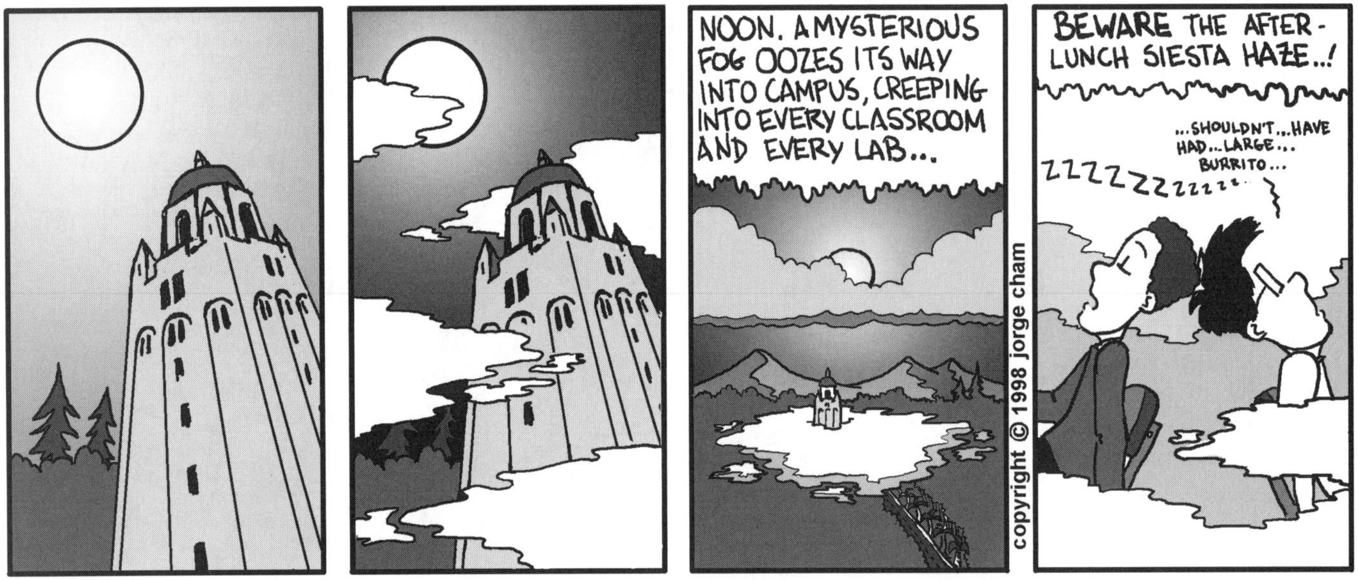
NOON. A MYSTERIOUS FOG OOZES ITS WAY INTO CAMPUS, CREEPING INTO EVERY CLASSROOM AND EVERY LAB...
copyright © 1998 jorge cham
BEWARE THE AFTER-LUNCH SIESTA HAZE...!
ZZZZZZzzzzz
...SHOULDN'T...HAVE HAD...LARGE... BURRITO...

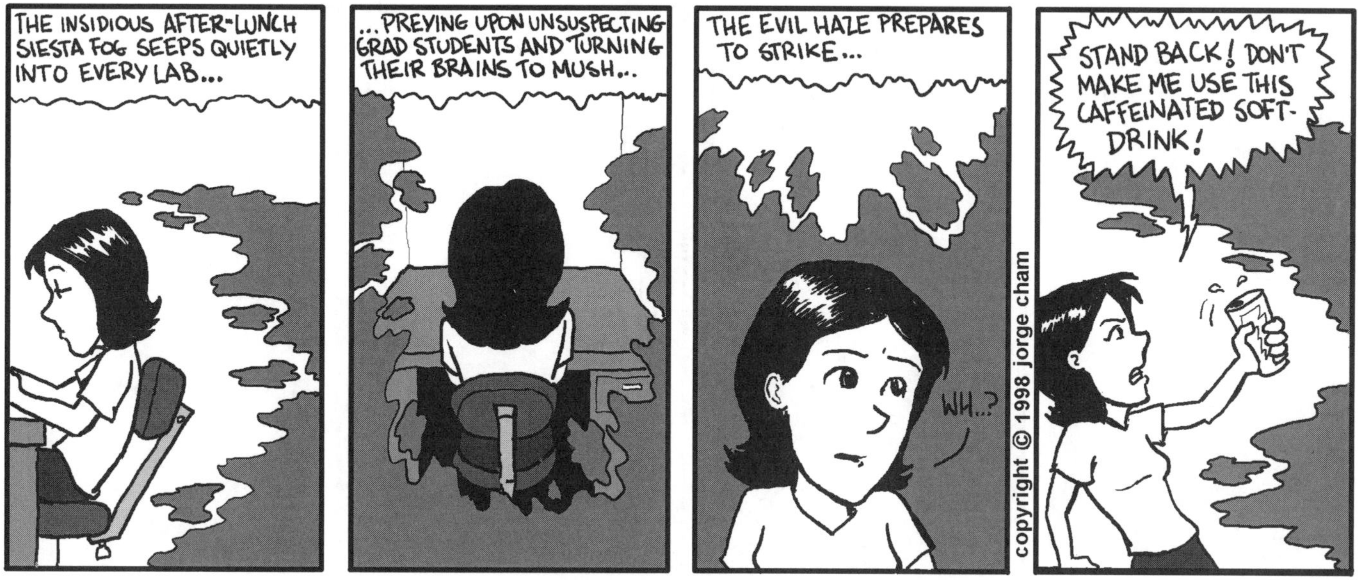
THE INSIDIOUS AFTER-LUNCH SIESTA FOG SEEPS QUIETLY INTO EVERY LAB...
...PREYING UPON UNSUSPECTING GRAD STUDENTS AND TURNING THEIR BRAINS TO MUSH...
THE EVIL HAZE PREPARES TO STRIKE...
WH..?
copyright © 1998 jorge cham
STAND BACK! DON'T MAKE ME USE THIS CAFFEINATED SOFT-DRINK!

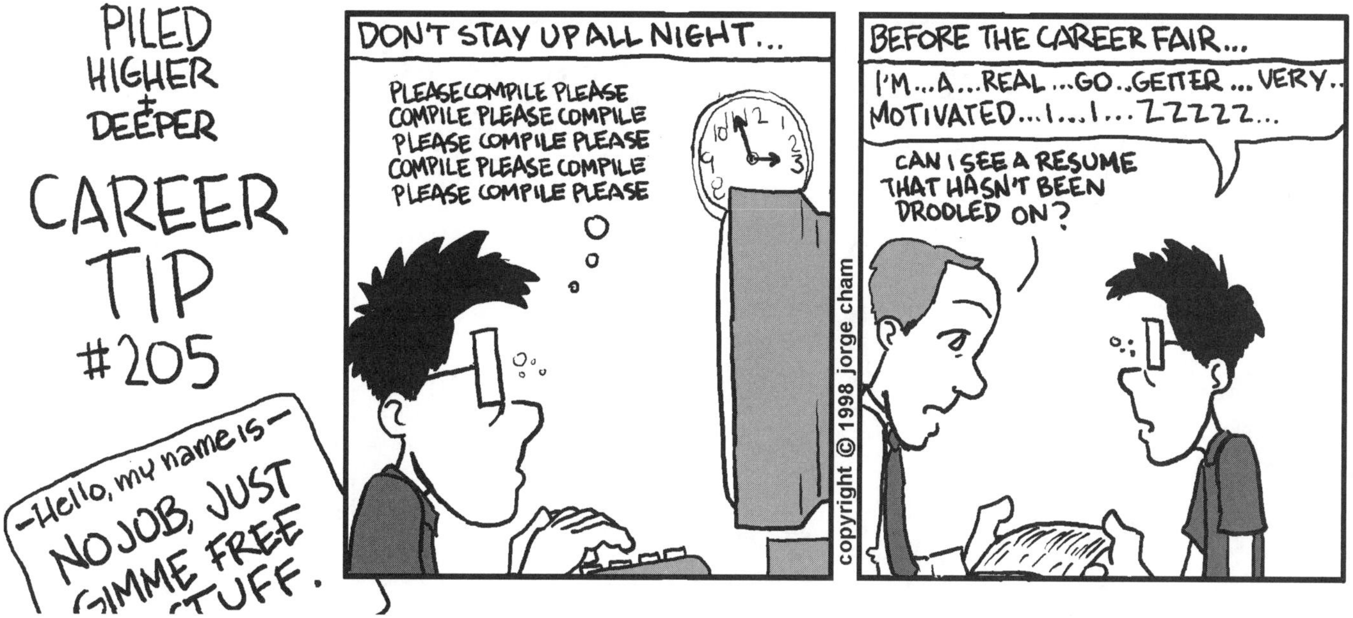
PILED HIGHER + DEEPER
CAREER TIP #205
-Hello, my name is-
NO JOB, JUST GIMME FREE STUFF.
DON'T STAY UP ALL NIGHT...
PLEASE COMPILE PLEASE COMPILE PLEASE COMPILE PLEASE COMPILE PLEASE COMPILE PLEASE COMPILE PLEASE
copyright © 1998 jorge cham
BEFORE THE CAREER FAIR...
I'M...A...REAL...GO..GETTER... VERY.. MOTIVATED...I...I...ZZZZZ...
CAN I SEE A RESUME THAT HASN'T BEEN DROOLED ON?

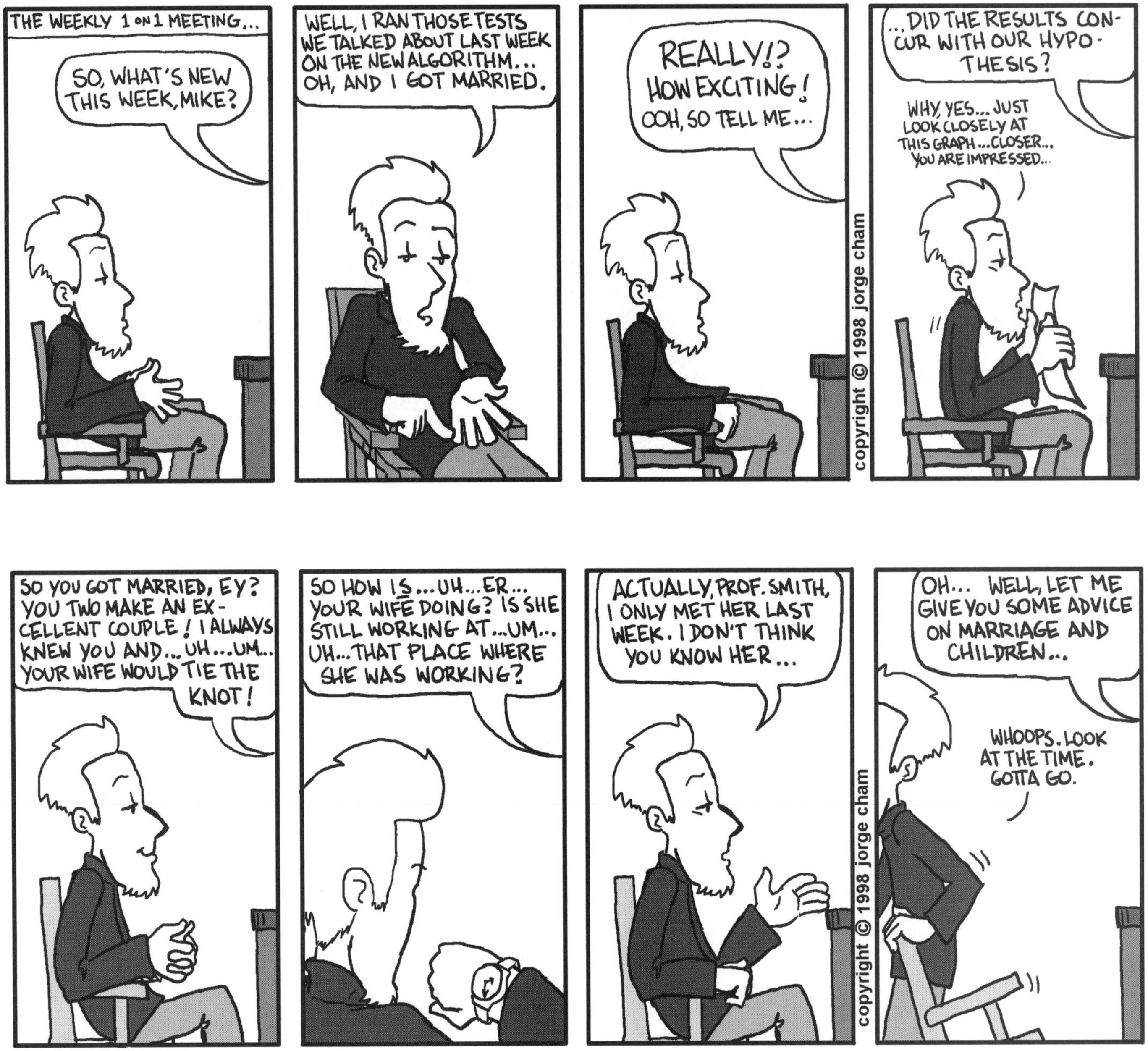
THE WEEKLY 1 ON 1 MEETING...
SO, WHAT'S NEW THIS WEEK, MIKE?
WELL, I RAN THOSE TESTS WE TALKED ABOUT LAST WEEK ON THE NEW ALGORITHM... OH, AND I GOT MARRIED.
REALLY!? HOW EXCITING! OOH, SO TELL ME...
...DID THE RESULTS CONCUR WITH OUR HYPOTHESIS?
WHY, YES... JUST LOOK CLOSELY AT THIS GRAPH... CLOSER... YOU ARE IMPRESSED...
copyright © 1998 jorge cham
SO YOU GOT MARRIED, EY? YOU TWO MAKE AN EXCELLENT COUPLE! I ALWAYS KNEW YOU AND... UH... UM... YOUR WIFE WOULD TIE THE KNOT!
SO HOW IS... UH... ER... YOUR WIFE DOING? IS SHE STILL WORKING AT... UM... UH... THAT PLACE WHERE SHE WAS WORKING?
ACTUALLY, PROF. SMITH, I ONLY MET HER LAST WEEK. I DON'T THINK YOU KNOW HER...
OH... WELL, LET ME GIVE YOU SOME ADVICE ON MARRIAGE AND CHILDREN...
WHOOPS. LOOK AT THE TIME. GOTTA GO.
copyright © 1998 jorge cham

PHD

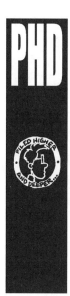

WARNING

The views expressed in this comic do not necessarily reflect the views of the authors. Any similarity between depicted characters or events and real advisors or research projects is purely coincidental and unintentional. **In fact**, the authors would like to express their extreme satisfaction and gratitude towards their advisor.

PROF. SMITH, I WANTED TO THANK YOU FOR LETTING ME WORK FOR YOU FOR CREDIT. I WANTED TO TALK TO YOU ABOUT JOINING YOU LAB AS AN R.A.
copyright © 1998 jorge cham
ACTUALLY, THE LAB WINDOWS ARE GETTING DIRTY AGAIN... WHAT WAS YOUR NAME AGAIN?

YOU WANTED TO SEE ME, PROF. SMITH?
YES, I HAVE GOOD NEWS... I FOUND FUNDING FOR YOU...
F-F...
...F-FUNDING...?
YES. NOW, THE PROJECT SPONSORS WANT YOU TO WEAR THIS JUMPSUIT WITH THEIR LOGOS WHENEVER YOU'RE IN THE LAB. I TOLD THEM IT'D BE NO PROBLEM...
MICROSCAPE
MATLAB
JUST DON'T
copyright © 1998 jorge cham
I ALSO TOOK THE LIBERTY OF SIGNING THIS CONTRACT FOR YOU. YOU DIDN'T REALLY WANT YOUR SOUL, RIGHT?
I HEREBY AGREE

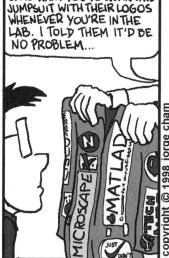

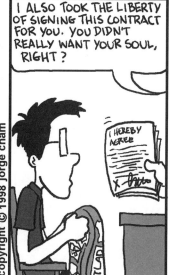

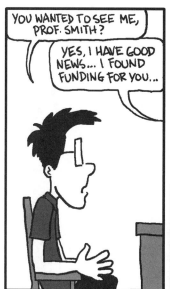

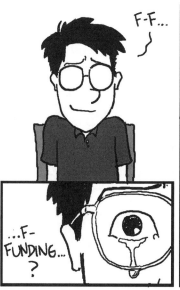

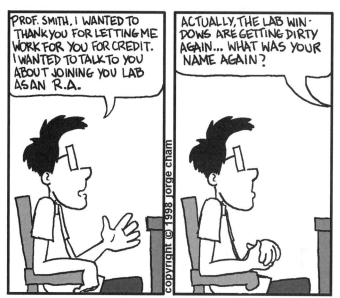

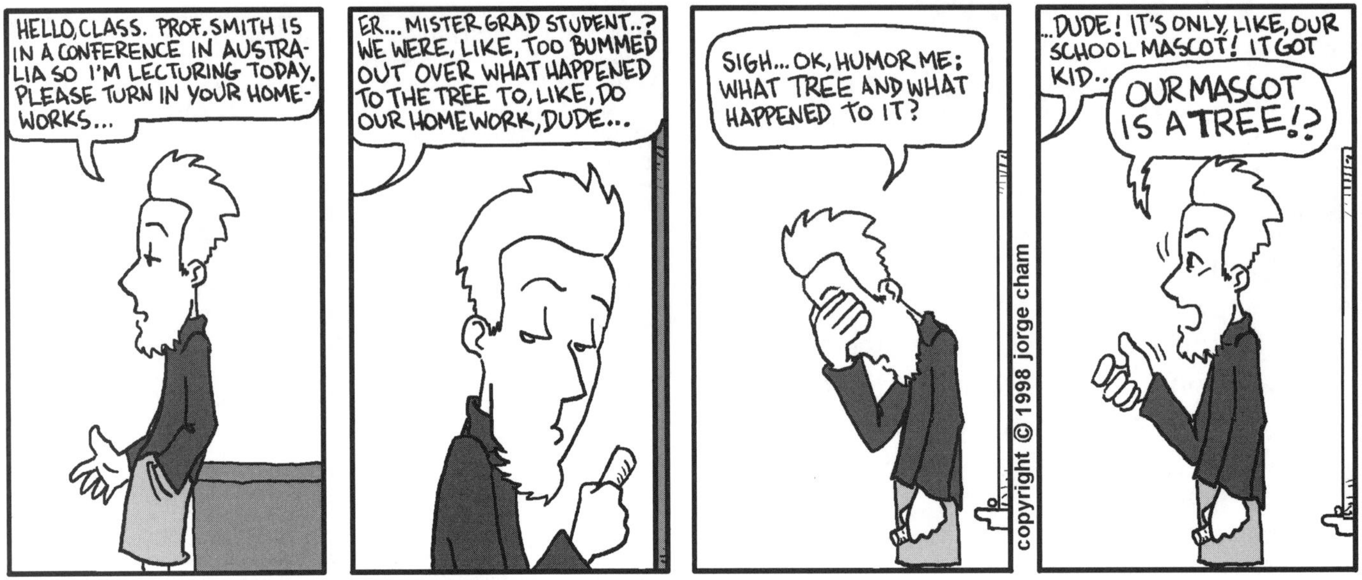
HELLO, CLASS. PROF. SMITH IS IN A CONFERENCE IN AUSTRALIA SO I'M LECTURING TODAY. PLEASE TURN IN YOUR HOMEWORKS...
ER... MISTER GRAD STUDENT..? WE WERE, LIKE, TOO BUMMED OUT OVER WHAT HAPPENED TO THE TREE TO, LIKE, DO OUR HOMEWORK, DUDE...
SIGH... OK, HUMOR ME; WHAT TREE AND WHAT HAPPENED TO IT?
copyright © 1998 jorge cham
...DUDE! IT'S ONLY, LIKE, OUR SCHOOL MASCOT! IT GOT KID...
OUR MASCOT IS A TREE!?

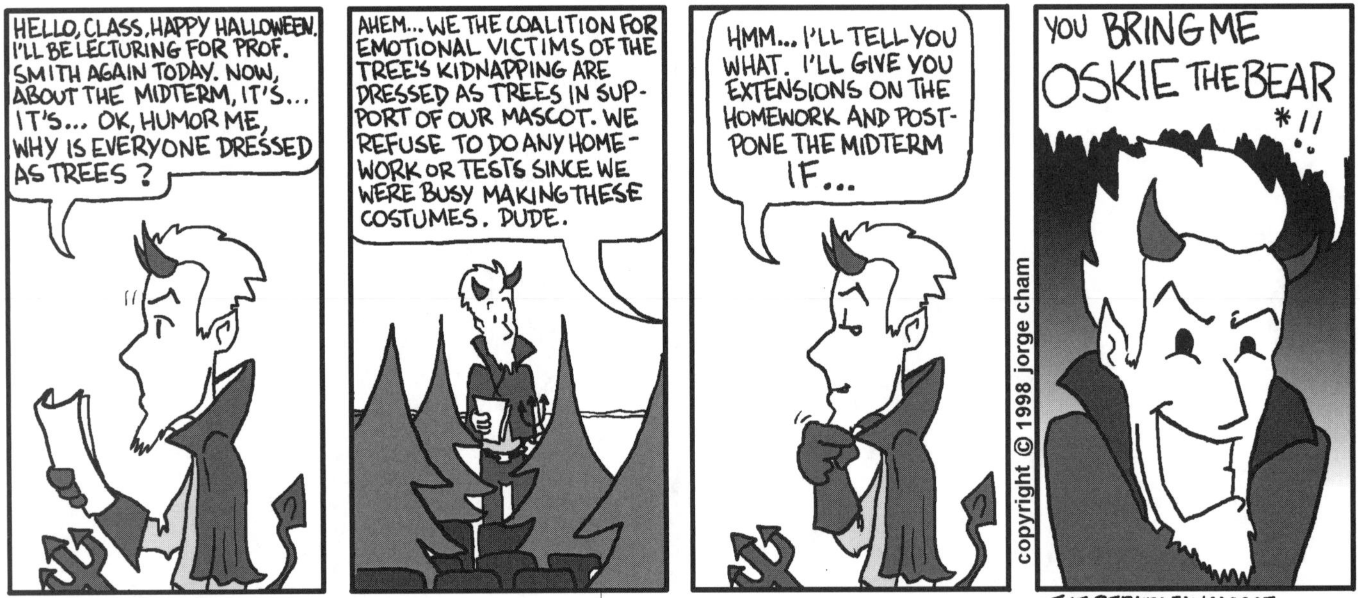
HELLO, CLASS, HAPPY HALLOWEEN. I'LL BE LECTURING FOR PROF. SMITH AGAIN TODAY. NOW, ABOUT THE MIDTERM, IT'S... IT'S... OK, HUMOR ME, WHY IS EVERYONE DRESSED AS TREES?
AHEM... WE THE COALITION FOR EMOTIONAL VICTIMS OF THE TREE'S KIDNAPPING ARE DRESSED AS TREES IN SUPPORT OF OUR MASCOT. WE REFUSE TO DO ANY HOMEWORK OR TESTS SINCE WE WERE BUSY MAKING THESE COSTUMES. DUDE.
HMM... I'LL TELL YOU WHAT. I'LL GIVE YOU EXTENSIONS ON THE HOMEWORK AND POSTPONE THE MIDTERM IF...
copyright © 1998 jorge cham
YOU BRING ME OSKIE THE BEAR*!!
*THE BERKELEY MASCOT.

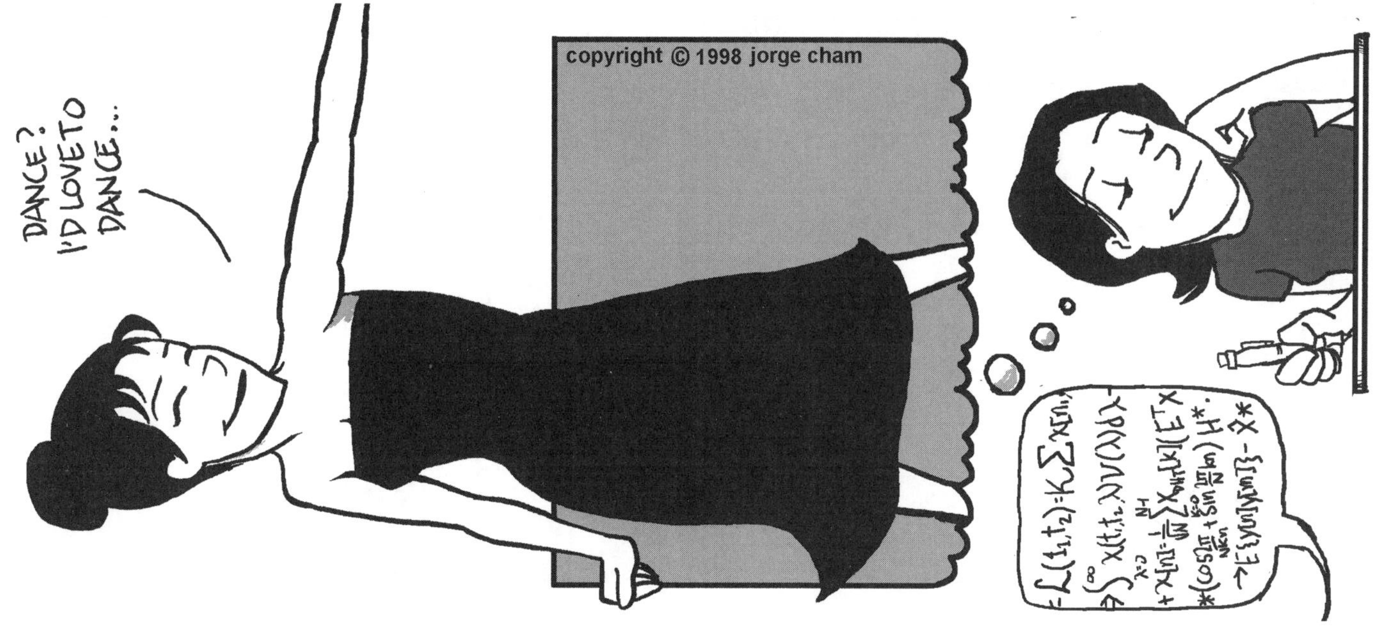
copyright © 1998 jorge cham
DANCE? I'D LOVE TO DANCE...

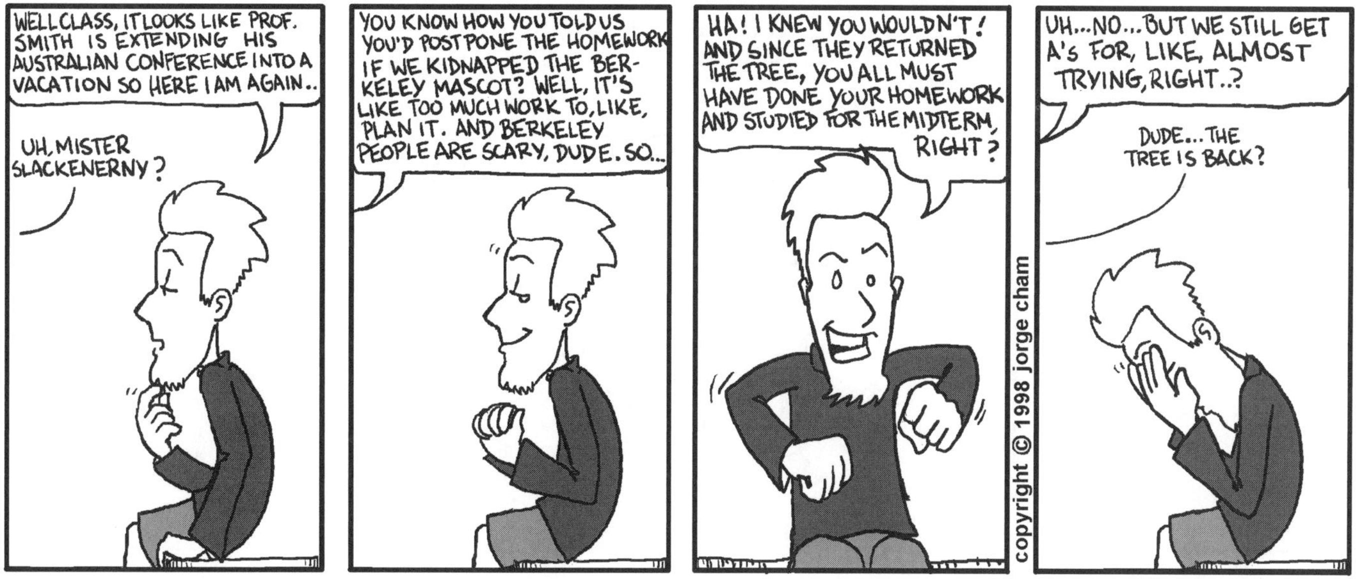
WELL CLASS, IT LOOKS LIKE PROF. SMITH IS EXTENDING HIS AUSTRALIAN CONFERENCE INTO A VACATION SO HERE I AM AGAIN..
UH, MISTER SLACKENERNY?
YOU KNOW HOW YOU TOLD US YOU'D POSTPONE THE HOMEWORK IF WE KIDNAPPED THE BERKELEY MASCOT? WELL, IT'S LIKE TOO MUCH WORK TO, LIKE, PLAN IT. AND BERKELEY PEOPLE ARE SCARY, DUDE. SO...
HA! I KNEW YOU WOULDN'T! AND SINCE THEY RETURNED THE TREE, YOU ALL MUST HAVE DONE YOUR HOMEWORK AND STUDIED FOR THE MIDTERM, RIGHT?
copyright © 1998 jorge cham
UH...NO...BUT WE STILL GET A's FOR, LIKE, ALMOST TRYING, RIGHT..?
DUDE... THE TREE IS BACK?

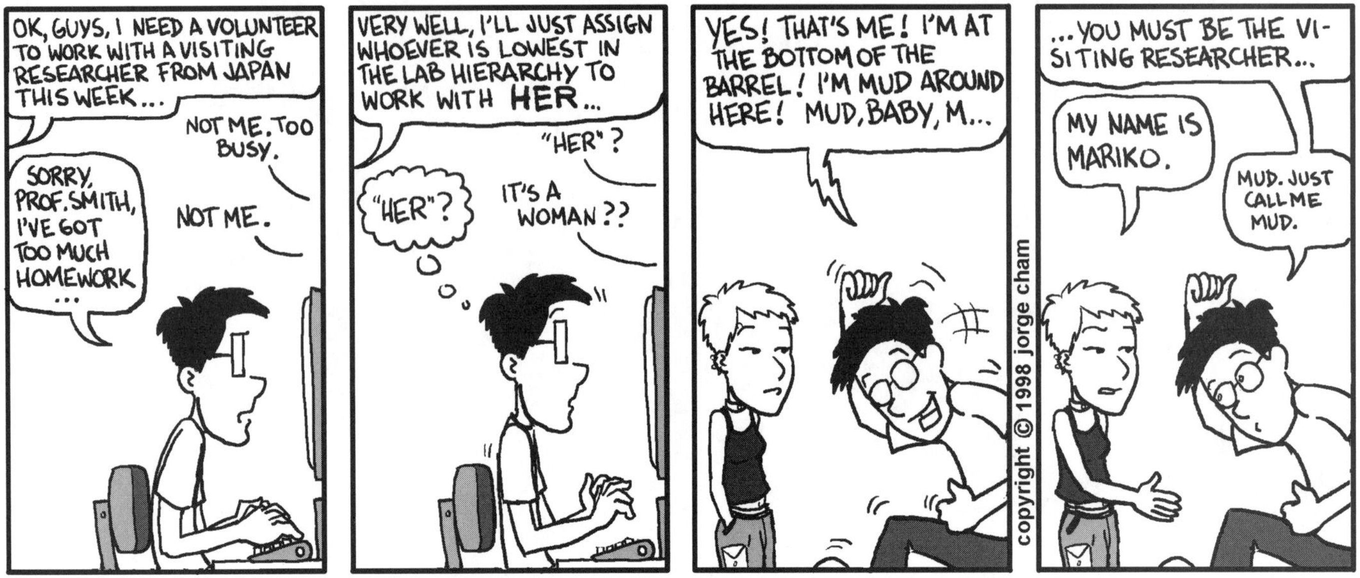
OK, GUYS, I NEED A VOLUNTEER TO WORK WITH A VISITING RESEARCHER FROM JAPAN THIS WEEK...
NOT ME. TOO BUSY.
SORRY, PROF. SMITH, I'VE GOT TOO MUCH HOMEWORK...
NOT ME.
VERY WELL, I'LL JUST ASSIGN WHOEVER IS LOWEST IN THE LAB HIERARCHY TO WORK WITH HER...
"HER"?
"HER"?
IT'S A WOMAN??
YES! THAT'S ME! I'M AT THE BOTTOM OF THE BARREL! I'M MUD AROUND HERE! MUD, BABY, M...
copyright © 1998 jorge cham
...YOU MUST BE THE VI-SITING RESEARCHER...
MY NAME IS MARIKO.
MUD. JUST CALL ME MUD.

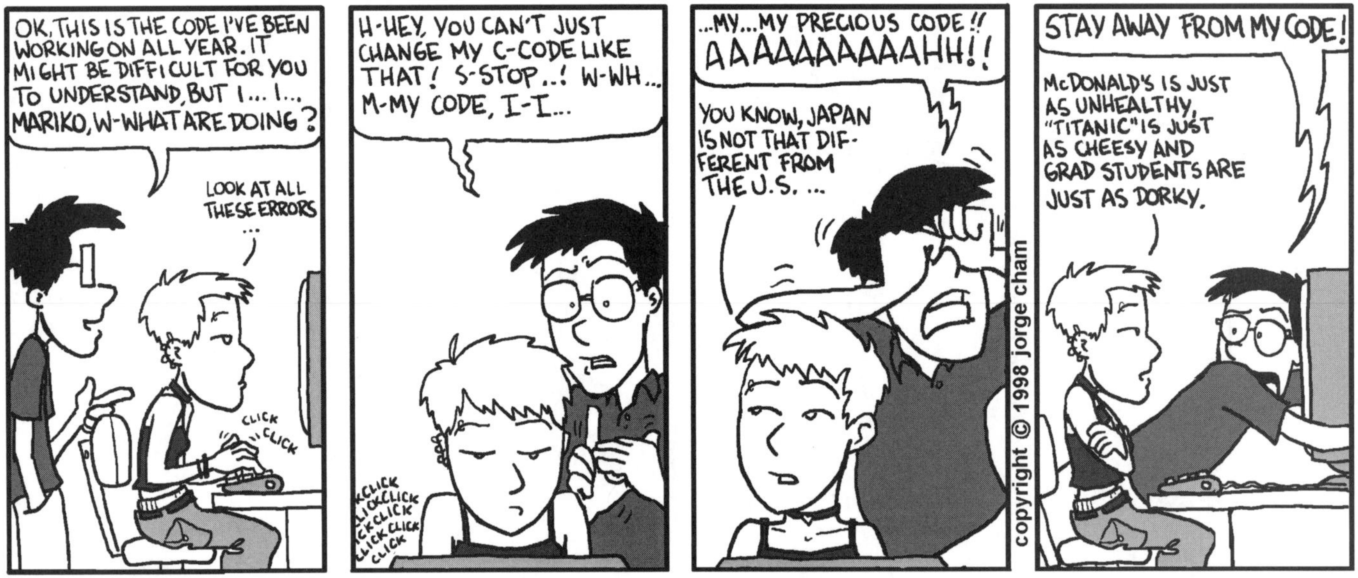
OK, THIS IS THE CODE I'VE BEEN WORKING ON ALL YEAR. IT MIGHT BE DIFFICULT FOR YOU TO UNDERSTAND, BUT I... I... MARIKO, W-WHAT ARE DOING?
LOOK AT ALL THESE ERRORS...
CLICK CLICK
H-HEY, YOU CAN'T JUST CHANGE MY C-CODE LIKE THAT! S-STOP..! W-WH... M-MY CODE, I-I...
CLICK CLICKCLICK CLICKCLICK CLICKCLICK CLICK
...MY...MY PRECIOUS CODE!!
AAAAAAAAAAHH!!
YOU KNOW, JAPAN IS NOT THAT DIF-FERENT FROM THE U.S. ...
copyright © 1998 jorge cham
STAY AWAY FROM MY CODE!
McDONALD'S IS JUST AS UNHEALTHY, "TITANIC" IS JUST AS CHEESY AND GRAD STUDENTS ARE JUST AS DORKY.

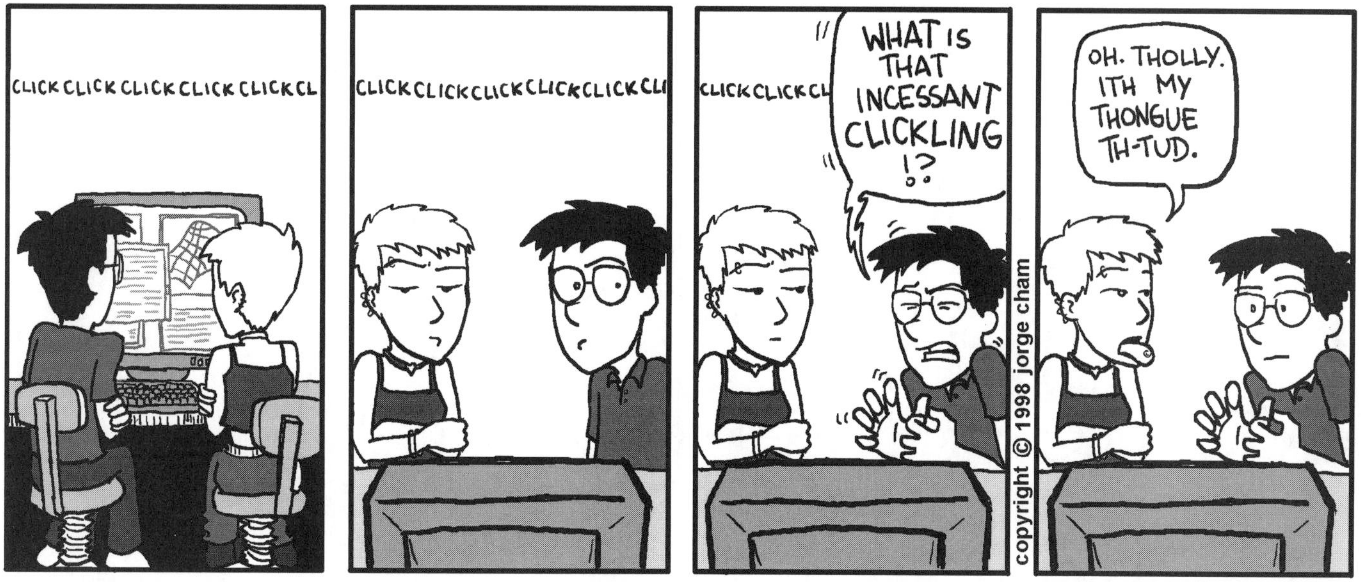
CLICK CLICK CLICK CLICK CLICK CL
CLICK CLICK CLICK CLICK CLICK CLI
CLICK CLICK CL
WHAT IS THAT INCESSANT CLICKLING !?
OH. THOLLY. ITH MY THONGUE TH-TUD.
copyright © 1998 jorge cham

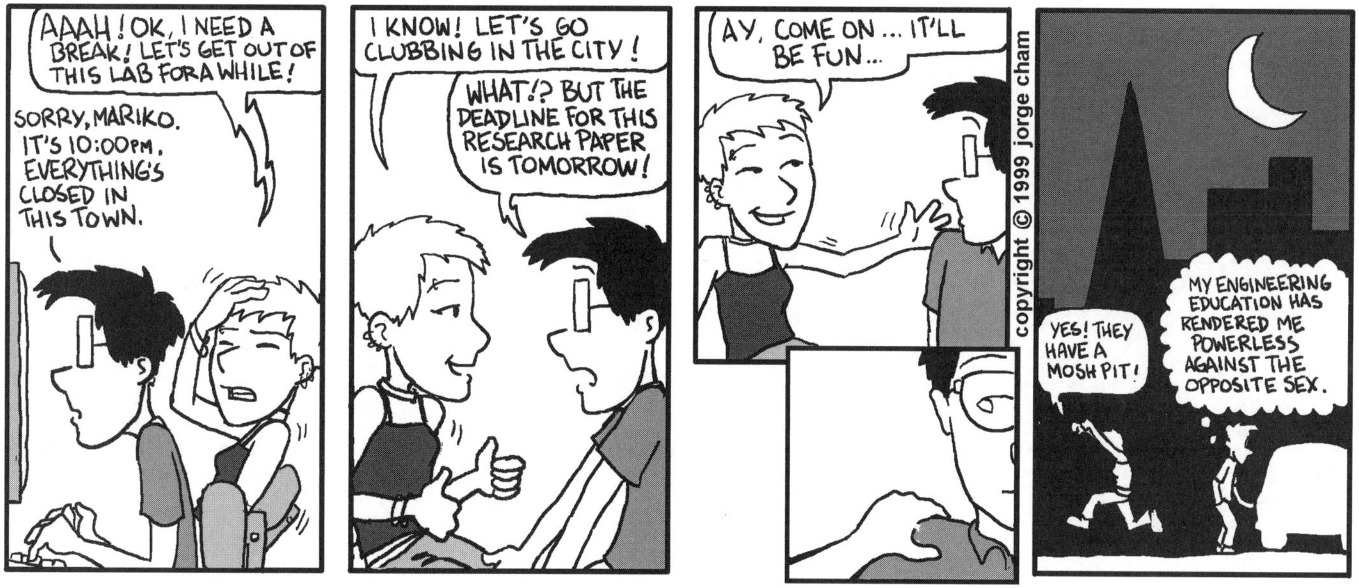
AAAH! OK, I NEED A BREAK! LET'S GET OUT OF THIS LAB FOR A WHILE!
SORRY, MARIKO. IT'S 10:00PM. EVERYTHING'S CLOSED IN THIS TOWN.
I KNOW! LET'S GO CLUBBING IN THE CITY!
WHAT!? BUT THE DEADLINE FOR THIS RESEARCH PAPER IS TOMORROW!
AY, COME ON ... IT'LL BE FUN...
copyright © 1999 jorge cham
YES! THEY HAVE A MOSH PIT!
MY ENGINEERING EDUCATION HAS RENDERED ME POWERLESS AGAINST THE OPPOSITE SEX.

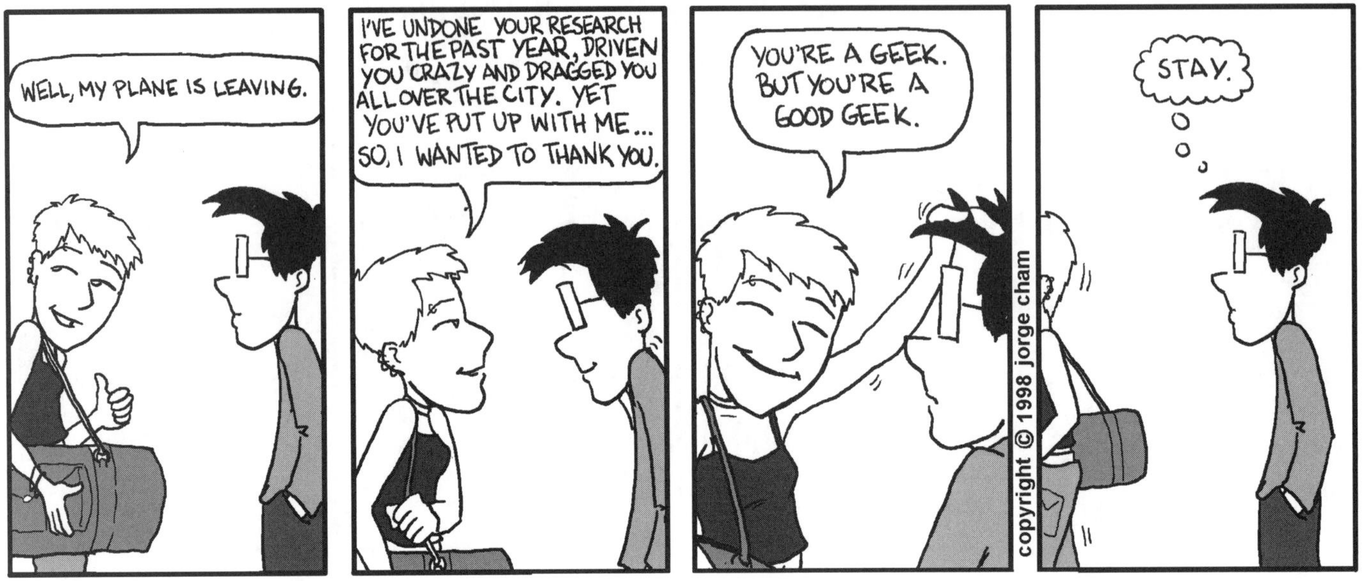
WELL, MY PLANE IS LEAVING.
I'VE UNDONE YOUR RESEARCH FOR THE PAST YEAR, DRIVEN YOU CRAZY AND DRAGGED YOU ALL OVER THE CITY. YET YOU'VE PUT UP WITH ME... SO, I WANTED TO THANK YOU.
YOU'RE A GEEK. BUT YOU'RE A GOOD GEEK.
copyright © 1998 jorge cham
STAY.

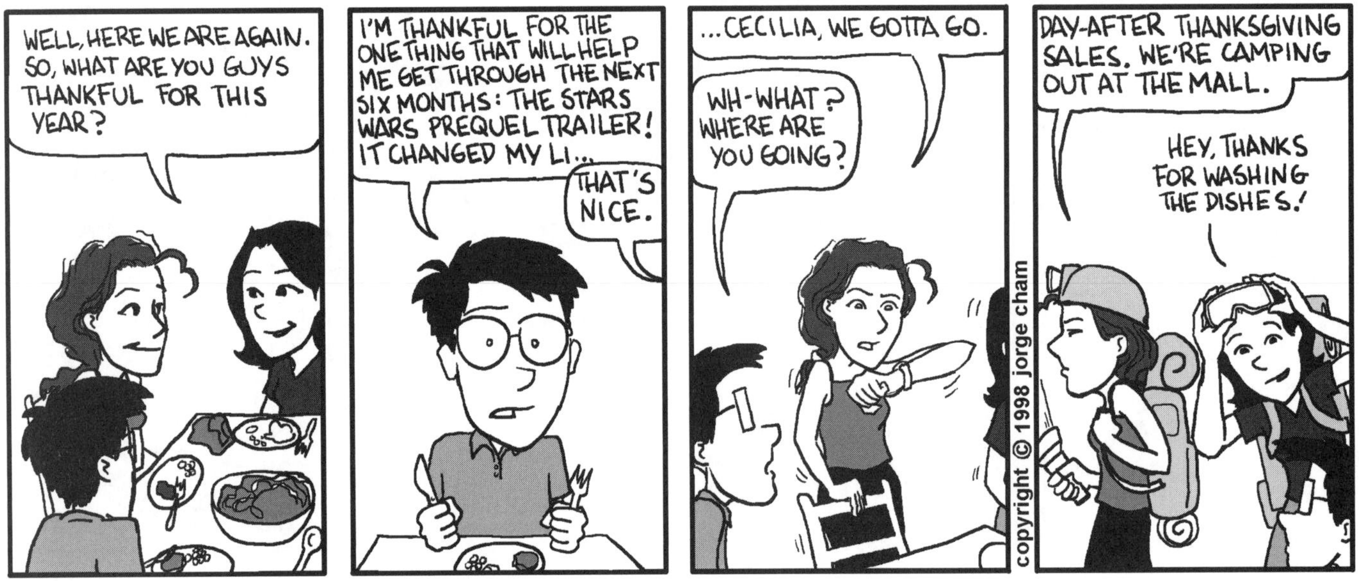
WELL, HERE WE ARE AGAIN. SO, WHAT ARE YOU GUYS THANKFUL FOR THIS YEAR?
I'M THANKFUL FOR THE ONE THING THAT WILL HELP ME GET THROUGH THE NEXT SIX MONTHS: THE STARS WARS PREQUEL TRAILER! IT CHANGED MY LI...
THAT'S NICE.
...CECILIA, WE GOTTA GO.
WH-WHAT? WHERE ARE YOU GOING?
copyright © 1998 jorge cham
DAY-AFTER THANKSGIVING SALES. WE'RE CAMPING OUT AT THE MALL.
HEY, THANKS FOR WASHING THE DISHES!

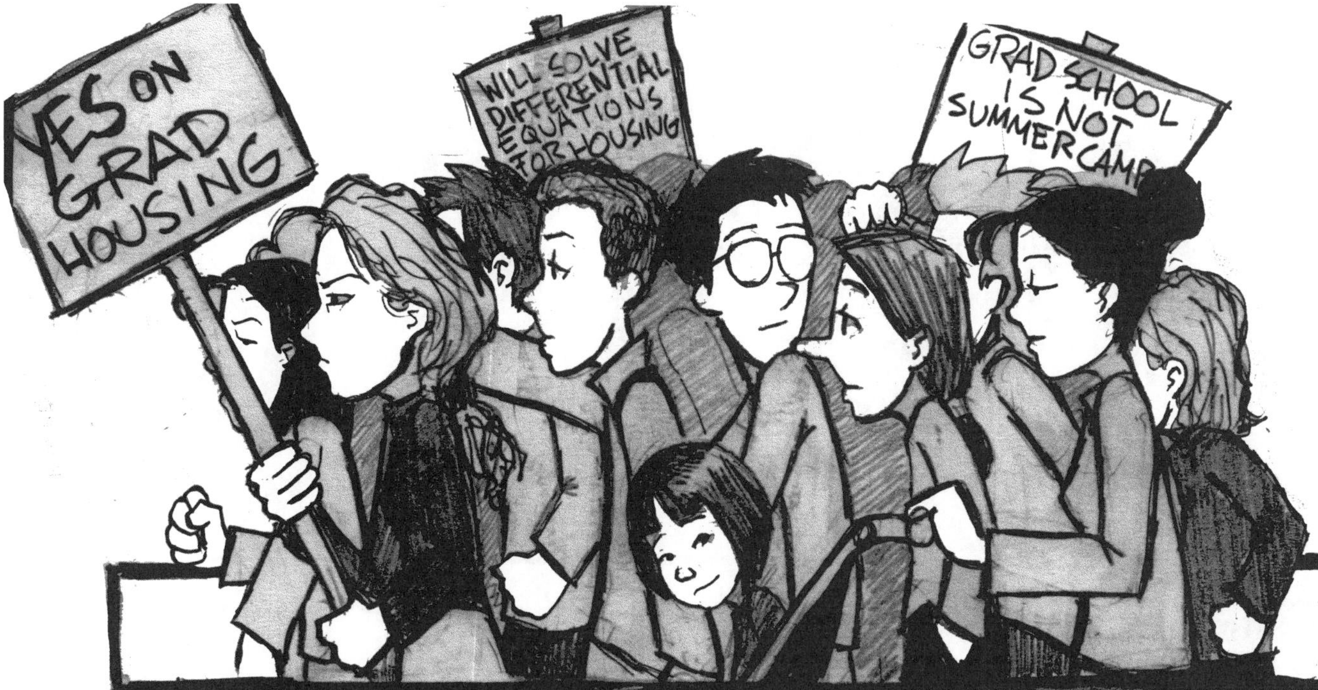
YES ON GRAD HOUSING
WILL SOLVE DIFFERENTIAL EQUATIONS FOR HOUSING
GRAD SCHOOL IS NOT SUMMER CAMP

THIS IS PHD REPORTING LIVE IN SUPPORT OF MORE GRAD HOUSING
TOWN HALL MEETING, 11/12/98

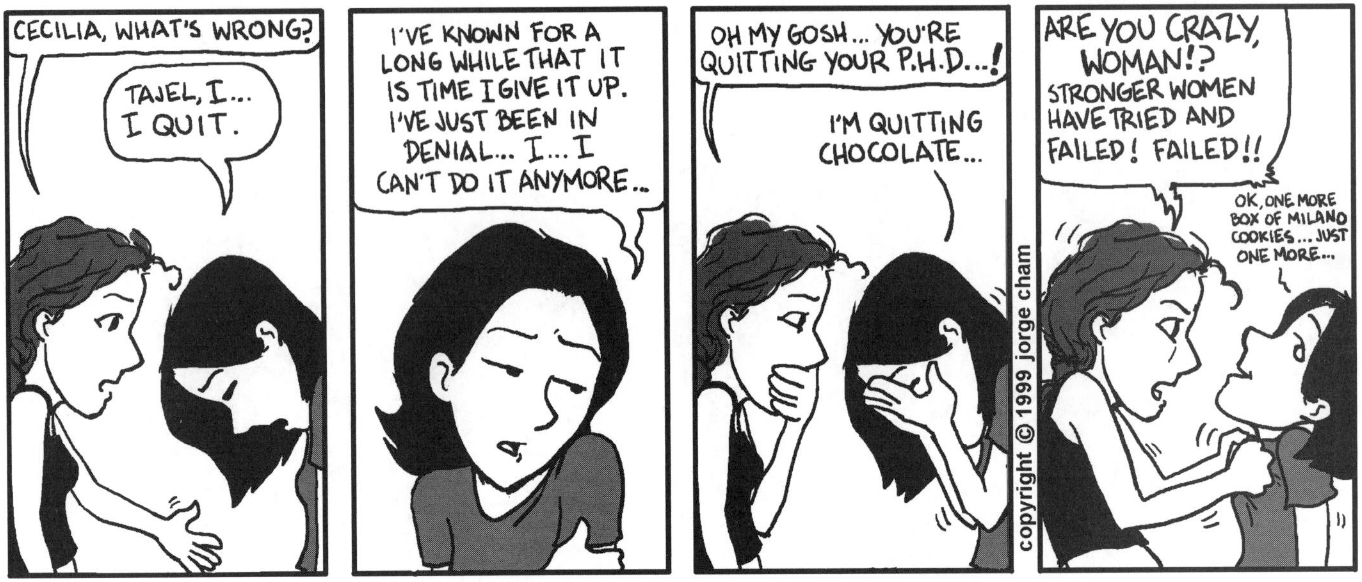
CECILIA, WHAT'S WRONG?
TAJEL, I... I QUIT.
I'VE KNOWN FOR A LONG WHILE THAT IT IS TIME I GIVE IT UP. I'VE JUST BEEN IN DENIAL... I... I CAN'T DO IT ANYMORE...
OH MY GOSH... YOU'RE QUITTING YOUR P.H.D...!
I'M QUITTING CHOCOLATE...
copyright © 1999 jorge cham
ARE YOU CRAZY, WOMAN!? STRONGER WOMEN HAVE TRIED AND FAILED! FAILED!!
OK, ONE MORE BOX OF MILANO COOKIES... JUST ONE MORE...

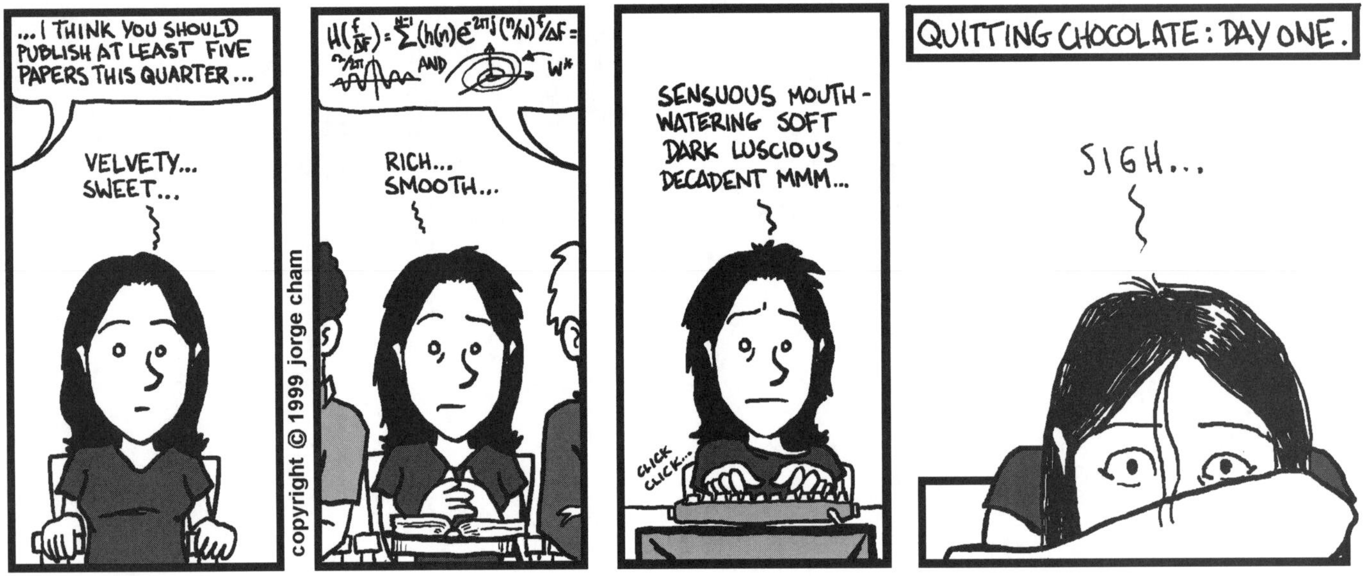
...I THINK YOU SHOULD PUBLISH AT LEAST FIVE PAPERS THIS QUARTER...
VELVETY... SWEET...
copyright © 1999 jorge cham
AND
W*
RICH... SMOOTH...
SENSUOUS MOUTH-WATERING SOFT DARK LUSCIOUS DECADENT MMM...
CLICK CLICK...
QUITTING CHOCOLATE: DAY ONE.
SIGH...

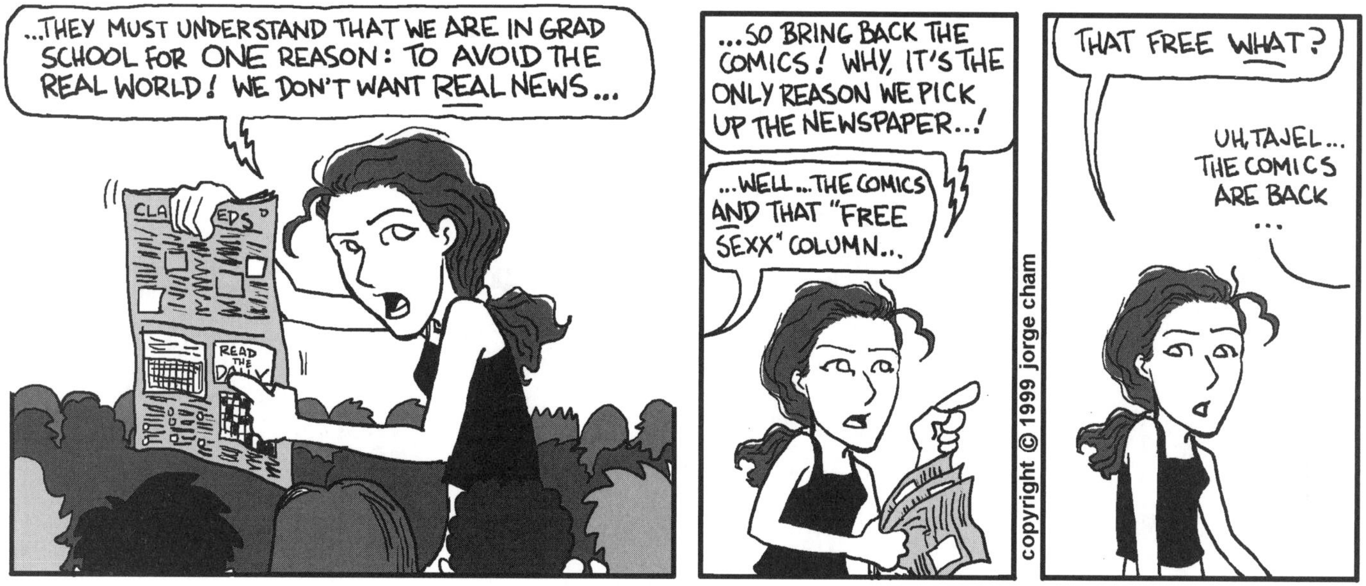
...THEY MUST UNDERSTAND THAT WE ARE IN GRAD SCHOOL FOR ONE REASON: TO AVOID THE REAL WORLD! WE DON'T WANT REAL NEWS...
...SO BRING BACK THE COMICS! WHY, IT'S THE ONLY REASON WE PICK UP THE NEWSPAPER...!
...WELL...THE COMICS AND THAT "FREE SEXX" COLUMN...
THAT FREE WHAT?
UH, TAJEL... THE COMICS ARE BACK ...
copyright © 1999 jorge cham

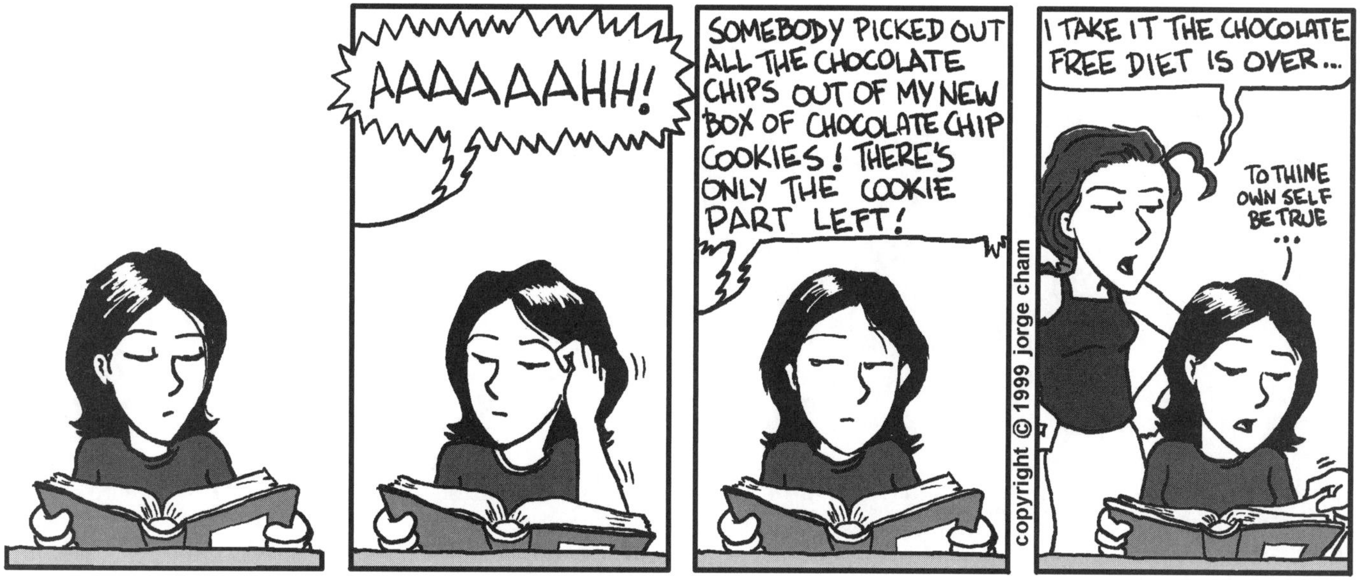
AAAAAAHH!
SOMEBODY PICKED OUT ALL THE CHOCOLATE CHIPS OUT OF MY NEW BOX OF CHOCOLATE CHIP COOKIES! THERE'S ONLY THE COOKIE PART LEFT!
I TAKE IT THE CHOCOLATE FREE DIET IS OVER...
TO THINE OWN SELF BE TRUE ...
copyright © 1999 jorge cham

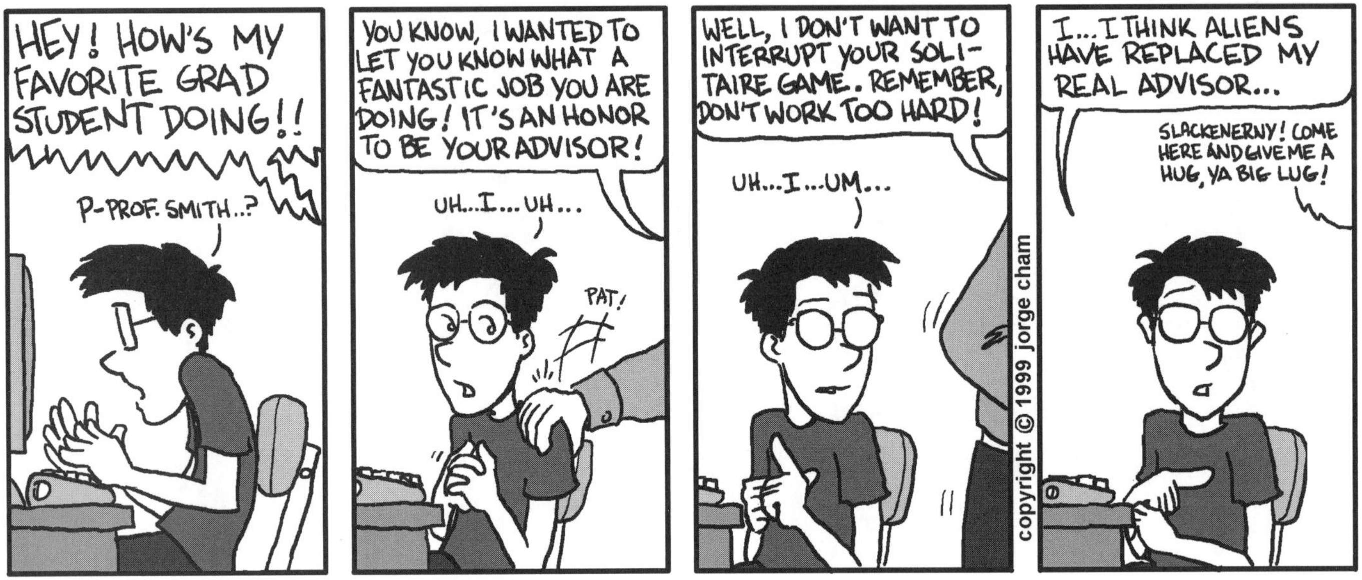
HEY! HOW'S MY FAVORITE GRAD STUDENT DOING!!
P-PROF. SMITH..?
YOU KNOW, I WANTED TO LET YOU KNOW WHAT A FANTASTIC JOB YOU ARE DOING! IT'S AN HONOR TO BE YOUR ADVISOR!
UH...I... UH...
PAT!
WELL, I DON'T WANT TO INTERRUPT YOUR SOLI-TAIRE GAME. REMEMBER, DON'T WORK TOO HARD!
UH...I...UM...
copyright © 1999 jorge cham
I...I THINK ALIENS HAVE REPLACED MY REAL ADVISOR...
SLACKENERNY! COME HERE AND GIVE ME A HUG, YA BIG LUG!

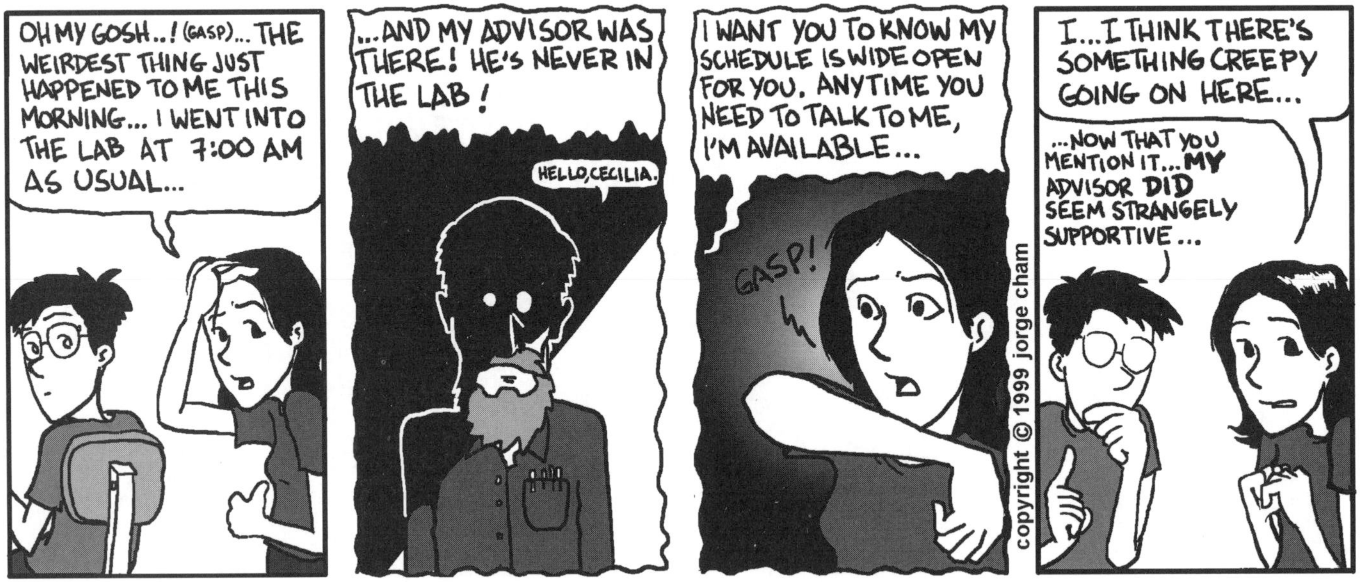
OH MY GOSH..! (GASP)... THE WEIRDEST THING JUST HAPPENED TO ME THIS MORNING... I WENT INTO THE LAB AT 7:00 AM AS USUAL...
...AND MY ADVISOR WAS THERE! HE'S NEVER IN THE LAB!
HELLO, CECILIA.
I WANT YOU TO KNOW MY SCHEDULE IS WIDE OPEN FOR YOU. ANYTIME YOU NEED TO TALK TO ME, I'M AVAILABLE...
GASP!
copyright © 1999 jorge cham
I...I THINK THERE'S SOMETHING CREEPY GOING ON HERE...
...NOW THAT YOU MENTION IT... MY ADVISOR DID SEEM STRANGELY SUPPORTIVE...

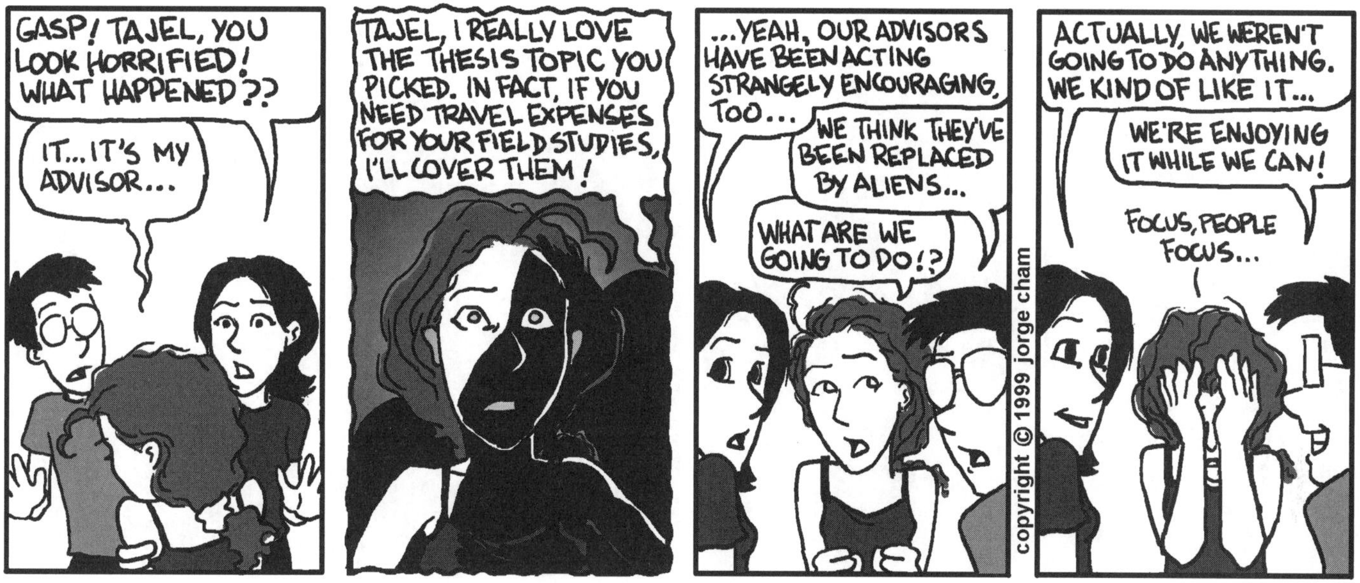
GASP! TAJEL, YOU LOOK HORRIFIED! WHAT HAPPENED??
IT...IT'S MY ADVISOR...
TAJEL, I REALLY LOVE THE THESIS TOPIC YOU PICKED. IN FACT, IF YOU NEED TRAVEL EXPENSES FOR YOUR FIELD STUDIES, I'LL COVER THEM!
...YEAH, OUR ADVISORS HAVE BEEN ACTING STRANGELY ENCOURAGING, TOO...
WE THINK THEY'VE BEEN REPLACED BY ALIENS...
WHAT ARE WE GOING TO DO!?
copyright © 1999 jorge cham
ACTUALLY, WE WEREN'T GOING TO DO ANYTHING. WE KIND OF LIKE IT...
WE'RE ENJOYING IT WHILE WE CAN!
FOCUS, PEOPLE FOCUS...

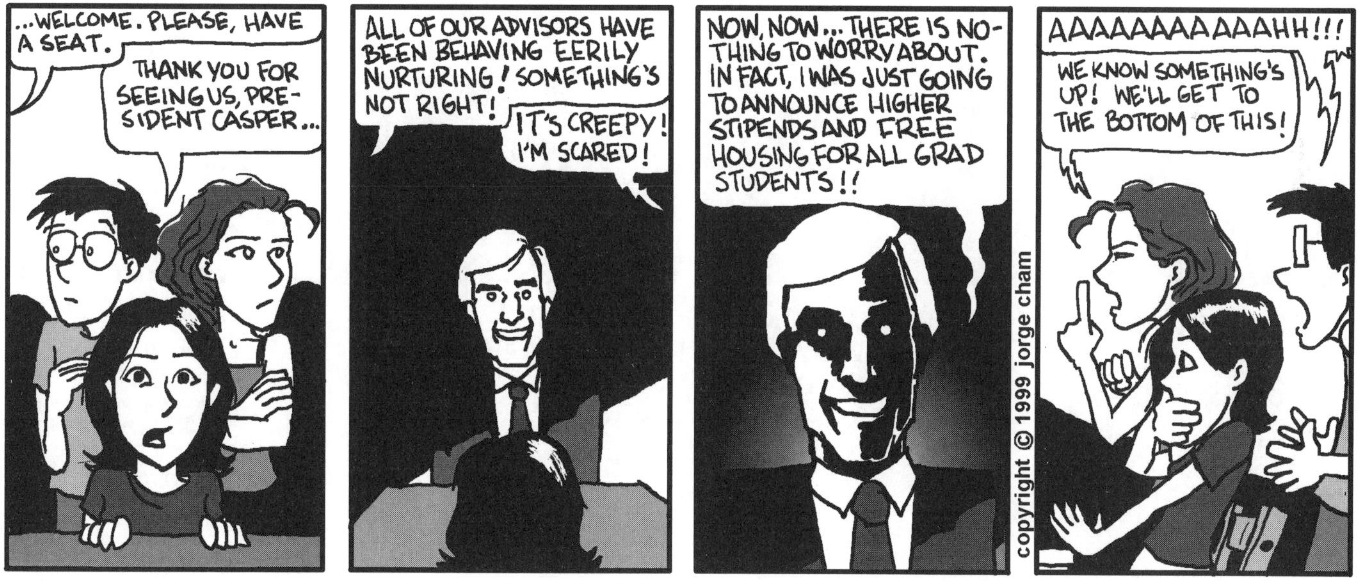
...WELCOME. PLEASE, HAVE A SEAT.
THANK YOU FOR SEEING US, PRESIDENT CASPER...
ALL OF OUR ADVISORS HAVE BEEN BEHAVING EERILY NURTURING! SOMETHING'S NOT RIGHT!
IT'S CREEPY! I'M SCARED!
NOW, NOW... THERE IS NOTHING TO WORRY ABOUT. IN FACT, I WAS JUST GOING TO ANNOUNCE HIGHER STIPENDS AND FREE HOUSING FOR ALL GRAD STUDENTS!!
copyright © 1999 jorge cham
AAAAAAAAAAAHH!!!
WE KNOW SOMETHING'S UP! WE'LL GET TO THE BOTTOM OF THIS!

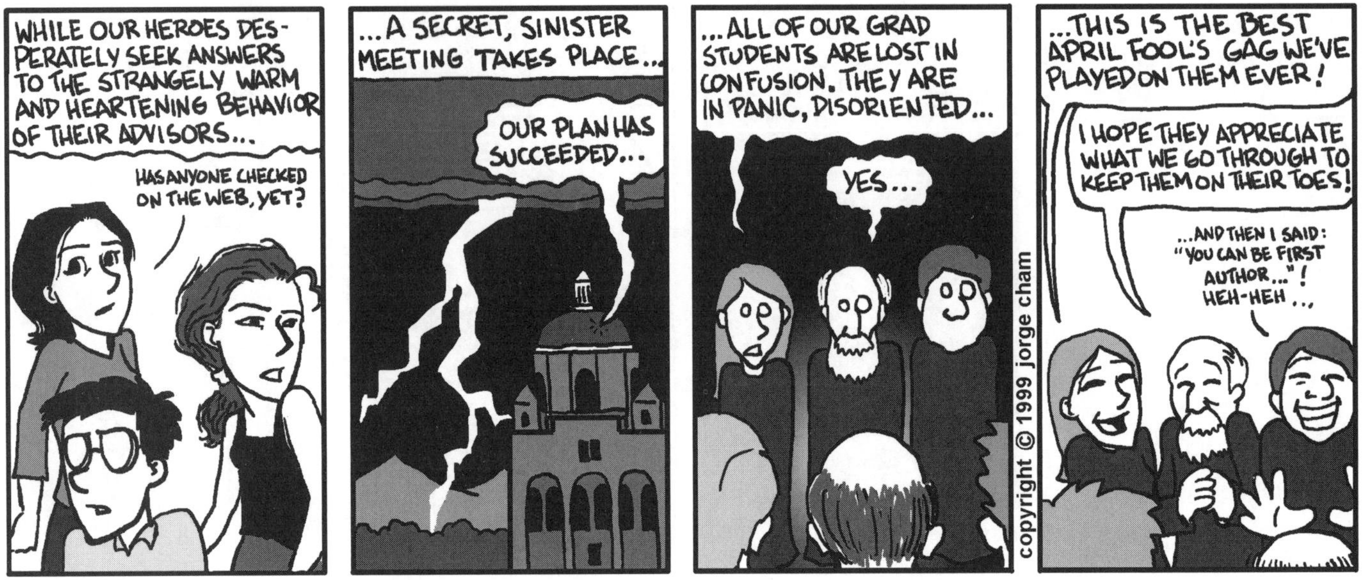
WHILE OUR HEROES DESPERATELY SEEK ANSWERS TO THE STRANGELY WARM AND HEARTENING BEHAVIOR OF THEIR ADVISORS...
HAS ANYONE CHECKED ON THE WEB, YET?
...A SECRET, SINISTER MEETING TAKES PLACE...
OUR PLAN HAS SUCCEEDED...
...ALL OF OUR GRAD STUDENTS ARE LOST IN CONFUSION. THEY ARE IN PANIC, DISORIENTED...
YES...
copyright © 1999 jorge cham
...THIS IS THE BEST APRIL FOOL'S GAG WE'VE PLAYED ON THEM EVER!
I HOPE THEY APPRECIATE WHAT WE GO THROUGH TO KEEP THEM ON THEIR TOES!
...AND THEN I SAID: "YOU CAN BE FIRST AUTHOR..."! HEH-HEH...

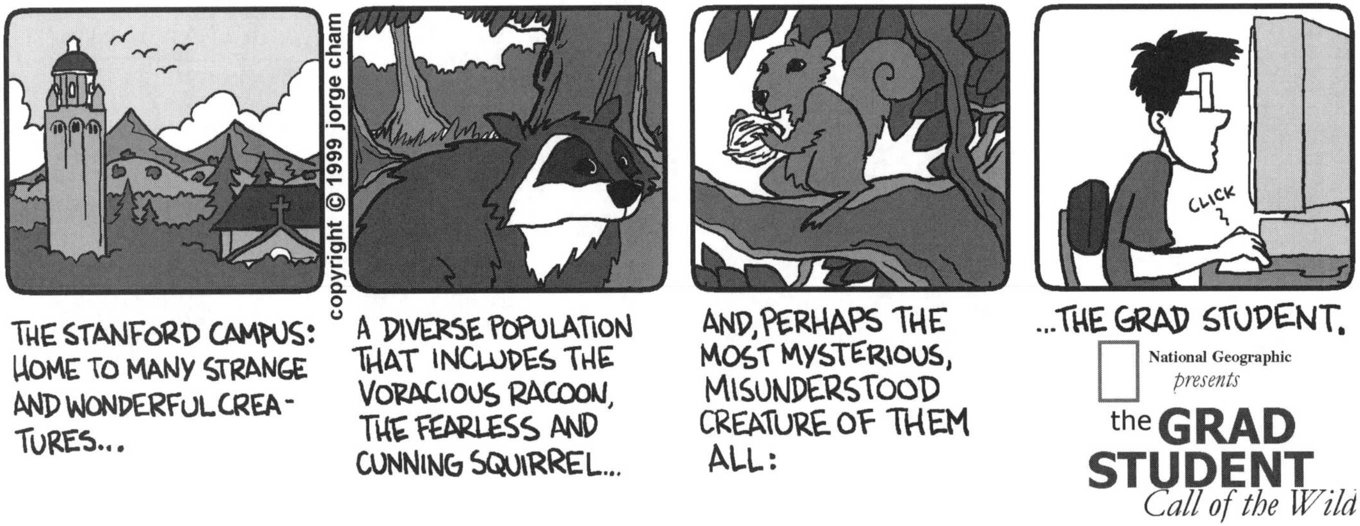
THE STANFORD CAMPUS: HOME TO MANY STRANGE AND WONDERFUL CREATURES...
copyright © 1999 jorge cham
A DIVERSE POPULATION THAT INCLUDES THE VORACIOUS RACOON, THE FEARLESS AND CUNNING SQUIRREL...
AND, PERHAPS THE MOST MYSTERIOUS, MISUNDERSTOOD CREATURE OF THEM ALL:
CLICK
...THE GRAD STUDENT.
National Geographic presents
the GRAD STUDENT
Call of the Wild

we now return to our feature documentary: "The Grad Student: Call of the Wild"...

THE MALE OF THE SPECIES CAN BE EASILY IDENTIFIED BY THE ALMOST UNNATURAL CURVATURE OF THE SPINE WHEN POISED IN ITS DWELLING AREA.

THE GRAD STUDENT FORMS DENSELY-PACKED COLONIES IN WHAT ARE KNOWN AS "STUDENT OFFICES" OR "LABS", THOUGH COMMUNICATION WITHIN THE SETTLEMENT IS RARE AND OFTEN CONSIDERED TABOO.

ONCE SETTLED, THE GRAD STUDENT ADDS ITEMS TO ITS HABITAT TO THE POINT WHERE IT CONTAINS ALL POSSIBLE NECESSITIES, THEREBY ELIMINATING THE NEED TO EVER VENTURE OUT.

A HIGHLY TERRITORIAL ANIMAL, THE GRAD STUDENT WILL FIERCELY DEFEND ITS DESK-SPACE BY EMITTING LOUD, WHINING SQUEALS AT ITS COMPETITORS...

we now return to our feature documentary: "The Grad Student: Call of the Wild"...

THOUGH A SIMPLE CREATURE, THE GRAD STUDENT HAS A COMPLEX FEEDING CYCLE...

ALWAYS HUNGRY, THE GRAD STUDENT PREYS UPON THE OCCASIONAL HERD OF PEOPLE CHATTING, SIGNIFYING WHAT ARE KNOWN AS "HAPPY HOURS" OR "SOCIAL EVENTS."

A MASTER OF CAMOUFLAGE, THE GRAD STUDENT EASILY BLENDS IN AND GORGES ON ITS SOLE SOURCE OF NUTRITION: A SUBSTANCE CALLED "FREE FOOD."

HAVING FEASTED, THE GRAD STUDENT ENTERS A LETHARGIC STATE CALLED "RESEARCHING," IN ANTICIPATION OF THE NEXT FREE MEAL.

when we return: the Grad Student's Mating Habits!

69

...WHY DON'T WE GO TO THE COHO TO DISCUSS THE REPERCUSSION OF THE EXISTENTIALIST DIASPHORA?
copyright © 1999 jorge cham
SO, WHAT DID YOU GET FOR PROBLEM 2?
I NEVER DREAMED OUR FIRST DATE'D BE THIS ROMANTIC...
...MUST... AVOID... EYE CONTACT...
I HAVE A BOYFRIEND
ARE YOU NEW TO SOCIAL DANCE? WATCH ME DO THE LINDY HOP...

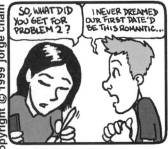

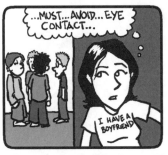

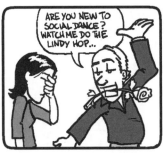

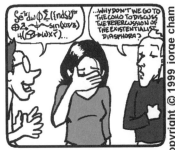

THE COURTSHIP PROCESS OF THE GRAD STUDENT, CONSIDERED BY MANY RESEARCHERS AS "AWKWARD" OR "EMBARRASSING", BEGINS WITH FUTILE, INCOMPREHENSIVE MATING CALLS BY THE MALES INTENDED TO IMPRESS THE FEMALE.

OUTNUMBERED BY AS MUCH AS TEN TO ONE, THE FEMALE OF THE SPECIES MUST ENDURE CONSTANT, OFTEN MISGUIDED, ATTEMPTS BY THE MALES...

...THUS FORCING THE FEMALE TO DEVELOP, THROUGH EVOLUTION, EVASSIVE AND FURTIVE TRAITS. OFTEN, DESPERATE MALES RESORT TO A COMPLICATED STRUTTING BEHAVIOR KNOWN AS...

..."BALLROOM DANCING". HOW EXACTLY HAS THIS SPECIES MANAGED TO AVOID EXTINCTION HAS BEEN, AND WILL LIKELY CONTINUE TO BE, A SOURCE OF AWE AND BAFFLEMENT TO EXPERTS WORLDWIDE.

UH... WELL, HELLO, PROF. SMITH!
copyright © 1999 jorge cham

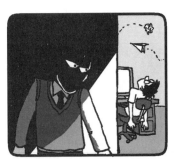

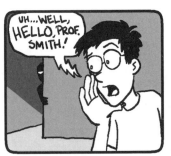

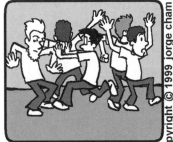

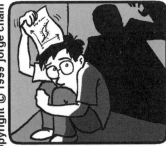

we now return to our feature documentary: "The Grad Student: Call of the Wild"...

WITHOUT MAKING A SOUND, THE GRAD STUDENT'S ONLY KNOWN PREDATOR, THE "RESEARCHUS ADVISORUS", PREPARES TO POUNCE ON AN UNSUSPECTING VICTIM.

SPOTTING THE IMPENDING PERIL, THE GRAD STUDENT ISSUES A WARNING CALL TO THE REST OF THE FLOCK. THIS IS THE ONLY KNOWN EXAMPLE OF COOPERATION IN THE OTHERWISE HERMIT-LIKE SPECIES.

THE GRAD STUDENT'S UNIFORM APPEARANCE, CHARACTERIZED BY WHITE T-SHIRT, JEANS AND WHITE SNEAKERS, HELP CONFUSE THE PREDATOR IN THE ENSUING WILD STAMPEDE.

ONCE CORNERED, THE GRAD STUDENT'S DEFENSE MECHANISM TRIGGERS UNCONTROLLABLE TECHNICAL WHIMPERINGS AND "GRAPH WAVING", TAKING REFUGE IN WHAT IT CALLS, "A HEAVY COURSE LOAD."

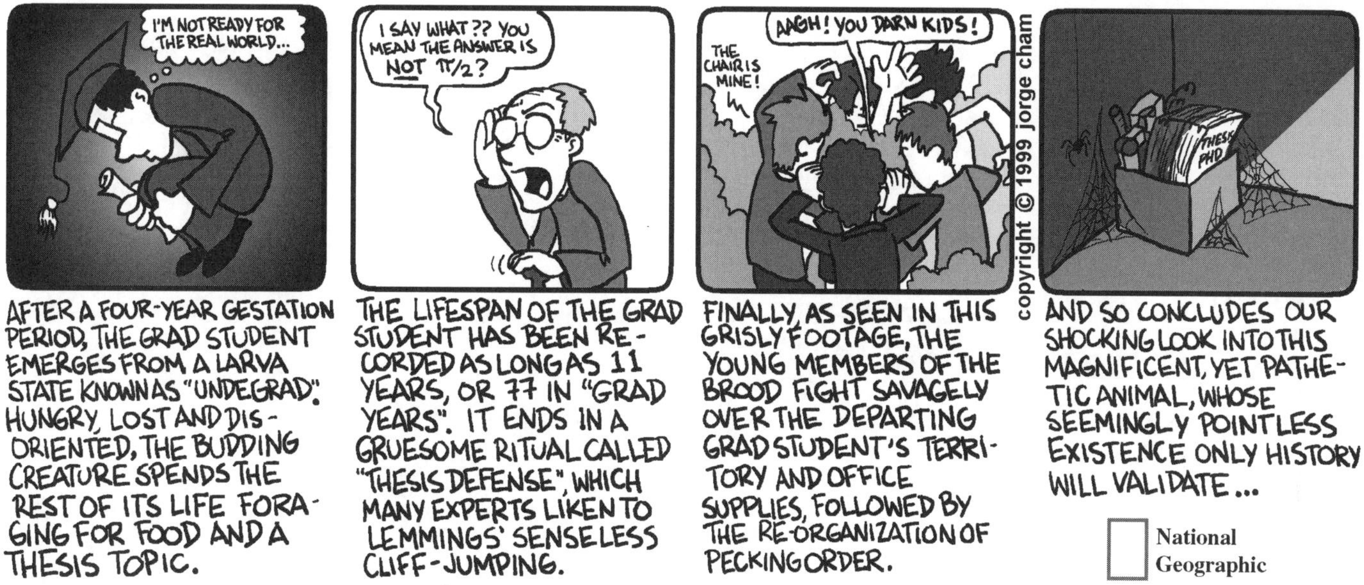
I'M NOT READY FOR THE REAL WORLD...
AFTER A FOUR-YEAR GESTATION PERIOD, THE GRAD STUDENT EMERGES FROM A LARVA STATE KNOWN AS "UNDEGRAD". HUNGRY, LOST AND DISORIENTED, THE BUDDING CREATURE SPENDS THE REST OF ITS LIFE FORAGING FOR FOOD AND A THESIS TOPIC.
I SAY WHAT?? YOU MEAN THE ANSWER IS NOT π/2?
THE LIFESPAN OF THE GRAD STUDENT HAS BEEN RECORDED AS LONG AS 11 YEARS, OR 77 IN "GRAD YEARS". IT ENDS IN A GRUESOME RITUAL CALLED "THESIS DEFENSE", WHICH MANY EXPERTS LIKEN TO LEMMINGS' SENSELESS CLIFF-JUMPING.
AAGH! YOU DARN KIDS!
THE CHAIR IS MINE!
FINALLY, AS SEEN IN THIS GRISLY FOOTAGE, THE YOUNG MEMBERS OF THE BROOD FIGHT SAVAGELY OVER THE DEPARTING GRAD STUDENT'S TERRITORY AND OFFICE SUPPLIES, FOLLOWED BY THE RE-ORGANIZATION OF PECKING ORDER.
copyright © 1999 jorge cham
THESIS PHD
AND SO CONCLUDES OUR SHOCKING LOOK INTO THIS MAGNIFICENT, YET PATHETIC ANIMAL, WHOSE SEEMINGLY POINTLESS EXISTENCE ONLY HISTORY WILL VALIDATE...
National Geographic

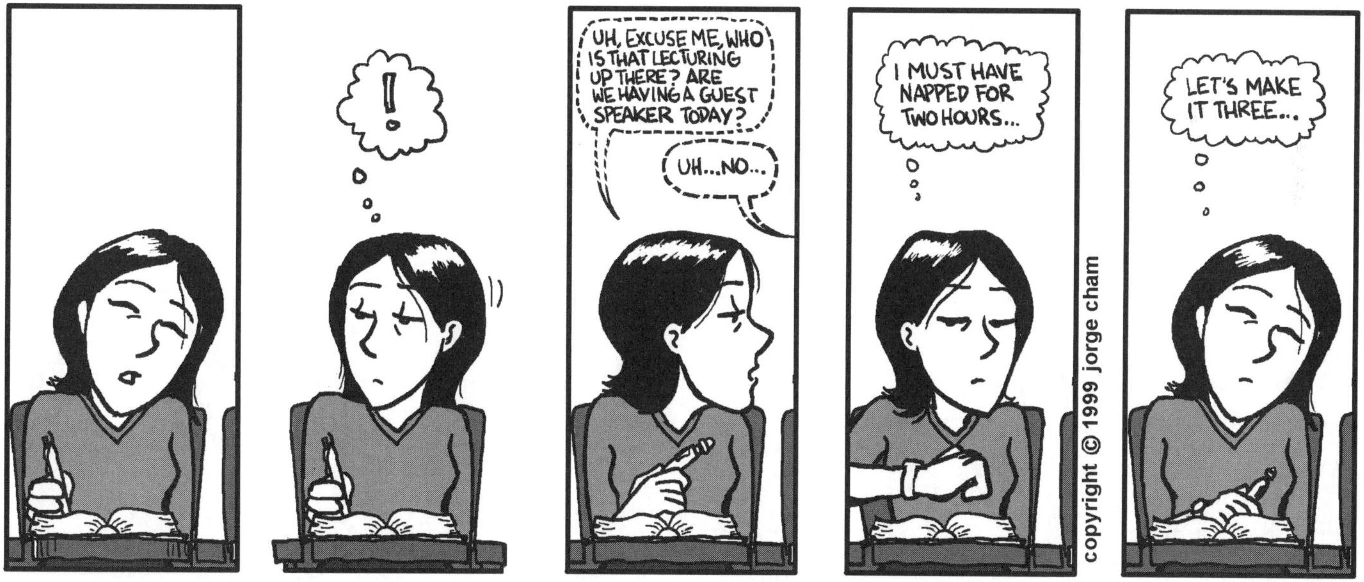
!
UH, EXCUSE ME, WHO IS THAT LECTURING UP THERE? ARE WE HAVING A GUEST SPEAKER TODAY?
UH...NO...
I MUST HAVE NAPPED FOR TWO HOURS...
copyright © 1999 jorge cham
LET'S MAKE IT THREE...

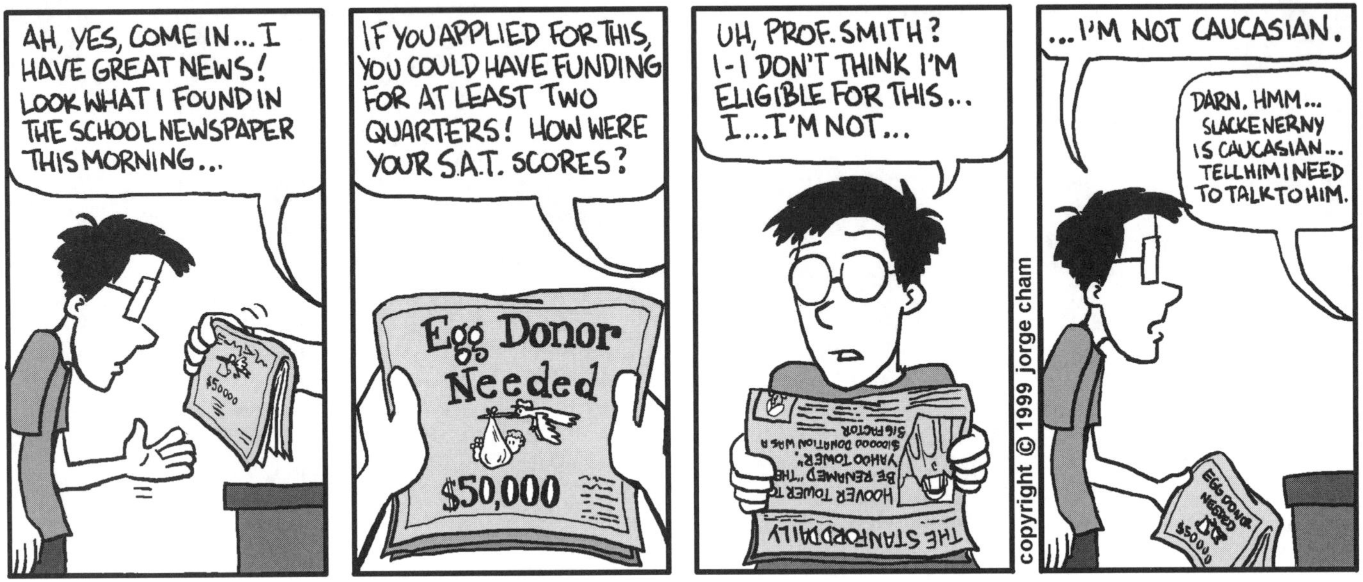
AH, YES, COME IN... I HAVE GREAT NEWS! LOOK WHAT I FOUND IN THE SCHOOL NEWSPAPER THIS MORNING...
$50000
IF YOU APPLIED FOR THIS, YOU COULD HAVE FUNDING FOR AT LEAST TWO QUARTERS! HOW WERE YOUR S.A.T. SCORES?
Egg Donor Needed
$50,000
UH, PROF. SMITH? I-I DON'T THINK I'M ELIGIBLE FOR THIS... I...I'M NOT...
THE STANFORD DAILY
HOOVER TOWER TO BE RENAMED "THE YAHOO TOWER". $100000 DONATION WAS A BIG FACTOR
...I'M NOT CAUCASIAN.
DARN. HMM... SLACKENERNY IS CAUCASIAN... TELL HIM I NEED TO TALK TO HIM.
copyright © 1999 jorge cham

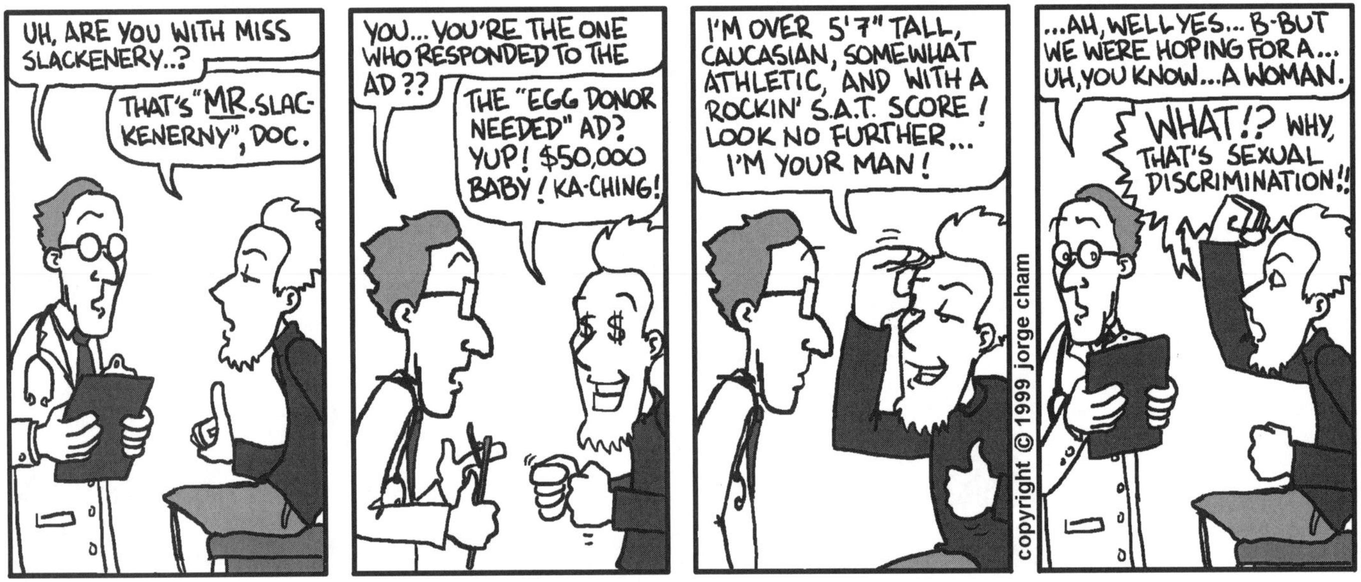
UH, ARE YOU WITH MISS SLACKENERY..?
THAT'S "MR. SLACKENERNY", DOC.
YOU... YOU'RE THE ONE WHO RESPONDED TO THE AD??
THE "EGG DONOR NEEDED" AD? YUP! $50,000 BABY! KA-CHING!
I'M OVER 5'7" TALL, CAUCASIAN, SOMEWHAT ATHLETIC, AND WITH A ROCKIN' S.A.T. SCORE! LOOK NO FURTHER... I'M YOUR MAN!
...AH, WELL YES... B-BUT WE WERE HOPING FOR A... UH, YOU KNOW...A WOMAN.
WHAT!? WHY, THAT'S SEXUAL DISCRIMINATION!!
copyright © 1999 jorge cham

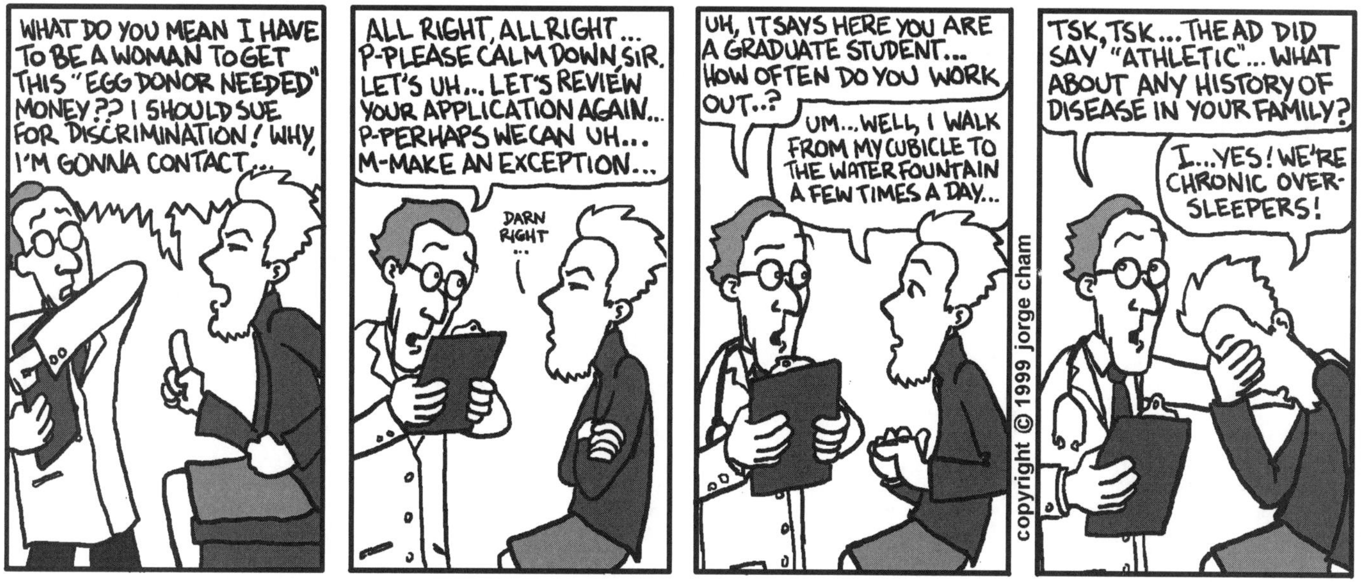
WHAT DO YOU MEAN I HAVE TO BE A WOMAN TO GET THIS "EGG DONOR NEEDED" MONEY?? I SHOULD SUE FOR DISCRIMINATION! WHY, I'M GONNA CONTACT...
ALL RIGHT, ALL RIGHT... P-PLEASE CALM DOWN, SIR. LET'S UH... LET'S REVIEW YOUR APPLICATION AGAIN... P-PERHAPS WE CAN UH... M-MAKE AN EXCEPTION...
DARN RIGHT ...
UH, IT SAYS HERE YOU ARE A GRADUATE STUDENT... HOW OFTEN DO YOU WORK OUT..?
UM... WELL, I WALK FROM MY CUBICLE TO THE WATER FOUNTAIN A FEW TIMES A DAY...
copyright © 1999 jorge cham
TSK, TSK... THE AD DID SAY "ATHLETIC"... WHAT ABOUT ANY HISTORY OF DISEASE IN YOUR FAMILY?
I... YES! WE'RE CHRONIC OVER-SLEEPERS!

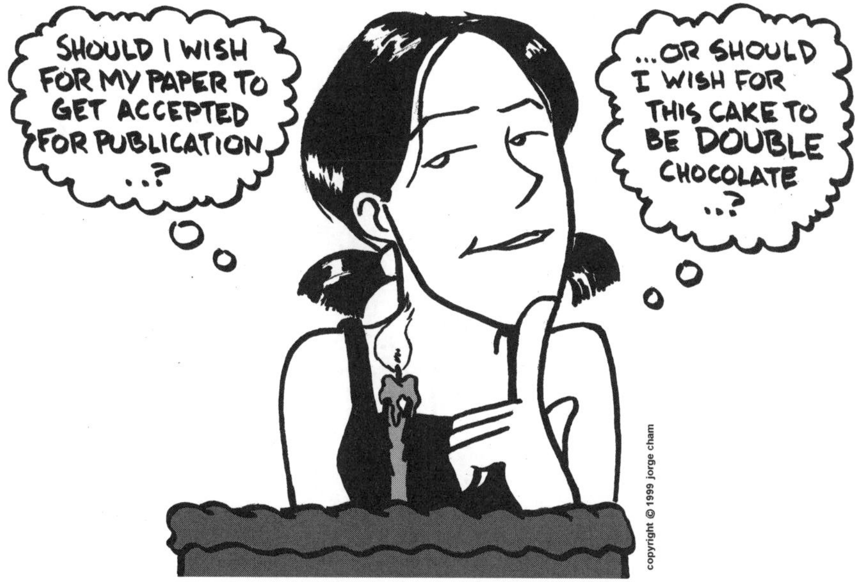
SHOULD I WISH FOR MY PAPER TO GET ACCEPTED FOR PUBLICATION ..?
...OR SHOULD I WISH FOR THIS CAKE TO BE DOUBLE CHOCOLATE ..?
copyright © 1999 jorge cham

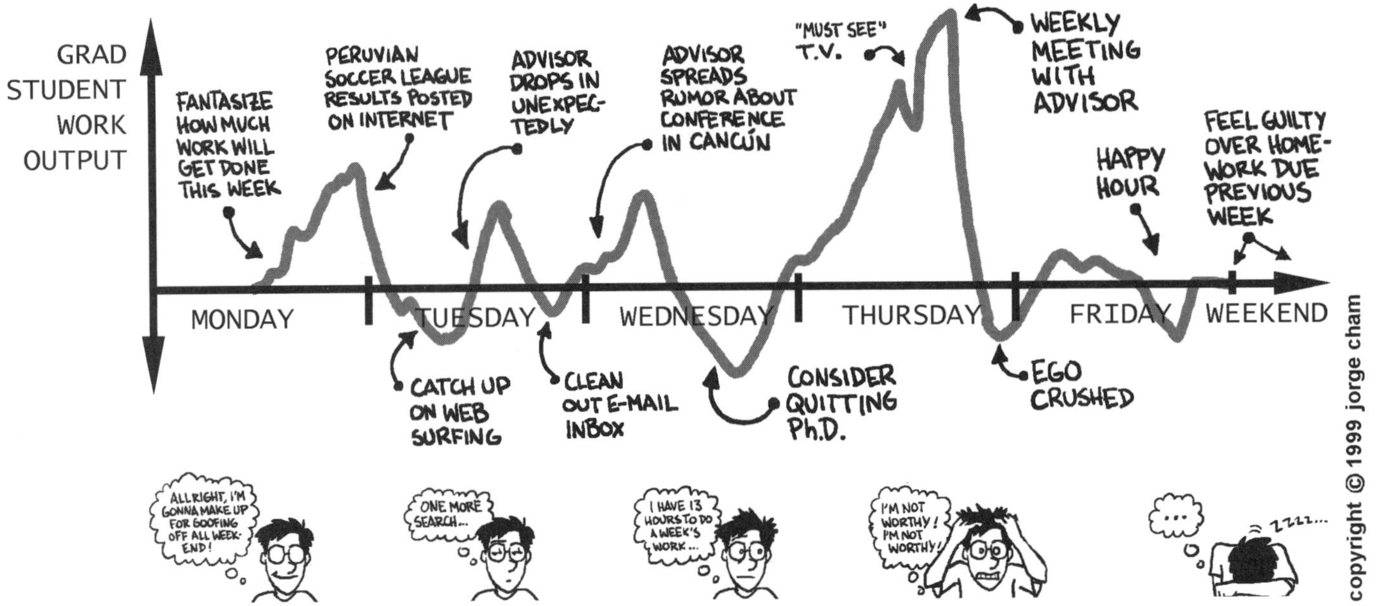
GRAD STUDENT WORK OUTPUT
MONDAY
TUESDAY
WEDNESDAY
THURSDAY
FRIDAY
WEEKEND
FANTASIZE HOW MUCH WORK WILL GET DONE THIS WEEK
PERUVIAN SOCCER LEAGUE RESULTS POSTED ON INTERNET
ADVISOR DROPS IN UNEXPEC-TEDLY
ADVISOR SPREADS RUMOR ABOUT CONFERENCE IN CANCÚN
"MUST SEE" T.V.
WEEKLY MEETING WITH ADVISOR
HAPPY HOUR
FEEL GUILTY OVER HOME-WORK DUE PREVIOUS WEEK
CATCH UP ON WEB SURFING
CLEAN OUT E-MAIL INBOX
CONSIDER QUITTING Ph.D.
EGO CRUSHED
ALL RIGHT, I'M GONNA MAKE UP FOR GOOFING OFF ALL WEEK-END!
ONE MORE SEARCH...
I HAVE 13 HOURS TO DO A WEEK'S WORK...
I'M NOT WORTHY! I'M NOT WORTHY!
...
ZZZZ...
copyright © 1999 jorge cham

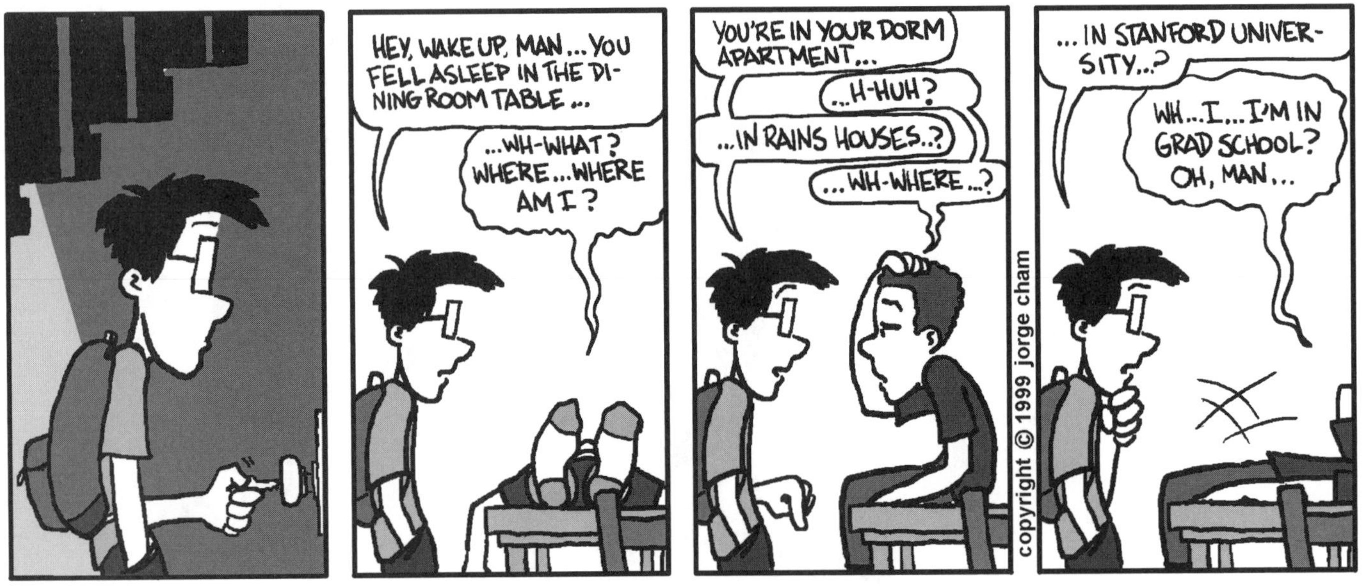
HEY, WAKE UP, MAN... YOU FELL ASLEEP IN THE DI-NING ROOM TABLE...
...WH-WHAT? WHERE... WHERE AM I?
YOU'RE IN YOUR DORM APARTMENT...
...H-HUH?
...IN RAINS HOUSES..?
...WH-WHERE...?
...IN STANFORD UNIVER-SITY...?
WH... I... I'M IN GRAD SCHOOL? OH, MAN...
copyright © 1999 jorge cham

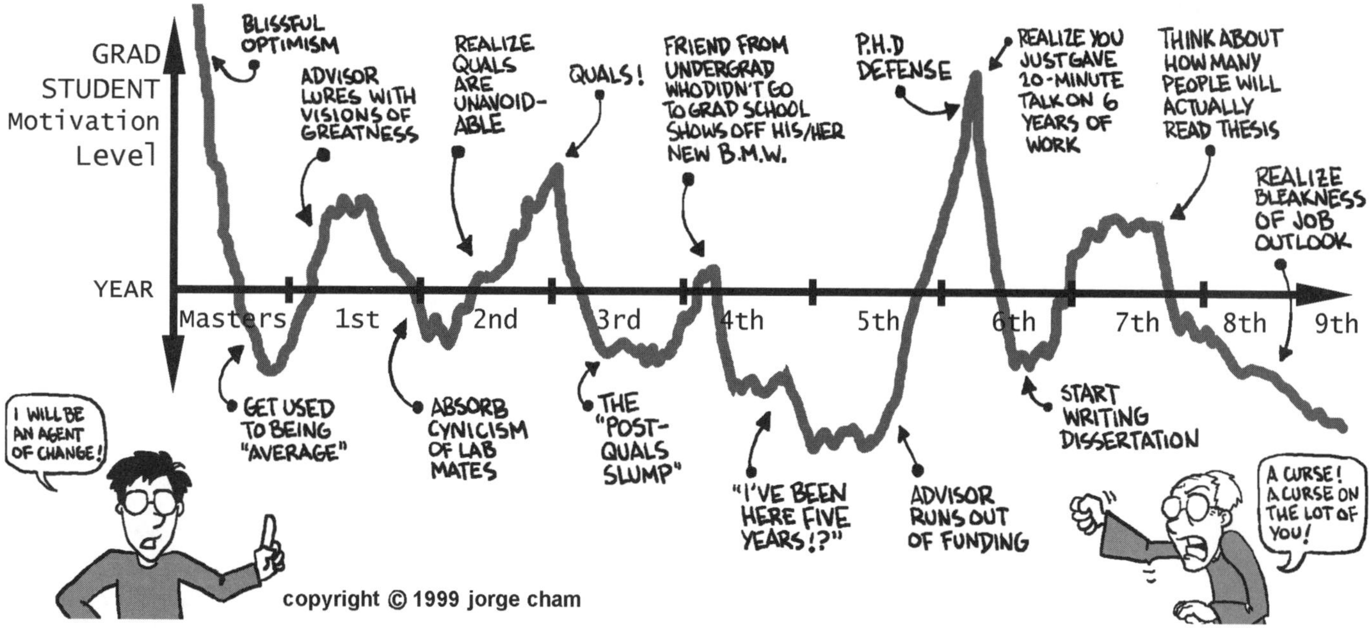
GRAD STUDENT Motivation Level
YEAR
Masters
1st
2nd
3rd
4th
5th
6th
7th
8th
9th
BLISSFUL OPTIMISM
ADVISOR LURES WITH VISIONS OF GREATNESS
REALIZE QUALS ARE UNAVOID-ABLE
QUALS!
FRIEND FROM UNDERGRAD WHO DIDN'T GO TO GRAD SCHOOL SHOWS OFF HIS/HER NEW B.M.W.
P.H.D DEFENSE
REALIZE YOU JUST GAVE 10-MINUTE TALK ON 6 YEARS OF WORK
THINK ABOUT HOW MANY PEOPLE WILL ACTUALLY READ THESIS
REALIZE BLEAKNESS OF JOB OUTLOOK
GET USED TO BEING "AVERAGE"
ABSORB CYNICISM OF LAB MATES
THE "POST-QUALS SLUMP"
"I'VE BEEN HERE FIVE YEARS!?"
ADVISOR RUNS OUT OF FUNDING
START WRITING DISSERTATION
I WILL BE AN AGENT OF CHANGE!
A CURSE! A CURSE ON THE LOT OF YOU!
copyright © 1999 jorge cham

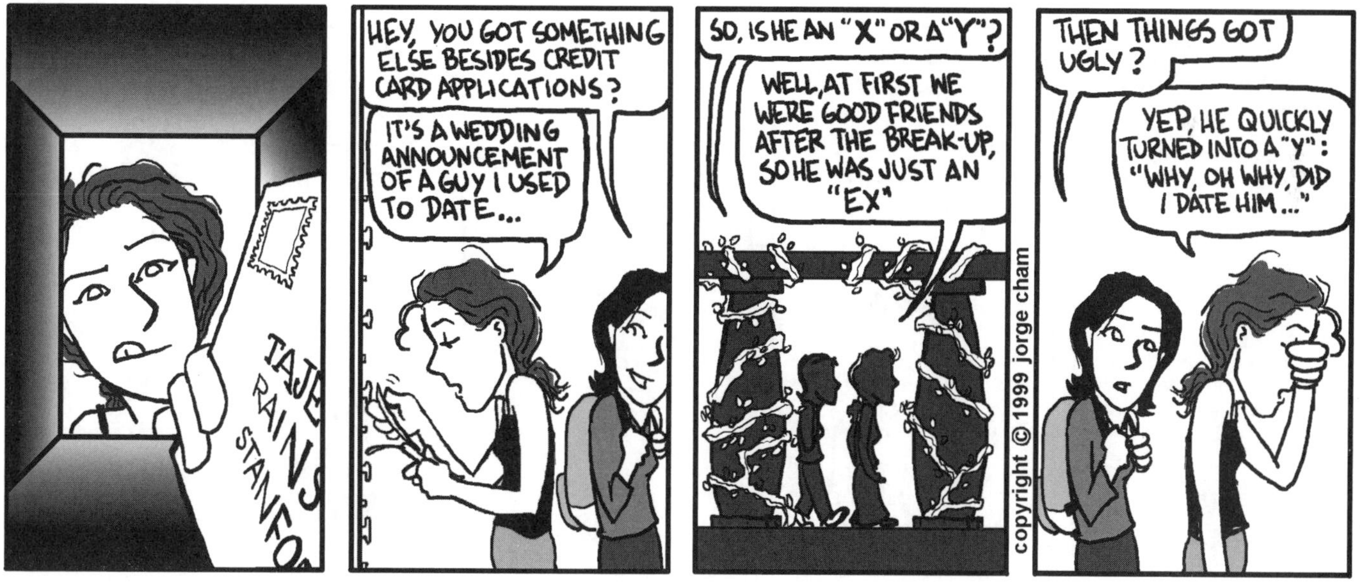
HEY, YOU GOT SOMETHING ELSE BESIDES CREDIT CARD APPLICATIONS?
IT'S A WEDDING ANNOUNCEMENT OF A GUY I USED TO DATE...
SO, IS HE AN "X" OR A "Y"?
WELL, AT FIRST WE WERE GOOD FRIENDS AFTER THE BREAK-UP, SO HE WAS JUST AN "EX"
copyright © 1999 jorge cham
THEN THINGS GOT UGLY?
YEP, HE QUICKLY TURNED INTO A "Y": "WHY, OH WHY, DID I DATE HIM..."

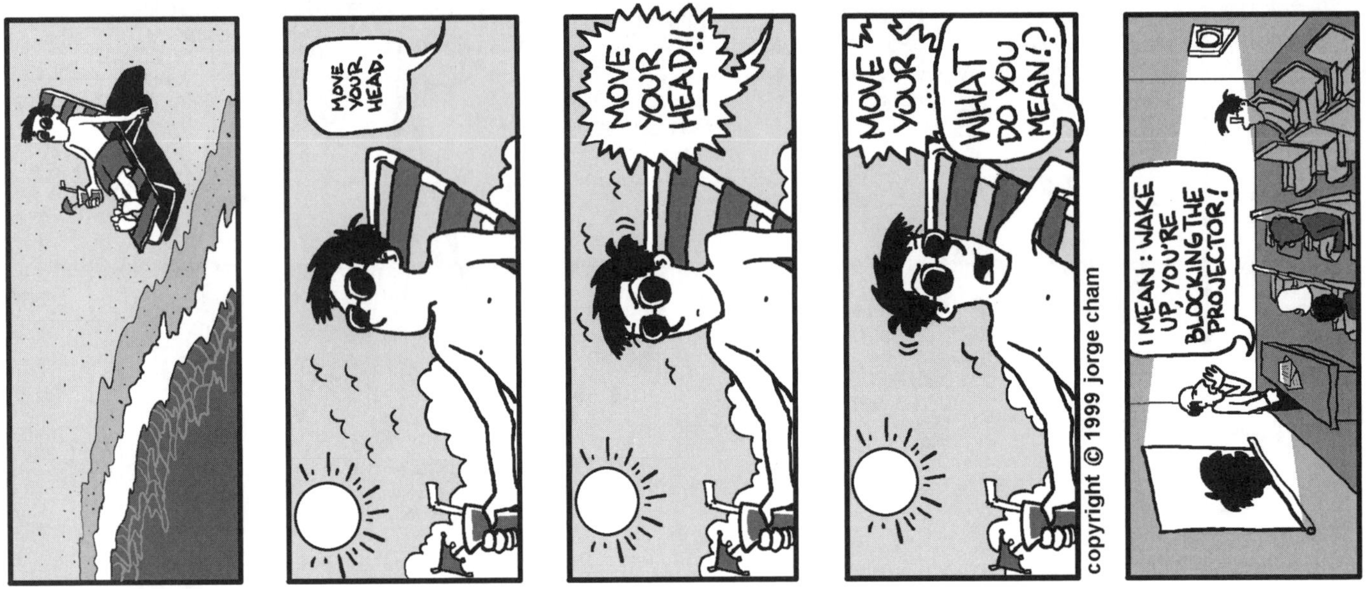
MOVE YOUR HEAD.
MOVE YOUR HEAD!!
MOVE YOUR ...
WHAT DO YOU MEAN!?
I MEAN: WAKE UP, YOU'RE BLOCKING THE PROJECTOR!
copyright © 1999 jorge cham

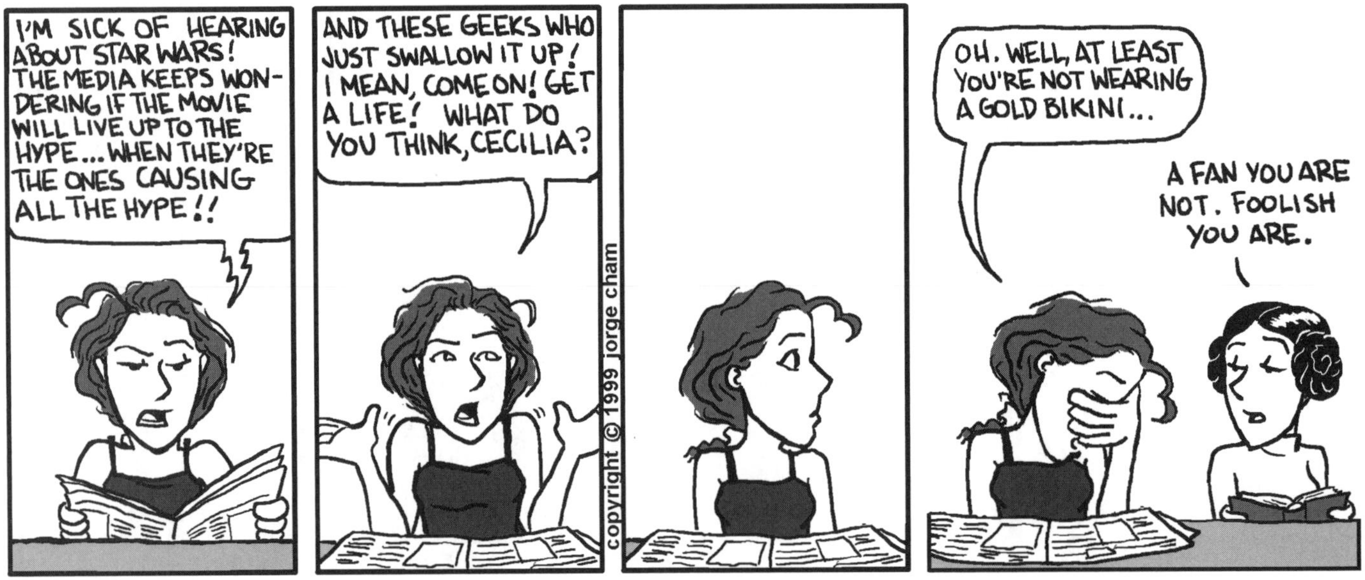
I'M SICK OF HEARING ABOUT STAR WARS! THE MEDIA KEEPS WONDERING IF THE MOVIE WILL LIVE UP TO THE HYPE... WHEN THEY'RE THE ONES CAUSING ALL THE HYPE!!
AND THESE GEEKS WHO JUST SWALLOW IT UP! I MEAN, COME ON! GET A LIFE! WHAT DO YOU THINK, CECILIA?
copyright © 1999 jorge cham
OH. WELL, AT LEAST YOU'RE NOT WEARING A GOLD BIKINI...
A FAN YOU ARE NOT. FOOLISH YOU ARE.

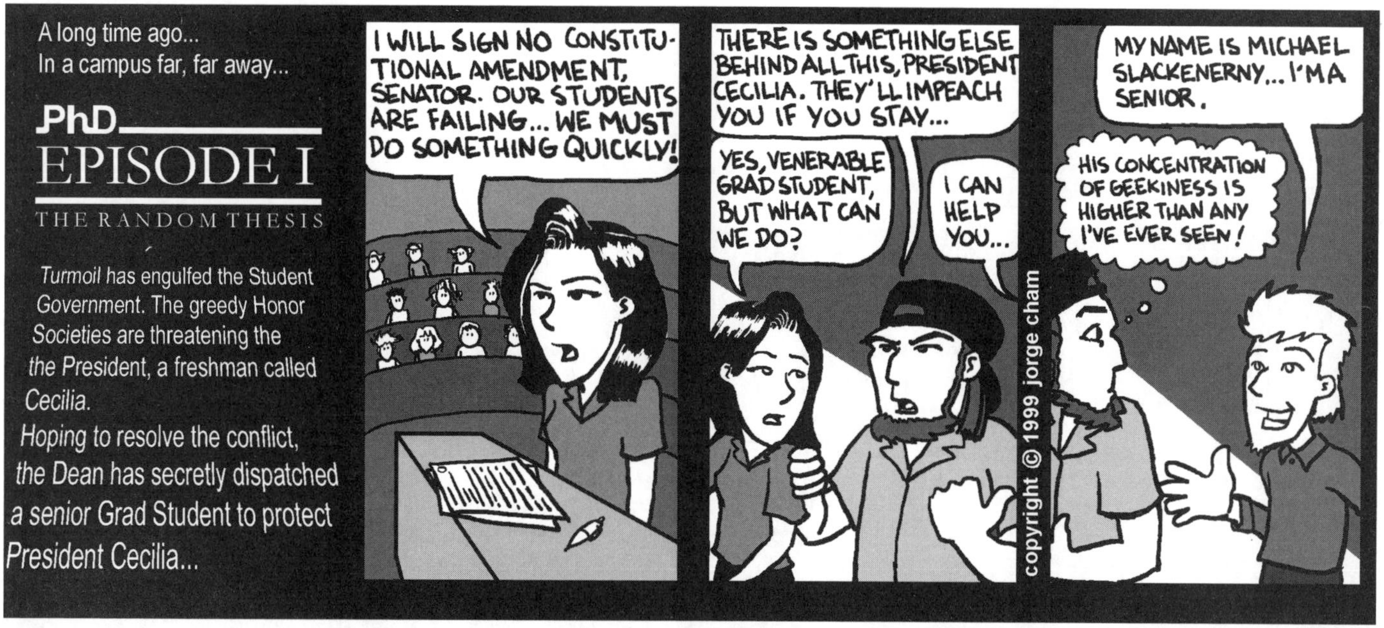
A long time ago...
In a campus far, far away...
PhD
EPISODE I
THE RANDOM THESIS
Turmoil has engulfed the Student Government. The greedy Honor Societies are threatening the the President, a freshman called Cecilia.
Hoping to resolve the conflict, the Dean has secretly dispatched a senior Grad Student to protect President Cecilia...
I WILL SIGN NO CONSTITUTIONAL AMENDMENT, SENATOR. OUR STUDENTS ARE FAILING... WE MUST DO SOMETHING QUICKLY!
THERE IS SOMETHING ELSE BEHIND ALL THIS, PRESIDENT CECILIA. THEY'LL IMPEACH YOU IF YOU STAY...
YES, VENERABLE GRAD STUDENT, BUT WHAT CAN WE DO?
I CAN HELP YOU...
copyright © 1999 jorge cham
MY NAME IS MICHAEL SLACKENERNY... I'M A SENIOR.
HIS CONCENTRATION OF GEEKINESS IS HIGHER THAN ANY I'VE EVER SEEN!

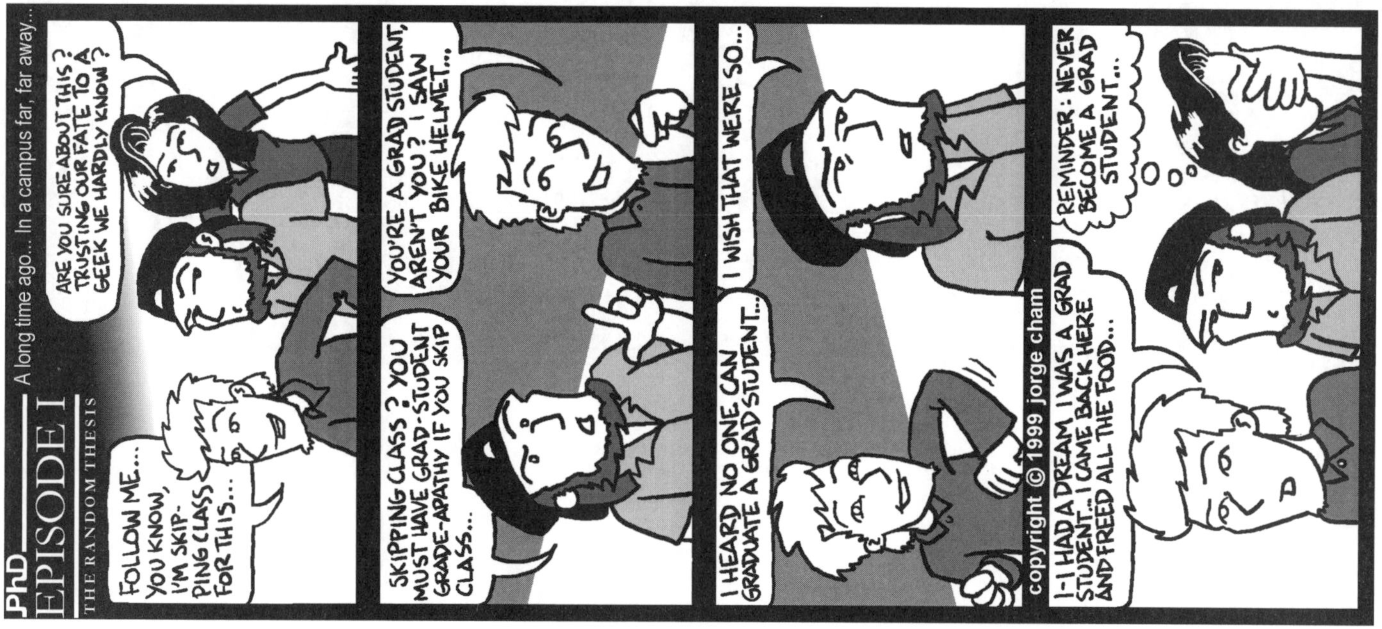
PhD
EPISODE I
THE RANDOM THESIS
A long time ago... In a campus far, far away...
FOLLOW ME.... YOU KNOW, I'M SKIP-PING CLASS FOR THIS....
ARE YOU SURE ABOUT THIS? TRUSTING OUR FATE TO A GEEK WE HARDLY KNOW?
SKIPPING CLASS? YOU MUST HAVE GRAD-STUDENT GRADE-APATHY IF YOU SKIP CLASS...
YOU'RE A GRAD STUDENT, AREN'T YOU? I SAW YOUR BIKE HELMET...
I HEARD NO ONE CAN GRADUATE A GRAD STUDENT...
I WISH THAT WERE SO...
copyright © 1999 jorge cham
I-I HAD A DREAM, I WAS A GRAD STUDENT... I CAME BACK HERE AND FREED ALL THE FOOD...
REMINDER: NEVER BECOME A GRAD STUDENT...

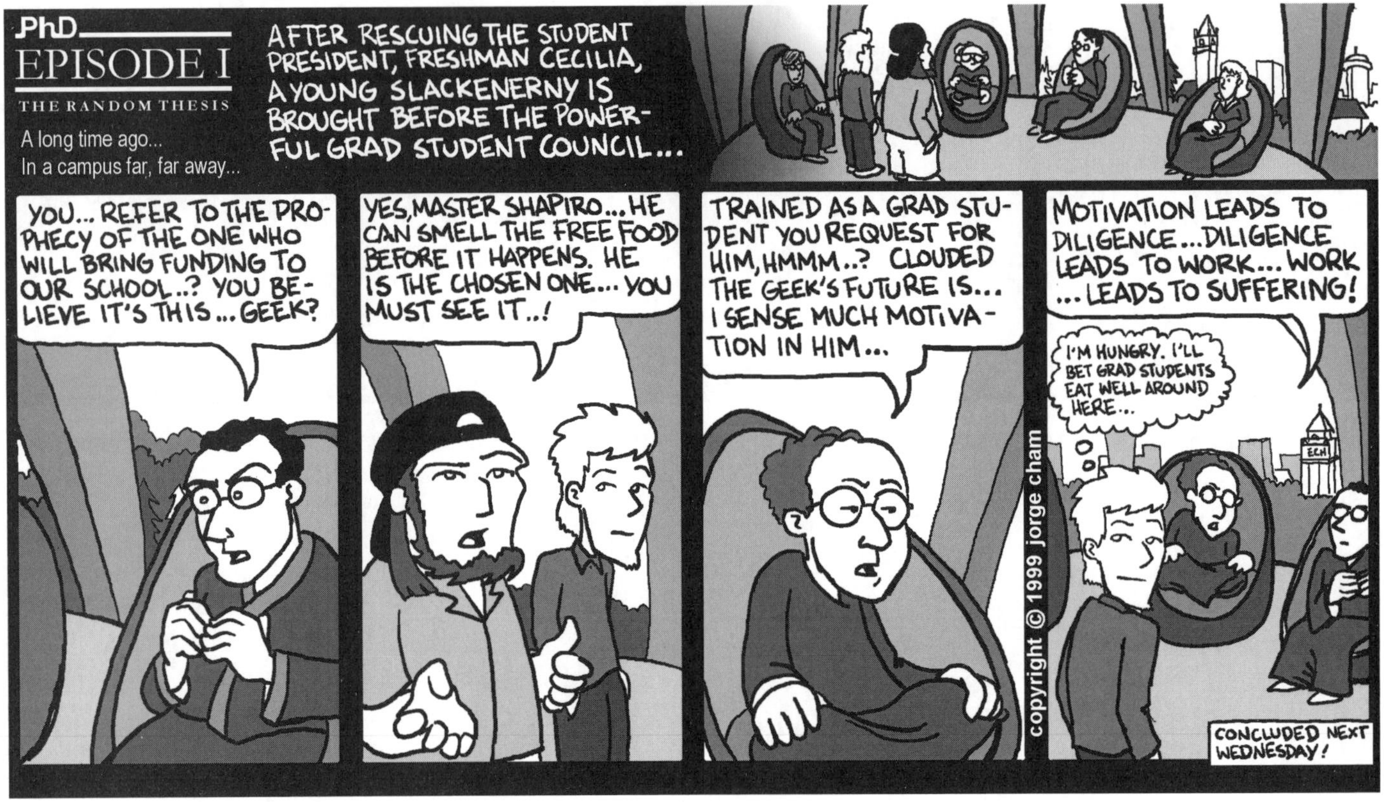
PhD
EPISODE I
THE RANDOM THESIS
A long time ago...
In a campus far, far away...
AFTER RESCUING THE STUDENT PRESIDENT, FRESHMAN CECILIA, A YOUNG SLACKENERNY IS BROUGHT BEFORE THE POWERFUL GRAD STUDENT COUNCIL...
YOU... REFER TO THE PROPHECY OF THE ONE WHO WILL BRING FUNDING TO OUR SCHOOL..? YOU BELIEVE IT'S THIS... GEEK?
YES, MASTER SHAPIRO... HE CAN SMELL THE FREE FOOD BEFORE IT HAPPENS. HE IS THE CHOSEN ONE... YOU MUST SEE IT..!
TRAINED AS A GRAD STUDENT YOU REQUEST FOR HIM, HMMM..? CLOUDED THE GEEK'S FUTURE IS... I SENSE MUCH MOTIVATION IN HIM...
copyright © 1999 jorge cham
MOTIVATION LEADS TO DILIGENCE... DILIGENCE LEADS TO WORK... WORK ... LEADS TO SUFFERING!
I'M HUNGRY. I'LL BET GRAD STUDENTS EAT WELL AROUND HERE...
ECH
CONCLUDED NEXT WEDNESDAY!

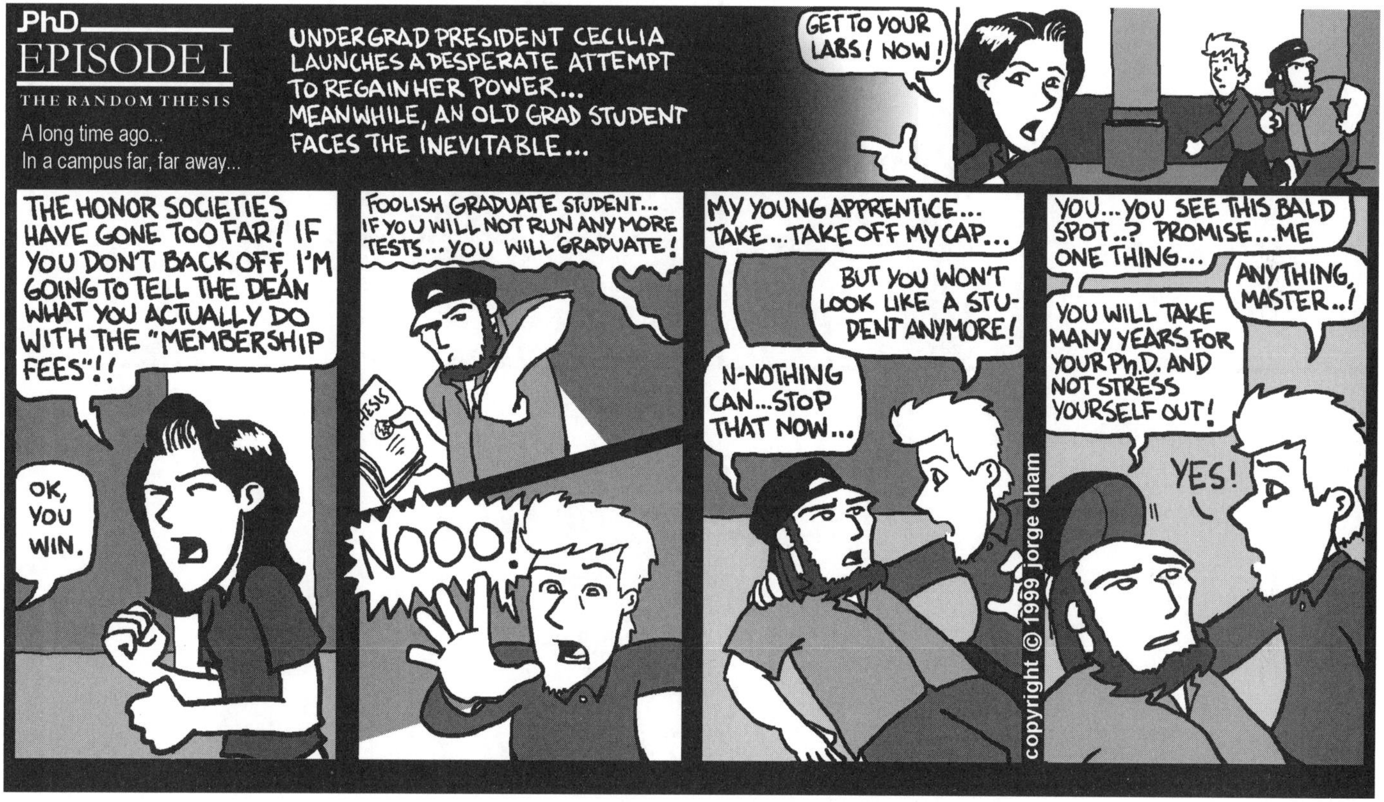
PhD
EPISODE I
THE RANDOM THESIS
A long time ago...
In a campus far, far away...
UNDERGRAD PRESIDENT CECILIA LAUNCHES A DESPERATE ATTEMPT TO REGAIN HER POWER... MEANWHILE, AN OLD GRAD STUDENT FACES THE INEVITABLE...
GET TO YOUR LABS! NOW!
THE HONOR SOCIETIES HAVE GONE TOO FAR! IF YOU DON'T BACK OFF, I'M GOING TO TELL THE DEAN WHAT YOU ACTUALLY DO WITH THE "MEMBERSHIP FEES"!!
OK, YOU WIN.
FOOLISH GRADUATE STUDENT... IF YOU WILL NOT RUN ANY MORE TESTS... YOU WILL GRADUATE!
THESIS
NOOO!
MY YOUNG APPRENTICE... TAKE... TAKE OFF MY CAP...
BUT YOU WON'T LOOK LIKE A STUDENT ANYMORE!
N-NOTHING CAN... STOP THAT NOW...
copyright © 1999 jorge cham
YOU... YOU SEE THIS BALD SPOT..? PROMISE... ME ONE THING...
ANYTHING, MASTER...!
YOU WILL TAKE MANY YEARS FOR YOUR Ph.D. AND NOT STRESS YOURSELF OUT!
YES!

P-PROF. SMITH..?

I DIDN'T SLEEP ALL WEEK, BUT I FINISHED THE PAPER FOR THAT CONFERENCE IN ITALY...

HUH? WHAT CONFERENCE?

WH..? UM... I-I THOUGHT YOU SAID IF I FINISHED THESE TESTS EARLY YOU WOULD PAY FOR FEES, PASSAGE AND ROOM IN PISA FOR THE MEETING ...

UH, NO... I SAID I'D PAY FOR A CHEESE, SAUSAGE AND MUSHROOM PIZZA FOR EATING...

OH. IS IT OK IF I TAKE A QUICK NAP ON YOUR RUG, SIR?

YEAR THREE
1999-2000

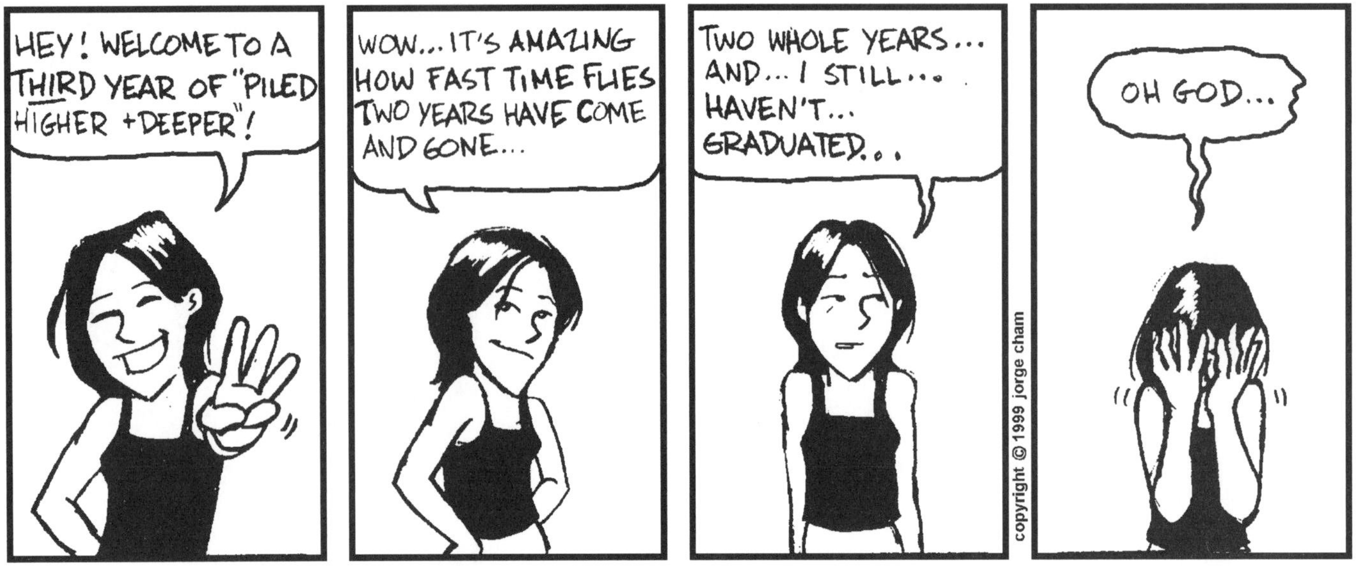
HEY! WELCOME TO A THIRD YEAR OF "PILED HIGHER + DEEPER"!
WOW... IT'S AMAZING HOW FAST TIME FLIES TWO YEARS HAVE COME AND GONE...
TWO WHOLE YEARS... AND... I STILL... HAVEN'T... GRADUATED...
OH GOD...
copyright © 1999 jorge cham

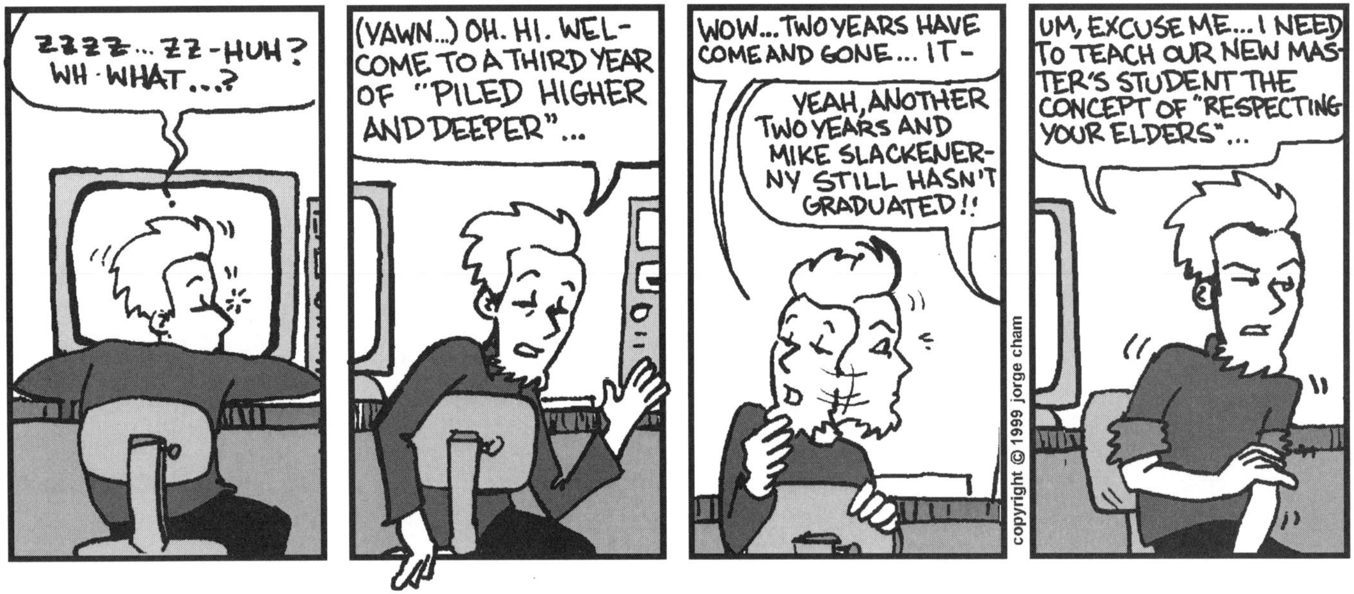
ZZZZ... ZZ-HUH? WH-WHAT...?
(YAWN...) OH. HI. WELCOME TO A THIRD YEAR OF "PILED HIGHER AND DEEPER"...
WOW... TWO YEARS HAVE COME AND GONE... IT-
YEAH, ANOTHER TWO YEARS AND MIKE SLACKENERNY STILL HASN'T GRADUATED!!
UM, EXCUSE ME... I NEED TO TEACH OUR NEW MASTER'S STUDENT THE CONCEPT OF "RESPECTING YOUR ELDERS"...
copyright © 1999 jorge cham

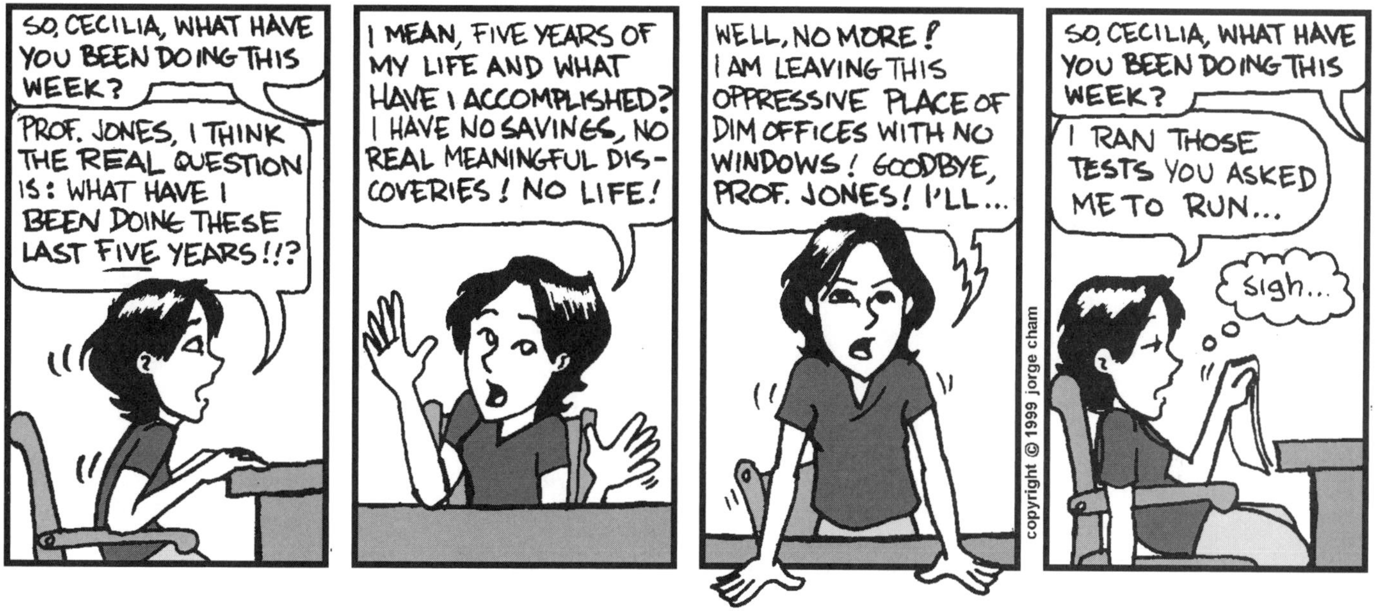
SO, CECILIA, WHAT HAVE YOU BEEN DOING THIS WEEK?
PROF. JONES, I THINK THE REAL QUESTION IS: WHAT HAVE I BEEN DOING THESE LAST FIVE YEARS!!?
I MEAN, FIVE YEARS OF MY LIFE AND WHAT HAVE I ACCOMPLISHED? I HAVE NO SAVINGS, NO REAL MEANINGFUL DISCOVERIES! NO LIFE!
WELL, NO MORE! I AM LEAVING THIS OPPRESSIVE PLACE OF DIM OFFICES WITH NO WINDOWS! GOODBYE, PROF. JONES! I'LL...
copyright © 1999 jorge cham
SO, CECILIA, WHAT HAVE YOU BEEN DOING THIS WEEK?
I RAN THOSE TESTS YOU ASKED ME TO RUN...
sigh...

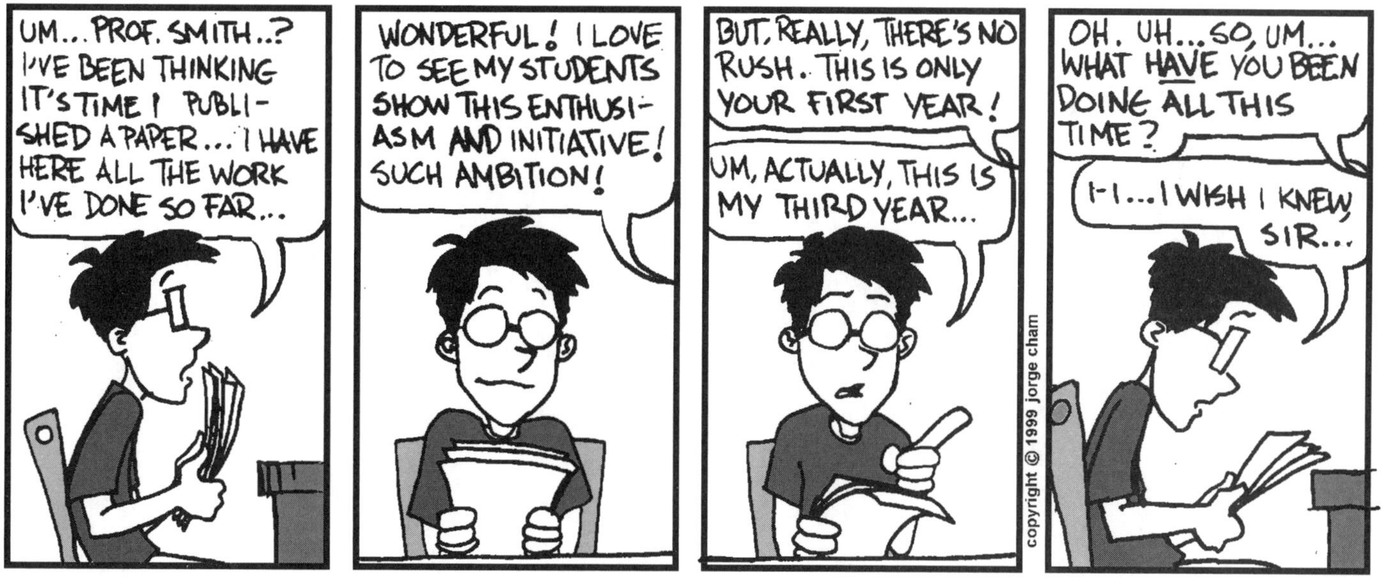
UM... PROF. SMITH..? I'VE BEEN THINKING IT'S TIME I PUBLISHED A PAPER... I HAVE HERE ALL THE WORK I'VE DONE SO FAR...
WONDERFUL! I LOVE TO SEE MY STUDENTS SHOW THIS ENTHUSIASM AND INITIATIVE! SUCH AMBITION!
BUT, REALLY, THERE'S NO RUSH. THIS IS ONLY YOUR FIRST YEAR!
UM, ACTUALLY, THIS IS MY THIRD YEAR...
copyright © 1999 jorge cham
OH. UH...SO, UM... WHAT HAVE YOU BEEN DOING ALL THIS TIME?
I-I...I WISH I KNEW, SIR...

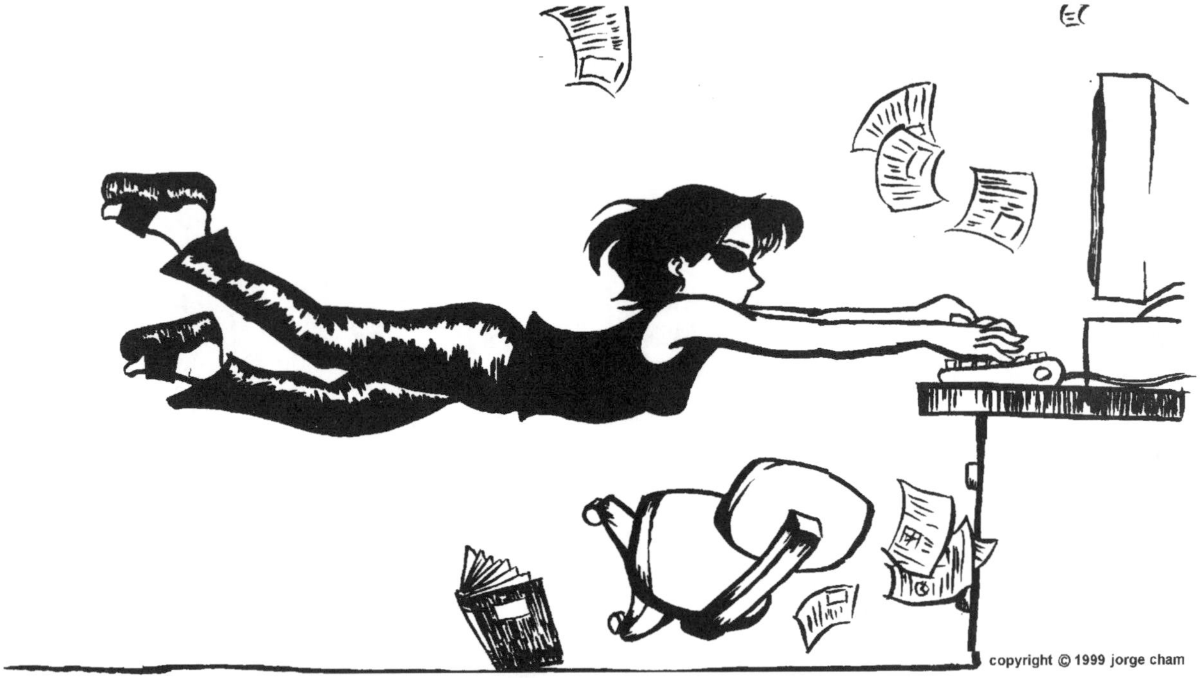
copyright © 1999 jorge cham

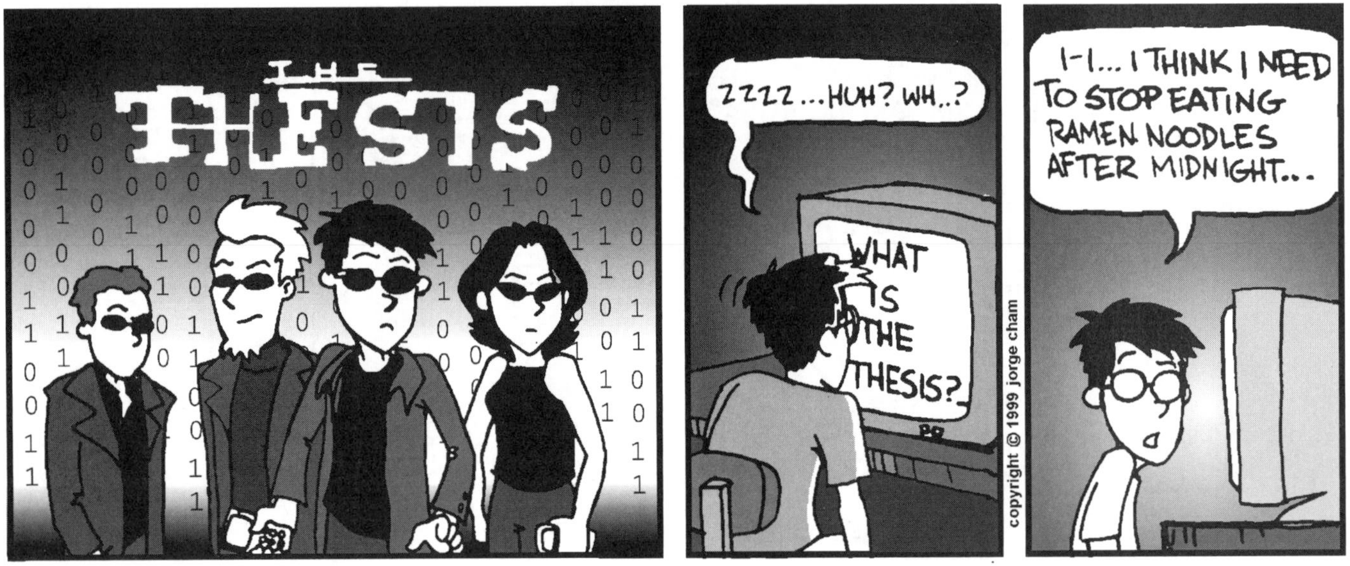
THE THESIS
ZZZZ...HUH? WH..?
WHAT IS THE THESIS?
copyright © 1999 jorge cham
I-I... I THINK I NEED TO STOP EATING RAMEN NOODLES AFTER MIDNIGHT...

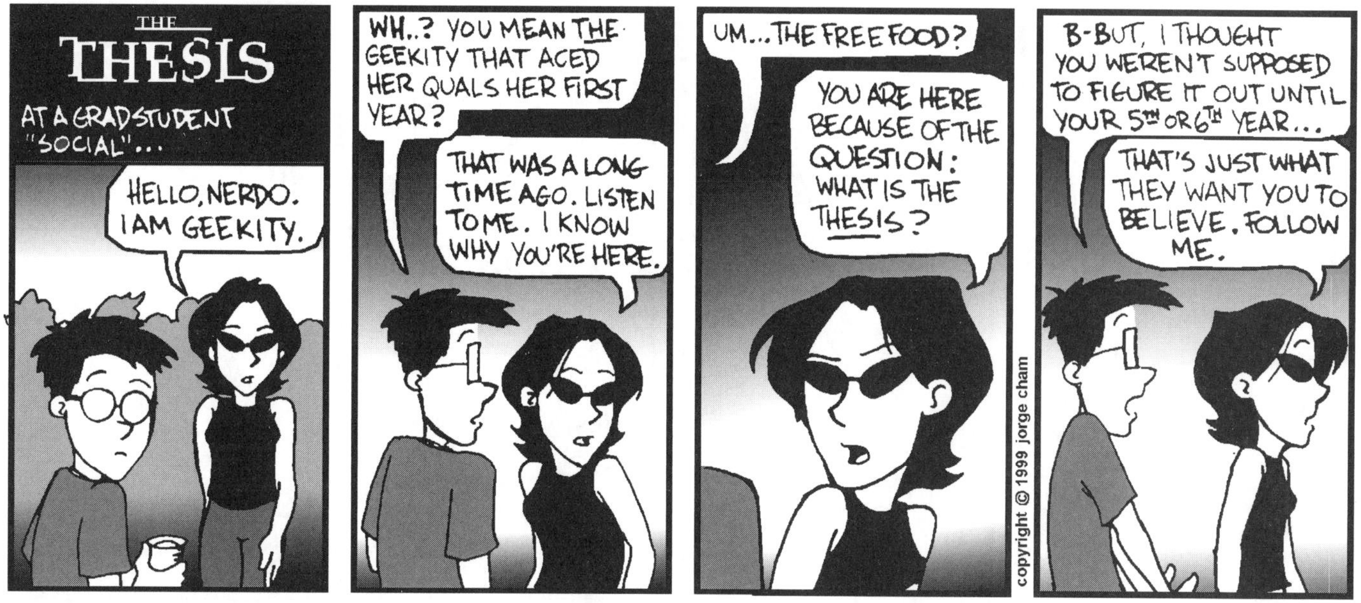
THE THESIS
AT A GRAD STUDENT "SOCIAL"...
HELLO, NERDO. I AM GEEKITY.
WH..? YOU MEAN THE GEEKITY THAT ACED HER QUALS HER FIRST YEAR?
THAT WAS A LONG TIME AGO. LISTEN TO ME. I KNOW WHY YOU'RE HERE.
UM... THE FREE FOOD?
YOU ARE HERE BECAUSE OF THE QUESTION: WHAT IS THE THESIS?
B-BUT, I THOUGHT YOU WEREN'T SUPPOSED TO FIGURE IT OUT UNTIL YOUR 5TH OR 6TH YEAR...
THAT'S JUST WHAT THEY WANT YOU TO BELIEVE. FOLLOW ME.
copyright © 1999 jorge cham

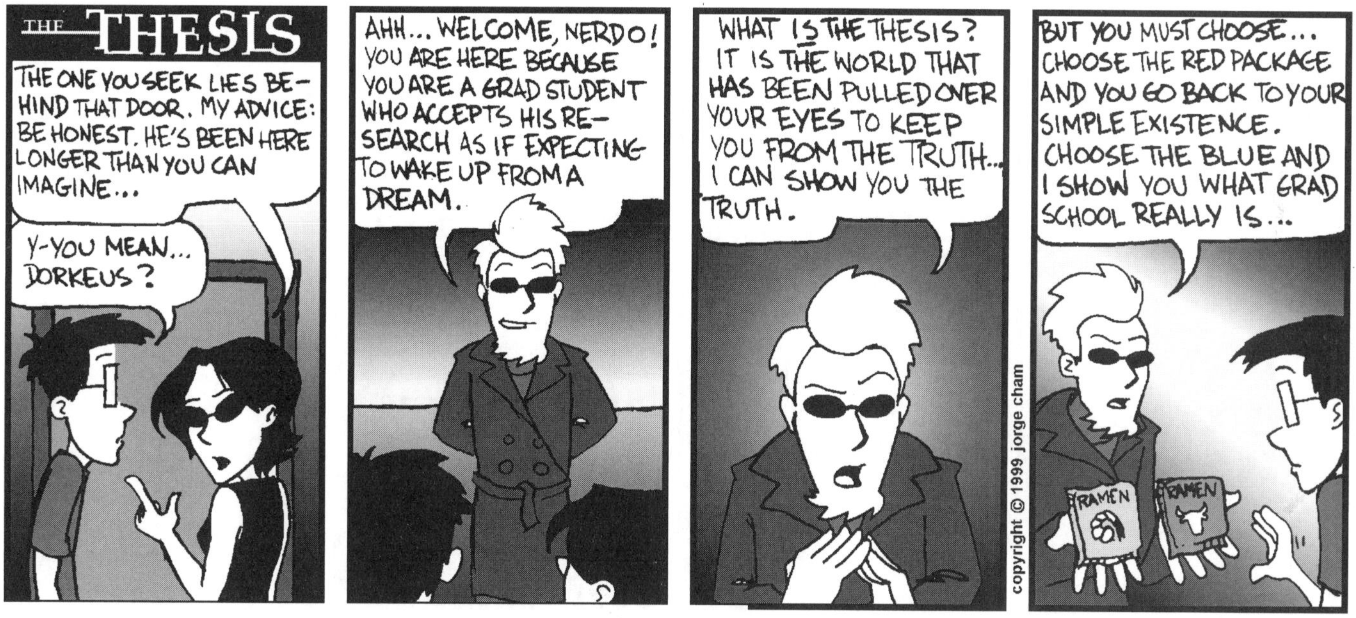
THE THESIS
THE ONE YOU SEEK LIES BEHIND THAT DOOR. MY ADVICE: BE HONEST. HE'S BEEN HERE LONGER THAN YOU CAN IMAGINE...
Y-YOU MEAN... DORKEUS?
AHH... WELCOME, NERDO! YOU ARE HERE BECAUSE YOU ARE A GRAD STUDENT WHO ACCEPTS HIS RESEARCH AS IF EXPECTING TO WAKE UP FROM A DREAM.
WHAT IS THE THESIS? IT IS THE WORLD THAT HAS BEEN PULLED OVER YOUR EYES TO KEEP YOU FROM THE TRUTH... I CAN SHOW YOU THE TRUTH.
BUT YOU MUST CHOOSE... CHOOSE THE RED PACKAGE AND YOU GO BACK TO YOUR SIMPLE EXISTENCE. CHOOSE THE BLUE AND I SHOW YOU WHAT GRAD SCHOOL REALLY IS...
RAMEN
RAMEN
copyright © 1999 jorge cham

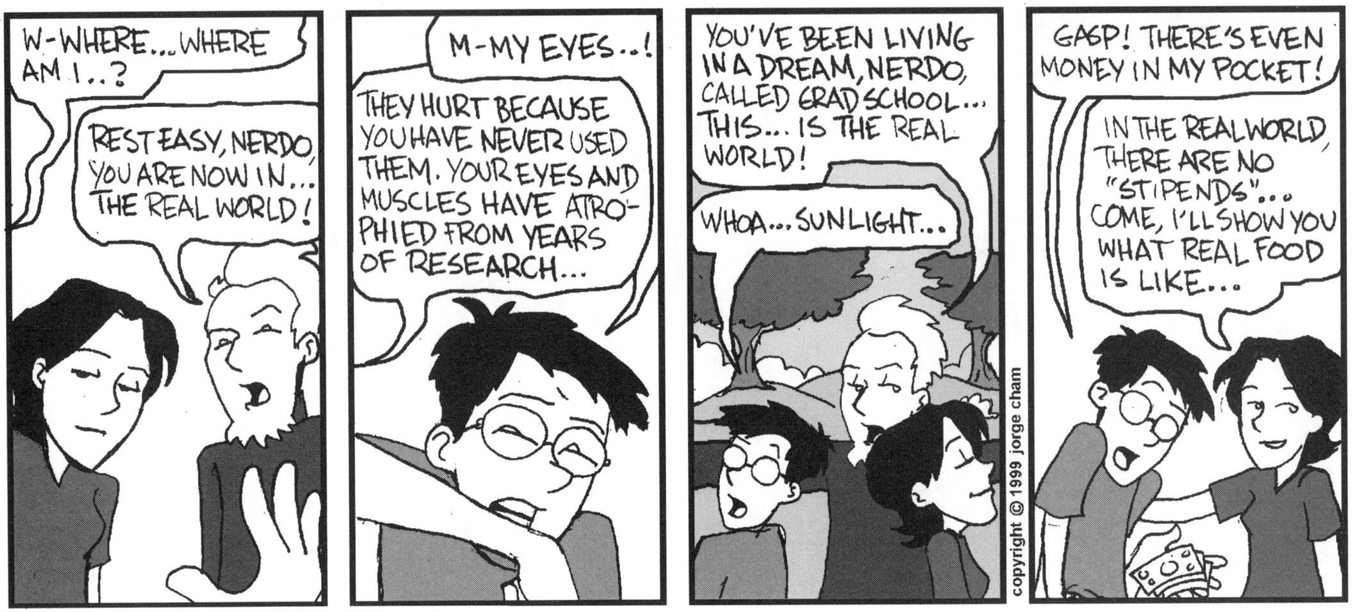
W-WHERE... WHERE AM I..?
REST EASY, NERDO, YOU ARE NOW IN... THE REAL WORLD!
M-MY EYES..!
THEY HURT BECAUSE YOU HAVE NEVER USED THEM. YOUR EYES AND MUSCLES HAVE ATROPHIED FROM YEARS OF RESEARCH...
YOU'VE BEEN LIVING IN A DREAM, NERDO, CALLED GRAD SCHOOL... THIS... IS THE REAL WORLD!
WHOA... SUNLIGHT...
copyright © 1999 jorge cham
GASP! THERE'S EVEN MONEY IN MY POCKET!
IN THE REAL WORLD, THERE ARE NO "STIPENDS"... COME, I'LL SHOW YOU WHAT REAL FOOD IS LIKE...

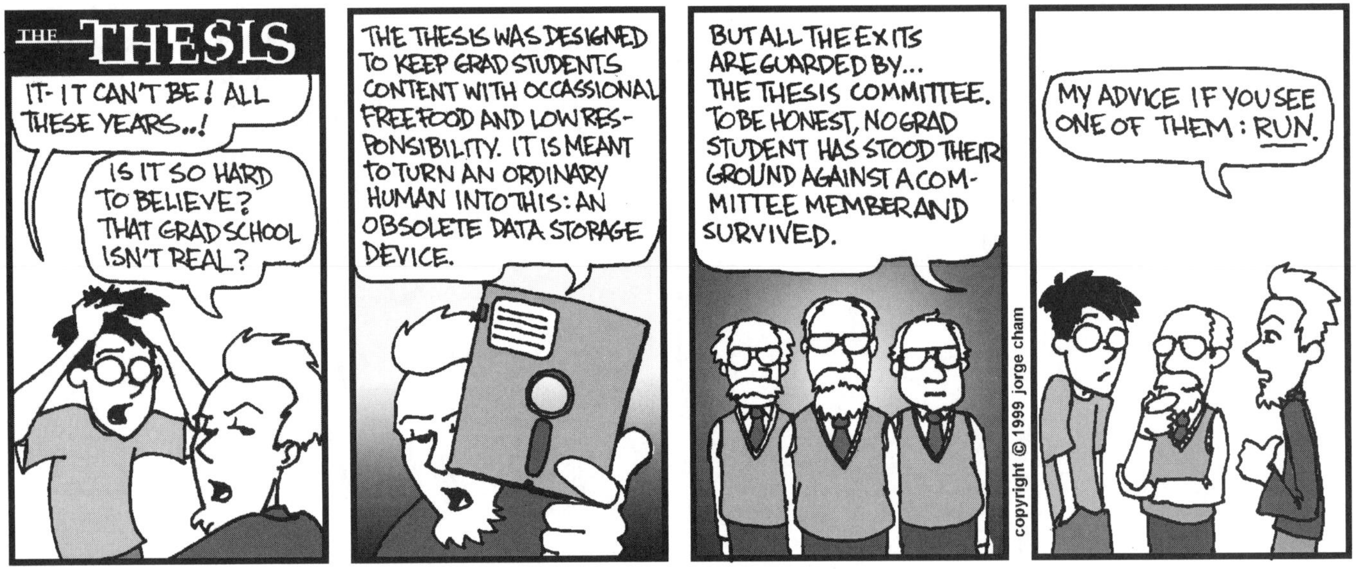
THE THESIS
IT- IT CAN'T BE! ALL THESE YEARS..!
IS IT SO HARD TO BELIEVE? THAT GRAD SCHOOL ISN'T REAL?
THE THESIS WAS DESIGNED TO KEEP GRAD STUDENTS CONTENT WITH OCCASSIONAL FREE FOOD AND LOW RESPONSIBILITY. IT IS MEANT TO TURN AN ORDINARY HUMAN INTO THIS: AN OBSOLETE DATA STORAGE DEVICE.
BUT ALL THE EXITS ARE GUARDED BY... THE THESIS COMMITTEE. TO BE HONEST, NO GRAD STUDENT HAS STOOD THEIR GROUND AGAINST A COMMITTEE MEMBER AND SURVIVED.
copyright © 1999 jorge cham
MY ADVICE IF YOU SEE ONE OF THEM: RUN.

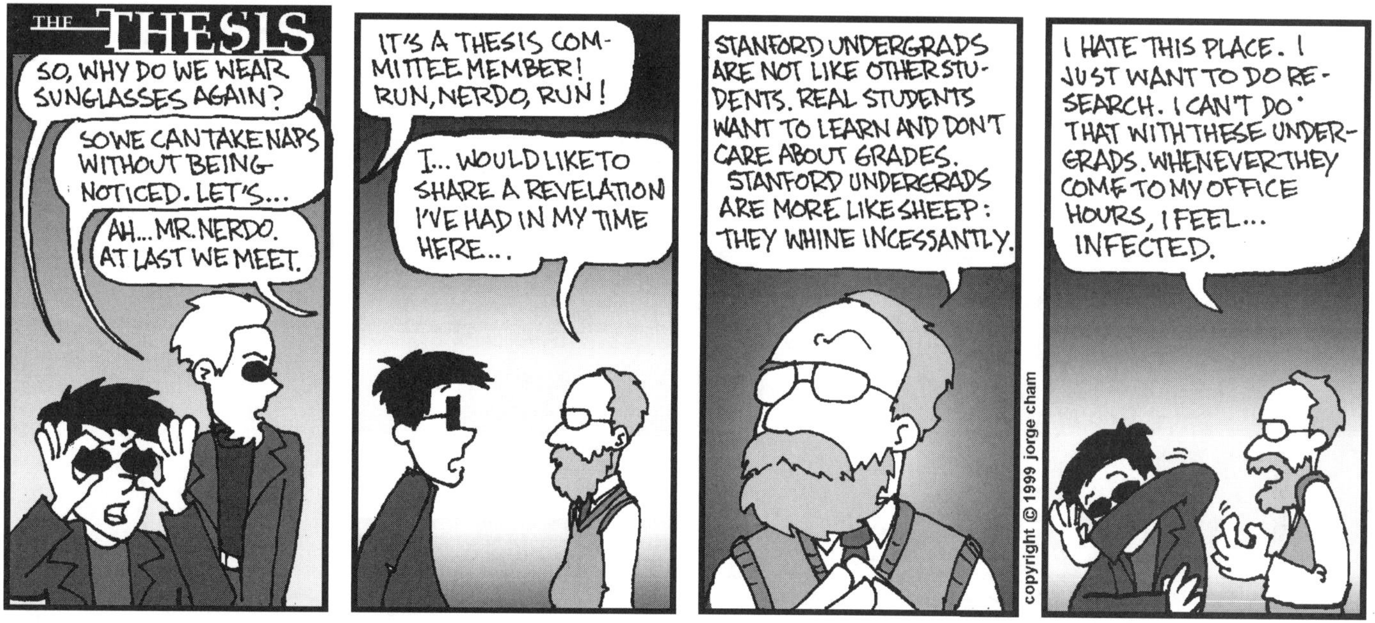
THE THESIS
SO, WHY DO WE WEAR SUNGLASSES AGAIN?
SO WE CAN TAKE NAPS WITHOUT BEING NOTICED. LET'S...
AH... MR. NERDO. AT LAST WE MEET.
IT'S A THESIS COMMITTEE MEMBER! RUN, NERDO, RUN!
I... WOULD LIKE TO SHARE A REVELATION I'VE HAD IN MY TIME HERE...
STANFORD UNDERGRADS ARE NOT LIKE OTHER STUDENTS. REAL STUDENTS WANT TO LEARN AND DON'T CARE ABOUT GRADES.
STANFORD UNDERGRADS ARE MORE LIKE SHEEP: THEY WHINE INCESSANTLY.
copyright © 1999 jorge cham
I HATE THIS PLACE. I JUST WANT TO DO RESEARCH. I CAN'T DO THAT WITH THESE UNDERGRADS. WHENEVER THEY COME TO MY OFFICE HOURS, I FEEL... INFECTED.

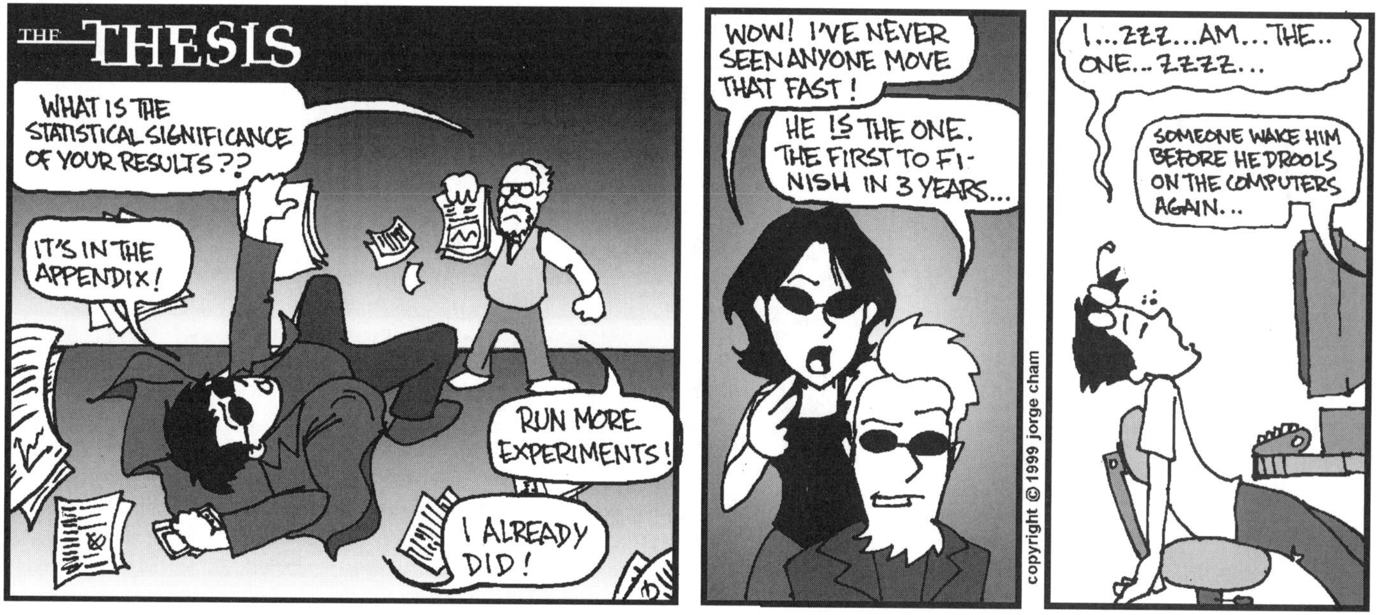
THE THESIS
WHAT IS THE STATISTICAL SIGNIFICANCE OF YOUR RESULTS??
IT'S IN THE APPENDIX!
RUN MORE EXPERIMENTS!
I ALREADY DID!
WOW! I'VE NEVER SEEN ANYONE MOVE THAT FAST!
HE IS THE ONE. THE FIRST TO FINISH IN 3 YEARS...
copyright © 1999 jorge cham
I...ZZZ...AM...THE...ONE...ZZZZ...
SOMEONE WAKE HIM BEFORE HE DROOLS ON THE COMPUTERS AGAIN...

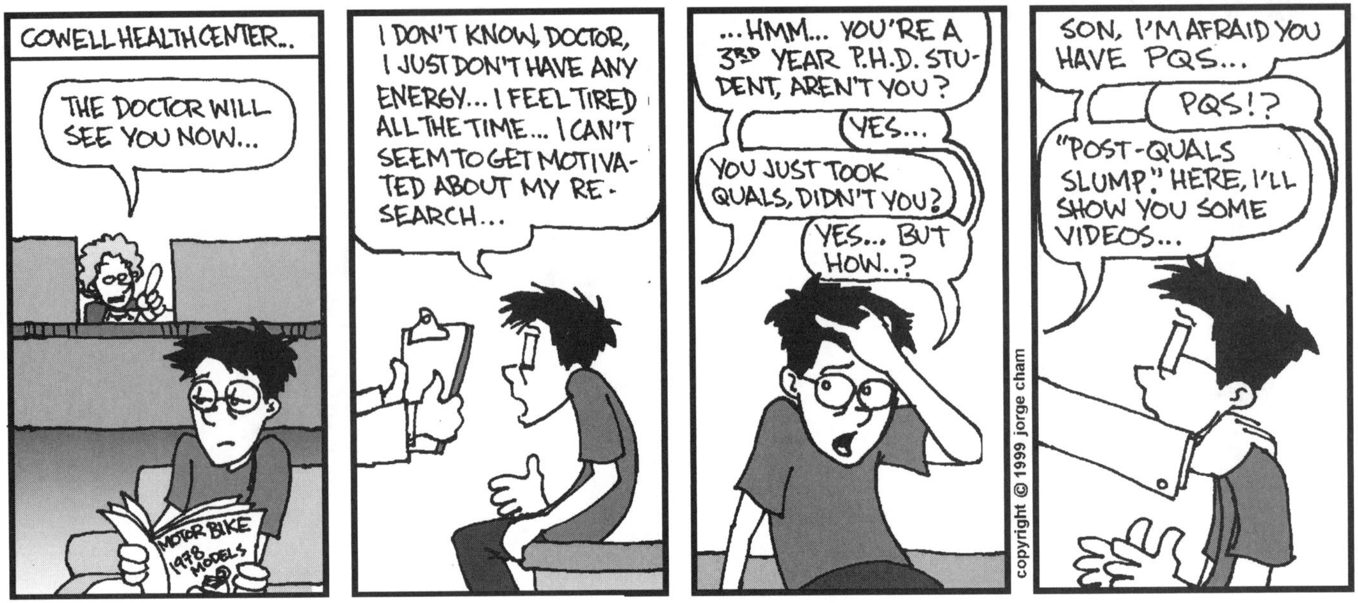
COWELL HEALTH CENTER..
THE DOCTOR WILL SEE YOU NOW...
MOTOR BIKE 1978 MODELS
I DON'T KNOW, DOCTOR, I JUST DON'T HAVE ANY ENERGY... I FEEL TIRED ALL THE TIME... I CAN'T SEEM TO GET MOTIVATED ABOUT MY RESEARCH...
...HMM... YOU'RE A 3RD YEAR P.H.D. STUDENT, AREN'T YOU?
YES...
YOU JUST TOOK QUALS, DIDN'T YOU?
YES... BUT HOW..?
copyright © 1999 jorge cham
SON, I'M AFRAID YOU HAVE PQS...
PQS!?
"POST-QUALS SLUMP." HERE, I'LL SHOW YOU SOME VIDEOS...

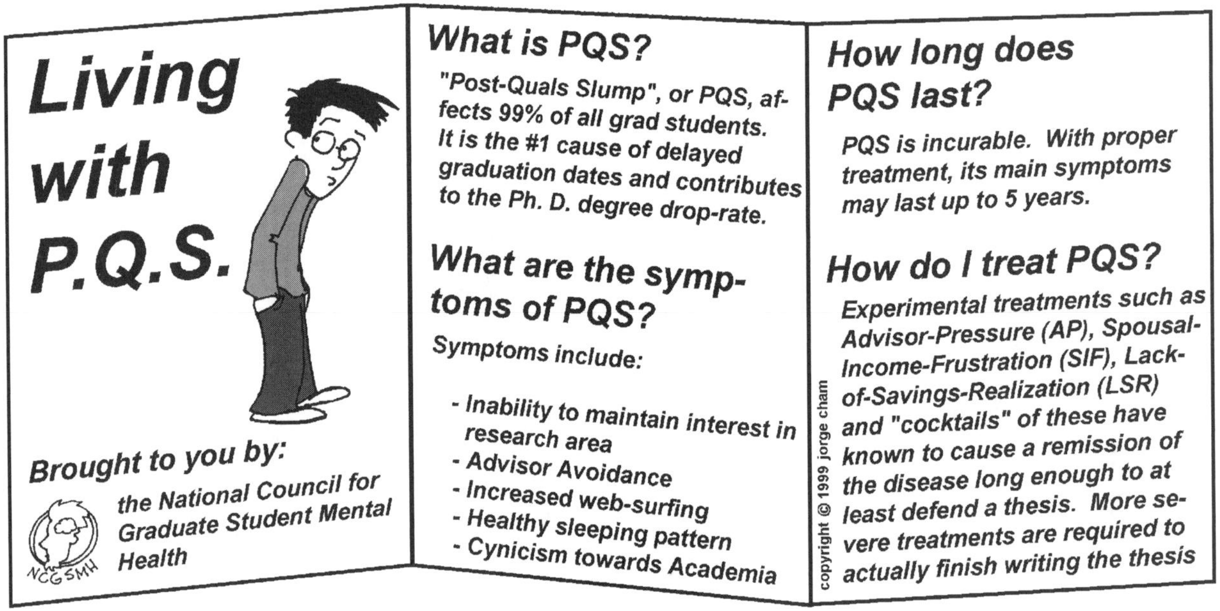
Living with P.Q.S.
Brought to you by:
the National Council for Graduate Student Mental Health
NCGSMH
What is PQS?
"Post-Quals Slump", or PQS, affects 99% of all grad students. It is the #1 cause of delayed graduation dates and contributes to the Ph. D. degree drop-rate.
What are the symptoms of PQS?
Symptoms include:
- Inability to maintain interest in research area
- Advisor Avoidance
- Increased web-surfing
- Healthy sleeping pattern
- Cynicism towards Academia
copyright © 1999 jorge cham
How long does PQS last?
PQS is incurable. With proper treatment, its main symptoms may last up to 5 years.
How do I treat PQS?
Experimental treatments such as Advisor-Pressure (AP), Spousal-Income-Frustration (SIF), Lack-of-Savings-Realization (LSR) and "cocktails" of these have known to cause a remission of the disease long enough to at least defend a thesis. More severe treatments are required to actually finish writing the thesis

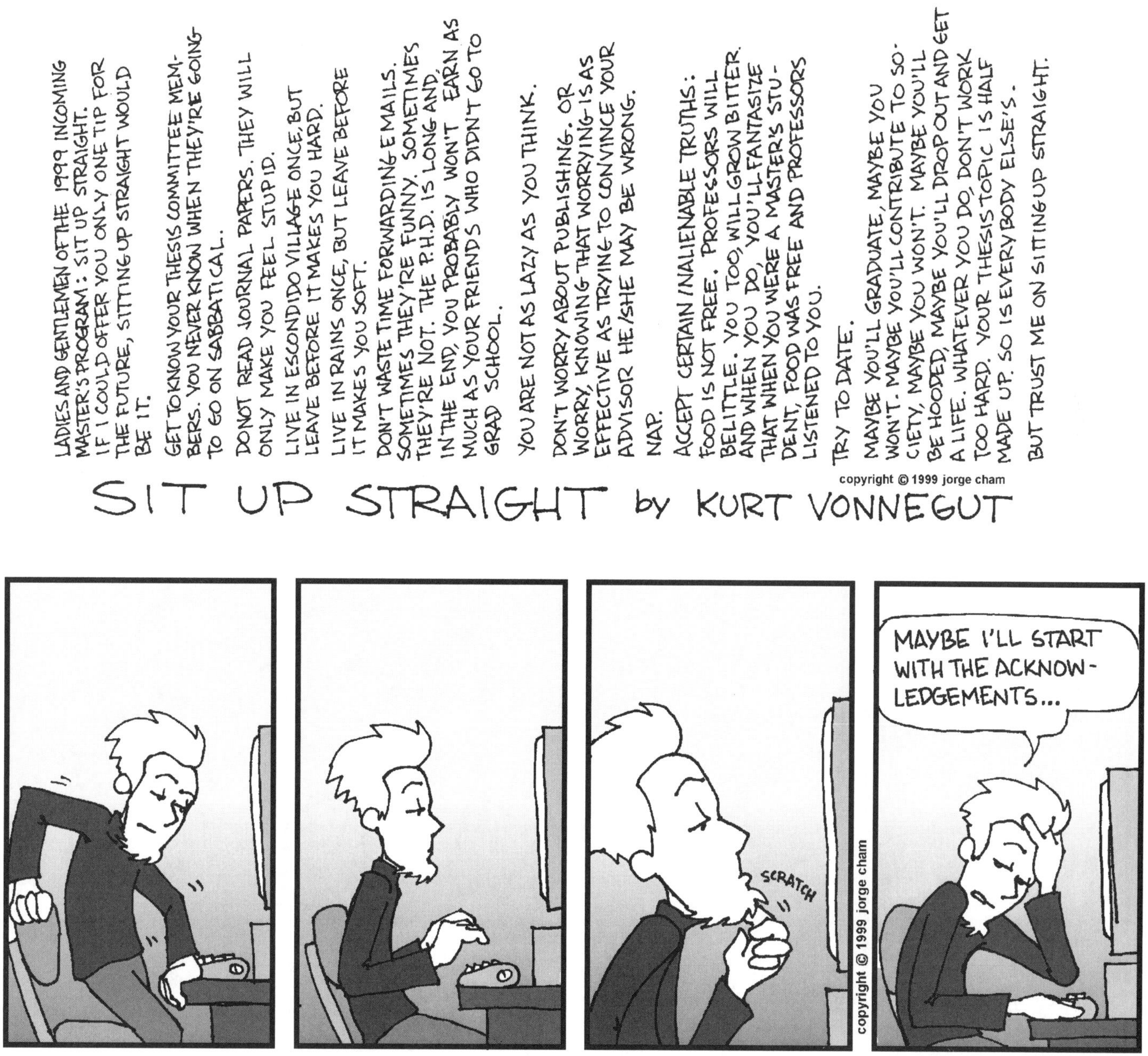
LADIES AND GENTLEMEN OF THE 1999 INCOMING MASTER'S PROGRAM: SIT UP STRAIGHT. IF I COULD OFFER YOU ONLY ONE TIP FOR THE FUTURE, SITTING UP STRAIGHT WOULD BE IT.
GET TO KNOW YOUR THESIS COMMITTEE MEMBERS. YOU NEVER KNOW WHEN THEY'RE GOING TO GO ON SABBATICAL.
DO NOT READ JOURNAL PAPERS. THEY WILL ONLY MAKE YOU FEEL STUPID.
LIVE IN ESCONDIDO VILLAGE ONCE, BUT LEAVE BEFORE IT MAKES YOU HARD.
LIVE IN RAINS ONCE, BUT LEAVE BEFORE IT MAKES YOU SOFT.
DON'T WASTE TIME FORWARDING EMAILS. SOMETIMES THEY'RE FUNNY. SOMETIMES THEY'RE NOT. THE P.H.D. IS LONG AND, IN THE END, YOU PROBABLY WON'T EARN AS MUCH AS YOUR FRIENDS WHO DIDN'T GO TO GRAD SCHOOL.
YOU ARE NOT AS LAZY AS YOU THINK.
DON'T WORRY ABOUT PUBLISHING. OR WORRY, KNOWING THAT WORRYING IS AS EFFECTIVE AS TRYING TO CONVINCE YOUR ADVISOR HE/SHE MAY BE WRONG.
NAP.
ACCEPT CERTAIN INALIENABLE TRUTHS: FOOD IS NOT FREE. PROFESSORS WILL BELITTLE. YOU TOO, WILL GROW BITTER. AND WHEN YOU DO, YOU'LL FANTASIZE THAT WHEN YOU WERE A MASTER'S STUDENT, FOOD WAS FREE AND PROFESSORS LISTENED TO YOU.
TRY TO DATE.
MAYBE YOU'LL GRADUATE, MAYBE YOU WON'T. MAYBE YOU'LL CONTRIBUTE TO SOCIETY, MAYBE YOU WON'T. MAYBE YOU'LL BE HOODED, MAYBE YOU'LL DROP OUT AND GET A LIFE. WHATEVER YOU DO, DON'T WORK TOO HARD. YOUR THESIS TOPIC IS HALF MADE UP. SO IS EVERYBODY ELSE'S.
BUT TRUST ME ON SITTING UP STRAIGHT.
copyright © 1999 jorge cham
SIT UP STRAIGHT by KURT VONNEGUT
SCRATCH
copyright © 1999 jorge cham
MAYBE I'LL START WITH THE ACKNOWLEDGEMENTS...

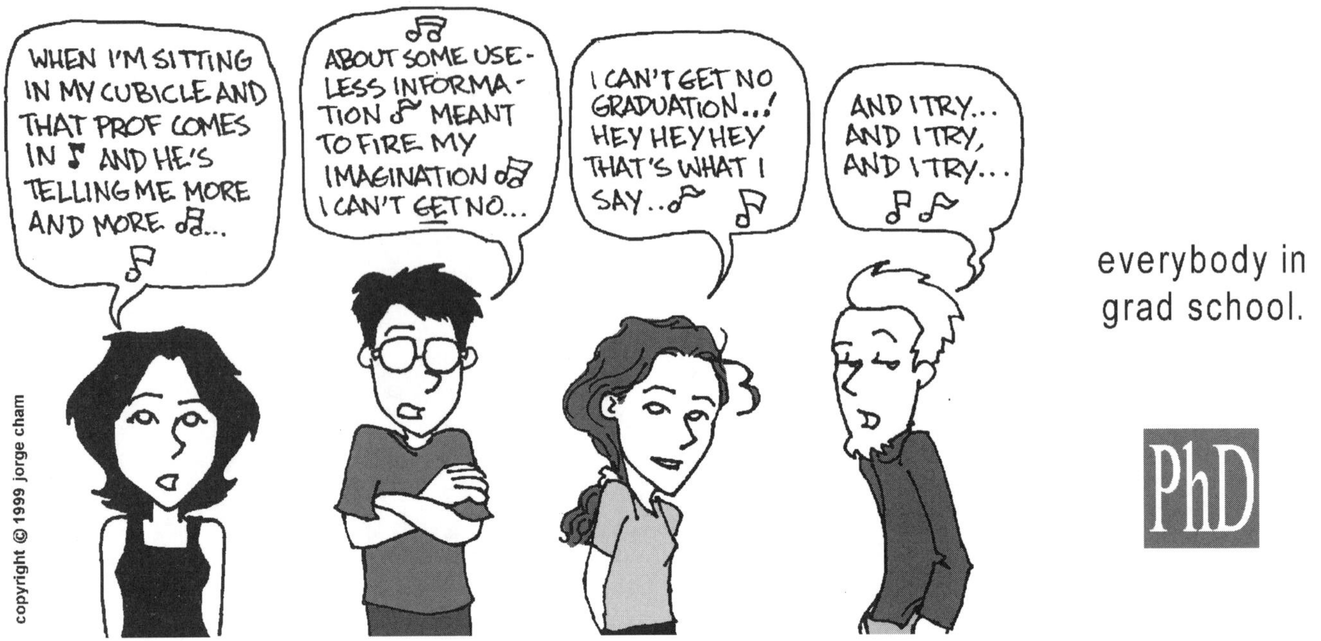
WHEN I'M SITTING IN MY CUBICLE AND THAT PROF COMES IN AND HE'S TELLING ME MORE AND MORE...
ABOUT SOME USELESS INFORMATION MEANT TO FIRE MY IMAGINATION I CAN'T GET NO...
I CAN'T GET NO GRADUATION...! HEY HEY HEY THAT'S WHAT I SAY...
AND I TRY... AND I TRY, AND I TRY...
everybody in grad school.
PhD
copyright © 1999 jorge cham

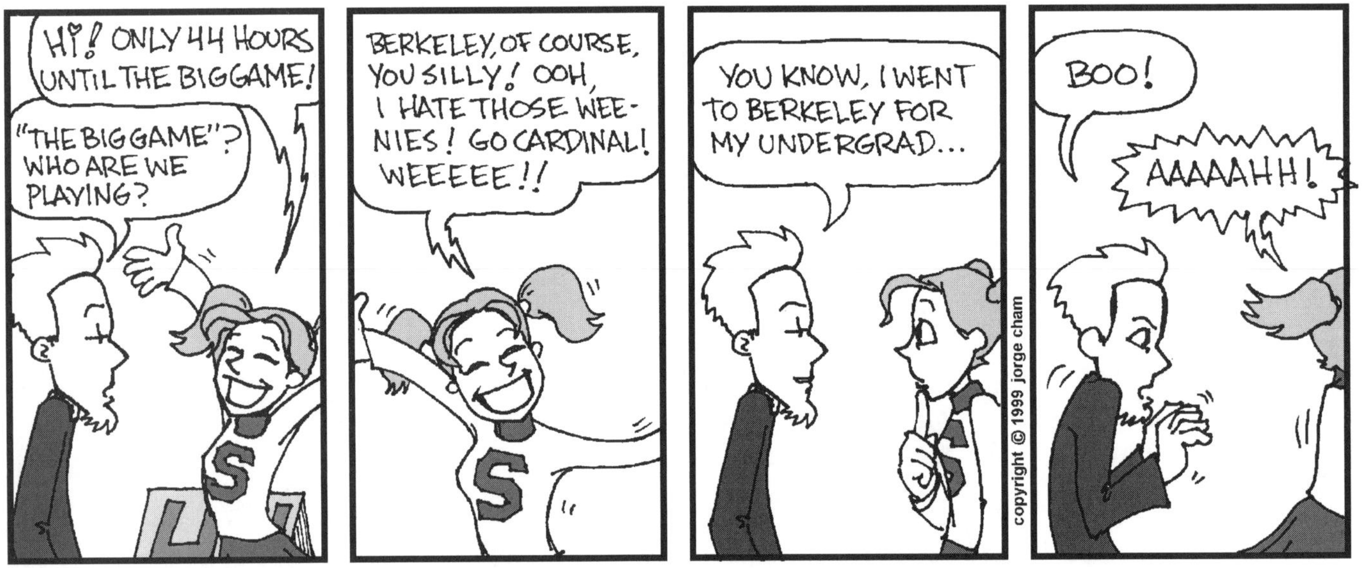
HI! ONLY 44 HOURS UNTIL THE BIG GAME!
"THE BIG GAME"? WHO ARE WE PLAYING?
BERKELEY, OF COURSE, YOU SILLY! OOH, I HATE THOSE WEENIES! GO CARDINAL! WEEEEE!!
YOU KNOW, I WENT TO BERKELEY FOR MY UNDERGRAD...
copyright © 1999 jorge cham
BOO!
AAAAAHH!

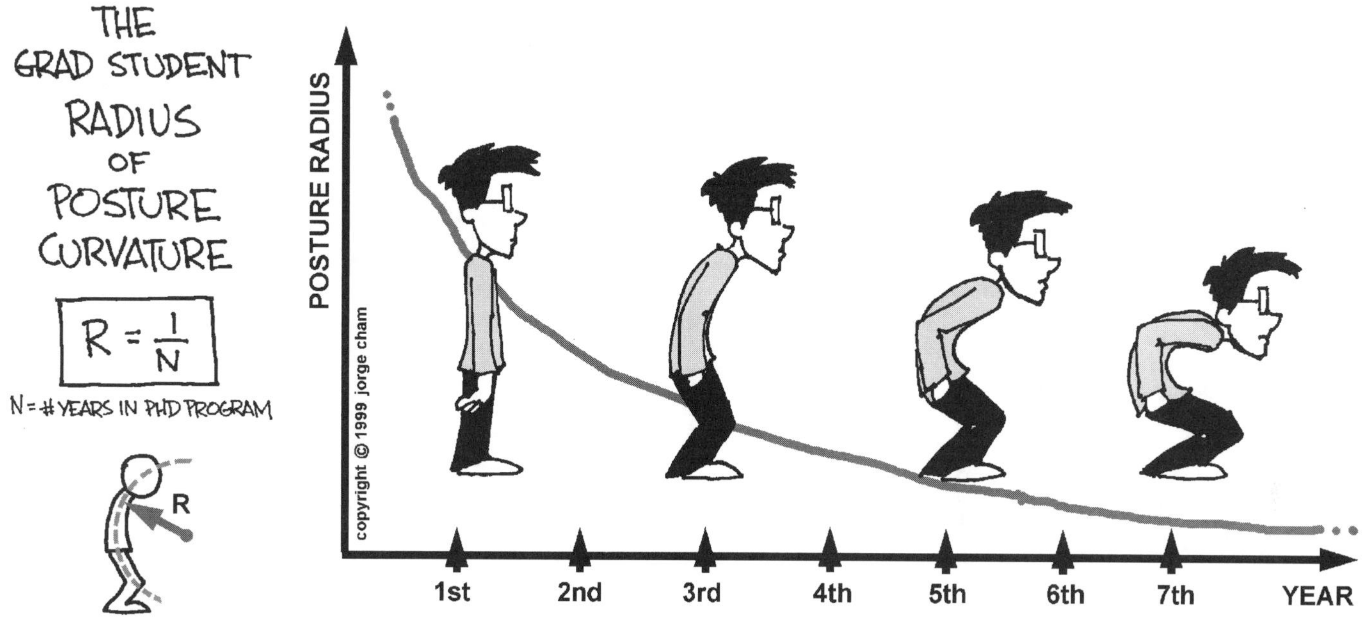
THE GRAD STUDENT RADIUS OF POSTURE CURVATURE
$R = \frac{1}{N}$
N = # YEARS IN PHD PROGRAM
R
POSTURE RADIUS
copyright © 1999 jorge cham
1st
2nd
3rd
4th
5th
6th
7th
YEAR

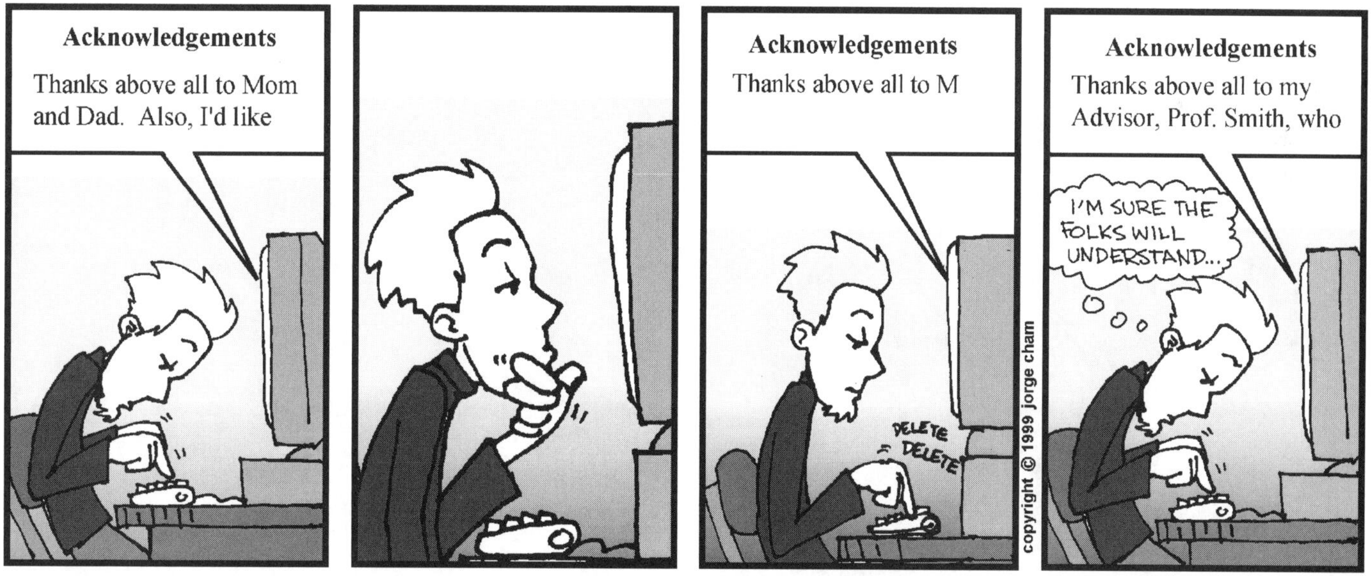
Acknowledgements
Thanks above all to Mom and Dad. Also, I'd like
Acknowledgements
Thanks above all to M
DELETE
DELETE
copyright © 1999 jorge cham
Acknowledgements
Thanks above all to my Advisor, Prof. Smith, who
I'M SURE THE FOLKS WILL UNDERSTAND...

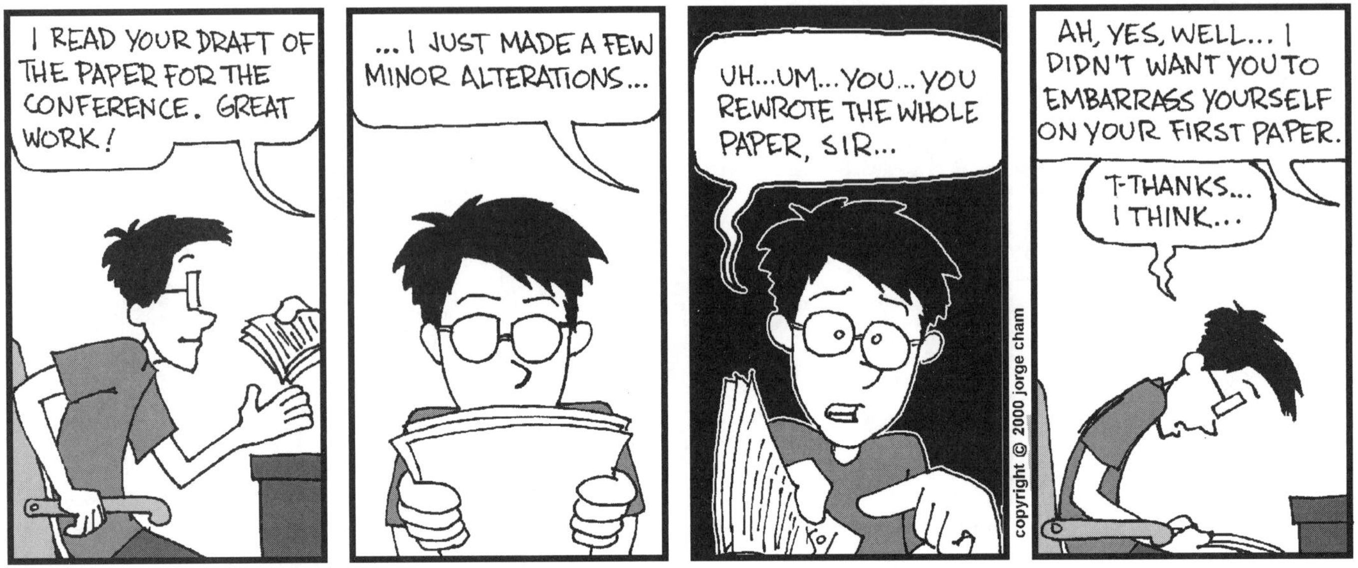
I READ YOUR DRAFT OF THE PAPER FOR THE CONFERENCE. GREAT WORK!
...I JUST MADE A FEW MINOR ALTERATIONS...
UH...UM...YOU...YOU REWROTE THE WHOLE PAPER, SIR...
copyright © 2000 jorge cham
AH, YES, WELL... I DIDN'T WANT YOU TO EMBARRASS YOURSELF ON YOUR FIRST PAPER.
T-THANKS... I THINK...

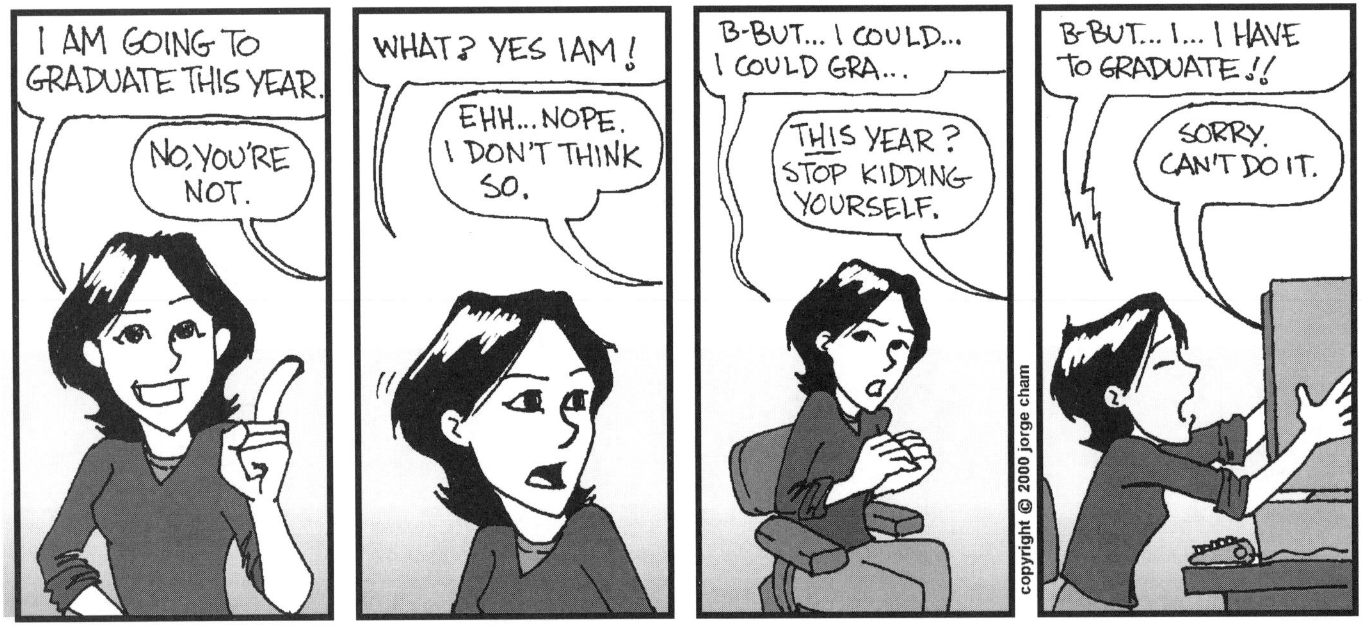
I AM GOING TO GRADUATE THIS YEAR.
NO, YOU'RE NOT.
WHAT? YES I AM!
EHH...NOPE. I DON'T THINK SO.
B-BUT... I COULD... I COULD GRA...
THIS YEAR? STOP KIDDING YOURSELF.
copyright © 2000 jorge cham
B-BUT... I... I HAVE TO GRADUATE!!
SORRY. CAN'T DO IT.

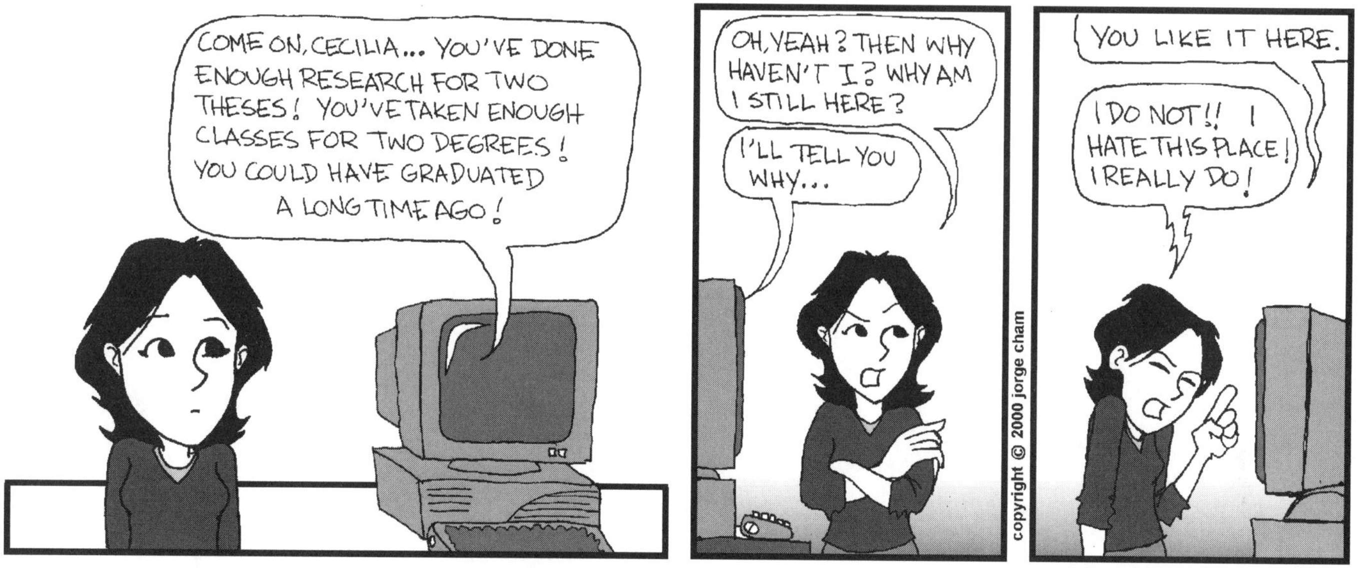
COME ON, CECILIA... YOU'VE DONE ENOUGH RESEARCH FOR TWO THESES! YOU'VE TAKEN ENOUGH CLASSES FOR TWO DEGREES! YOU COULD HAVE GRADUATED A LONG TIME AGO!
OH, YEAH? THEN WHY HAVEN'T I? WHY AM I STILL HERE?
I'LL TELL YOU WHY...
copyright © 2000 jorge cham
YOU LIKE IT HERE.
I DO NOT!! I HATE THIS PLACE! I REALLY DO!

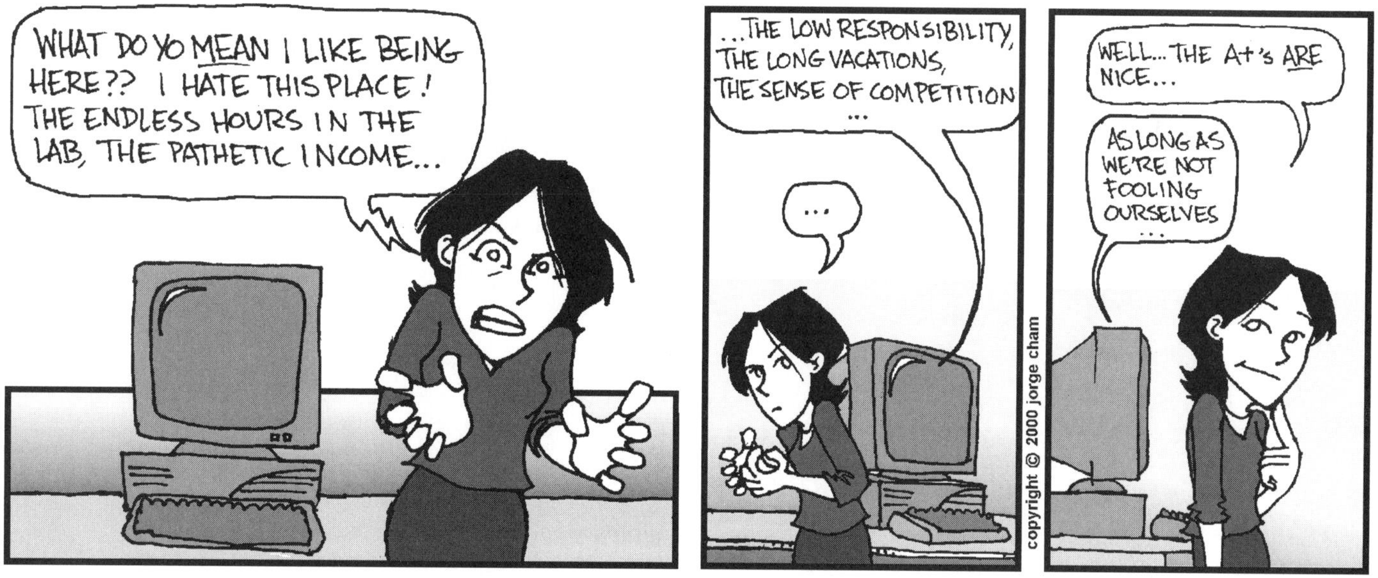
WHAT DO YO MEAN I LIKE BEING HERE?? I HATE THIS PLACE! THE ENDLESS HOURS IN THE LAB, THE PATHETIC INCOME...
...THE LOW RESPONSIBILITY, THE LONG VACATIONS, THE SENSE OF COMPETITION...
...
copyright © 2000 jorge cham
WELL... THE A+'s ARE NICE...
AS LONG AS WE'RE NOT FOOLING OURSELVES...

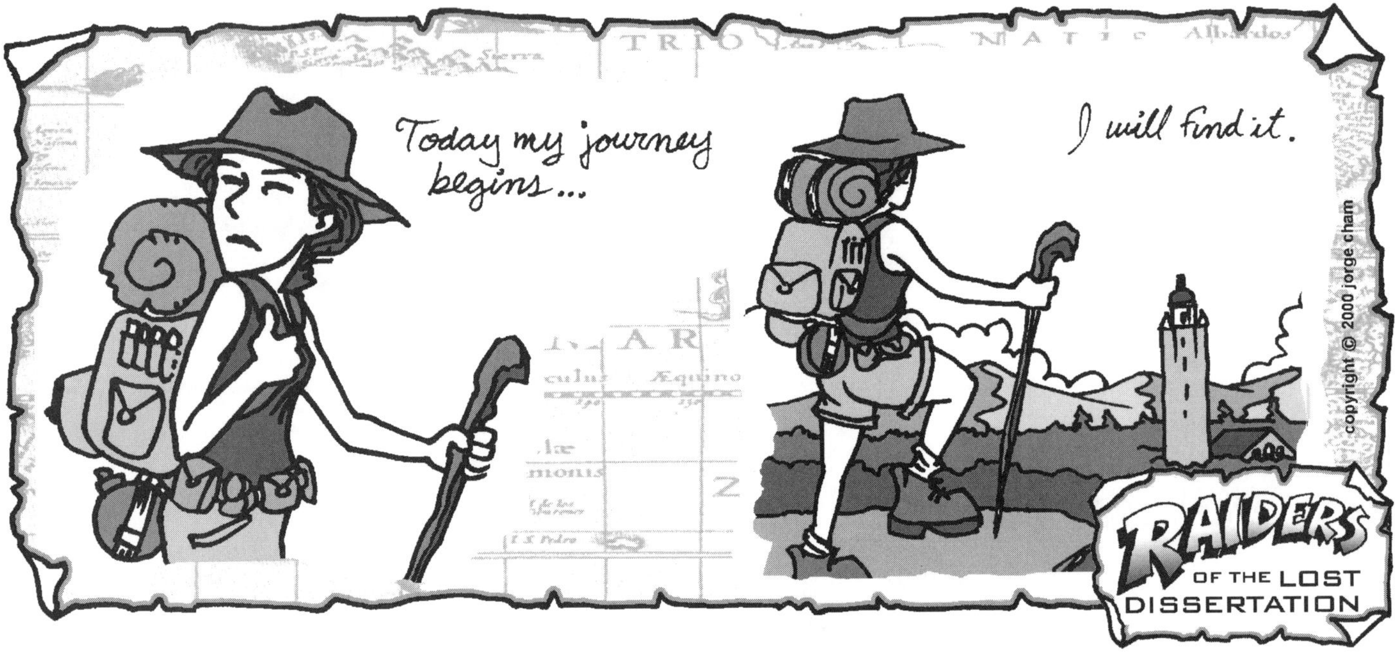
Today my journey begins...
I will find it.
copyright © 2000 jorge cham
RAIDERS OF THE LOST DISSERTATION

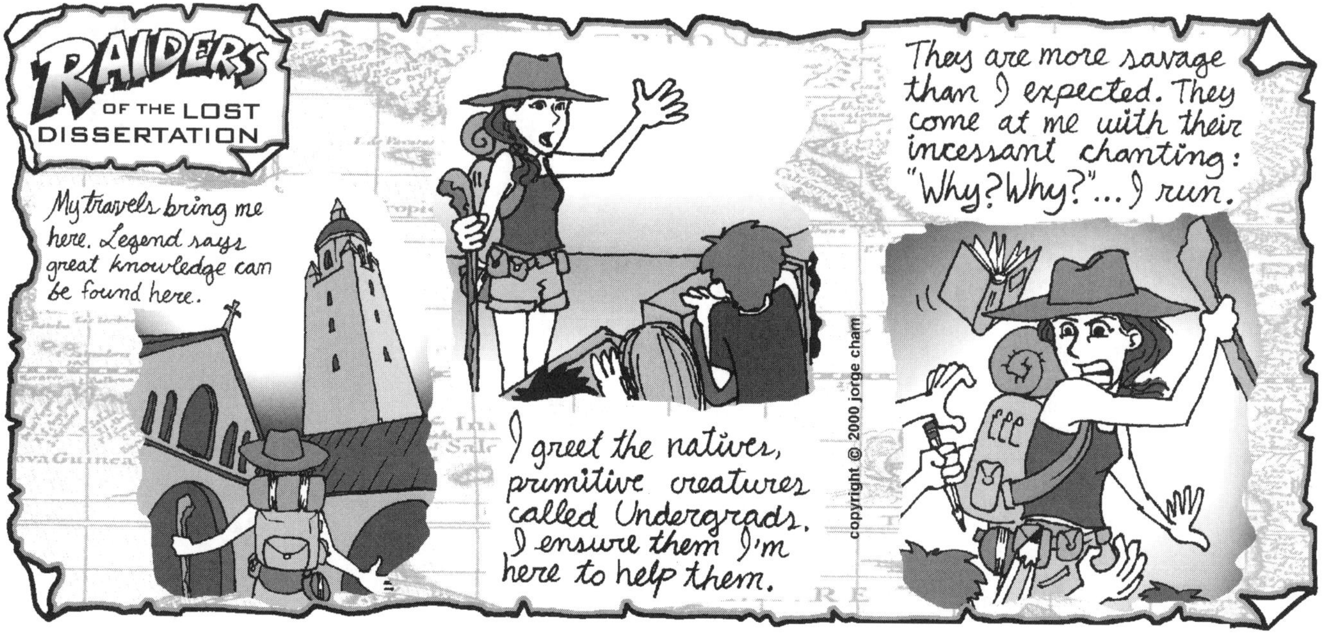
RAIDERS OF THE LOST DISSERTATION
My travels bring me here. Legend says great knowledge can be found here.
I greet the natives, primitive creatures called Undergrads. I ensure them I'm here to help them.
copyright © 2000 jorge cham
They are more savage than I expected. They come at me with their incessant chanting: "Why? Why?"... I run.

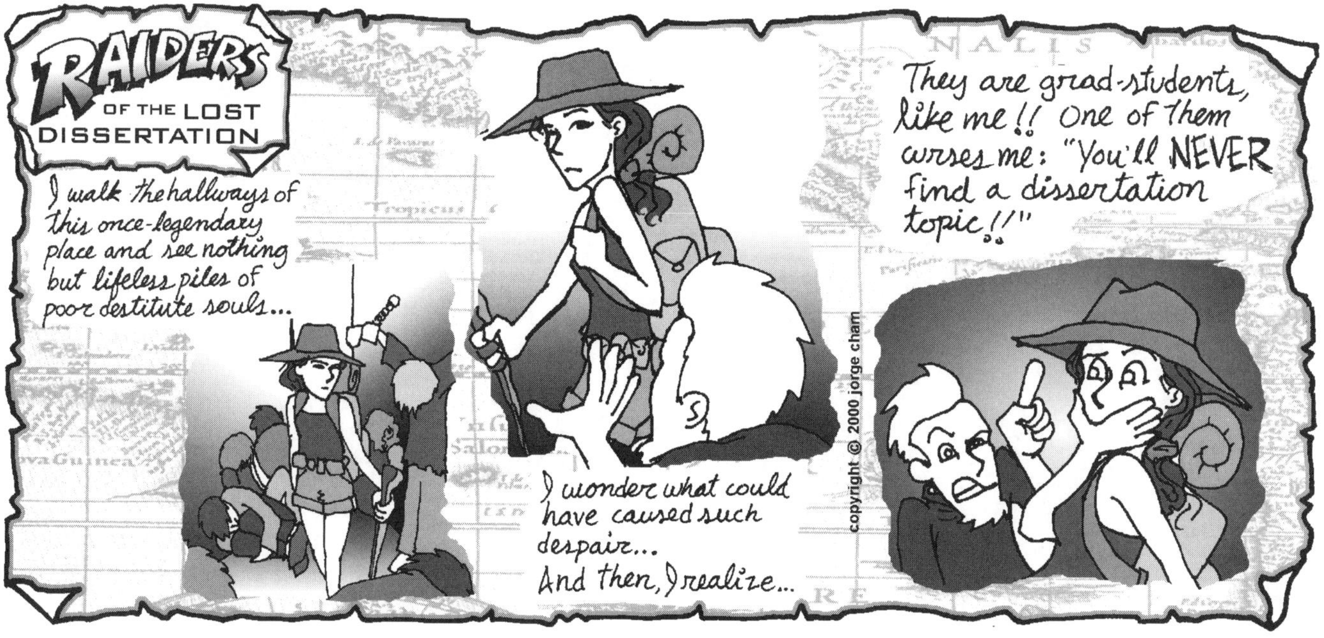
RAIDERS OF THE LOST DISSERTATION
I walk the hallways of this once-legendary place and see nothing but lifeless piles of poor destitute souls...
I wonder what could have caused such despair...
And then, I realize...
copyright © 2000 jorge cham
They are grad-students, like me!! One of them curses me: "You'll NEVER find a dissertation topic!!"

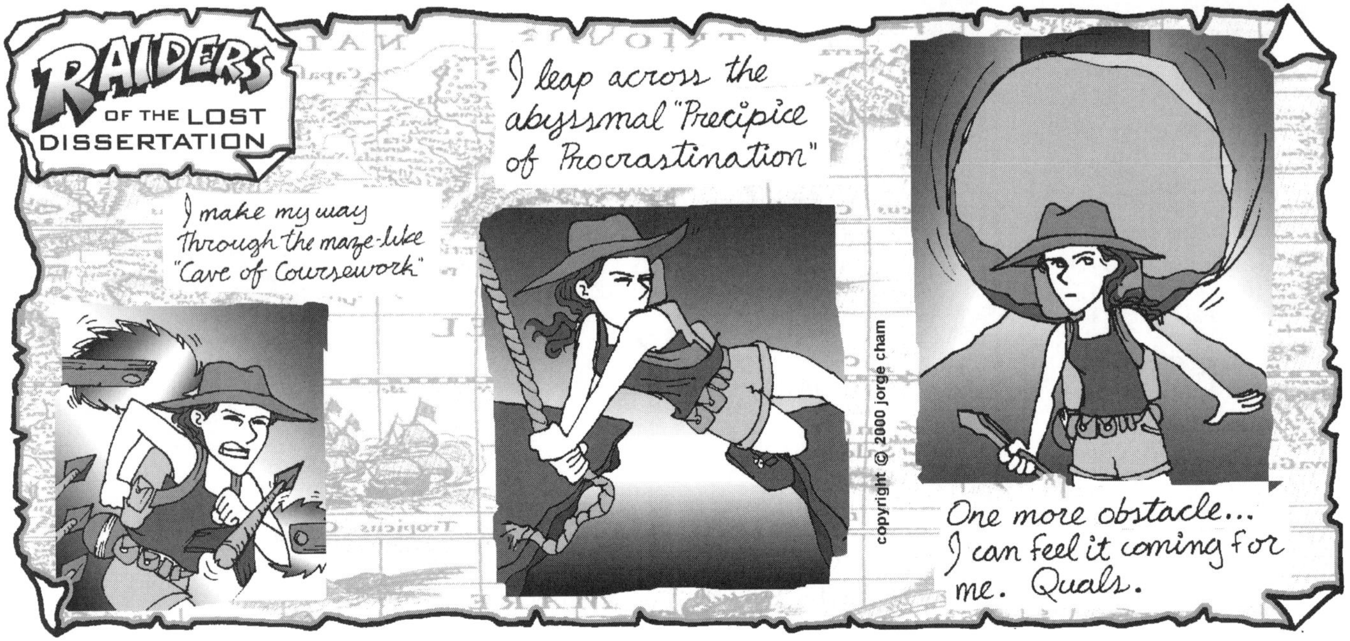
RAIDERS OF THE LOST DISSERTATION
I make my way Through the maze-like "Cave of Coursework"
I leap across the abyssmal "Precipice of Procrastination"
copyright © 2000 jorge cham
One more obstacle... I can feel it coming for me. Quals.

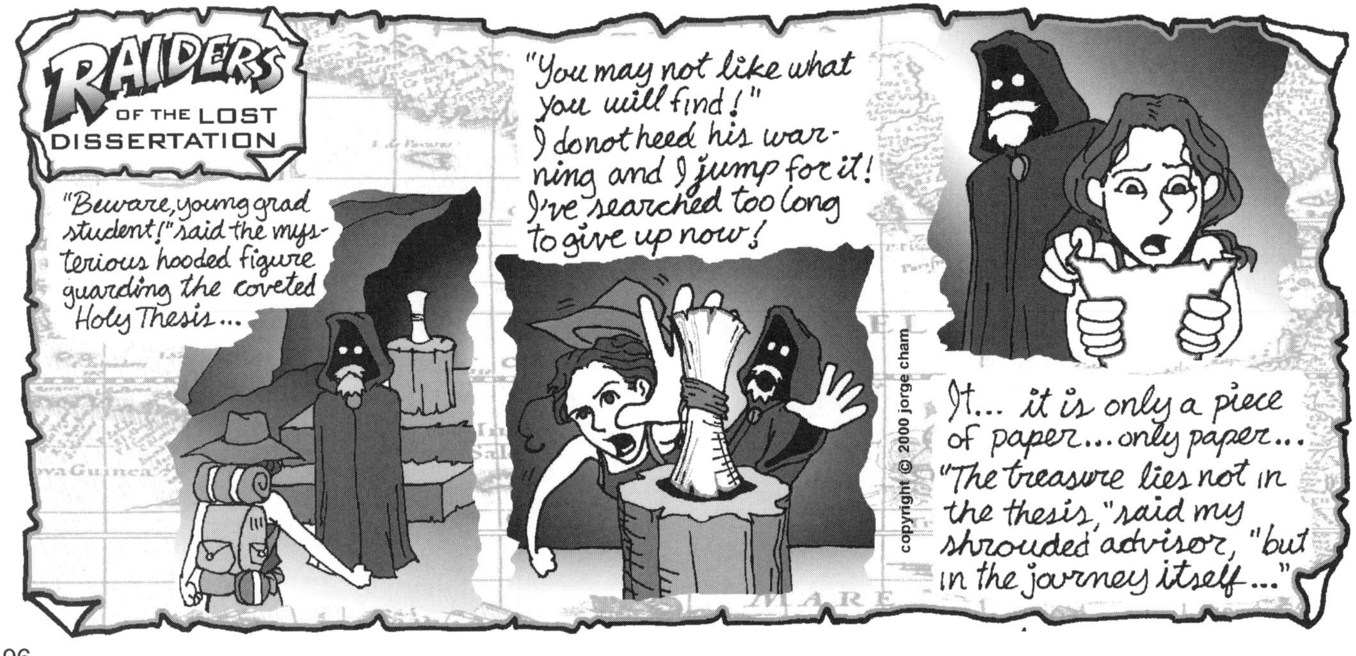
RAIDERS OF THE LOST DISSERTATION
"Beware, young grad student!" said the mysterious hooded figure guarding the coveted Holy Thesis...
"You may not like what you will find!" I do not heed his warning and I jump for it! I've searched too long to give up now!
copyright © 2000 jorge cham
It... it is only a piece of paper... only paper... "The treasure lies not in the thesis," said my shrouded advisor, "but in the journey itself..."

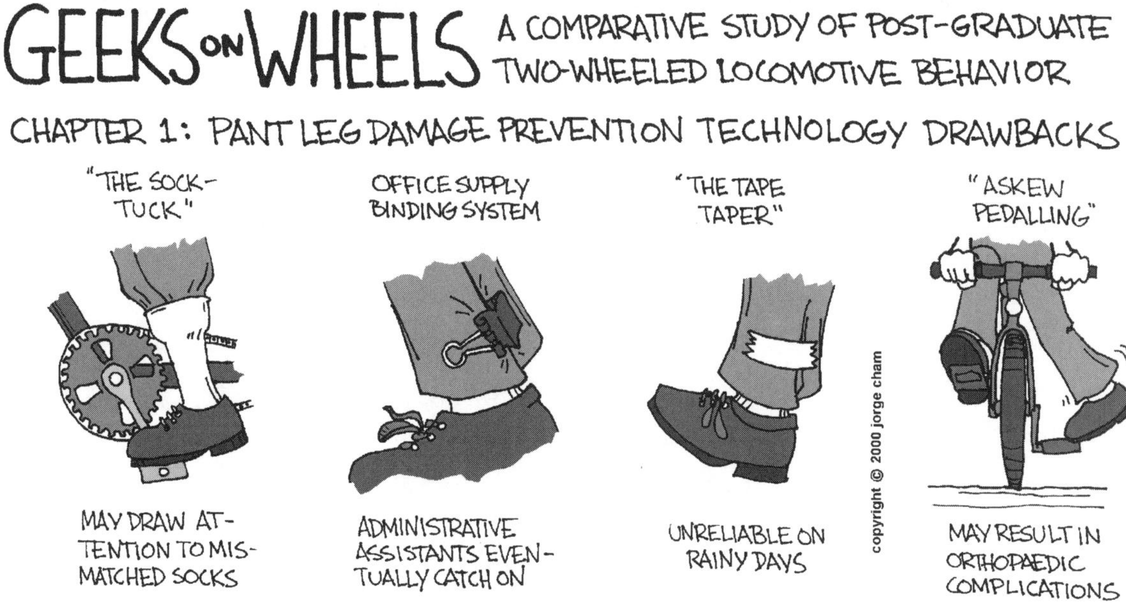
GEEKS ON WHEELS
A COMPARATIVE STUDY OF POST-GRADUATE TWO-WHEELED LOCOMOTIVE BEHAVIOR
CHAPTER 1: PANT LEG DAMAGE PREVENTION TECHNOLOGY DRAWBACKS
"THE SOCK-TUCK"
OFFICE SUPPLY BINDING SYSTEM
"THE TAPE TAPER"
"ASKEW PEDALLING"
MAY DRAW AT-TENTION TO MIS-MATCHED SOCKS
ADMINISTRATIVE ASSISTANTS EVEN-TUALLY CATCH ON
UNRELIABLE ON RAINY DAYS
MAY RESULT IN ORTHOPAEDIC COMPLICATIONS
copyright © 2000 jorge cham

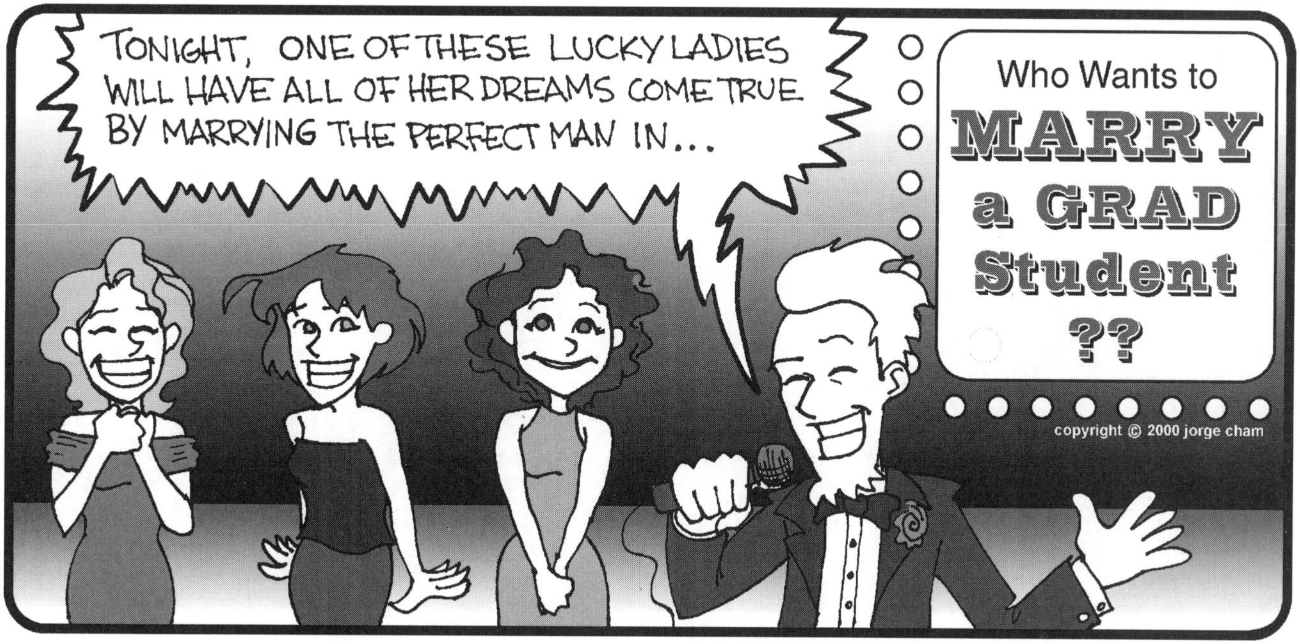
TONIGHT, ONE OF THESE LUCKY LADIES WILL HAVE ALL OF HER DREAMS COME TRUE BY MARRYING THE PERFECT MAN IN...
Who Wants to MARRY a GRAD Student ??
copyright © 2000 jorge cham

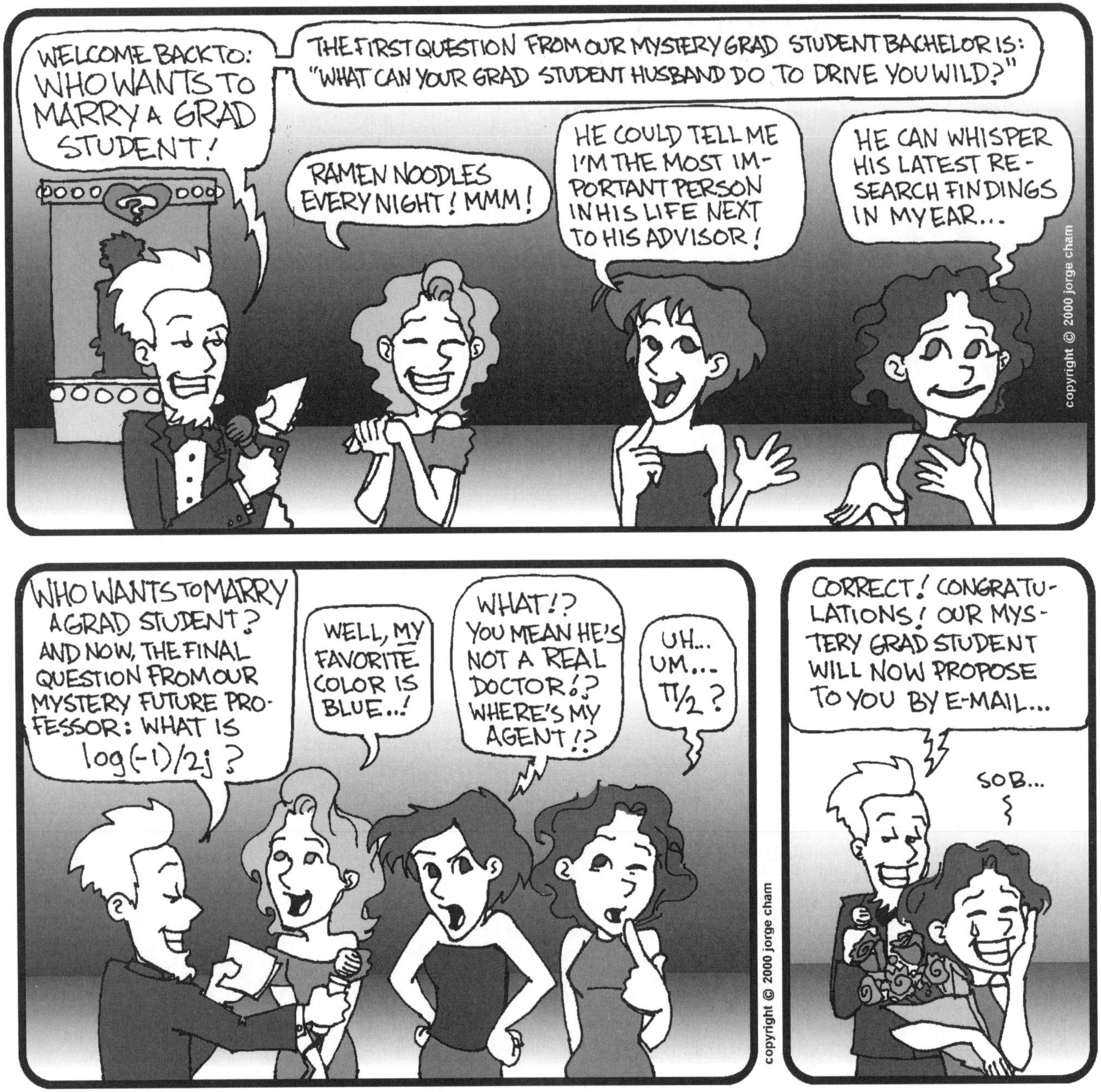
WELCOME BACK TO: WHO WANTS TO MARRY A GRAD STUDENT!
THE FIRST QUESTION FROM OUR MYSTERY GRAD STUDENT BACHELOR IS: "WHAT CAN YOUR GRAD STUDENT HUSBAND DO TO DRIVE YOU WILD?"
RAMEN NOODLES EVERY NIGHT! MMM!
HE COULD TELL ME I'M THE MOST IMPORTANT PERSON IN HIS LIFE NEXT TO HIS ADVISOR!
HE CAN WHISPER HIS LATEST RESEARCH FINDINGS IN MY EAR...
copyright © 2000 jorge cham
WHO WANTS TO MARRY A GRAD STUDENT? AND NOW, THE FINAL QUESTION FROM OUR MYSTERY FUTURE PROFESSOR: WHAT IS log(-1)/2j ?
WELL, MY FAVORITE COLOR IS BLUE...!
WHAT!? YOU MEAN HE'S NOT A REAL DOCTOR!? WHERE'S MY AGENT!?
UH... UM... π/2 ?
copyright © 2000 jorge cham
CORRECT! CONGRATULATIONS! OUR MYSTERY GRAD STUDENT WILL NOW PROPOSE TO YOU BY E-MAIL...
SOB...

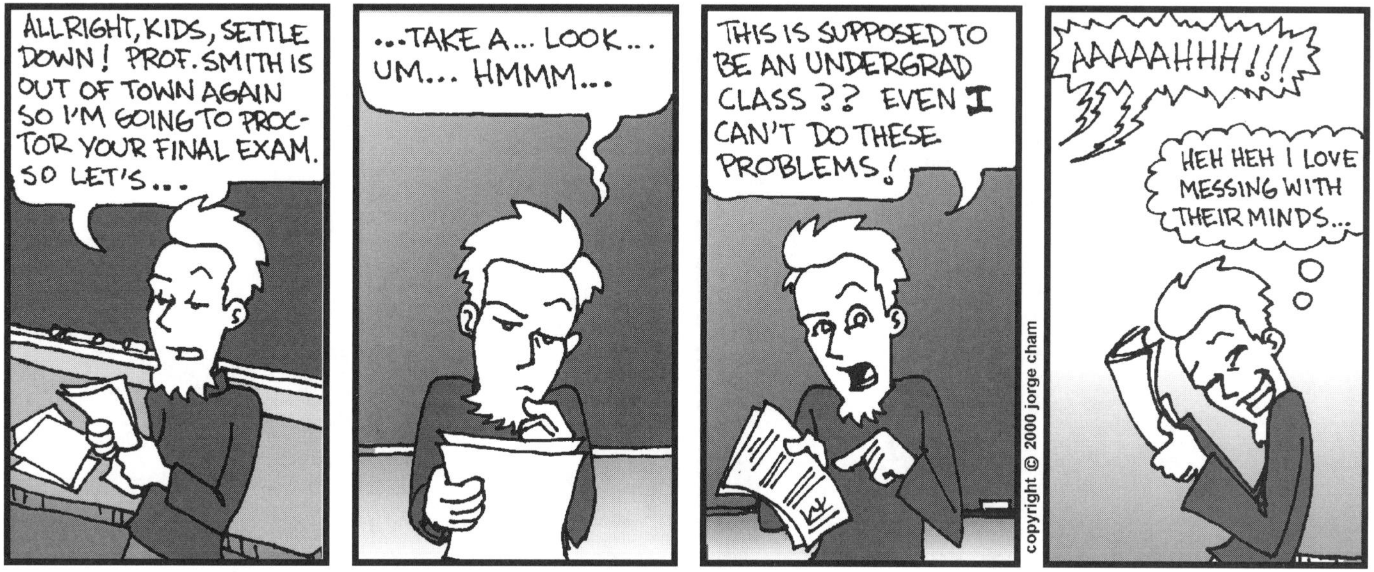
ALLRIGHT, KIDS, SETTLE DOWN! PROF. SMITH IS OUT OF TOWN AGAIN SO I'M GOING TO PROCTOR YOUR FINAL EXAM. SO LET'S...
...TAKE A... LOOK... UM... HMMM...
THIS IS SUPPOSED TO BE AN UNDERGRAD CLASS?? EVEN I CAN'T DO THESE PROBLEMS!
copyright © 2000 jorge cham
AAAAAHHH!!!
HEH HEH I LOVE MESSING WITH THEIR MINDS...

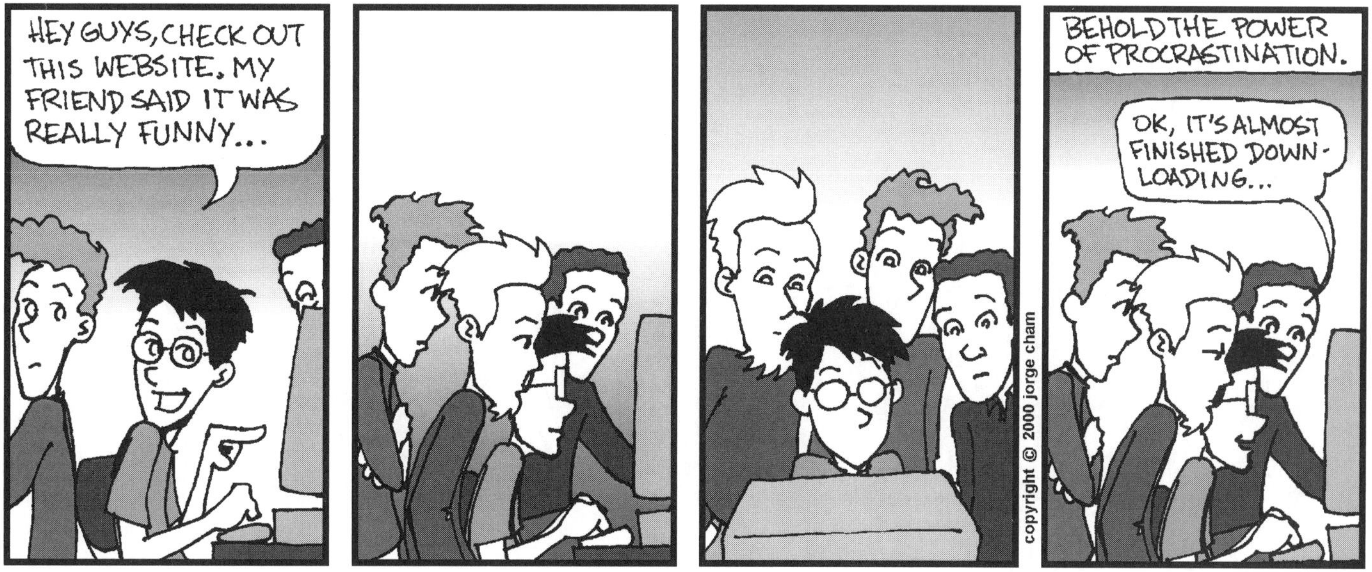
HEY GUYS, CHECK OUT THIS WEBSITE. MY FRIEND SAID IT WAS REALLY FUNNY...
copyright © 2000 jorge cham
BEHOLD THE POWER OF PROCRASTINATION.
OK, IT'S ALMOST FINISHED DOWNLOADING...

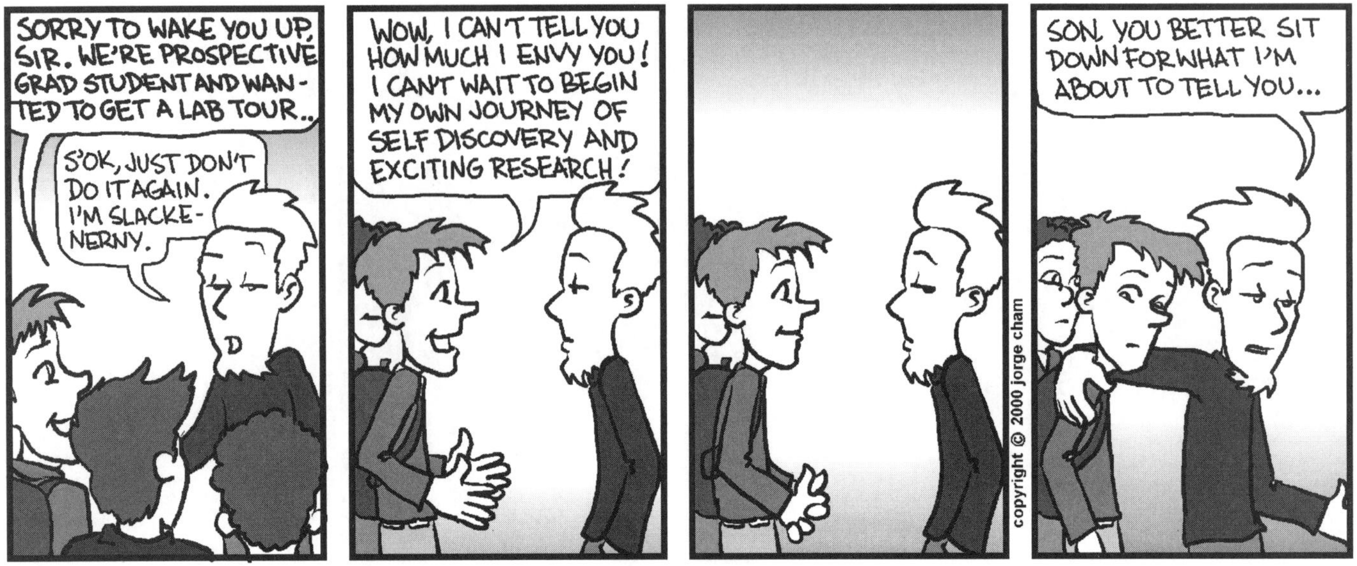
SORRY TO WAKE YOU UP, SIR. WE'RE PROSPECTIVE GRAD STUDENT AND WANTED TO GET A LAB TOUR..
S'OK, JUST DON'T DO IT AGAIN. I'M SLACKENERNY.
WOW, I CAN'T TELL YOU HOW MUCH I ENVY YOU! I CAN'T WAIT TO BEGIN MY OWN JOURNEY OF SELF DISCOVERY AND EXCITING RESEARCH!
copyright © 2000 jorge cham
SON, YOU BETTER SIT DOWN FOR WHAT I'M ABOUT TO TELL YOU...

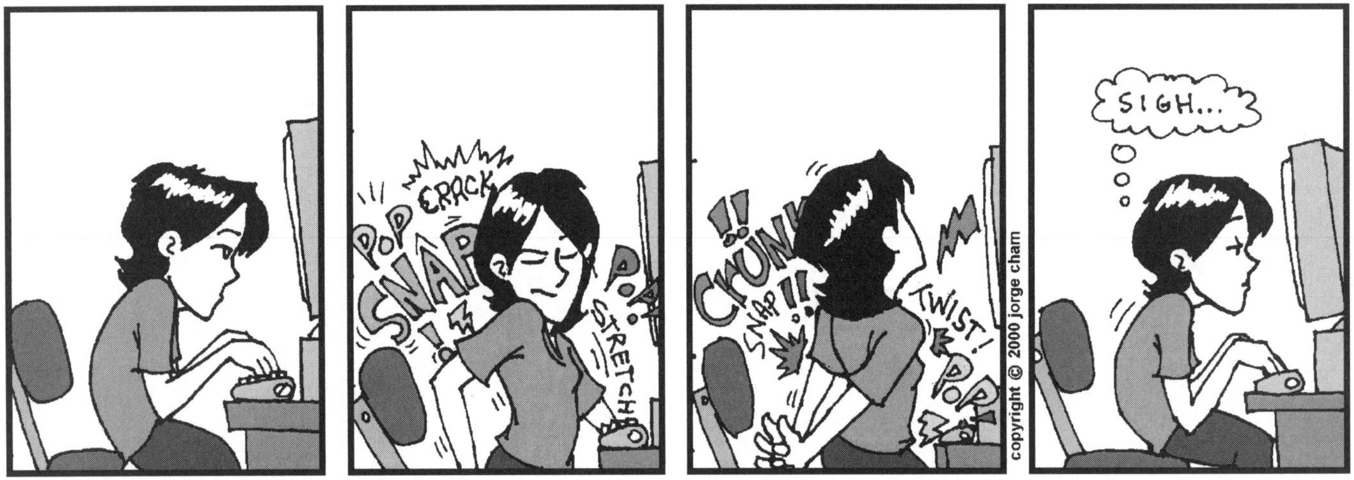
POP
CRACK
SNAP
POP
STRETCH
CHUNK
SNAP!!
TWIST!
POP
copyright © 2000 jorge cham
SIGH...

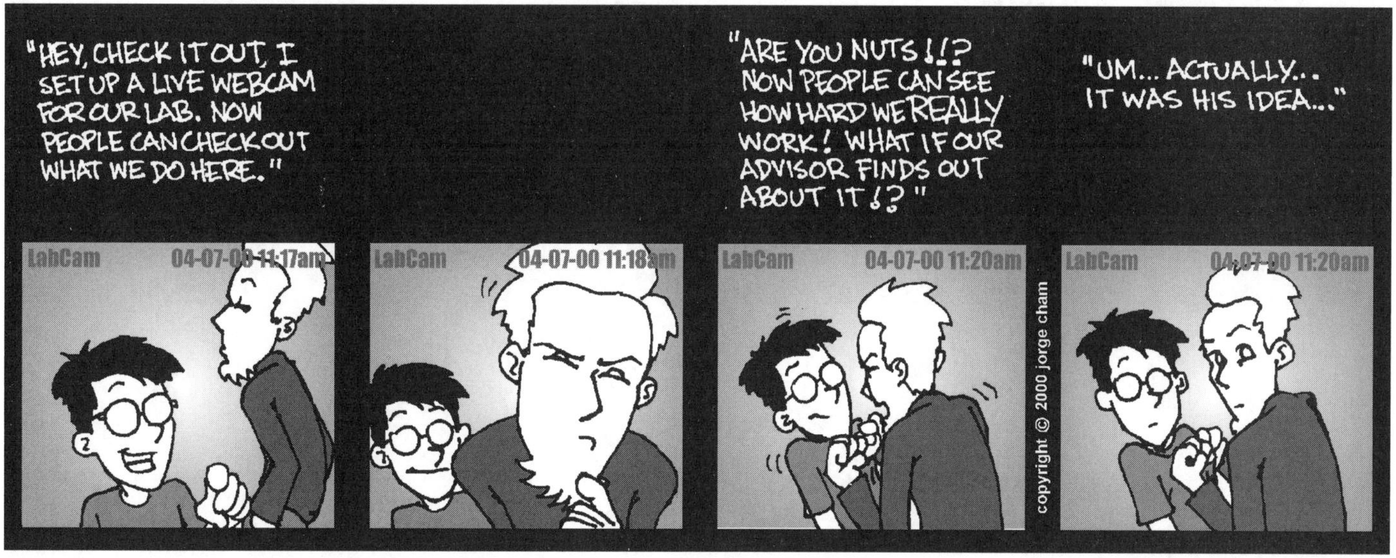
"HEY, CHECK IT OUT, I SET UP A LIVE WEBCAM FOR OUR LAB. NOW PEOPLE CAN CHECK OUT WHAT WE DO HERE."
"ARE YOU NUTS ¡!? NOW PEOPLE CAN SEE HOW HARD WE REALLY WORK! WHAT IF OUR ADVISOR FINDS OUT ABOUT IT¿?"
"UM... ACTUALLY.. IT WAS HIS IDEA..."
LabCam 04-07-00 11:17am
LabCam 04-07-00 11:18am
LabCam 04-07-00 11:20am
copyright © 2000 jorge cham
LabCam 04-07-00 11:20am

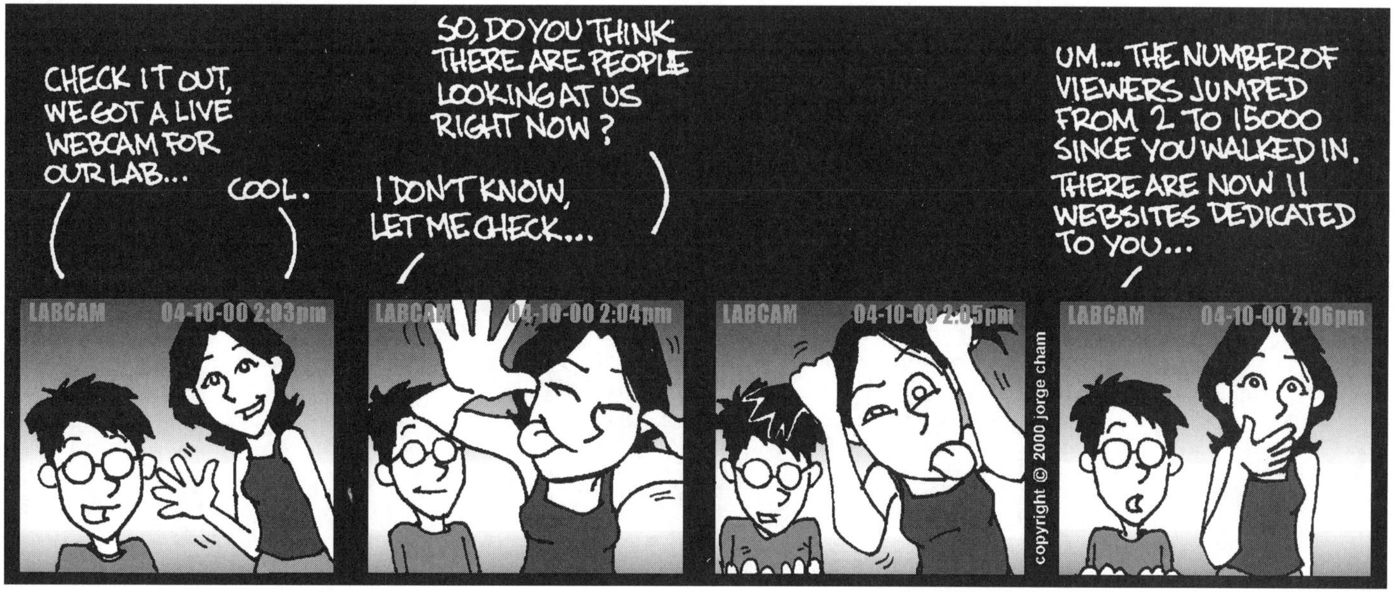
CHECK IT OUT, WE GOT A LIVE WEBCAM FOR OUR LAB...
COOL.
SO, DO YOU THINK THERE ARE PEOPLE LOOKING AT US RIGHT NOW?
I DON'T KNOW, LET ME CHECK...
UM... THE NUMBER OF VIEWERS JUMPED FROM 2 TO 15000 SINCE YOU WALKED IN. THERE ARE NOW 11 WEBSITES DEDICATED TO YOU...
LABCAM 04-10-00 2:03pm
LABCAM 04-10-00 2:04pm
LABCAM 04-10-00 2:05pm
copyright © 2000 jorge cham
LABCAM 04-10-00 2:06pm

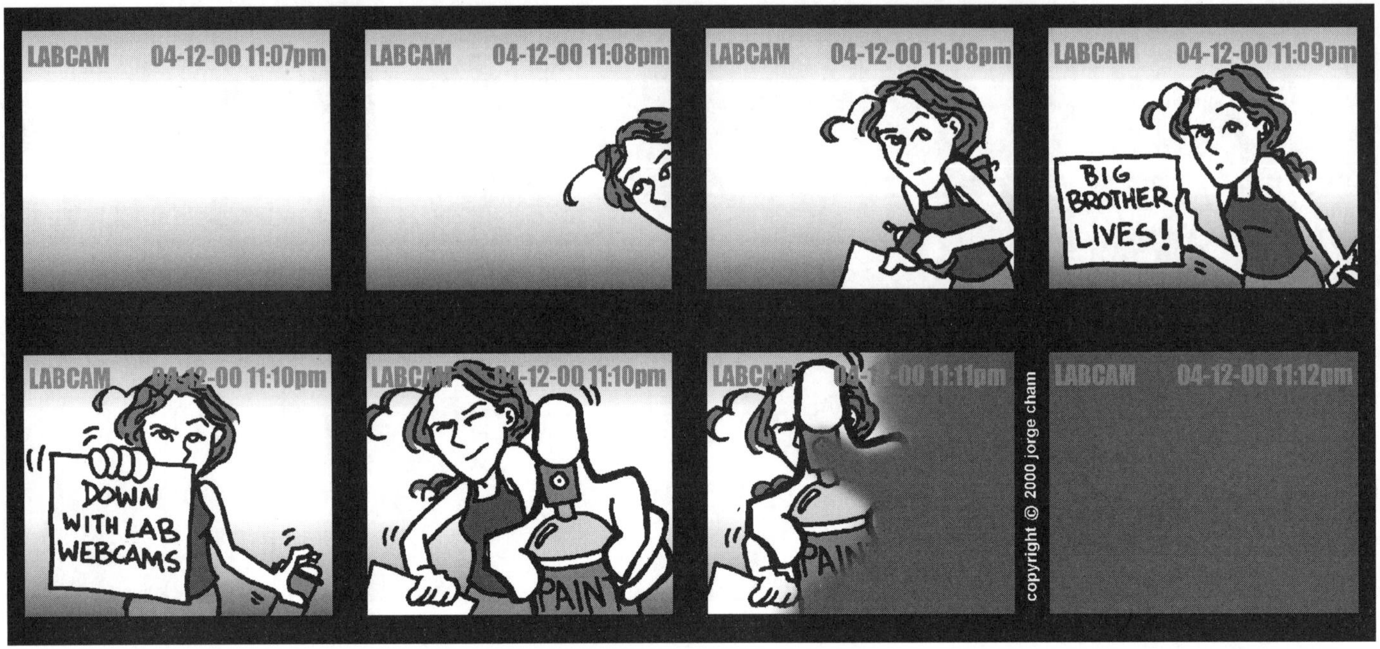
LABCAM 04-12-00 11:07pm
LABCAM 04-12-00 11:08pm
LABCAM 04-12-00 11:08pm
LABCAM 04-12-00 11:09pm
BIG BROTHER LIVES!
LABCAM 04-12-00 11:10pm
DOWN WITH LAB WEBCAMS
LABCAM 04-12-00 11:10pm
PAINT
LABCAM 04-12-00 11:11pm
LABCAM 04-12-00 11:12pm
copyright © 2000 jorge cham

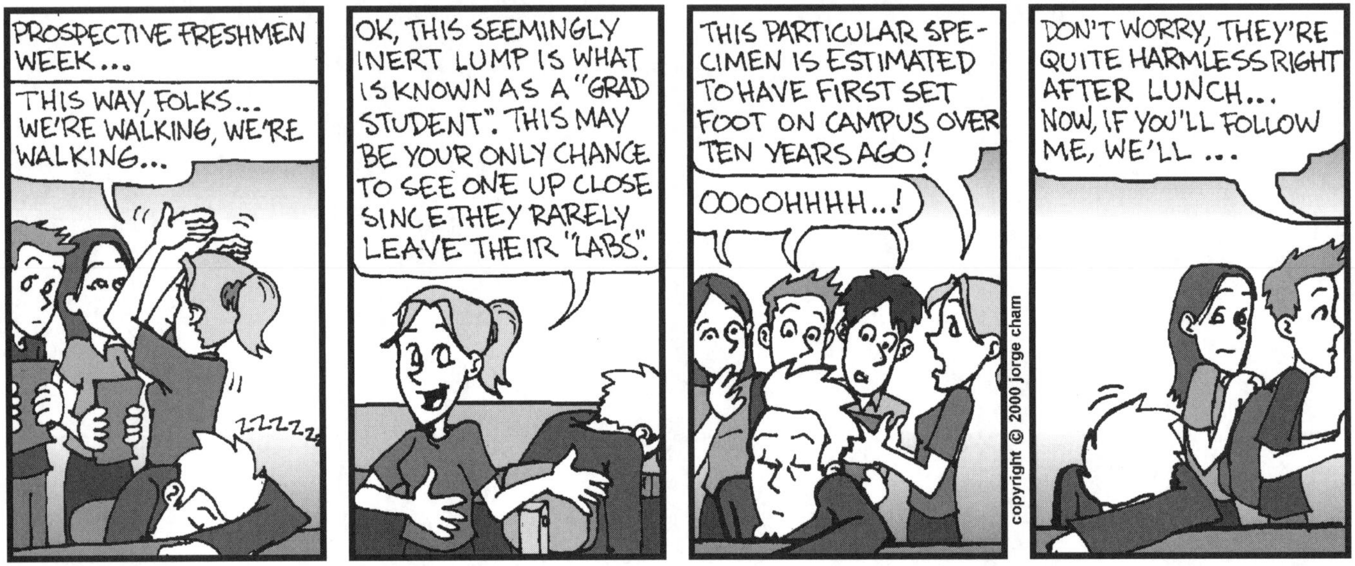
PROSPECTIVE FRESHMEN WEEK...
THIS WAY, FOLKS... WE'RE WALKING, WE'RE WALKING...
ZZZZZ
OK, THIS SEEMINGLY INERT LUMP IS WHAT IS KNOWN AS A "GRAD STUDENT". THIS MAY BE YOUR ONLY CHANCE TO SEE ONE UP CLOSE SINCE THEY RARELY LEAVE THEIR "LABS".
THIS PARTICULAR SPECIMEN IS ESTIMATED TO HAVE FIRST SET FOOT ON CAMPUS OVER TEN YEARS AGO!
OOOOHHHH...!
copyright © 2000 jorge cham
DON'T WORRY, THEY'RE QUITE HARMLESS RIGHT AFTER LUNCH... NOW, IF YOU'LL FOLLOW ME, WE'LL ...

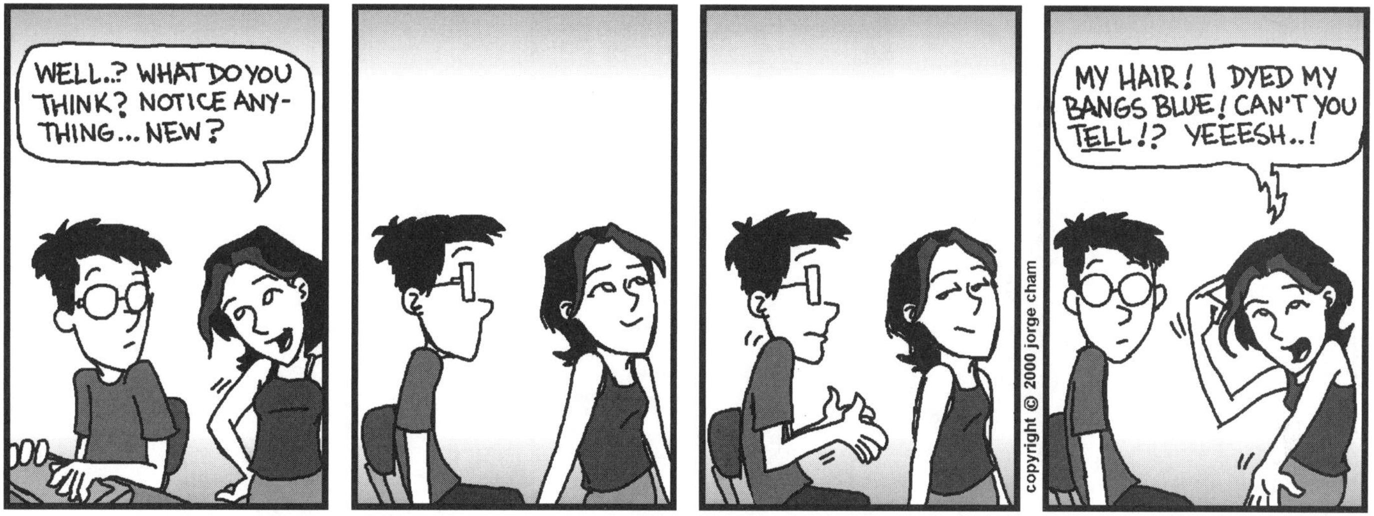
WELL..? WHAT DO YOU THINK? NOTICE ANYTHING... NEW?
MY HAIR! I DYED MY BANGS BLUE! CAN'T YOU TELL!? YEEESH..!
copyright © 2000 jorge cham

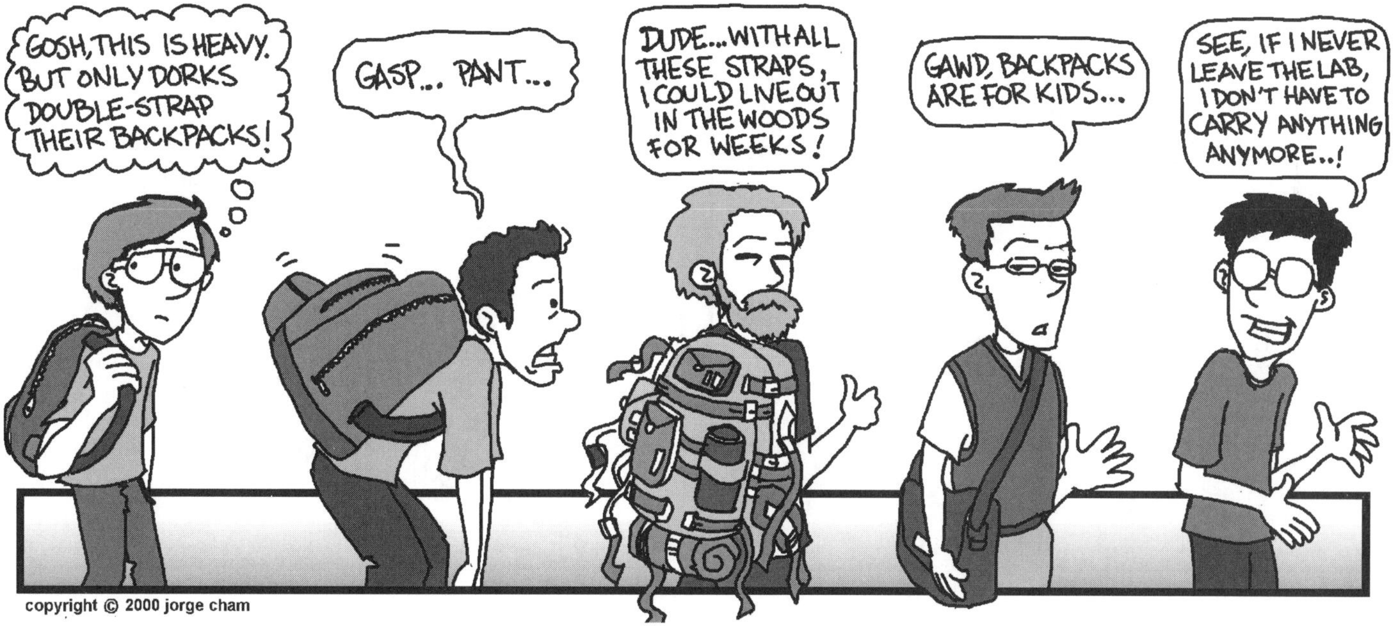
GOSH, THIS IS HEAVY. BUT ONLY DORKS DOUBLE-STRAP THEIR BACKPACKS!
GASP... PANT...
DUDE... WITH ALL THESE STRAPS, I COULD LIVE OUT IN THE WOODS FOR WEEKS!
GAWD, BACKPACKS ARE FOR KIDS...
SEE, IF I NEVER LEAVE THE LAB, I DON'T HAVE TO CARRY ANYTHING ANYMORE..!
copyright © 2000 jorge cham

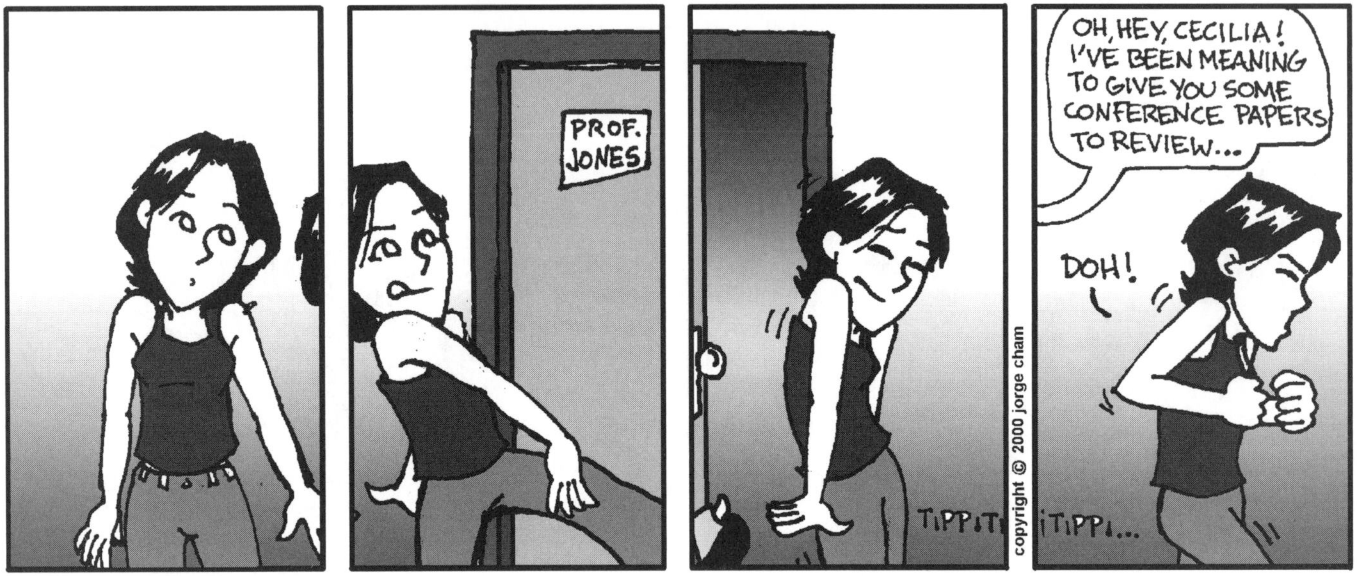
PROF. JONES
OH, HEY, CECILIA! I'VE BEEN MEANING TO GIVE YOU SOME CONFERENCE PAPERS TO REVIEW...
DOH!
TIPPITIPPITIPPI...
copyright © 2000 jorge cham

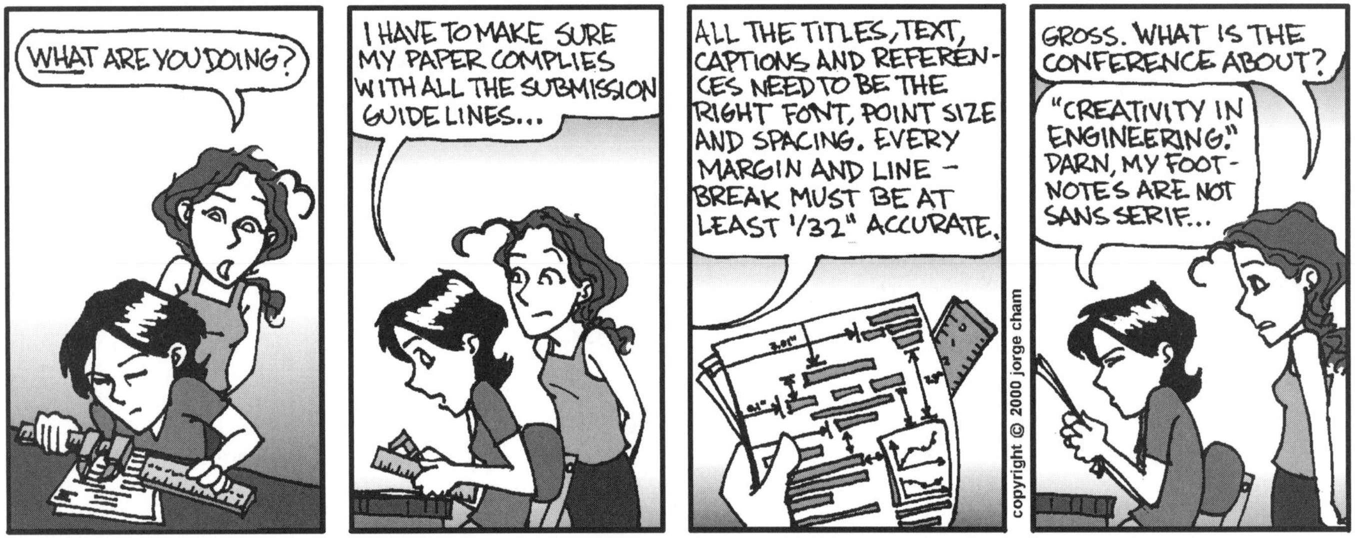
WHAT ARE YOU DOING?
I HAVE TO MAKE SURE MY PAPER COMPLIES WITH ALL THE SUBMISSION GUIDELINES...
ALL THE TITLES, TEXT, CAPTIONS AND REFERENCES NEED TO BE THE RIGHT FONT, POINT SIZE AND SPACING. EVERY MARGIN AND LINE-BREAK MUST BE AT LEAST 1/32" ACCURATE.
GROSS. WHAT IS THE CONFERENCE ABOUT?
"CREATIVITY IN ENGINEERING." DARN, MY FOOTNOTES ARE NOT SANS SERIF...
copyright © 2000 jorge cham

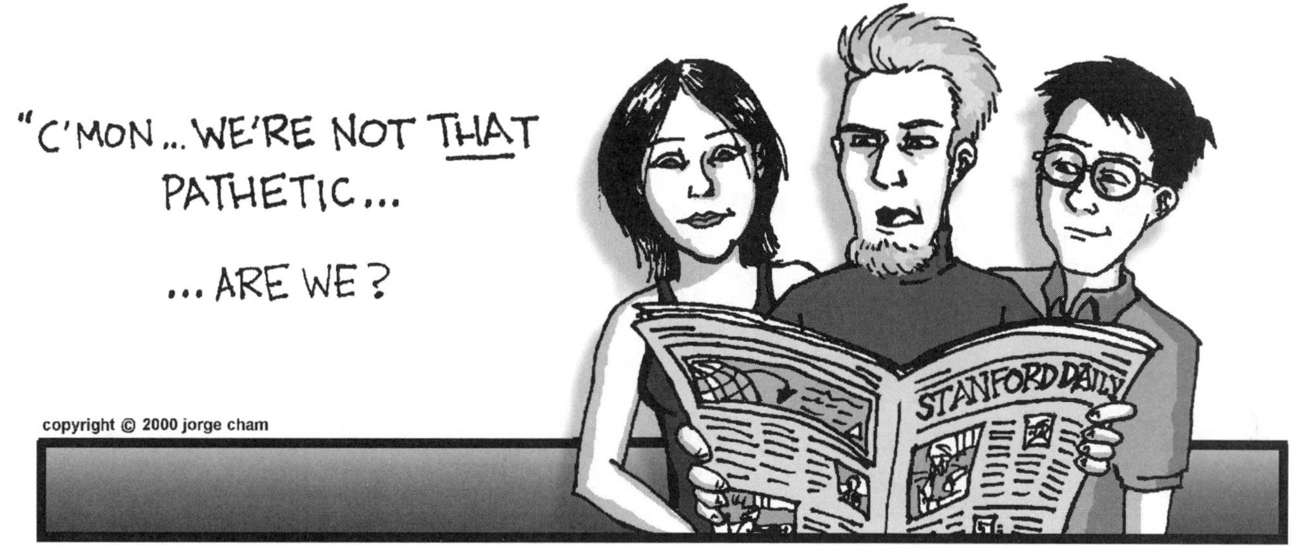
"C'MON... WE'RE NOT THAT PATHETIC...
...ARE WE?
STANFORD DAILY
copyright © 2000 jorge cham

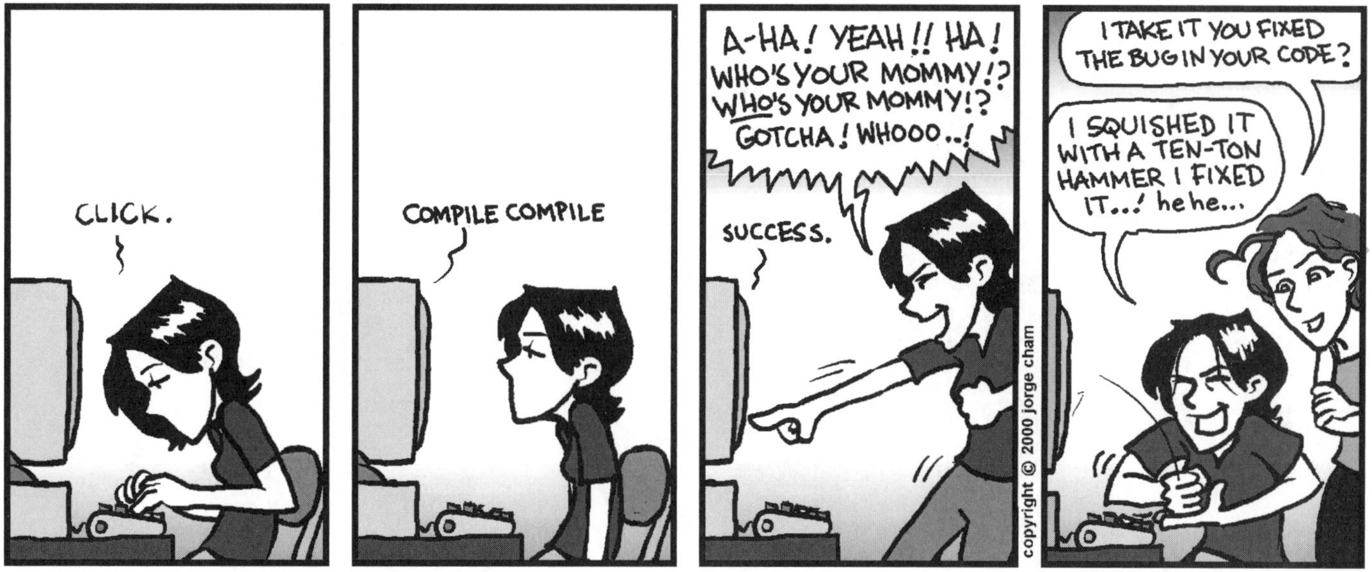
CLICK.
COMPILE COMPILE
A-HA! YEAH!! HA! WHO'S YOUR MOMMY!? WHO'S YOUR MOMMY!? GOTCHA! WHOOO..!
SUCCESS.
copyright © 2000 jorge cham
I TAKE IT YOU FIXED THE BUG IN YOUR CODE?
I SQUISHED IT WITH A TEN-TON HAMMER I FIXED IT..! he he...

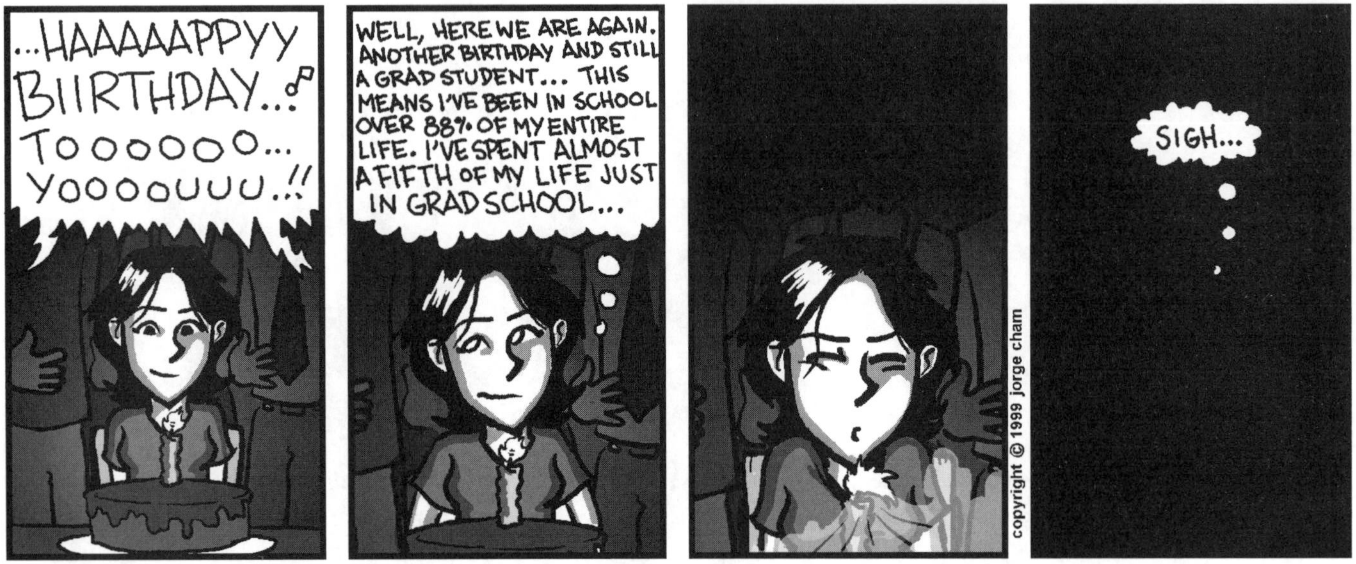
...HAAAAAPPYY BIIRTHDAY...
TOOOOOO... YOOOOUUU..!!
WELL, HERE WE ARE AGAIN. ANOTHER BIRTHDAY AND STILL A GRAD STUDENT... THIS MEANS I'VE BEEN IN SCHOOL OVER 88% OF MY ENTIRE LIFE. I'VE SPENT ALMOST A FIFTH OF MY LIFE JUST IN GRAD SCHOOL...
SIGH...
copyright © 1999 jorge cham

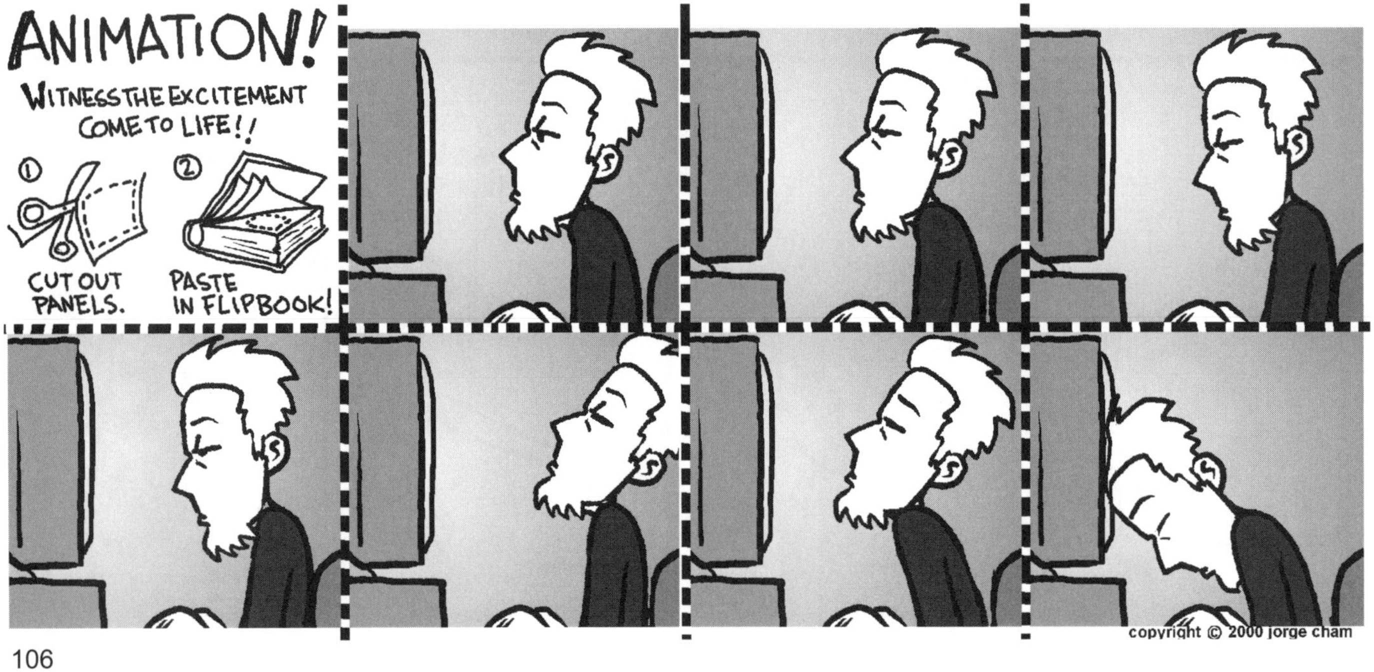
ANIMATION!
WITNESS THE EXCITEMENT COME TO LIFE!!
① CUT OUT PANELS.
② PASTE IN FLIPBOOK!
copyright © 2000 jorge cham

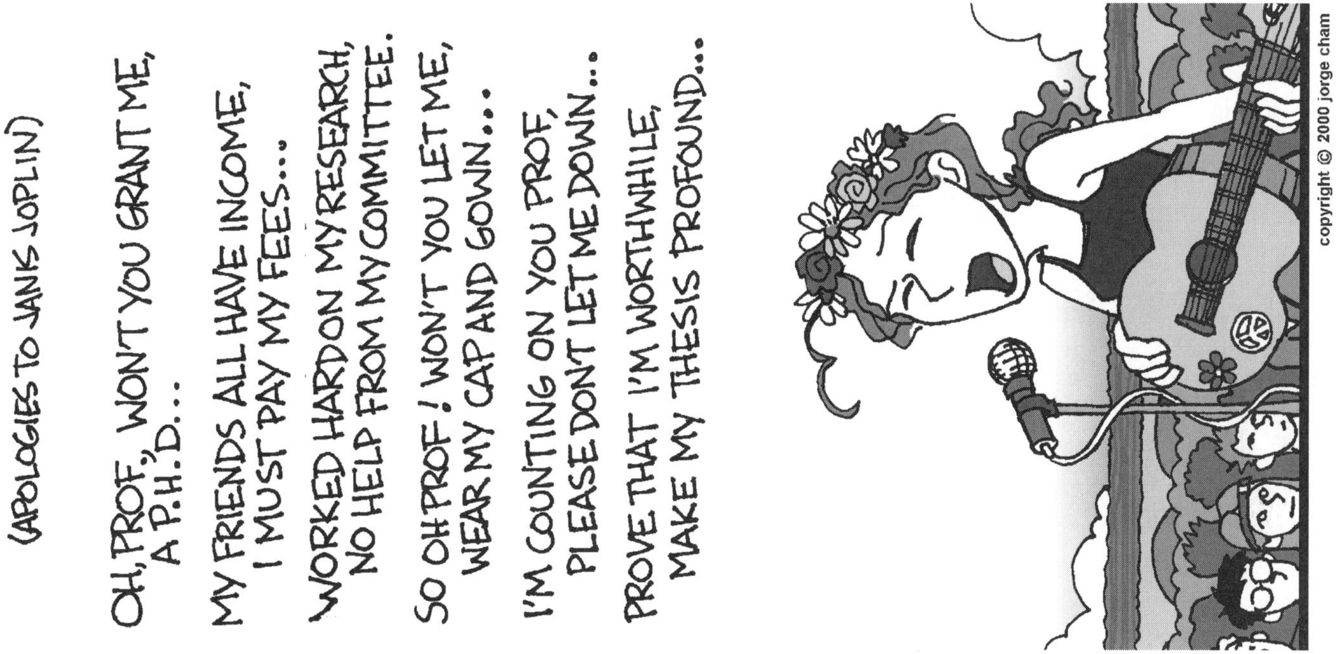
(APOLOGIES TO JANIS JOPLIN)
OH, PROF., WON'T YOU GRANT ME, A P.H.D...
MY FRIENDS ALL HAVE INCOME, I MUST PAY MY FEES....
WORKED HARD ON MY RESEARCH, NO HELP FROM MY COMMITTEE.
SO OH PROF! WON'T YOU LET ME, WEAR MY CAP AND GOWN...
I'M COUNTING ON YOU PROF, PLEASE DON'T LET ME DOWN...
PROVE THAT I'M WORTHWHILE, MAKE MY THESIS PROFOUND...
copyright © 2000 jorge cham

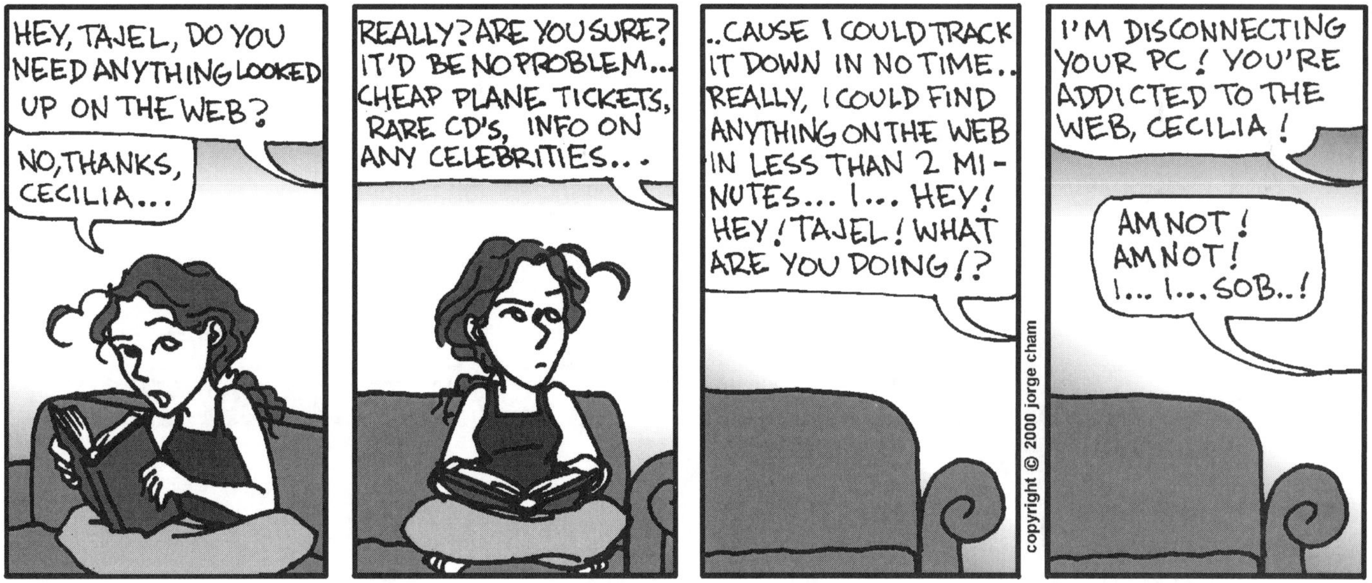
HEY, TAJEL, DO YOU NEED ANYTHING LOOKED UP ON THE WEB?
NO, THANKS, CECILIA...
REALLY? ARE YOU SURE? IT'D BE NO PROBLEM... CHEAP PLANE TICKETS, RARE CD'S, INFO ON ANY CELEBRITIES...
..CAUSE I COULD TRACK IT DOWN IN NO TIME.. REALLY, I COULD FIND ANYTHING ON THE WEB IN LESS THAN 2 MINUTES... I... HEY! HEY! TAJEL! WHAT ARE YOU DOING!?
I'M DISCONNECTING YOUR PC! YOU'RE ADDICTED TO THE WEB, CECILIA!
AM NOT! AM NOT! I... I... SOB..!
copyright © 2000 jorge cham

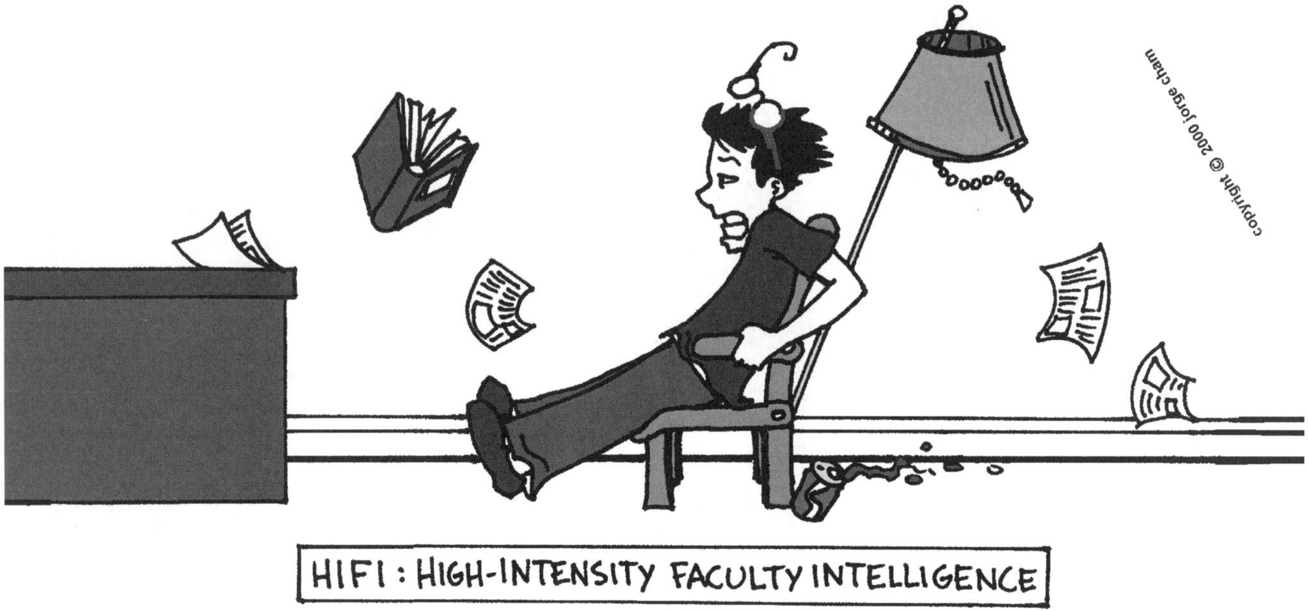
copyright © 2000 jorge cham
HIFI: HIGH-INTENSITY FACULTY INTELLIGENCE

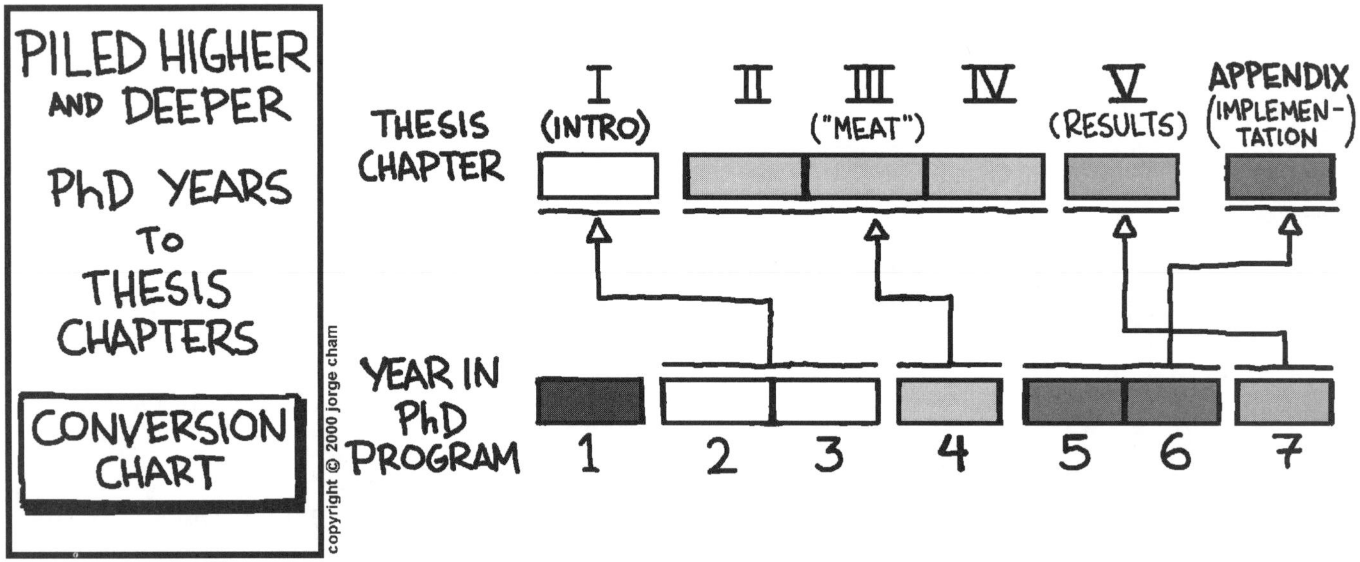
PILED HIGHER AND DEEPER
PhD YEARS TO THESIS CHAPTERS
CONVERSION CHART
copyright © 2000 jorge cham
THESIS CHAPTER
I (INTRO)
II
III ("MEAT")
IV
V (RESULTS)
APPENDIX (IMPLEMENTATION)
YEAR IN PhD PROGRAM
1
2
3
4
5
6
7

THE LIGHT AT THE END OF THE THESIS.

CAN <u>YOU</u> SEE IT?

copyright © 2000 jorge cham

PILED HIGHER AND DEEPER

LAB AGE PERCEPTION CHART

FROM PEDIATRIC TO GERIATRIC IN JUST 5 YEARS!

AS PERCEIVED BY OLDER GRAD STUDENTS

AS PERCEIVED BY NEW MASTER'S STUDENTS

TIME IN LAB

ACTUAL AGE:	23	25	27
AGE IN "LAB YEARS"	2	37	79

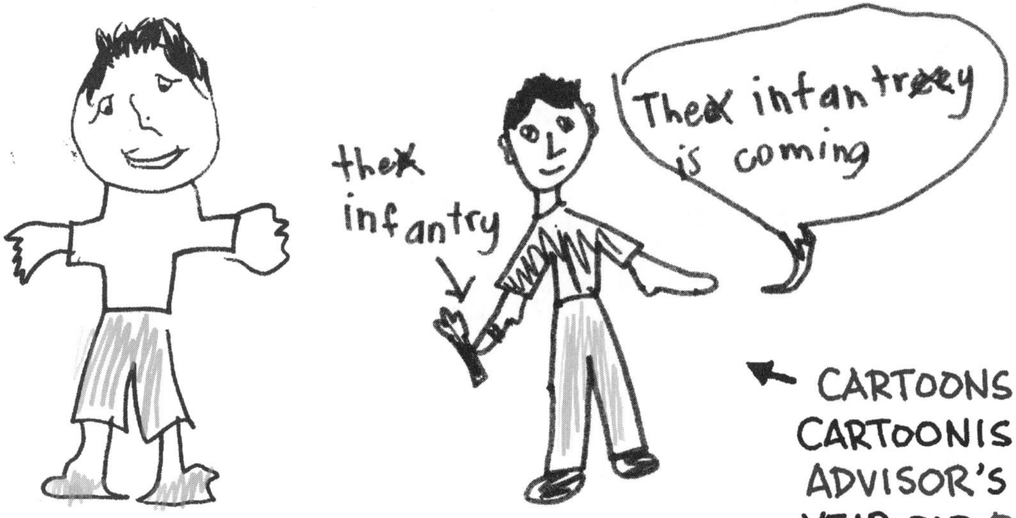

the~~x~~ infantry
The~~x~~ infantr~~ee~~y is coming

CARTOONS OF THE CARTOONIST BY HIS ADVISOR'S 6 AND 7 YEAR-OLD DAUGHTERS.

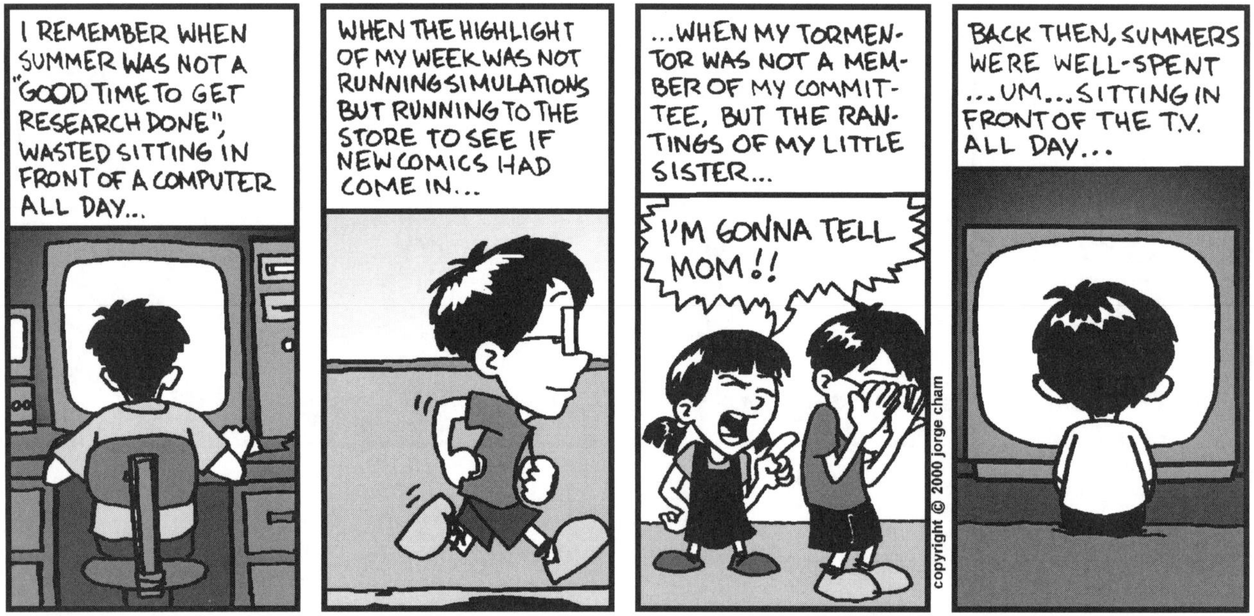

I REMEMBER WHEN SUMMER WAS NOT A "GOOD TIME TO GET RESEARCH DONE", WASTED SITTING IN FRONT OF A COMPUTER ALL DAY...
WHEN THE HIGHLIGHT OF MY WEEK WAS NOT RUNNING SIMULATIONS BUT RUNNING TO THE STORE TO SEE IF NEW COMICS HAD COME IN...
...WHEN MY TORMENTOR WAS NOT A MEMBER OF MY COMMITTEE, BUT THE RANTINGS OF MY LITTLE SISTER...
I'M GONNA TELL MOM!!
copyright © 2000 jorge cham
BACK THEN, SUMMERS WERE WELL-SPENT ...UM...SITTING IN FRONT OF THE T.V. ALL DAY...

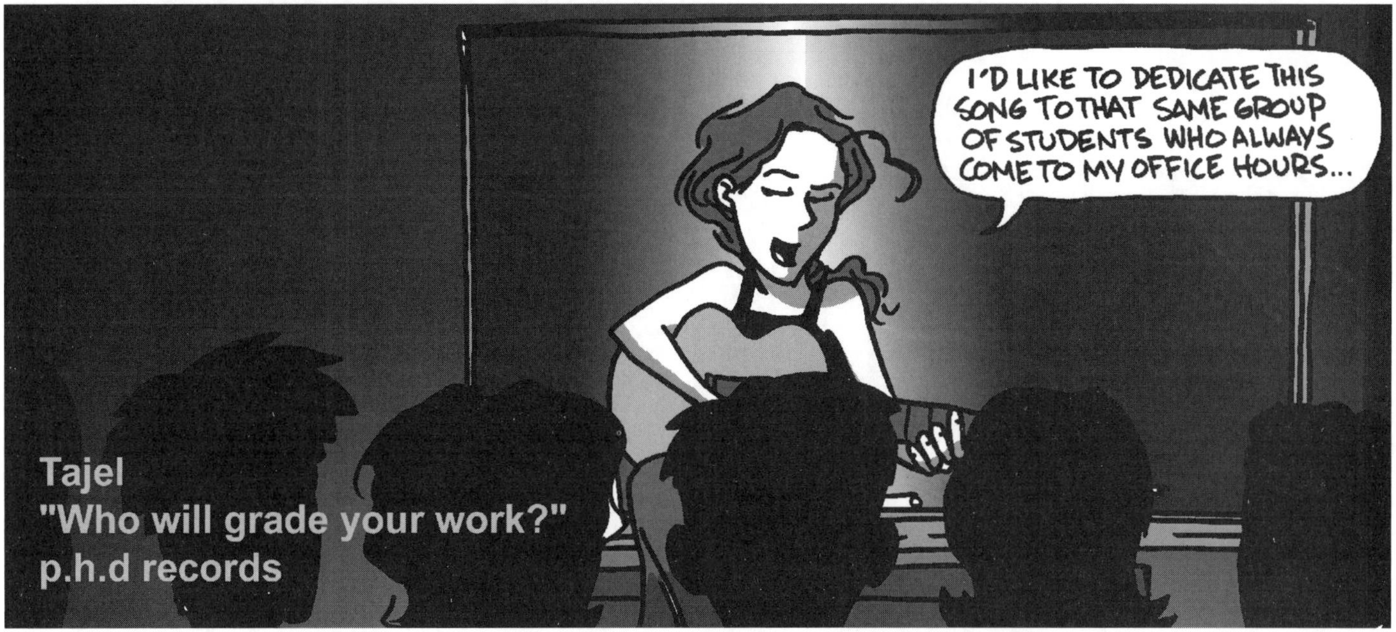
I'D LIKE TO DEDICATE THIS SONG TO THAT SAME GROUP OF STUDENTS WHO ALWAYS COME TO MY OFFICE HOURS...
Tajel
"Who will grade your work?"
p.h.d records

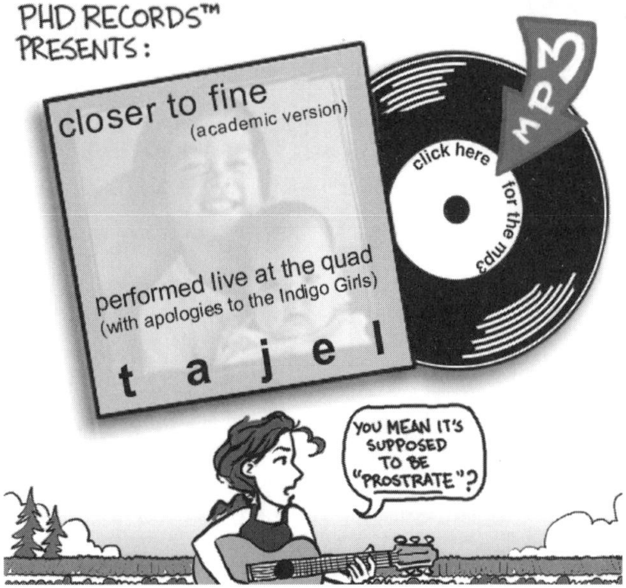
PHD RECORDS™ PRESENTS:
closer to fine
(academic version)
performed live at the quad
(with apologies to the Indigo Girls)
t a j e l
click here for the mp3
MP3
YOU MEAN IT'S SUPPOSED TO BE "PROSTRATE"?

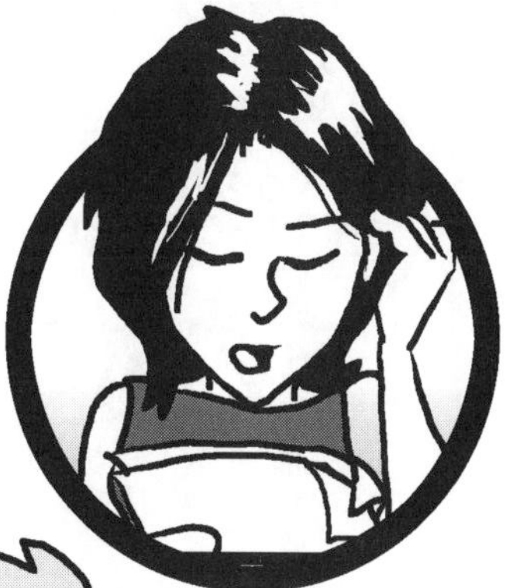

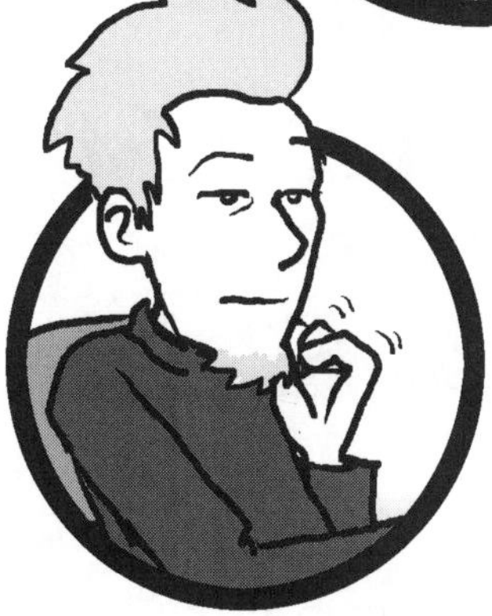

YEAR FOUR
2000-2001

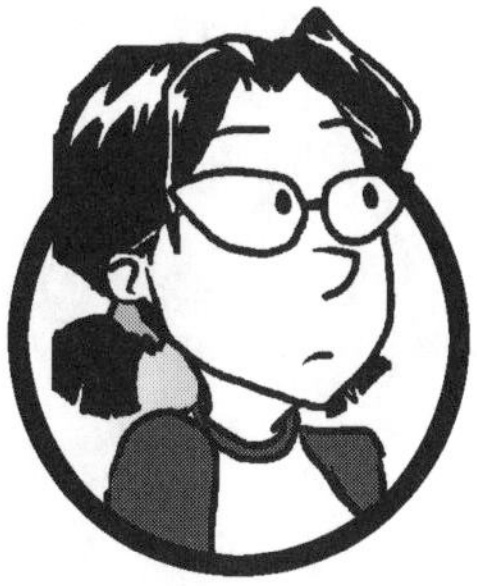

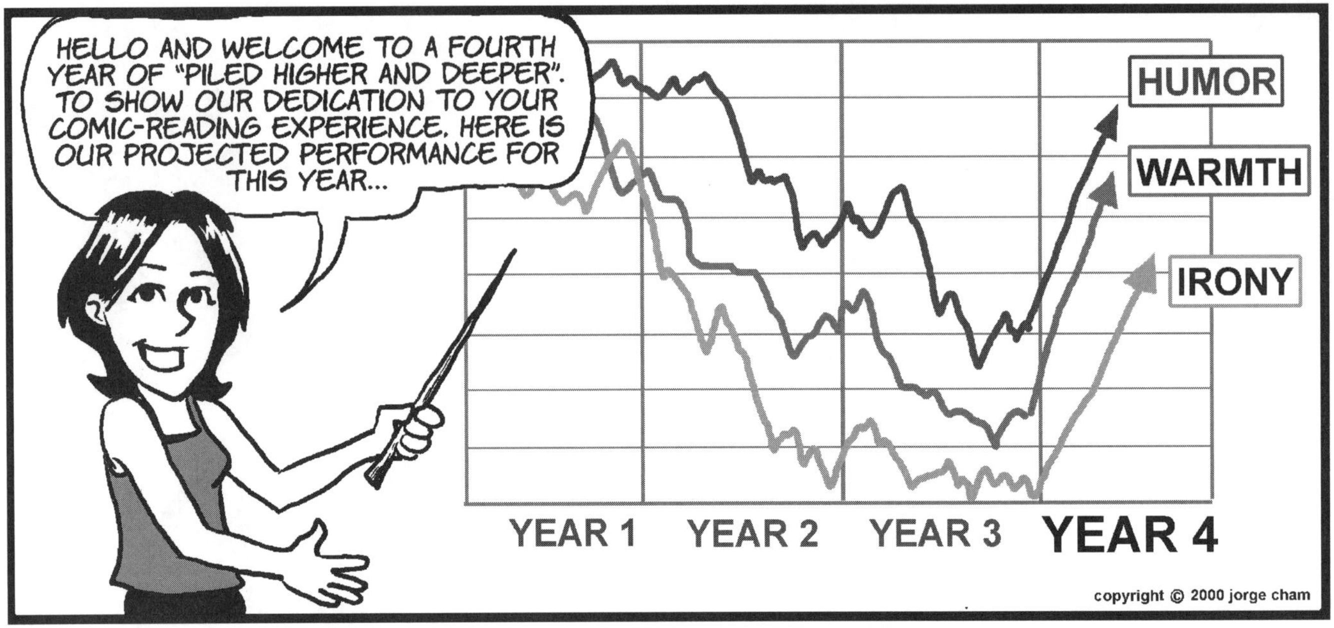
HELLO AND WELCOME TO A FOURTH YEAR OF "PILED HIGHER AND DEEPER". TO SHOW OUR DEDICATION TO YOUR COMIC-READING EXPERIENCE, HERE IS OUR PROJECTED PERFORMANCE FOR THIS YEAR...
HUMOR
WARMTH
IRONY
YEAR 1
YEAR 2
YEAR 3
YEAR 4
copyright © 2000 jorge cham

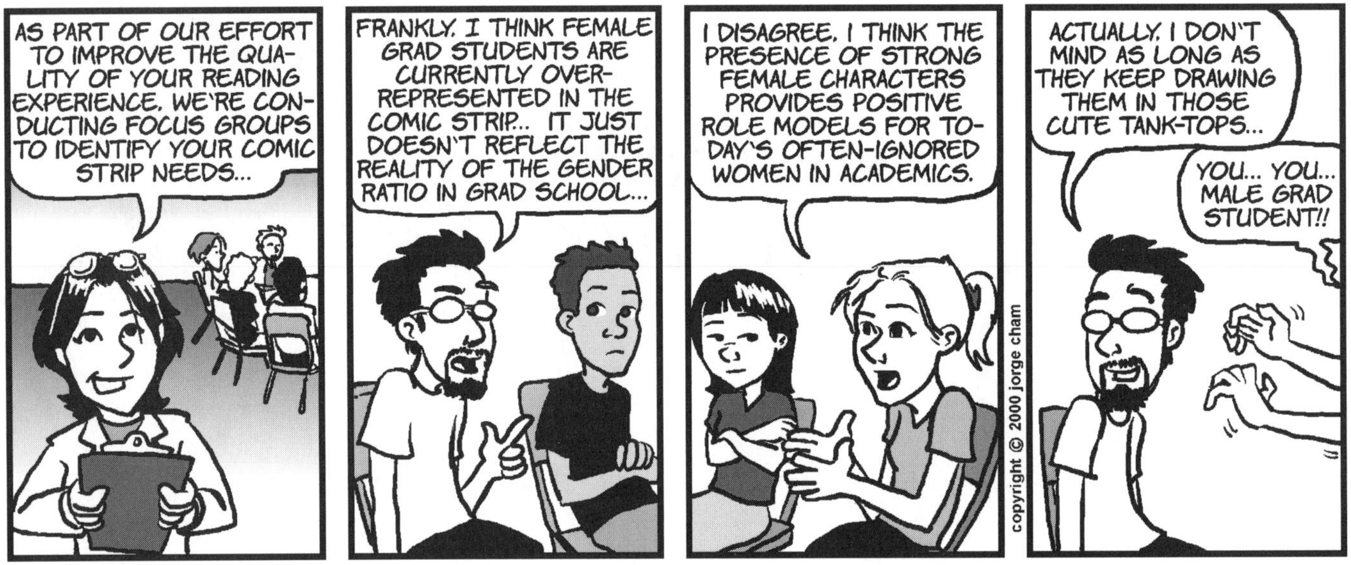
AS PART OF OUR EFFORT TO IMPROVE THE QUALITY OF YOUR READING EXPERIENCE, WE'RE CONDUCTING FOCUS GROUPS TO IDENTIFY YOUR COMIC STRIP NEEDS...
FRANKLY, I THINK FEMALE GRAD STUDENTS ARE CURRENTLY OVER-REPRESENTED IN THE COMIC STRIP... IT JUST DOESN'T REFLECT THE REALITY OF THE GENDER RATIO IN GRAD SCHOOL...
I DISAGREE. I THINK THE PRESENCE OF STRONG FEMALE CHARACTERS PROVIDES POSITIVE ROLE MODELS FOR TODAY'S OFTEN-IGNORED WOMEN IN ACADEMICS.
copyright © 2000 jorge cham
ACTUALLY, I DON'T MIND AS LONG AS THEY KEEP DRAWING THEM IN THOSE CUTE TANK-TOPS...
YOU... YOU... MALE GRAD STUDENT!!

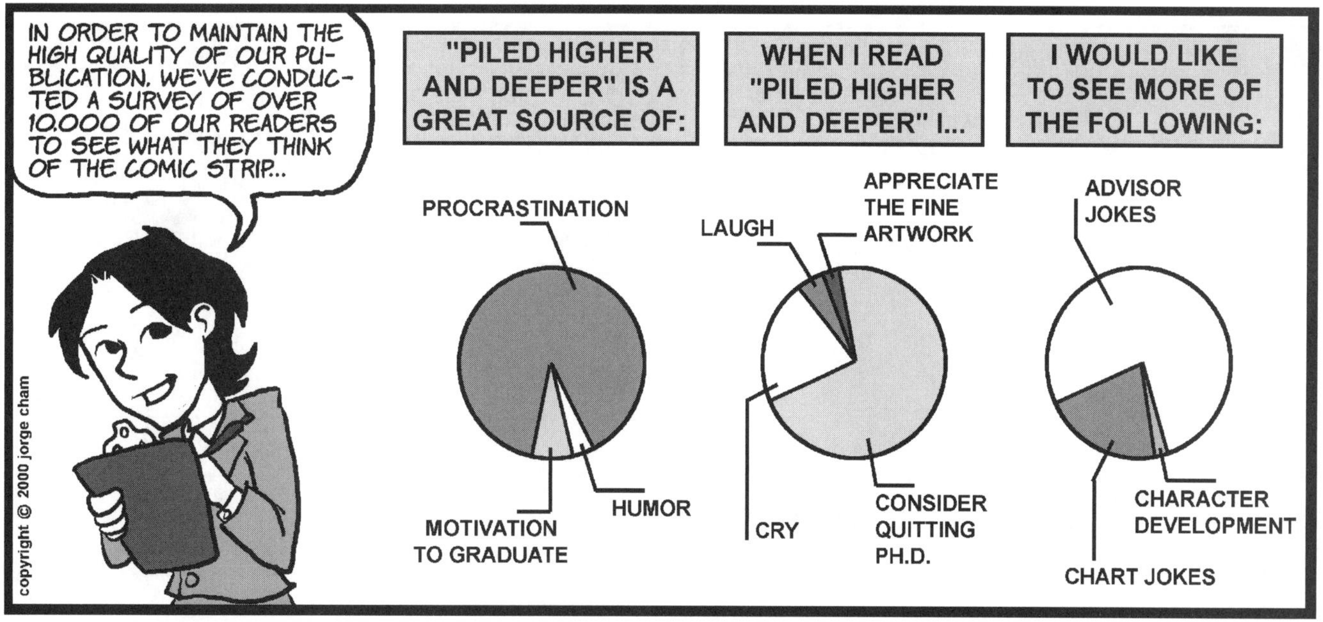
IN ORDER TO MAINTAIN THE HIGH QUALITY OF OUR PUBLICATION, WE'VE CONDUCTED A SURVEY OF OVER 10,000 OF OUR READERS TO SEE WHAT THEY THINK OF THE COMIC STRIP...
"PILED HIGHER AND DEEPER" IS A GREAT SOURCE OF:
PROCRASTINATION
MOTIVATION TO GRADUATE
HUMOR
WHEN I READ "PILED HIGHER AND DEEPER" I...
APPRECIATE THE FINE ARTWORK
LAUGH
CRY
CONSIDER QUITTING PH.D.
I WOULD LIKE TO SEE MORE OF THE FOLLOWING:
ADVISOR JOKES
CHARACTER DEVELOPMENT
CHART JOKES
copyright © 2000 jorge cham

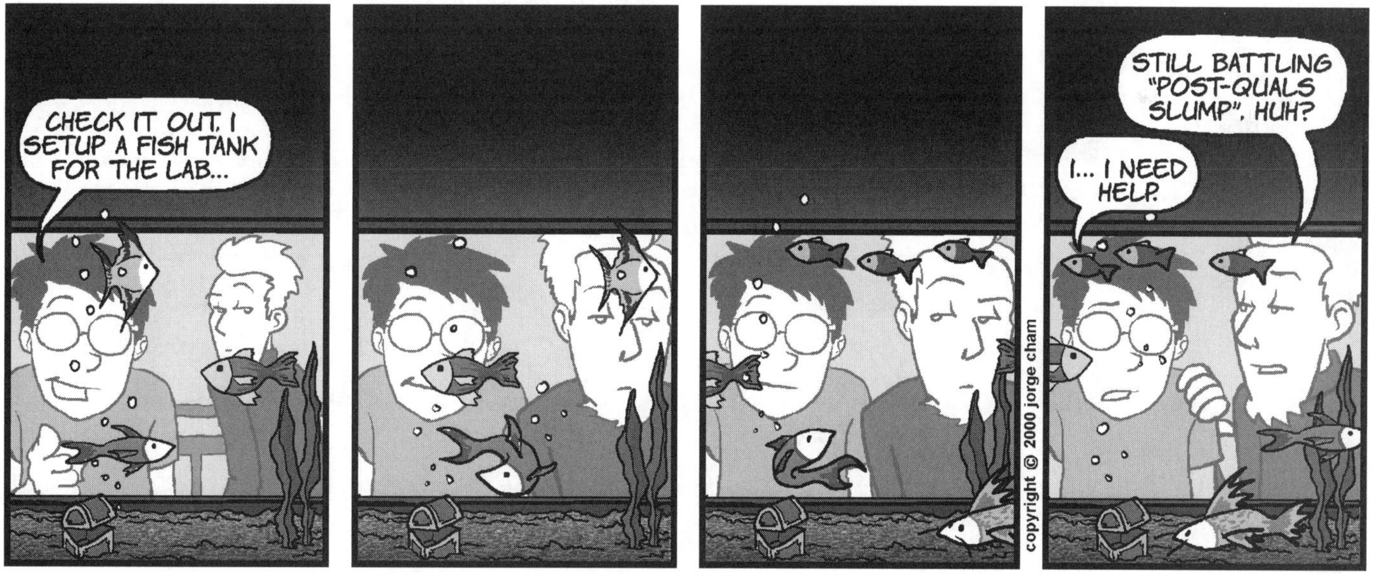
CHECK IT OUT. I SETUP A FISH TANK FOR THE LAB...
copyright © 2000 jorge cham
STILL BATTLING "POST-QUALS SLUMP", HUH?
I... I NEED HELP.

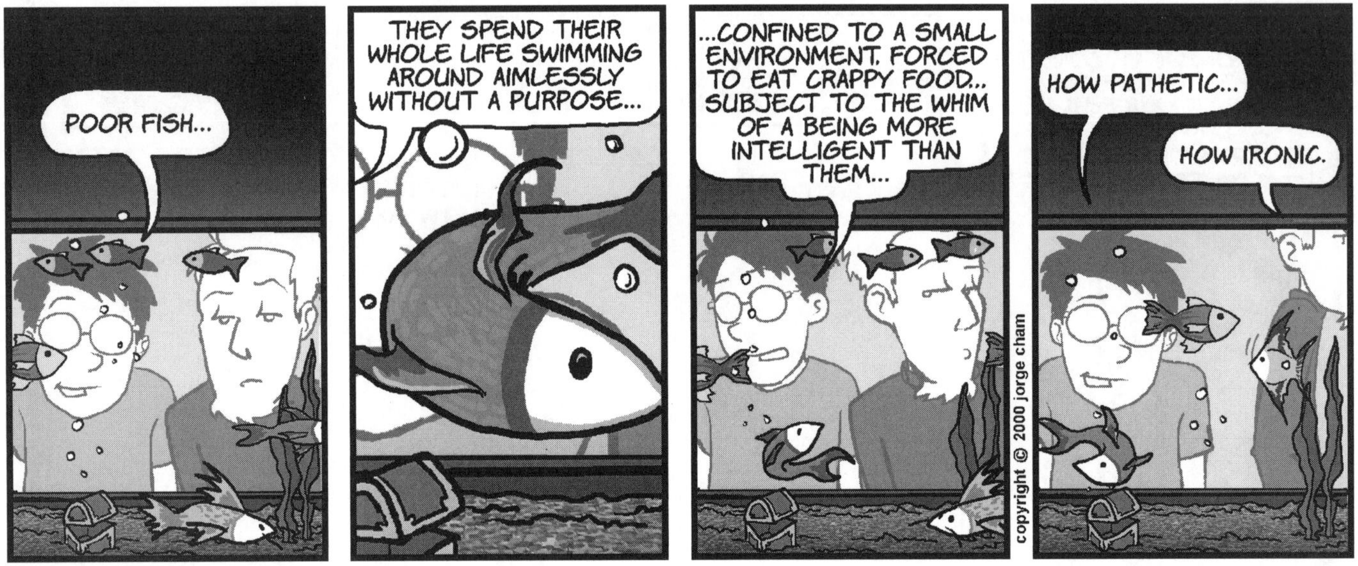
POOR FISH...
THEY SPEND THEIR WHOLE LIFE SWIMMING AROUND AIMLESSLY WITHOUT A PURPOSE...
...CONFINED TO A SMALL ENVIRONMENT. FORCED TO EAT CRAPPY FOOD... SUBJECT TO THE WHIM OF A BEING MORE INTELLIGENT THAN THEM...
copyright © 2000 jorge cham
HOW PATHETIC...
HOW IRONIC.

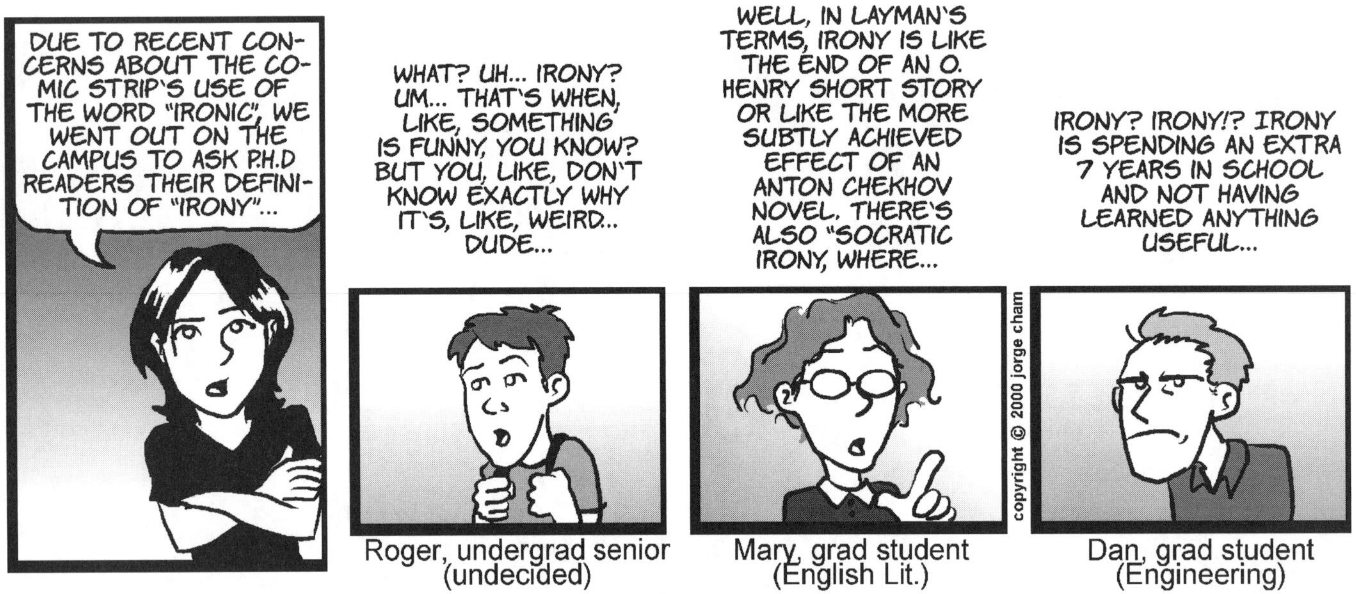
DUE TO RECENT CONCERNS ABOUT THE COMIC STRIP'S USE OF THE WORD "IRONIC", WE WENT OUT ON THE CAMPUS TO ASK P.H.D READERS THEIR DEFINITION OF "IRONY"...
WHAT? UH... IRONY? UM... THAT'S WHEN, LIKE, SOMETHING IS FUNNY, YOU KNOW? BUT YOU, LIKE, DON'T KNOW EXACTLY WHY IT'S, LIKE, WEIRD... DUDE...
Roger, undergrad senior (undecided)
WELL, IN LAYMAN'S TERMS, IRONY IS LIKE THE END OF AN O. HENRY SHORT STORY OR LIKE THE MORE SUBTLY ACHIEVED EFFECT OF AN ANTON CHEKHOV NOVEL. THERE'S ALSO "SOCRATIC IRONY, WHERE...
Mary, grad student (English Lit.)
copyright © 2000 jorge cham
IRONY? IRONY!? IRONY IS SPENDING AN EXTRA 7 YEARS IN SCHOOL AND NOT HAVING LEARNED ANYTHING USEFUL...
Dan, grad student (Engineering)

IRONY and GENERATION Ph.D.

LANDMARK USES OF THE WORD "IRONY" THAT HELPED DEFINE OUR "CULTURE"

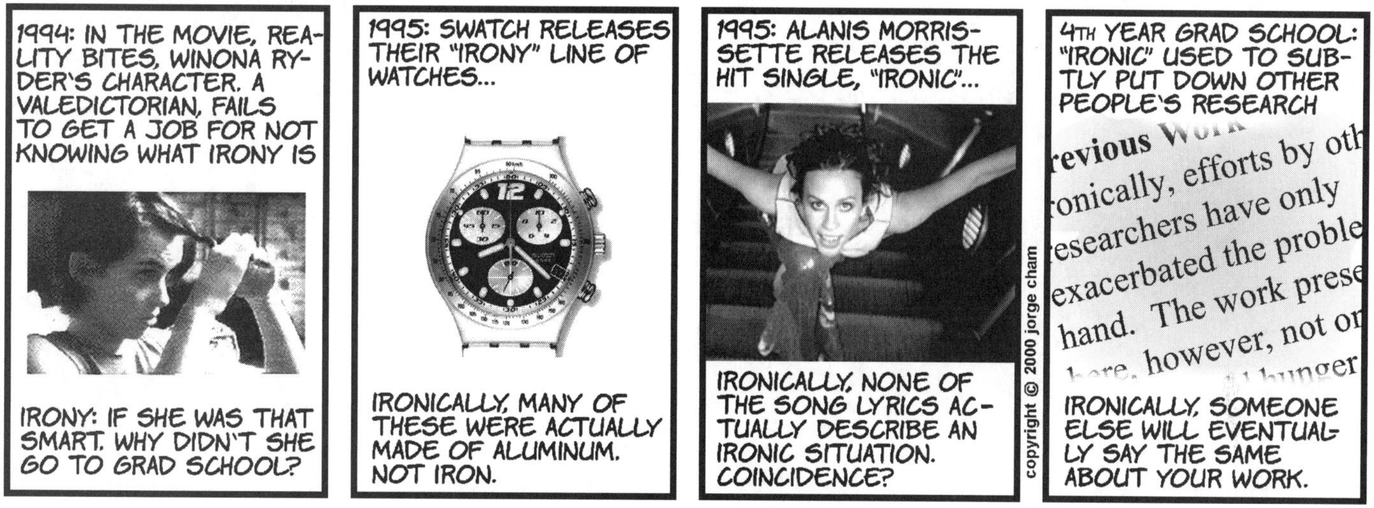
1994: IN THE MOVIE, REALITY BITES, WINONA RYDER'S CHARACTER, A VALEDICTORIAN, FAILS TO GET A JOB FOR NOT KNOWING WHAT IRONY IS
IRONY: IF SHE WAS THAT SMART, WHY DIDN'T SHE GO TO GRAD SCHOOL?
1995: SWATCH RELEASES THEIR "IRONY" LINE OF WATCHES...
12
IRONICALLY, MANY OF THESE WERE ACTUALLY MADE OF ALUMINUM, NOT IRON.
1995: ALANIS MORRISSETTE RELEASES THE HIT SINGLE, "IRONIC"...
IRONICALLY, NONE OF THE SONG LYRICS ACTUALLY DESCRIBE AN IRONIC SITUATION. COINCIDENCE?
copyright © 2000 jorge cham
4TH YEAR GRAD SCHOOL: "IRONIC" USED TO SUBTLY PUT DOWN OTHER PEOPLE'S RESEARCH
revious Work
ronically, efforts by oth
researchers have only
exacerbated the proble
hand. The work prese
here, however, not or
IRONICALLY, SOMEONE ELSE WILL EVENTUALLY SAY THE SAME ABOUT YOUR WORK.

(images copyright of their respective owners)

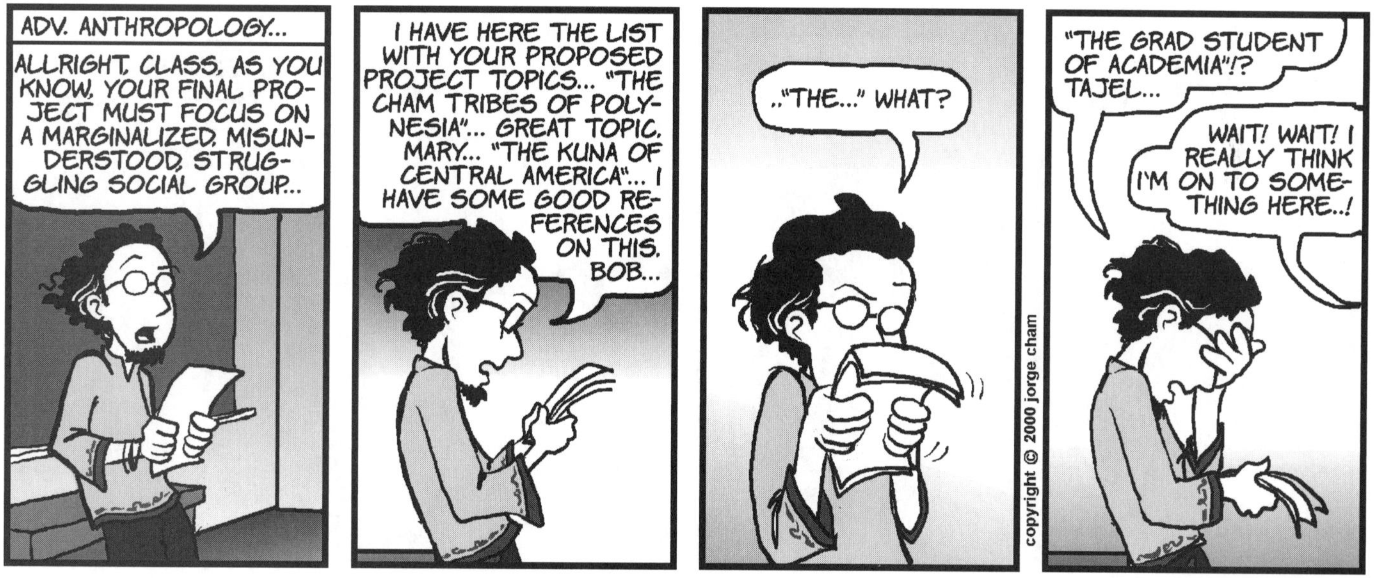
ADV. ANTHROPOLOGY...
ALLRIGHT, CLASS, AS YOU KNOW, YOUR FINAL PROJECT MUST FOCUS ON A MARGINALIZED, MISUNDERSTOOD, STRUGGLING SOCIAL GROUP...
I HAVE HERE THE LIST WITH YOUR PROPOSED PROJECT TOPICS... "THE CHAM TRIBES OF POLYNESIA"... GREAT TOPIC, MARY... "THE KUNA OF CENTRAL AMERICA"... I HAVE SOME GOOD REFERENCES ON THIS, BOB...
.."THE..." WHAT?
copyright © 2000 jorge cham
"THE GRAD STUDENT OF ACADEMIA"!? TAJEL...
WAIT! WAIT! I REALLY THINK I'M ON TO SOMETHING HERE..!

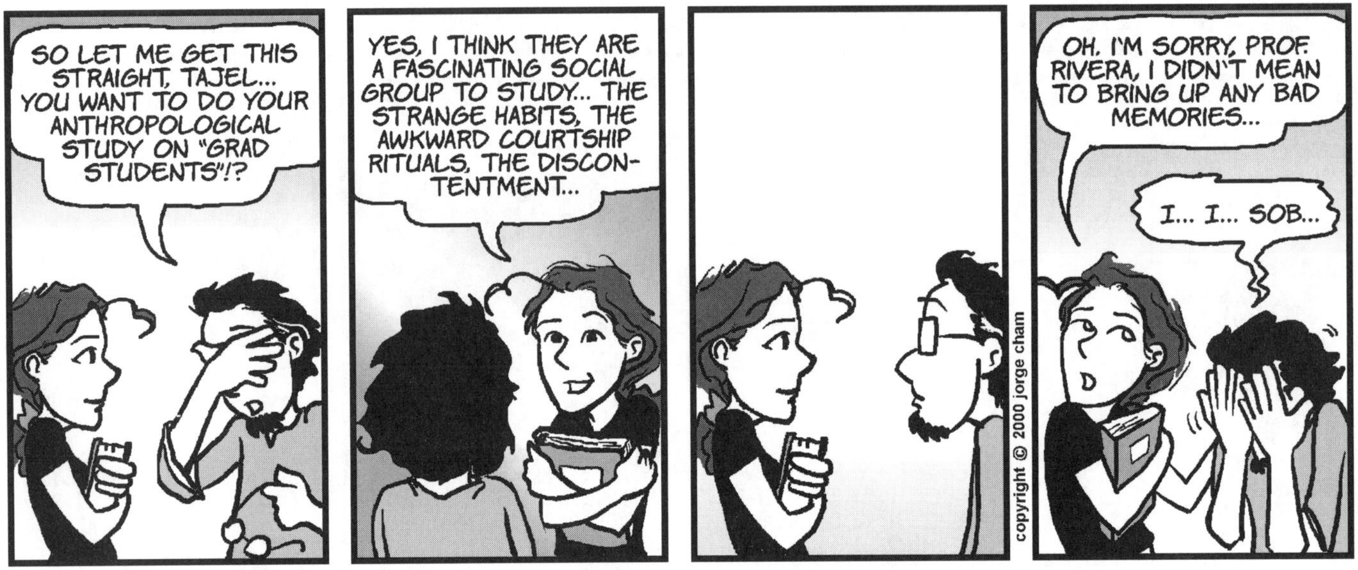
SO LET ME GET THIS STRAIGHT, TAJEL... YOU WANT TO DO YOUR ANTHROPOLOGICAL STUDY ON "GRAD STUDENTS"!?
YES, I THINK THEY ARE A FASCINATING SOCIAL GROUP TO STUDY... THE STRANGE HABITS, THE AWKWARD COURTSHIP RITUALS, THE DISCONTENTMENT...
copyright © 2000 jorge cham
OH, I'M SORRY, PROF. RIVERA, I DIDN'T MEAN TO BRING UP ANY BAD MEMORIES...
I... I... SOB...

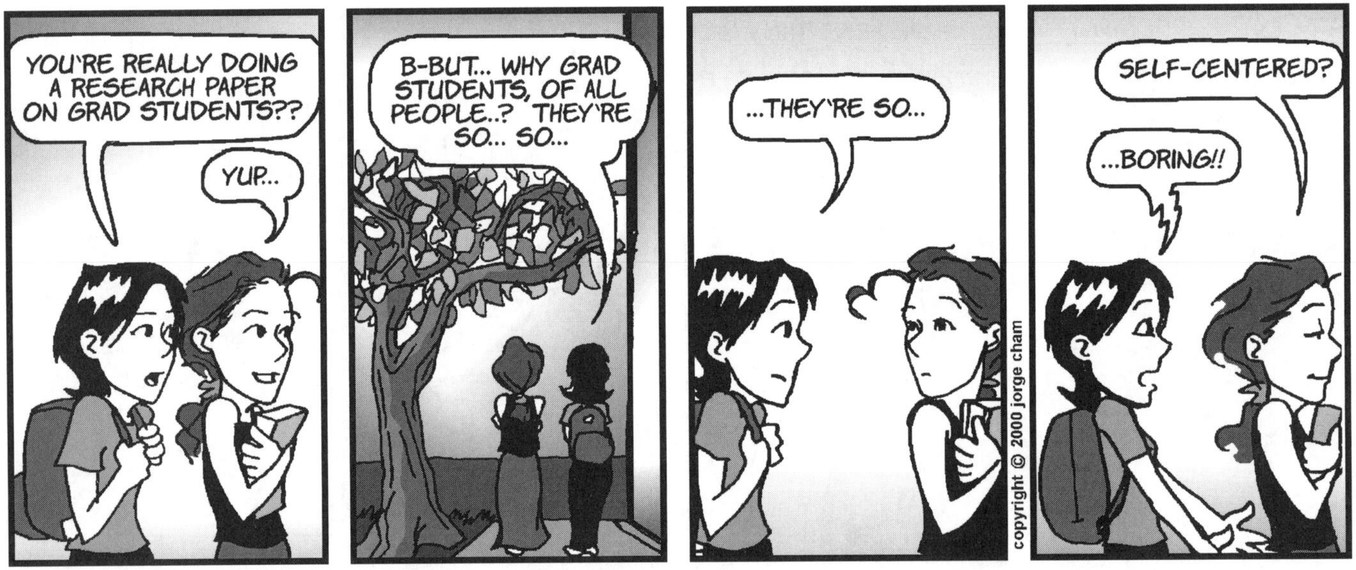
YOU'RE REALLY DOING A RESEARCH PAPER ON GRAD STUDENTS??
YUP...
B-BUT... WHY GRAD STUDENTS, OF ALL PEOPLE..? THEY'RE SO... SO...
...THEY'RE SO...
copyright © 2000 jorge cham
SELF-CENTERED?
...BORING!!

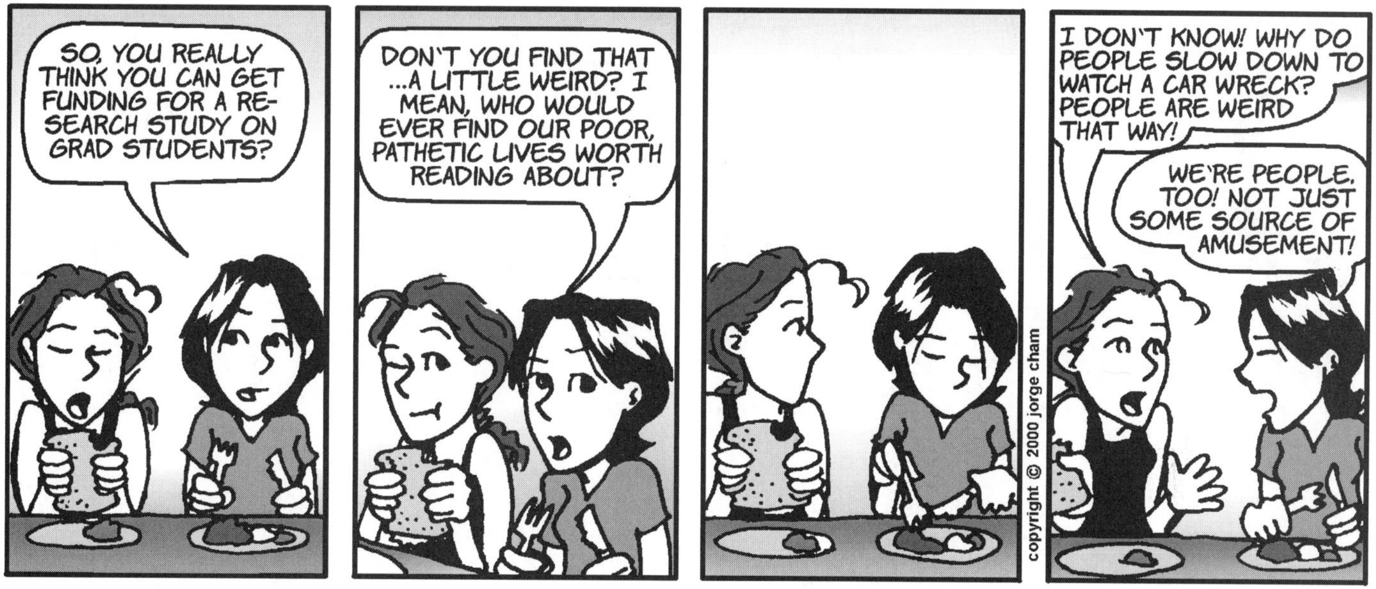
SO, YOU REALLY THINK YOU CAN GET FUNDING FOR A RE-SEARCH STUDY ON GRAD STUDENTS?
DON'T YOU FIND THAT ...A LITTLE WEIRD? I MEAN, WHO WOULD EVER FIND OUR POOR, PATHETIC LIVES WORTH READING ABOUT?
I DON'T KNOW! WHY DO PEOPLE SLOW DOWN TO WATCH A CAR WRECK? PEOPLE ARE WEIRD THAT WAY!
WE'RE PEOPLE, TOO! NOT JUST SOME SOURCE OF AMUSEMENT!
copyright © 2000 jorge cham

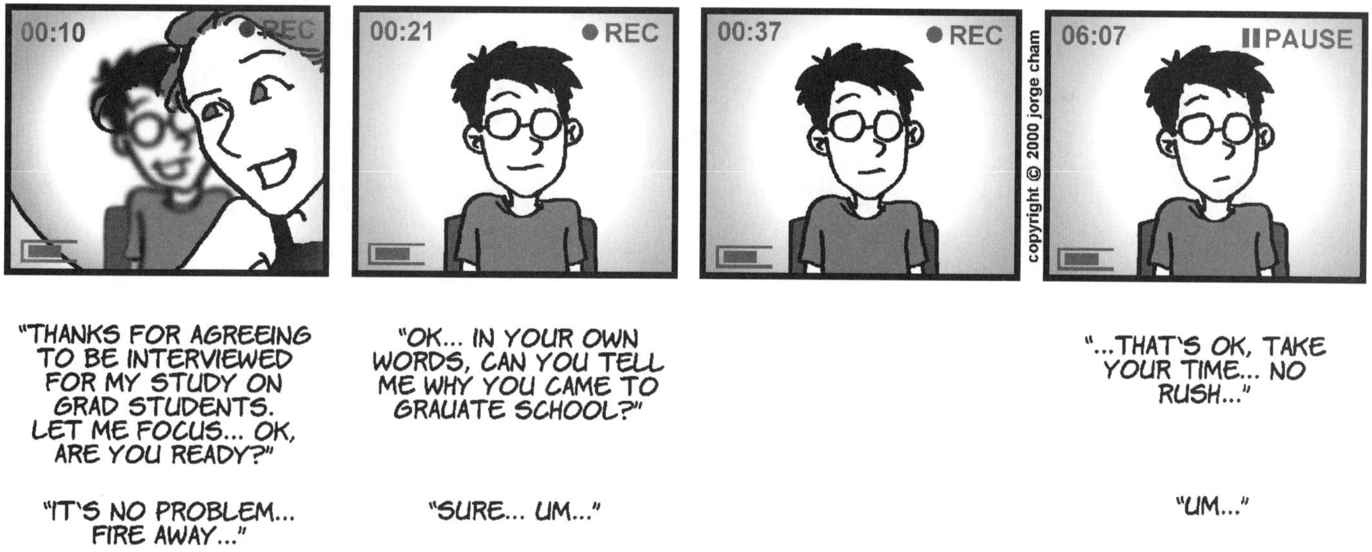
00:10
REC
00:21
REC
00:37
REC
06:07
PAUSE
copyright © 2000 jorge cham
"THANKS FOR AGREEING TO BE INTERVIEWED FOR MY STUDY ON GRAD STUDENTS. LET ME FOCUS... OK, ARE YOU READY?"
"IT'S NO PROBLEM... FIRE AWAY..."
"OK... IN YOUR OWN WORDS, CAN YOU TELL ME WHY YOU CAME TO GRAUATE SCHOOL?"
"SURE... UM..."
"...THAT'S OK, TAKE YOUR TIME... NO RUSH..."
"UM..."

07:23 ● REC
LINUX
08:01 ● REC
LINUX
09:17 ● REC
LINUX
copyright © 2000 jorge cham
10:42 ● REC

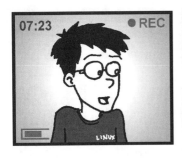

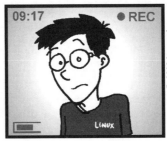

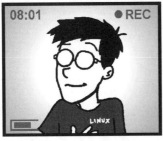

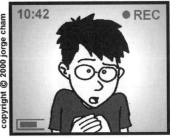

"WELL, I SUPPOSE IF I WERE HONEST I'D SAY I CAME TO GRADUATE SCHOOL FOR THE TITLE: 'P.H.D'... 'DOCTOR'... 'PROFESSOR'..."

"I WAS ATTRACTED TO THE GLAMOUR, THE EXCITEMENT OF BEING A PROFESSOR... THE RESPECT, THE SWOONING WOMEN, THE MONEY..."

"SO, WOULD YOU SAY IT'S BEEN A DISSAPOINTING EXPERIENCE, THEN?"

"W-WHY? Y-YOU... YOU MEAN IT... IT'S NOT TRUE??"

00:39 ● REC
01:01 ● REC
02:07 ● REC
copyright © 2000 jorge cham
02:46 ● REC

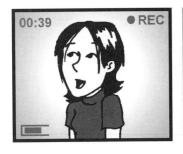

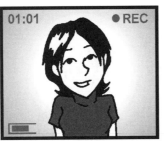

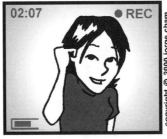

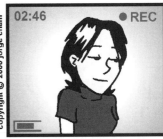

"WHY I CAME TO GRAD SCHOOL? GOSH... I DON'T EVEN REMEMBER MAKING THAT CHOICE... I GUESS... I GUESS I ALWAYS KNEW. IT WAS ALWAYS PART OF THE PLAN..."

"AND THE RESEARCH... THE RESEARCH IS KIND OF INTERESTING. I SUPPOSE IT COULD BE WORSE..."

"MY... MY FATHER WAS A PROFESSOR, YOU KNOW? HE WAS VERY RESPECTED AND A GREAT TEACHER..."

"...A REALLY GREAT TEACHER..."

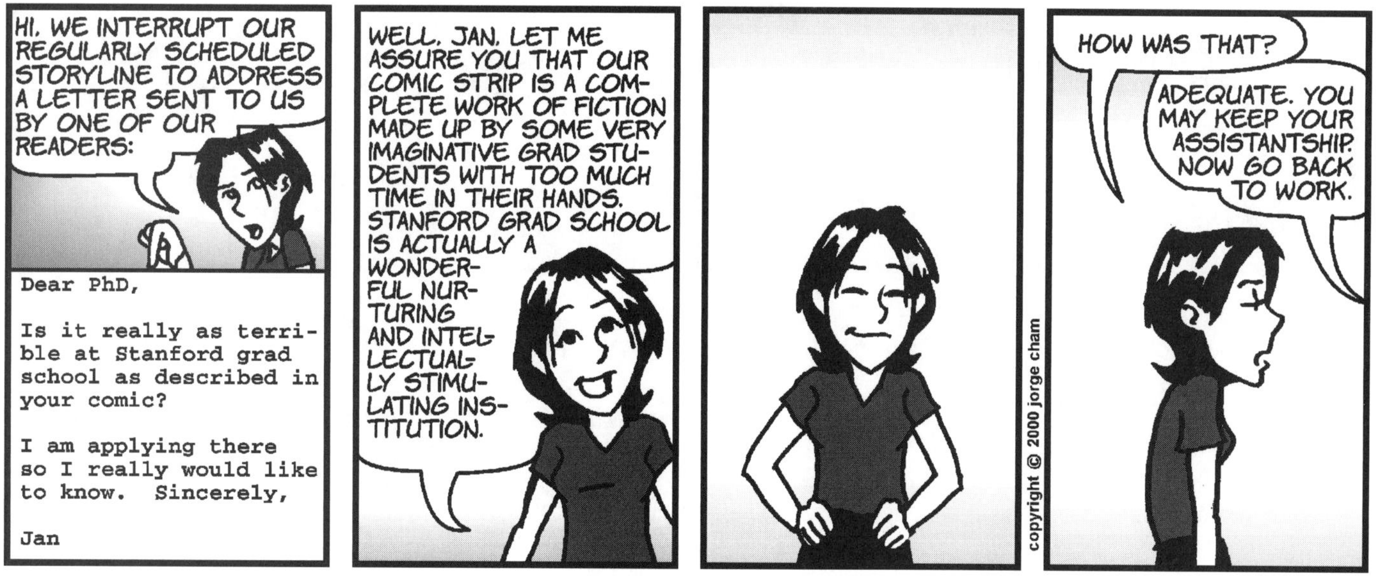
HI, WE INTERRUPT OUR REGULARLY SCHEDULED STORYLINE TO ADDRESS A LETTER SENT TO US BY ONE OF OUR READERS:
Dear PhD,
Is it really as terrible at Stanford grad school as described in your comic?
I am applying there so I really would like to know. Sincerely,
Jan
WELL, JAN, LET ME ASSURE YOU THAT OUR COMIC STRIP IS A COMPLETE WORK OF FICTION MADE UP BY SOME VERY IMAGINATIVE GRAD STUDENTS WITH TOO MUCH TIME IN THEIR HANDS. STANFORD GRAD SCHOOL IS ACTUALLY A WONDERFUL NURTURING AND INTELLECTUALLY STIMULATING INSTITUTION.
copyright © 2000 jorge cham
HOW WAS THAT?
ADEQUATE. YOU MAY KEEP YOUR ASSISTANTSHIP. NOW GO BACK TO WORK.

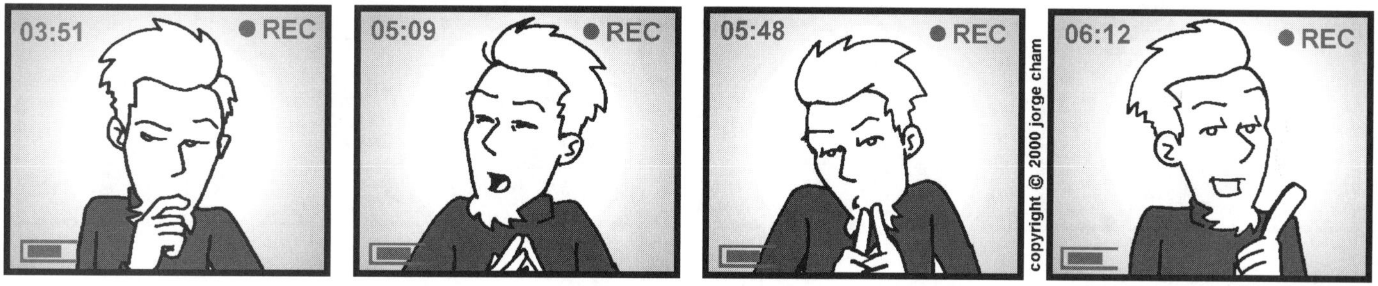
03:51
REC
05:09
REC
05:48
REC
copyright © 2000 jorge cham
06:12
REC

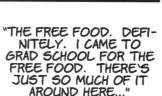

"THE FREE FOOD. DEFINITELY. I CAME TO GRAD SCHOOL FOR THE FREE FOOD. THERE'S JUST SO MUCH OF IT AROUND HERE..."

"BUT MIKE, IF YOU WEREN'T IN GRAD SCHOOL, YOU COULD GET A PAYING JOB AND YOU COULD BUY ALL THE FOOD YOU EVER WANTED..."

"YES, BUT THEN YOU'D ACTUALLY HAVE TO WORK, WOULDN'T YOU?"

11:29
REC
13:02
REC
14:18
REC
copyright © 2000 jorge cham
14:27
REC

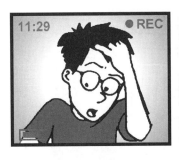

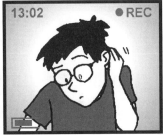

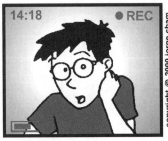

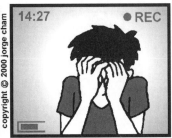

"S-SO YOU'RE SAYING A PH.D. W-WILL NOT BRING ME FAME AND P-PRESTIGE..? WO-MEN DON'T GO NUTS OVER PROFESSORS..?"

"I'M AFRAID NOT..."

"BUT AT LEAST I'LL STILL BE RICH, RIGHT?"

"ACTUALLY, WITH TODAY'S STARTING SALARIES FOR PH.D'S, YOU'LL NEVER CATCH UP TO SOMEONE WHO STARTED WORKING AFTER THEIR BACHELOR'S"

23:10
REC
23:57
REC
24:14
REC
copyright © 2001 jorge cham
26:09
STOP

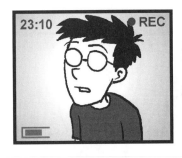

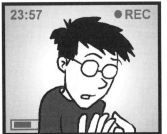

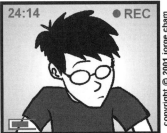

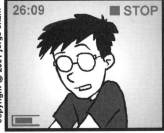

"I... WELL... AT LEAST THE RESEARCH IS STILL VERY EXCITING... FIN-DING NEW IDEAS AND CONCEPTS AND SUCH..."

"THAT'S GREAT! SO TELL ME, WHAT IS THE LATEST NEW IDEA YOU'VE DISCOVERED?"

"UM... WELL... IT'S ON-LY MY... FOURTH YEAR HERE SO... I HAVEN'T REALLY..."

"THAT'S OK. WELL I'M SURE THE EVERYDAY SEARCH FOR INNOVA-TION MUST BE PRETTY COOL... FOR EXAM-PLE, WHAT DID YOU DO TODAY AT THE LAB?"

"TODAY..? UM... LET'S SEE... I... HMMM...
...
...
HMMM..."

"OH YEAH, THE LAB FLOOR WAS PRETTY DIRTY SO PROF. SMITH ASKED ME TO..."

"OK. I THINK THAT ENDS OUR INTERVIEW. THANK YOU VERY MUCH."

'TWAS THE NIGHT BEFORE WINTER BREAK
  AND ALL THROUGH THE RESEARCH CENTER
NOT A SOUND COULD BE HEARD
  NOT EVEN A KEYBOARD "ENTER"

THE GRAPHS WERE ALL HUNG
  BY THE BULLETIN BOARD WITH CARE,
WEARY THAT PROFESSOR SMITH
  SOON WOULD BE THERE.

THE GRAD STUDENTS WERE NESTLED
  ALL SNUG IN THEIR DESKS,
WITH VISIONS OF DIPLOMAS
  THAT WERE SLIGHTLY KAFKAESQUE

THEY DREAMED OF ONE DAY WEARING
  A BLACK GOWN AND CAP,
BUT TIRED, LAZY, HAD SETTLED DOWN
  FOR A LONG WINTER'S NAP.

WHEN OUT ON THE QUAD
  THERE AROSE SUCH A COMMOTION.♪
THE STUDENTS SPRANG UP TO THEIR FEET
  WITH MUSCLES SORE FROM LACK OF MOTION.

FROM THEIR BASEMENT OFFICES
  THEY FLEW LIKE A FLASH♪
AFTER MAKING A BACKUP, OF COURSE
  LEST THE SYSTEM CRASH...

AND WITH DARTING EYES,
  SO LIVELY AND FULL OF WIT,
IN CAME THEIR ADVISOR,
  IN CAME PROFESSOR SMITH♪

MORE RAPID THAN AN EAGLE
  HIS WISDOM CAME.
AND HE WHISTLED, AND SHOUTED,
  FOR THEIR WORK NOT TO WANE:

"NOW, REGRESSIONS♪ NOW, GRAPHS♪
  NOW, RESULTS AND CONCLUSIONS♪
ON, REFERENCES♪ ON, SURVEYS♪
  ON, TRANSFORMS AND CONVOLUTIONS♪

TO THE TOP OF THE RANKINGS♪
  TO A PRESTIGIOUS JOURNAL♪
NOW WORK AWAY♪ WORK AWAY♪
  WORK AWAY ALL♪"

AS DRY LEAVES THAT
  BEFORE THE WILD HURRICANE FLY,
THE GRAD STUDENTS TYPED AND TYPED
  FEARING TO EVEN ASK WHY...

SO UP THE IVORY TOWER
  THE ADVISOR FLEW,
WITH A HANDFUL OF PAPER DRAFTS
  TO EDIT AND REVIEW.

BUT I HEARD HIM EXCLAIM,
  ERE HE DROVE OUT SMIRKING,
"HAPPY WINTER BREAK TO ALL,
  BUT TO ALL: KEEP WORKING♪"

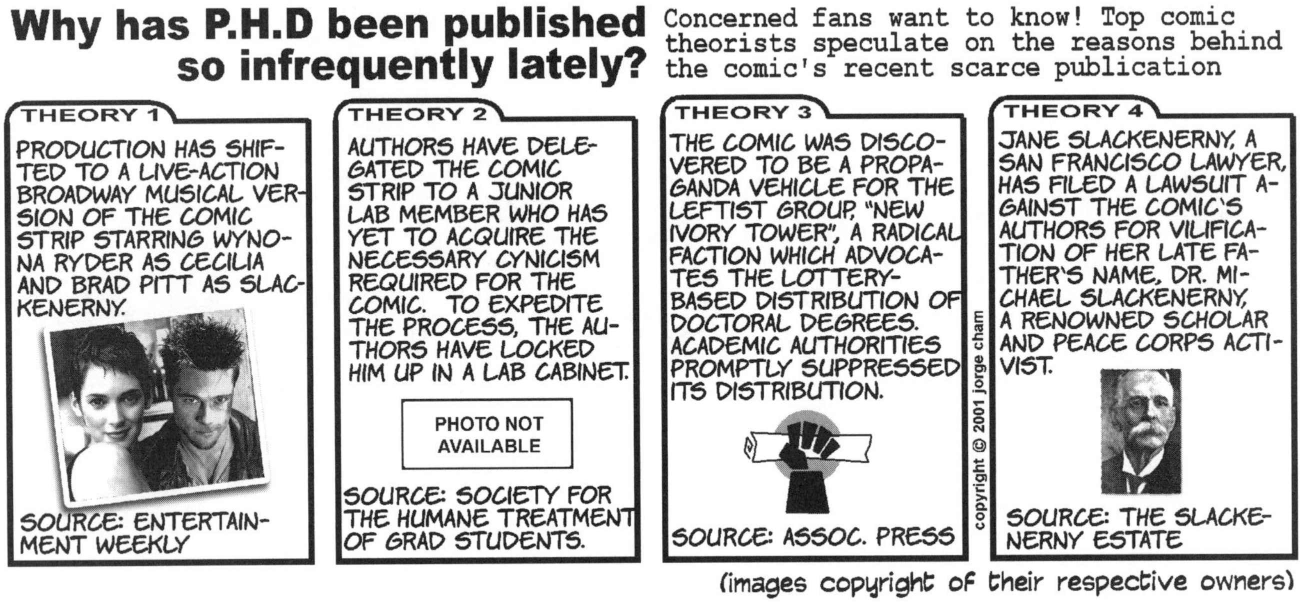
Why has P.H.D been published so infrequently lately?
Concerned fans want to know! Top comic theorists speculate on the reasons behind the comic's recent scarce publication
THEORY 1
PRODUCTION HAS SHIFTED TO A LIVE-ACTION BROADWAY MUSICAL VERSION OF THE COMIC STRIP STARRING WYNONA RYDER AS CECILIA AND BRAD PITT AS SLACKENERNY.
SOURCE: ENTERTAINMENT WEEKLY
THEORY 2
AUTHORS HAVE DELEGATED THE COMIC STRIP TO A JUNIOR LAB MEMBER WHO HAS YET TO ACQUIRE THE NECESSARY CYNICISM REQUIRED FOR THE COMIC. TO EXPEDITE THE PROCESS, THE AUTHORS HAVE LOCKED HIM UP IN A LAB CABINET.
PHOTO NOT AVAILABLE
SOURCE: SOCIETY FOR THE HUMANE TREATMENT OF GRAD STUDENTS.
THEORY 3
THE COMIC WAS DISCOVERED TO BE A PROPAGANDA VEHICLE FOR THE LEFTIST GROUP, "NEW IVORY TOWER", A RADICAL FACTION WHICH ADVOCATES THE LOTTERY-BASED DISTRIBUTION OF DOCTORAL DEGREES. ACADEMIC AUTHORITIES PROMPTLY SUPPRESSED ITS DISTRIBUTION.
SOURCE: ASSOC. PRESS
copyright © 2001 jorge cham
THEORY 4
JANE SLACKENERNY, A SAN FRANCISCO LAWYER, HAS FILED A LAWSUIT AGAINST THE COMIC'S AUTHORS FOR VILIFICATION OF HER LATE FATHER'S NAME, DR. MICHAEL SLACKENERNY, A RENOWNED SCHOLAR AND PEACE CORPS ACTIVIST.
SOURCE: THE SLACKENERNY ESTATE
(images copyright of their respective owners)

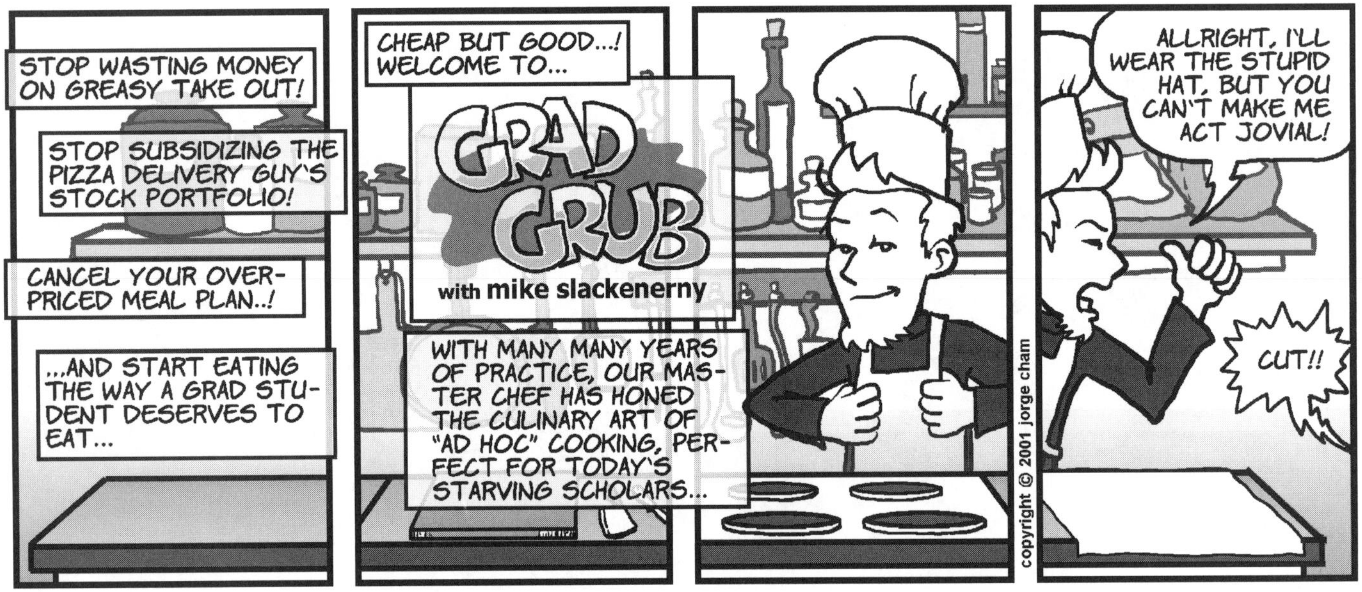
STOP WASTING MONEY ON GREASY TAKE OUT!
STOP SUBSIDIZING THE PIZZA DELIVERY GUY'S STOCK PORTFOLIO!
CANCEL YOUR OVERPRICED MEAL PLAN..!
...AND START EATING THE WAY A GRAD STUDENT DESERVES TO EAT...
CHEAP BUT GOOD...! WELCOME TO...
GRAD GRUB
with mike slackenerny
WITH MANY MANY YEARS OF PRACTICE, OUR MASTER CHEF HAS HONED THE CULINARY ART OF "AD HOC" COOKING, PERFECT FOR TODAY'S STARVING SCHOLARS...
copyright © 2001 jorge cham
ALLRIGHT, I'LL WEAR THE STUPID HAT, BUT YOU CAN'T MAKE ME ACT JOVIAL!
CUT!!

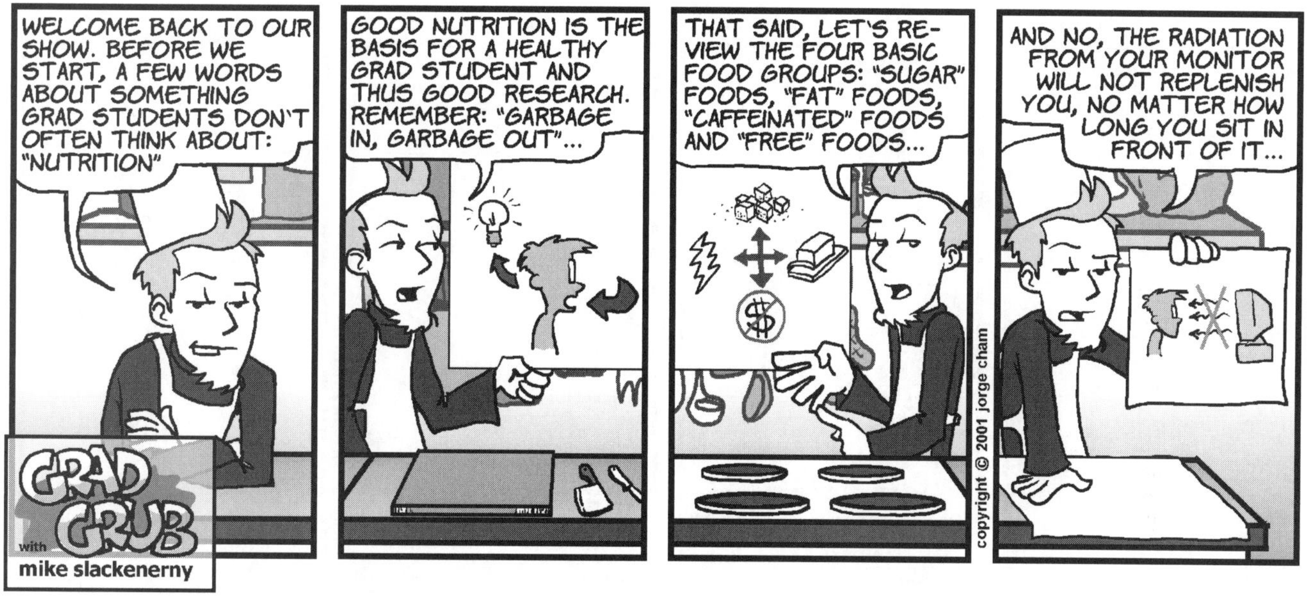
WELCOME BACK TO OUR SHOW. BEFORE WE START, A FEW WORDS ABOUT SOMETHING GRAD STUDENTS DON'T OFTEN THINK ABOUT: "NUTRITION"
GRAD GRUB with mike slackenerny
GOOD NUTRITION IS THE BASIS FOR A HEALTHY GRAD STUDENT AND THUS GOOD RESEARCH. REMEMBER: "GARBAGE IN, GARBAGE OUT"...
THAT SAID, LET'S RE-VIEW THE FOUR BASIC FOOD GROUPS: "SUGAR" FOODS, "FAT" FOODS, "CAFFEINATED" FOODS AND "FREE" FOODS...
copyright © 2001 jorge cham
AND NO, THE RADIATION FROM YOUR MONITOR WILL NOT REPLENISH YOU, NO MATTER HOW LONG YOU SIT IN FRONT OF IT...

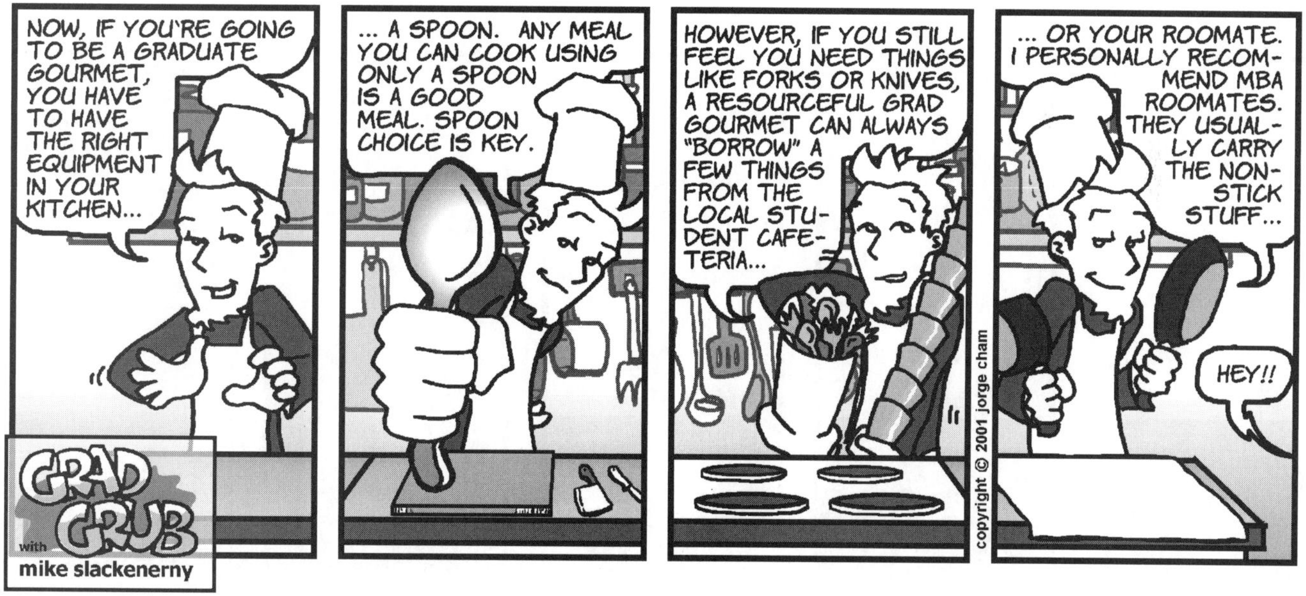
NOW, IF YOU'RE GOING TO BE A GRADUATE GOURMET, YOU HAVE TO HAVE THE RIGHT EQUIPMENT IN YOUR KITCHEN...
GRAD GRUB with mike slackenerny
... A SPOON. ANY MEAL YOU CAN COOK USING ONLY A SPOON IS A GOOD MEAL. SPOON CHOICE IS KEY.
HOWEVER, IF YOU STILL FEEL YOU NEED THINGS LIKE FORKS OR KNIVES, A RESOURCEFUL GRAD GOURMET CAN ALWAYS "BORROW" A FEW THINGS FROM THE LOCAL STU-DENT CAFE-TERIA...
copyright © 2001 jorge cham
... OR YOUR ROOMATE. I PERSONALLY RECOM-MEND MBA ROOMATES. THEY USUAL-LY CARRY THE NON-STICK STUFF...
HEY!!

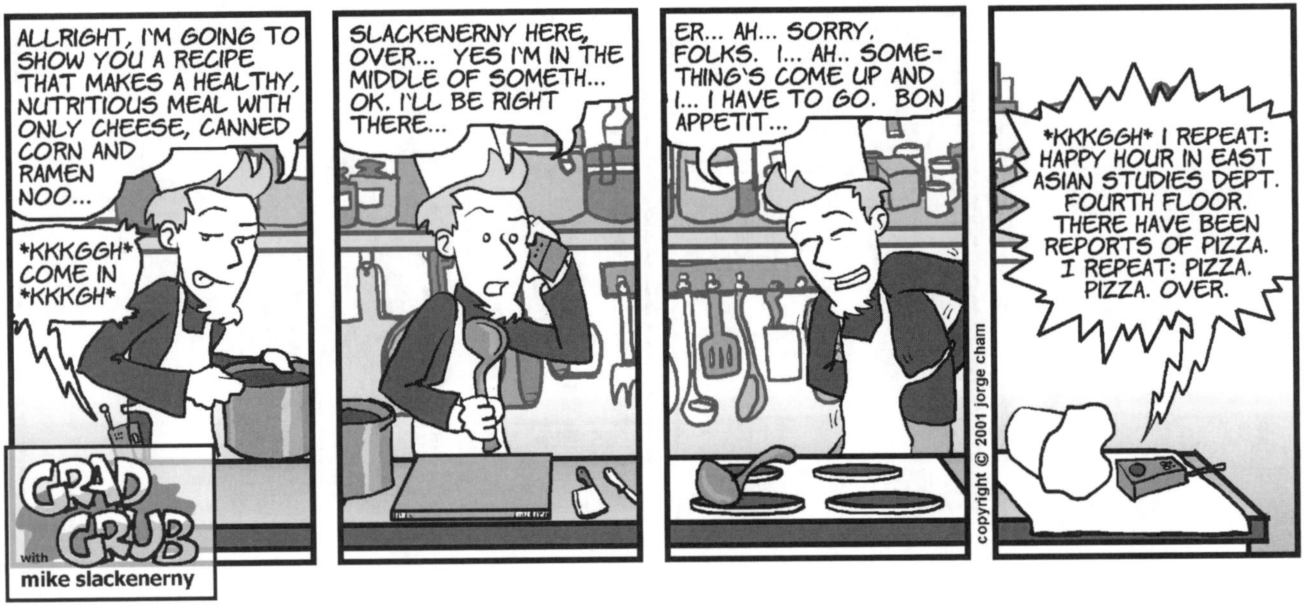
ALLRIGHT, I'M GOING TO SHOW YOU A RECIPE THAT MAKES A HEALTHY, NUTRITIOUS MEAL WITH ONLY CHEESE, CANNED CORN AND RAMEN NOO...
KKKGGH COME IN *KKKGH*
GRAD GRUB with mike slackenerny
SLACKENERNY HERE, OVER... YES I'M IN THE MIDDLE OF SOMETH... OK. I'LL BE RIGHT THERE...
ER... AH... SORRY, FOLKS. I... AH.. SOMETHING'S COME UP AND I... I HAVE TO GO. BON APPETIT...
copyright © 2001 jorge cham
KKKGGH I REPEAT: HAPPY HOUR IN EAST ASIAN STUDIES DEPT. FOURTH FLOOR. THERE HAVE BEEN REPORTS OF PIZZA. I REPEAT: PIZZA. PIZZA. OVER.

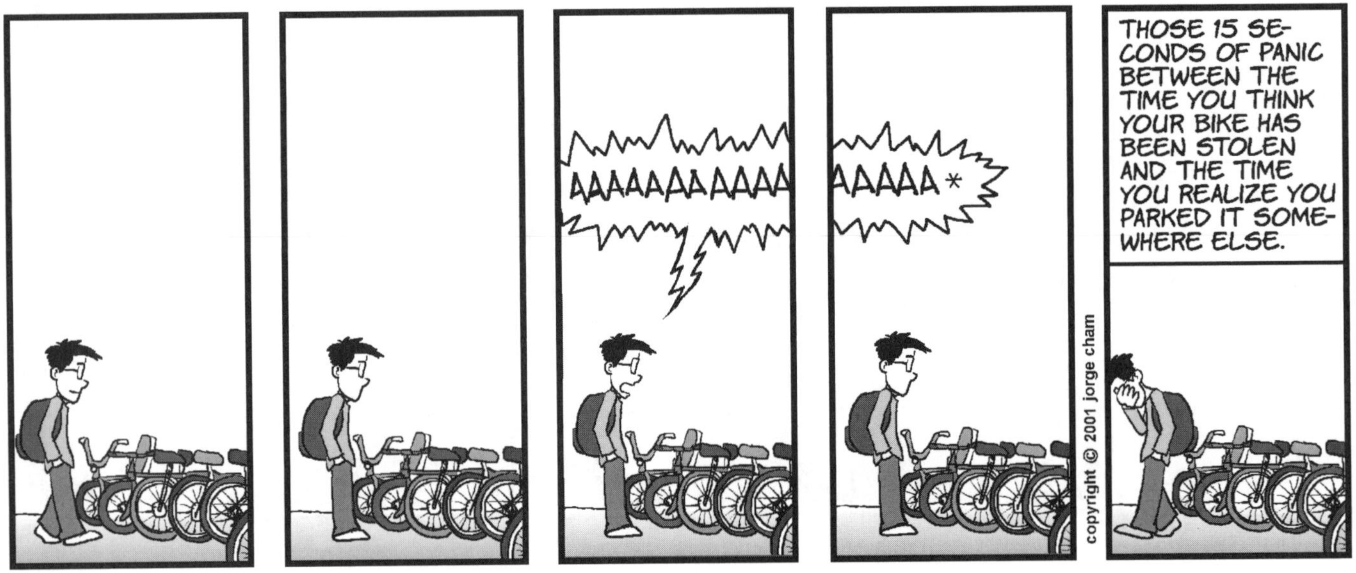
AAAAAAAAAAAAAAAAA*
copyright © 2001 jorge cham
THOSE 15 SECONDS OF PANIC BETWEEN THE TIME YOU THINK YOUR BIKE HAS BEEN STOLEN AND THE TIME YOU REALIZE YOU PARKED IT SOMEWHERE ELSE.

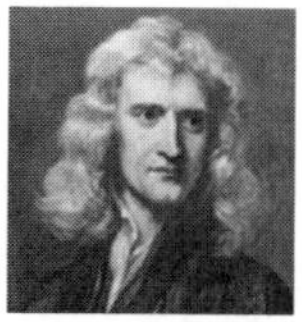

NEWTON'S THREE LAWS OF GRADUATION

Though famous for his seminal work in Mechanics, Isaac Newton's theories on the prediction of a doctoral graduation formulated while still a grad student at Cambridge remain his most important contribution to academia.

FIRST LAW

"*A grad student in procrastination tends to stay in procrastination unless an external force is applied to it*"

This postulate is known as the "***Law of Inertia***" and was originally discovered experimentally by Galileo four years before Newton was born when he threatened to cut his grad student's funding. This resulted in a quickening of the student's research progress.

Galileo's observations were later perfected by Descartes through the application of "Weekly Meetings."

Before Galileo's time, it was wrongfully thought that grad students would rest only as long as no work was required of them and that in the absence of external forces, they would graduate by themselves.

(From Encyclopaedia Britannica)

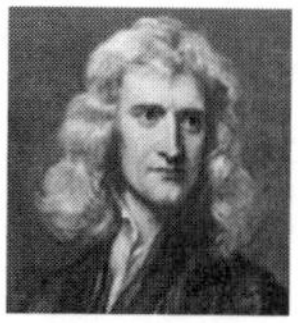

NEWTON'S THREE LAWS OF GRADUATION

First published in 1679, Isaac Newton's "***Procrastinare Unnaturalis Principia Mathematica***" is often considered one of the most important single works in the history of science. Its Second Law is the most powerful of the three, allowing mathematical calculation of the duration of a doctoral degree.

SECOND LAW

"*The age,* **a**, *of a doctoral process is directly proportional to the flexibility,* **f**, *given by the advisor and inversely proportional to the student's motivation,* **m**"

Mathematically, this postulate translates to:

$$age_{PhD} = \frac{flexibility}{motivation}$$

$$\mathbf{a} = \mathbf{F} / \mathbf{m}$$

$$\therefore \mathbf{F} = \mathbf{m}\,\mathbf{a}$$

This Law is a quantitative description of the effect of the forces experienced by a grad student. A highly motivated student may still remain in grad school given enough flexibility. As motivation goes to zero, the duration of the PhD goes to infinity.

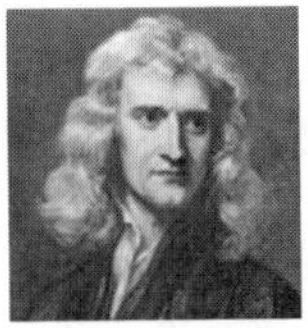

NEWTON'S THREE LAWS OF GRADUATION

Having postulated the first two Laws of Graduation, Isaac Newton the grad student was still perplexed by this paradox: If indeed the first two Laws accounted for the forces which delayed graduation, why doesn't explicit awareness of these forces allow a grad student to graduate?

It is believed that Newton practically abandoned his graduate research in Celestial Mechanics to pursue this paradox and develop his Third Law.

THIRD LAW

"For every action towards graduation there is an equal and opposite distraction"

This Law states that, regardless of the nature of the interaction with the advisor, every force for productivity acting on a grad student is accompanied by an equal and opposing useless activity such that the net advancement in thesis progress is zero.

Newton's Laws of Graduation were ultimately shown to be an approximation of the more complete description of Graduation Mechanics given by Einstein's Special Theory of Research Inactivity.

Einstein's theory, developed during his graduate work in Zurich, explains the general phenomena that, relative to the grad student, time slows down to nearly a standstill.

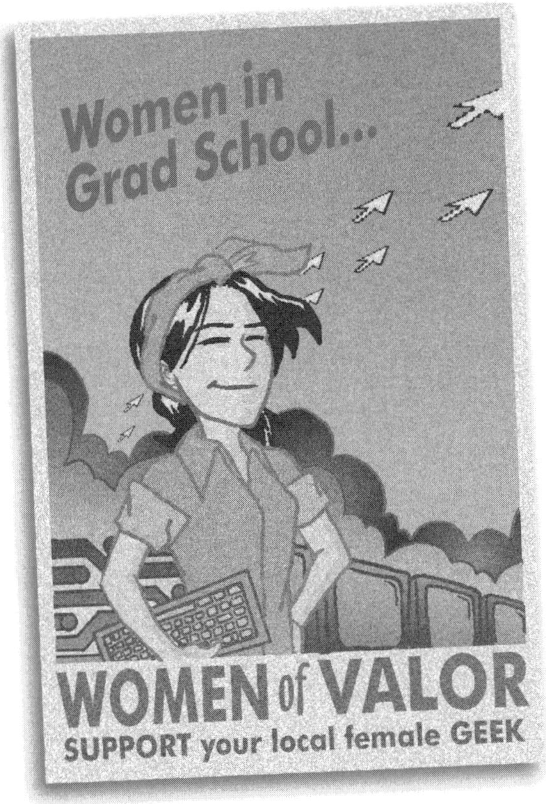
Women in
Grad School...
WOMEN of VALOR
SUPPORT your local female GEEK

P.H.D. PROPAGANDA

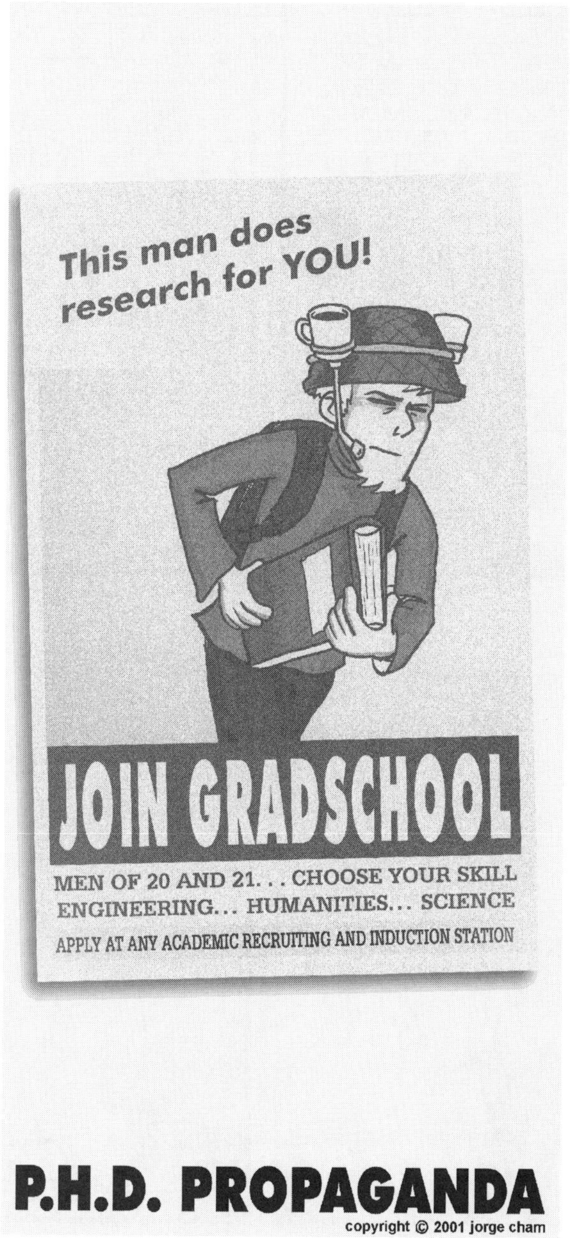
This man does research for YOU!
JOIN GRADSCHOOL
MEN OF 20 AND 21. . . CHOOSE YOUR SKILL
ENGINEERING. . . HUMANITIES. . . SCIENCE
APPLY AT ANY ACADEMIC RECRUITING AND INDUCTION STATION
P.H.D. PROPAGANDA
copyright © 2001 jorge cham

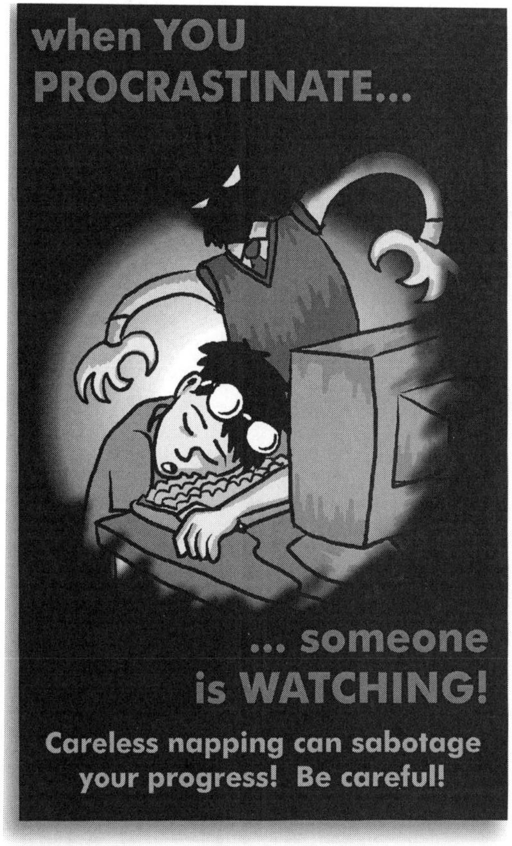
when YOU PROCRASTINATE...
... someone is WATCHING!
Careless napping can sabotage your progress! Be careful!

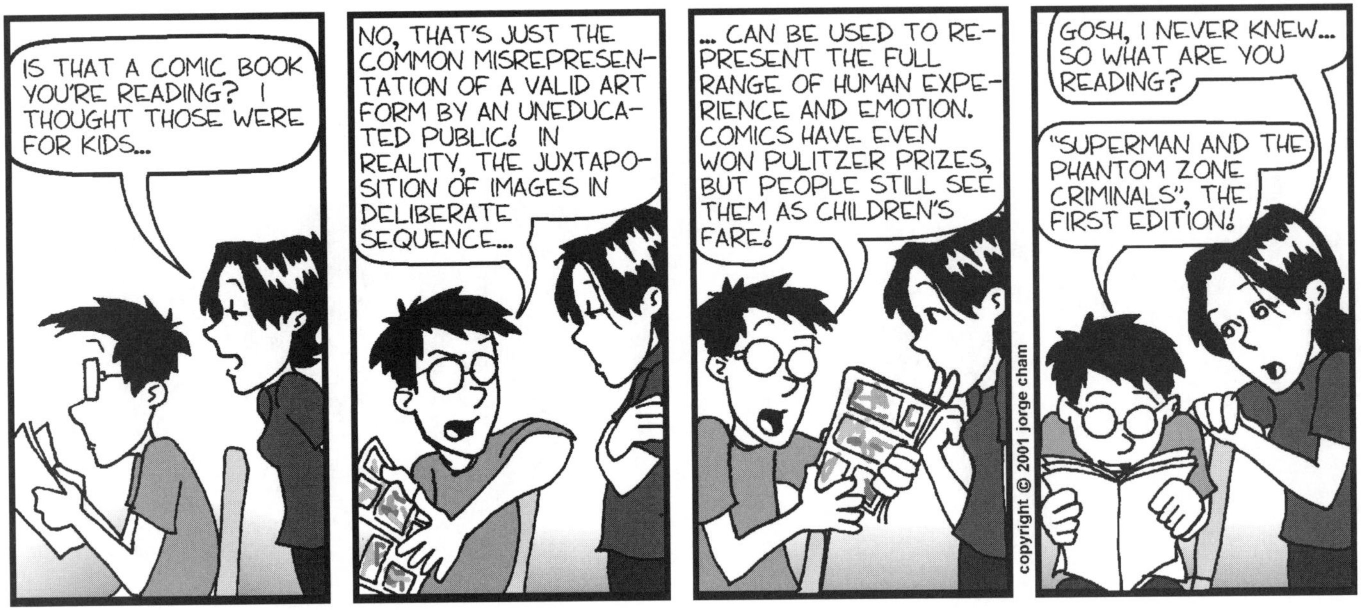
IS THAT A COMIC BOOK YOU'RE READING? I THOUGHT THOSE WERE FOR KIDS...
NO, THAT'S JUST THE COMMON MISREPRESENTATION OF A VALID ART FORM BY AN UNEDUCATED PUBLIC! IN REALITY, THE JUXTAPOSITION OF IMAGES IN DELIBERATE SEQUENCE...
... CAN BE USED TO REPRESENT THE FULL RANGE OF HUMAN EXPERIENCE AND EMOTION. COMICS HAVE EVEN WON PULITZER PRIZES, BUT PEOPLE STILL SEE THEM AS CHILDREN'S FARE!
copyright © 2001 jorge cham
GOSH, I NEVER KNEW... SO WHAT ARE YOU READING?
"SUPERMAN AND THE PHANTOM ZONE CRIMINALS", THE FIRST EDITION!

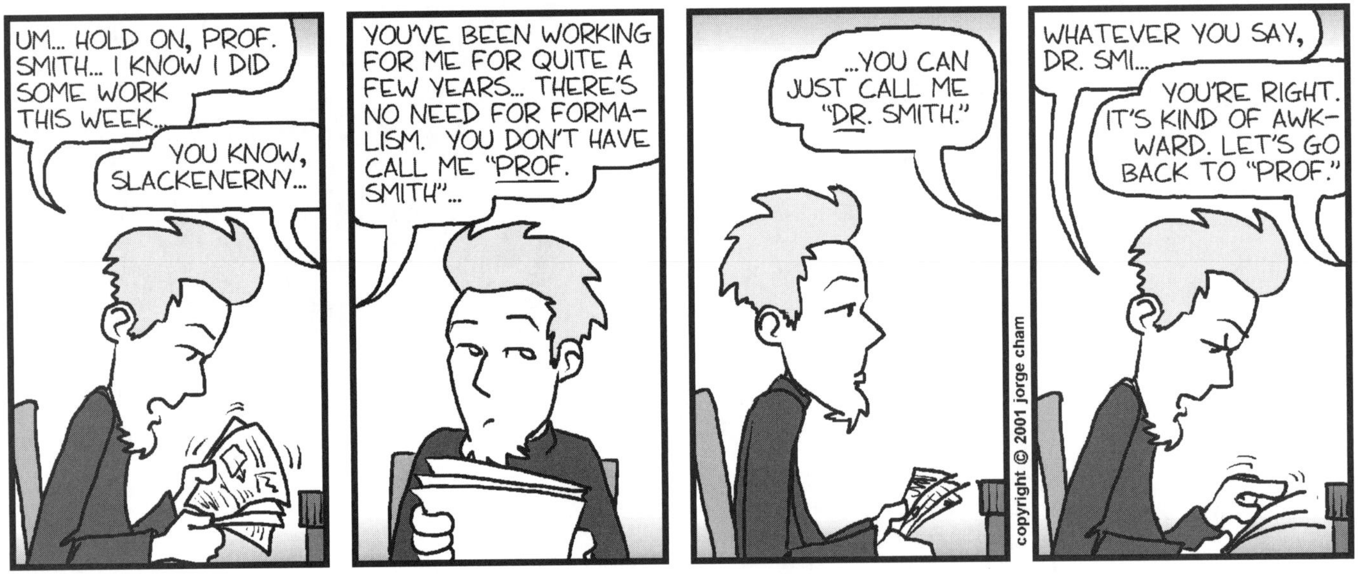
UM... HOLD ON, PROF. SMITH... I KNOW I DID SOME WORK THIS WEEK...
YOU KNOW, SLACKENERNY...
YOU'VE BEEN WORKING FOR ME FOR QUITE A FEW YEARS... THERE'S NO NEED FOR FORMALISM. YOU DON'T HAVE CALL ME "PROF. SMITH"...
...YOU CAN JUST CALL ME "DR. SMITH."
copyright © 2001 jorge cham
WHATEVER YOU SAY, DR. SMI...
YOU'RE RIGHT. IT'S KIND OF AWKWARD. LET'S GO BACK TO "PROF."

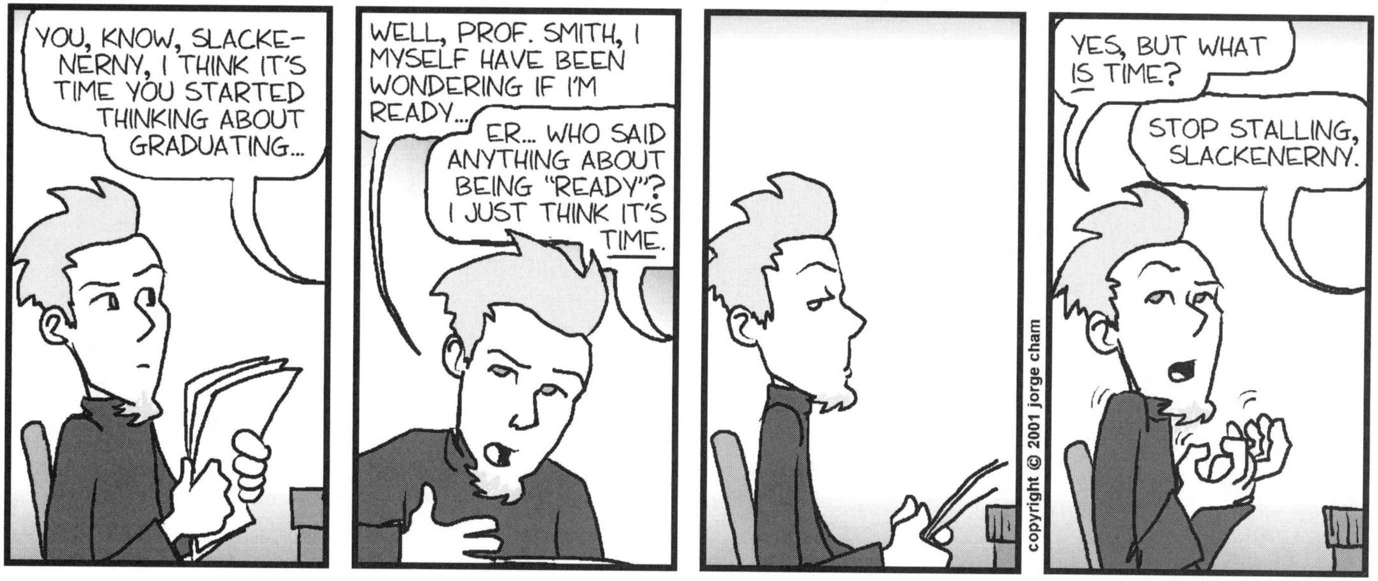
YOU, KNOW, SLACKE-NERNY, I THINK IT'S TIME YOU STARTED THINKING ABOUT GRADUATING...
WELL, PROF. SMITH, I MYSELF HAVE BEEN WONDERING IF I'M READY...
ER... WHO SAID ANYTHING ABOUT BEING "READY"? I JUST THINK IT'S TIME.
YES, BUT WHAT IS TIME?
STOP STALLING, SLACKENERNY.
copyright © 2001 jorge cham

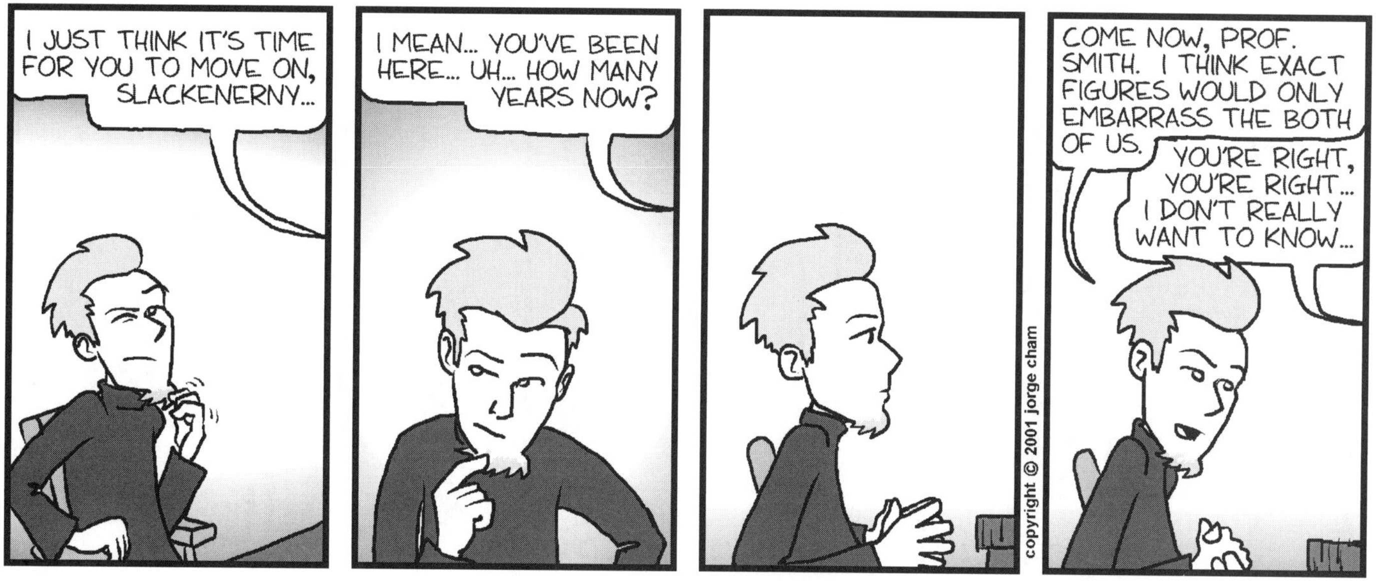
I JUST THINK IT'S TIME FOR YOU TO MOVE ON, SLACKENERNY...
I MEAN... YOU'VE BEEN HERE... UH... HOW MANY YEARS NOW?
COME NOW, PROF. SMITH. I THINK EXACT FIGURES WOULD ONLY EMBARRASS THE BOTH OF US.
YOU'RE RIGHT, YOU'RE RIGHT... I DON'T REALLY WANT TO KNOW...
copyright © 2001 jorge cham

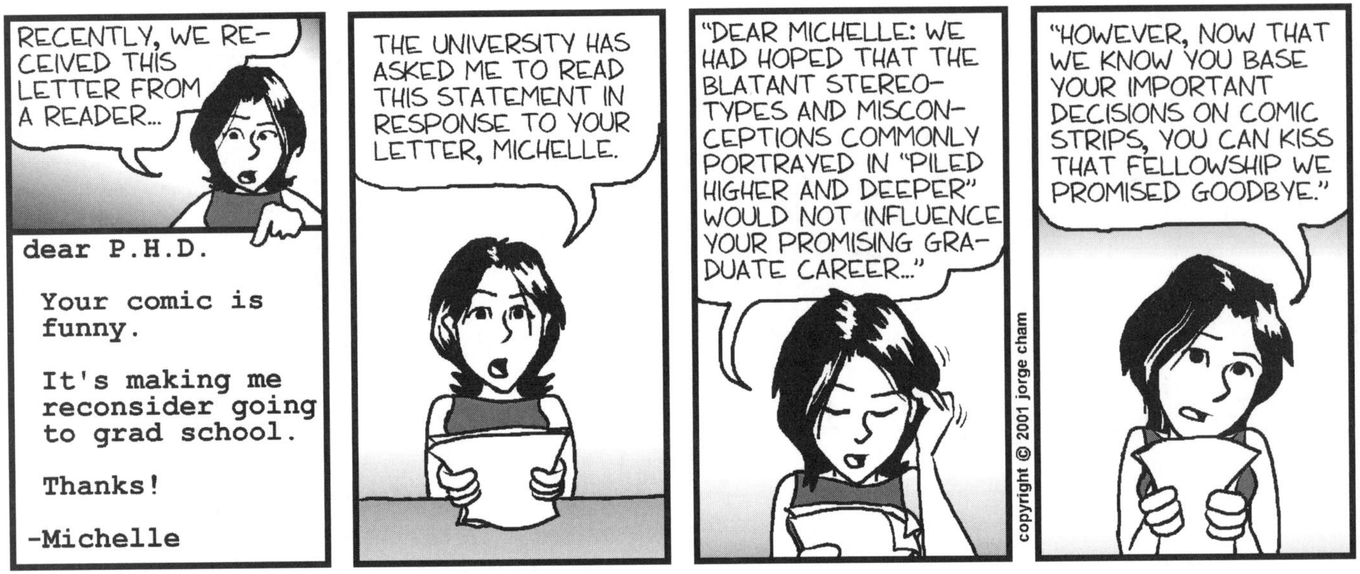
RECENTLY, WE RECEIVED THIS LETTER FROM A READER...
dear P.H.D.
Your comic is funny.
It's making me reconsider going to grad school.
Thanks!
-Michelle
THE UNIVERSITY HAS ASKED ME TO READ THIS STATEMENT IN RESPONSE TO YOUR LETTER, MICHELLE.
"DEAR MICHELLE: WE HAD HOPED THAT THE BLATANT STEREOTYPES AND MISCONCEPTIONS COMMONLY PORTRAYED IN "PILED HIGHER AND DEEPER" WOULD NOT INFLUENCE YOUR PROMISING GRADUATE CAREER..."
copyright © 2001 jorge cham
"HOWEVER, NOW THAT WE KNOW YOU BASE YOUR IMPORTANT DECISIONS ON COMIC STRIPS, YOU CAN KISS THAT FELLOWSHIP WE PROMISED GOODBYE."

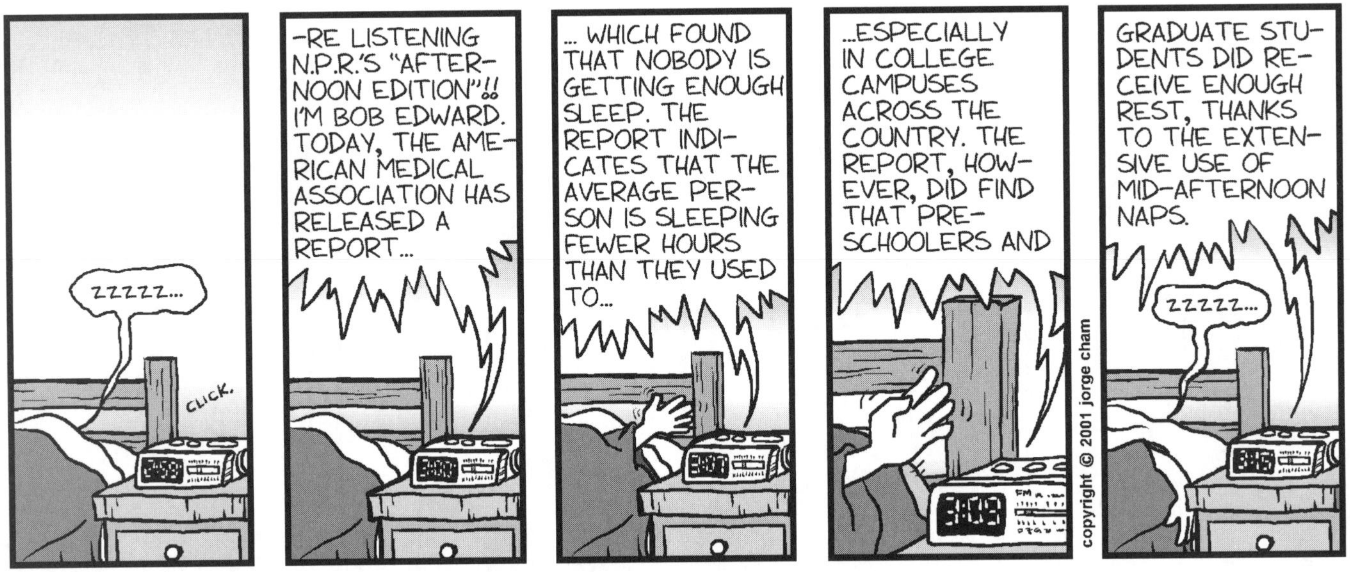
ZZZZZ...
CLICK.
-RE LISTENING N.P.R.'S "AFTERNOON EDITION"!! I'M BOB EDWARD. TODAY, THE AMERICAN MEDICAL ASSOCIATION HAS RELEASED A REPORT...
... WHICH FOUND THAT NOBODY IS GETTING ENOUGH SLEEP. THE REPORT INDICATES THAT THE AVERAGE PERSON IS SLEEPING FEWER HOURS THAN THEY USED TO...
...ESPECIALLY IN COLLEGE CAMPUSES ACROSS THE COUNTRY. THE REPORT, HOWEVER, DID FIND THAT PRESCHOOLERS AND
copyright © 2001 jorge cham
GRADUATE STUDENTS DID RECEIVE ENOUGH REST, THANKS TO THE EXTENSIVE USE OF MID-AFTERNOON NAPS.
ZZZZZ...

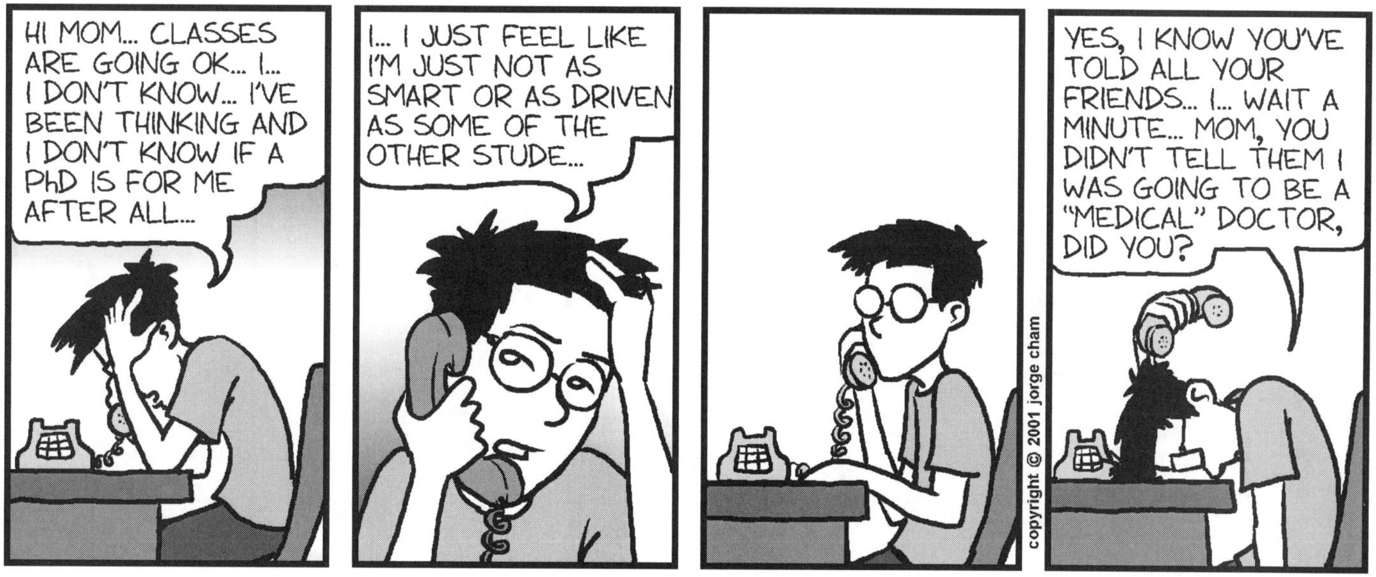
HI MOM... CLASSES ARE GOING OK... I... I DON'T KNOW... I'VE BEEN THINKING AND I DON'T KNOW IF A PhD IS FOR ME AFTER ALL...
I... I JUST FEEL LIKE I'M JUST NOT AS SMART OR AS DRIVEN AS SOME OF THE OTHER STUDE...
copyright © 2001 jorge cham
YES, I KNOW YOU'VE TOLD ALL YOUR FRIENDS... I... WAIT A MINUTE... MOM, YOU DIDN'T TELL THEM I WAS GOING TO BE A "MEDICAL" DOCTOR, DID YOU?

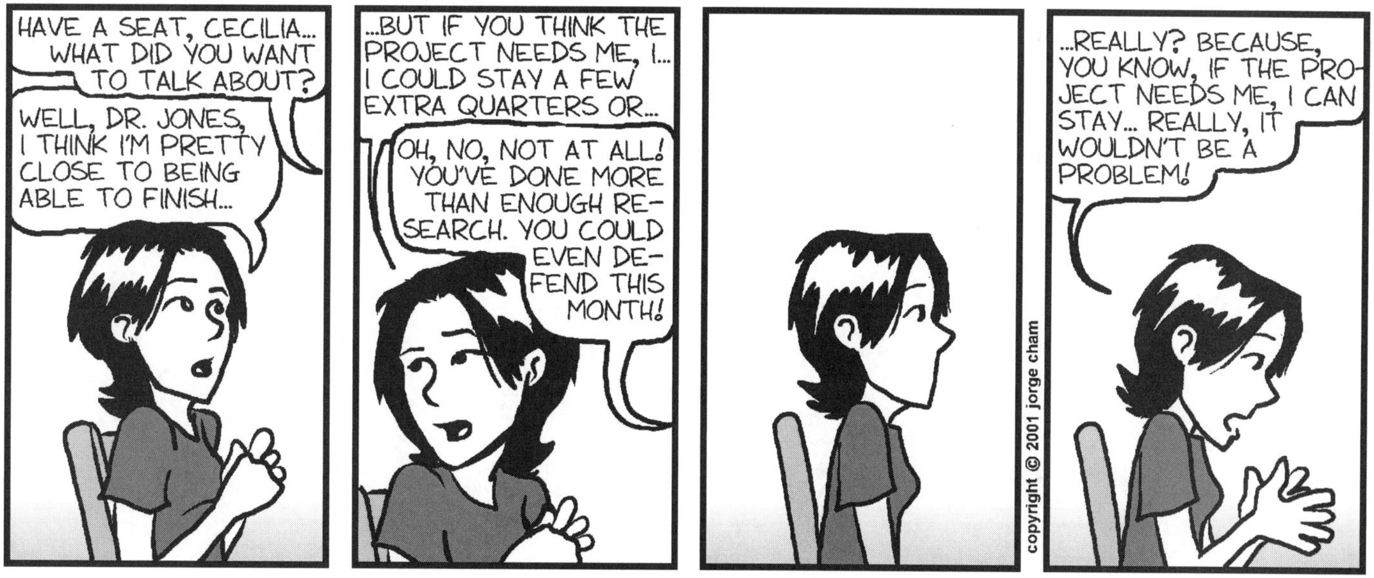
HAVE A SEAT, CECILIA... WHAT DID YOU WANT TO TALK ABOUT?
WELL, DR. JONES, I THINK I'M PRETTY CLOSE TO BEING ABLE TO FINISH...
...BUT IF YOU THINK THE PROJECT NEEDS ME, I... I COULD STAY A FEW EXTRA QUARTERS OR...
OH, NO, NOT AT ALL! YOU'VE DONE MORE THAN ENOUGH RESEARCH. YOU COULD EVEN DEFEND THIS MONTH!
copyright © 2001 jorge cham
...REALLY? BECAUSE, YOU KNOW, IF THE PROJECT NEEDS ME, I CAN STAY... REALLY, IT WOULDN'T BE A PROBLEM!

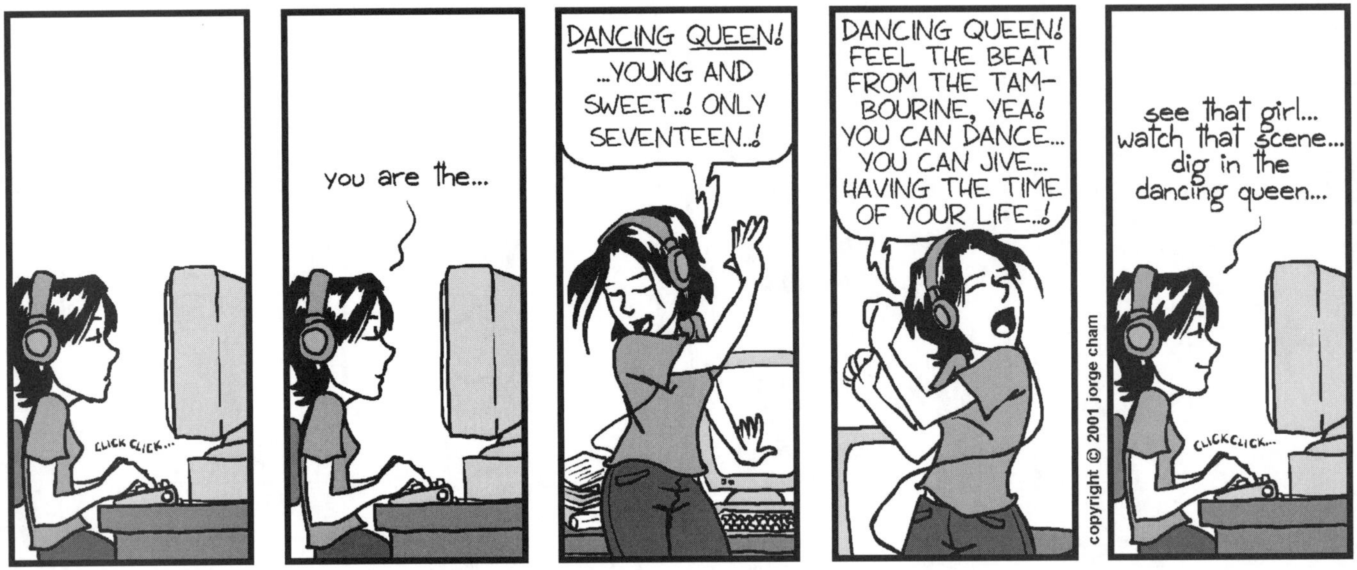
CLICK CLICK...
you are the...
DANCING QUEEN! ...YOUNG AND SWEET..! ONLY SEVENTEEN..!
DANCING QUEEN! FEEL THE BEAT FROM THE TAM-BOURINE, YEA! YOU CAN DANCE... YOU CAN JIVE... HAVING THE TIME OF YOUR LIFE..!
copyright © 2001 jorge cham
see that girl... watch that scene... dig in the dancing queen...
CLICKCLICK...

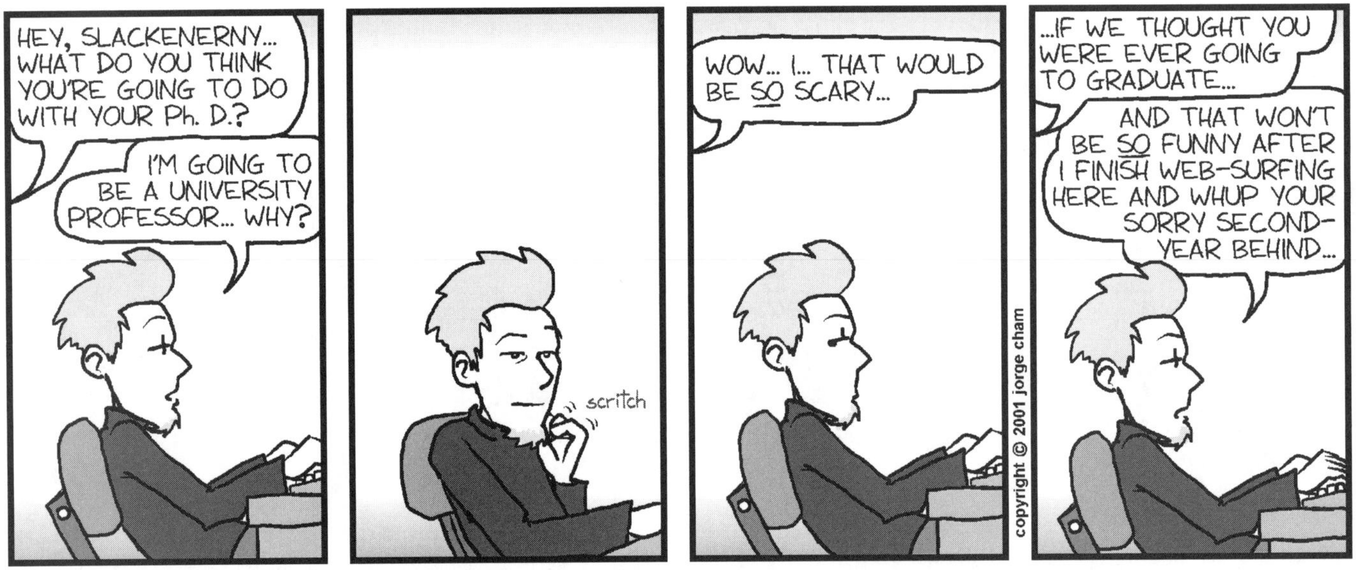
HEY, SLACKENERNY... WHAT DO YOU THINK YOU'RE GOING TO DO WITH YOUR Ph. D.?
I'M GOING TO BE A UNIVERSITY PROFESSOR... WHY?
scritch
WOW... I... THAT WOULD BE SO SCARY...
copyright © 2001 jorge cham
...IF WE THOUGHT YOU WERE EVER GOING TO GRADUATE...
AND THAT WON'T BE SO FUNNY AFTER I FINISH WEB-SURFING HERE AND WHUP YOUR SORRY SECOND-YEAR BEHIND...

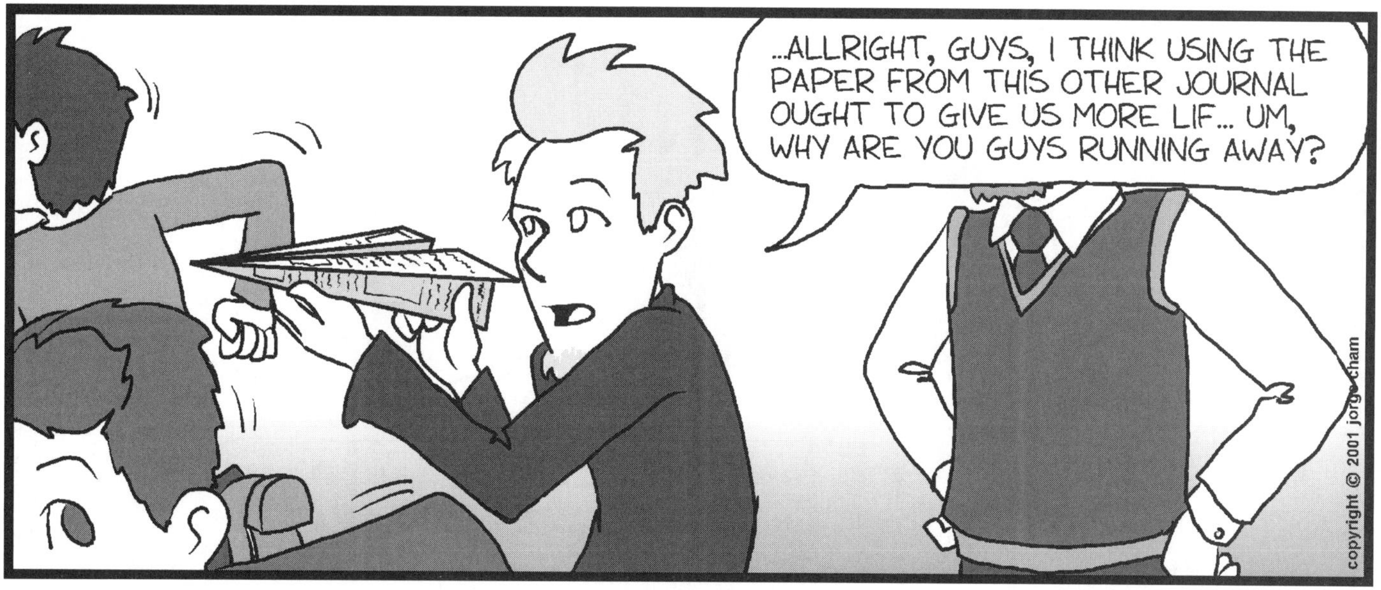
...ALLRIGHT, GUYS, I THINK USING THE PAPER FROM THIS OTHER JOURNAL OUGHT TO GIVE US MORE LIF... UM, WHY ARE YOU GUYS RUNNING AWAY?
copyright © 2001 jorge cham

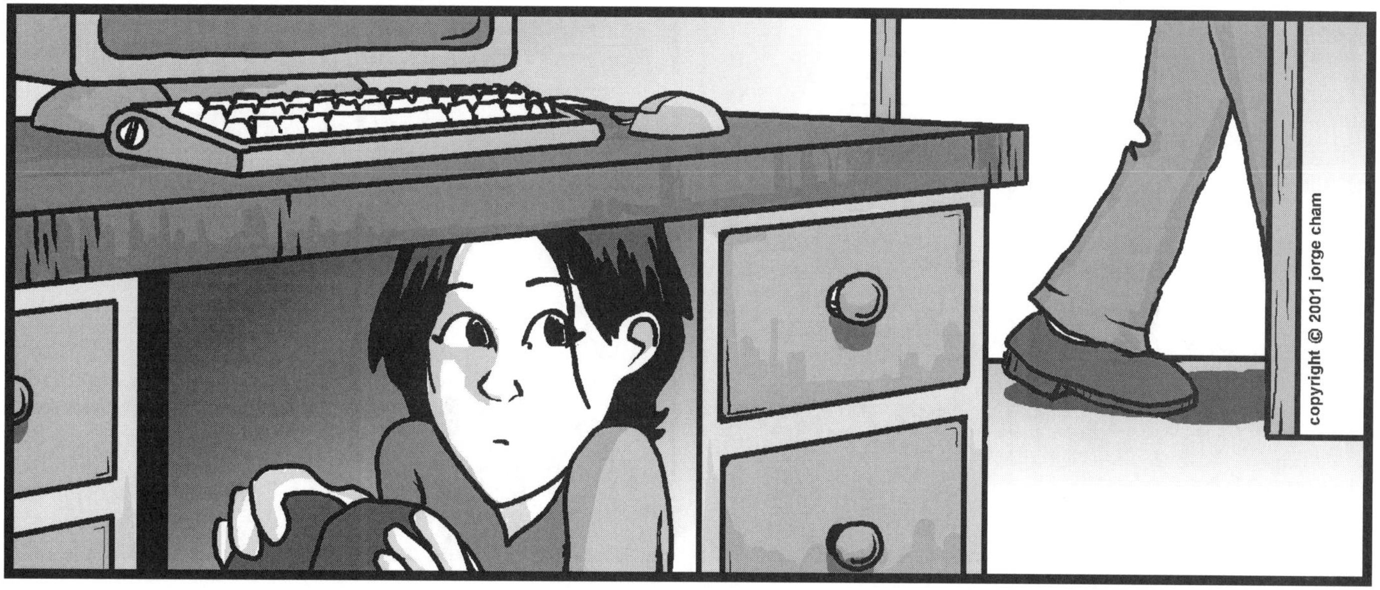
copyright © 2001 jorge cham

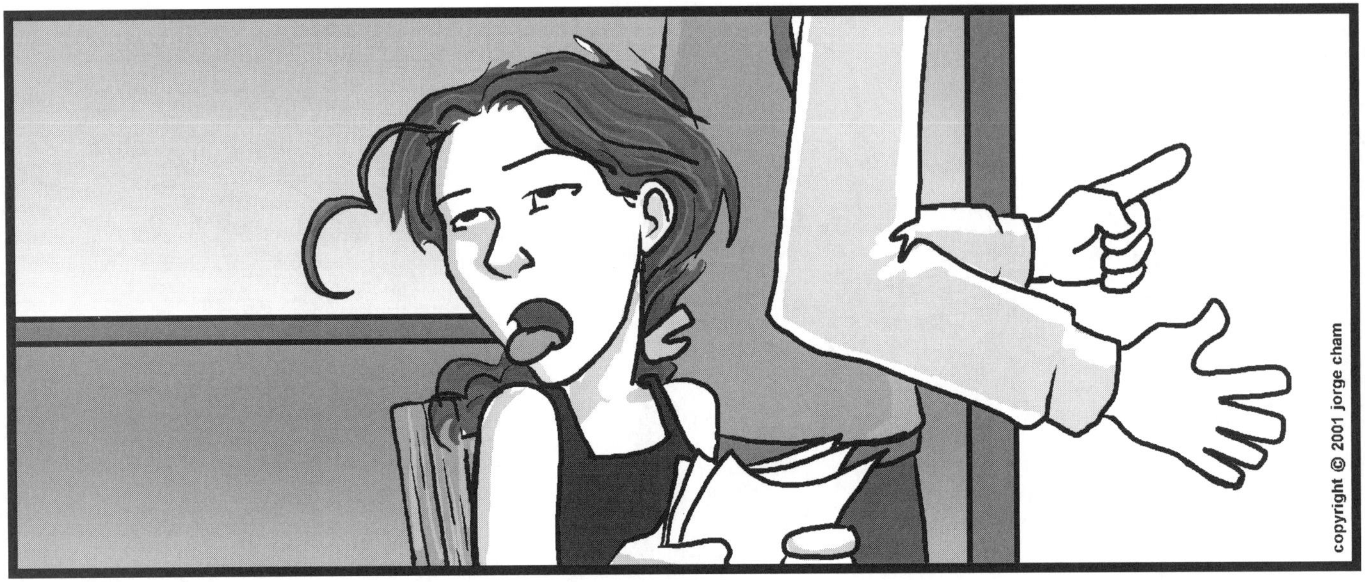
copyright © 2001 jorge cham

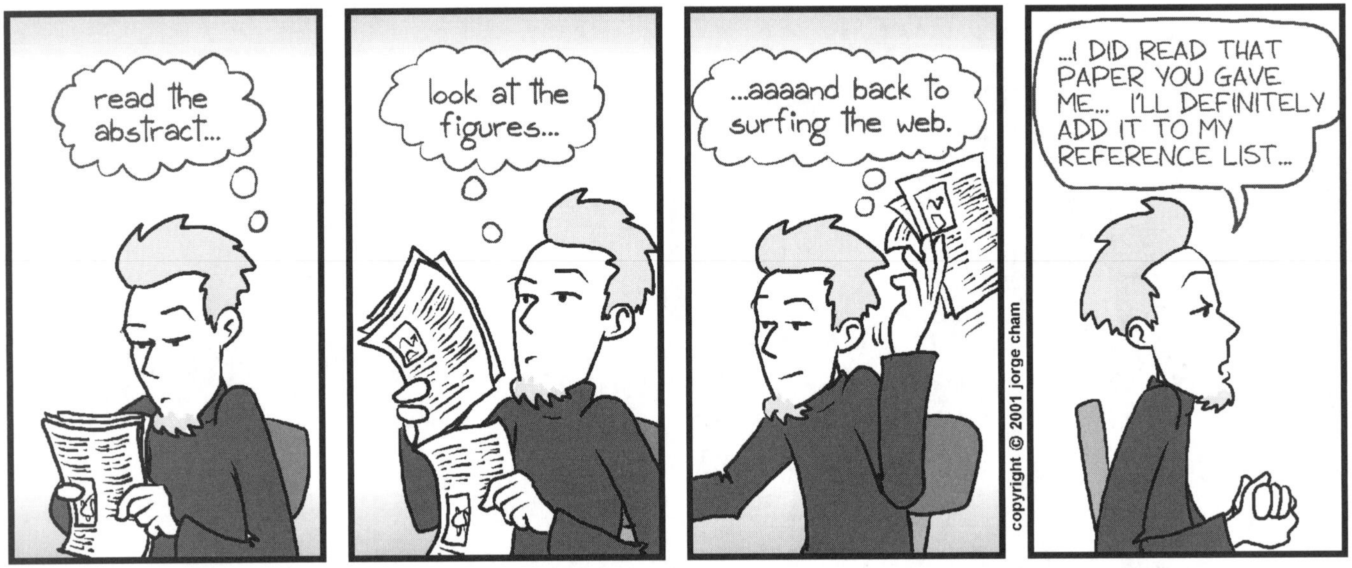
read the abstract...
look at the figures...
...aaaand back to surfing the web.
copyright © 2001 jorge cham
...I DID READ THAT PAPER YOU GAVE ME... I'LL DEFINITELY ADD IT TO MY REFERENCE LIST...

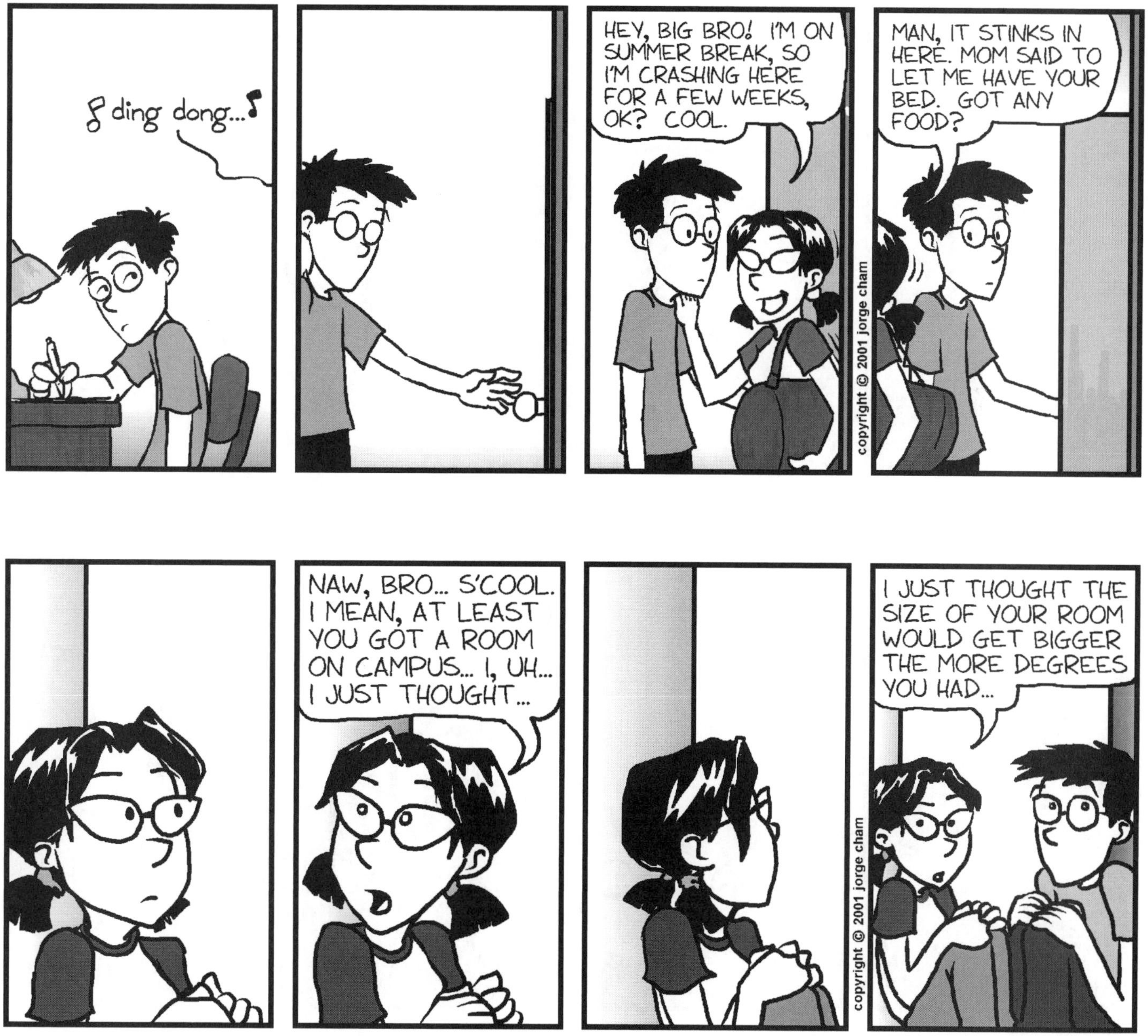
ding dong...
HEY, BIG BRO! I'M ON SUMMER BREAK, SO I'M CRASHING HERE FOR A FEW WEEKS, OK? COOL.
copyright © 2001 jorge cham
MAN, IT STINKS IN HERE. MOM SAID TO LET ME HAVE YOUR BED. GOT ANY FOOD?
NAW, BRO... S'COOL. I MEAN, AT LEAST YOU GOT A ROOM ON CAMPUS... I, UH... I JUST THOUGHT...
copyright © 2001 jorge cham
I JUST THOUGHT THE SIZE OF YOUR ROOM WOULD GET BIGGER THE MORE DEGREES YOU HAD...

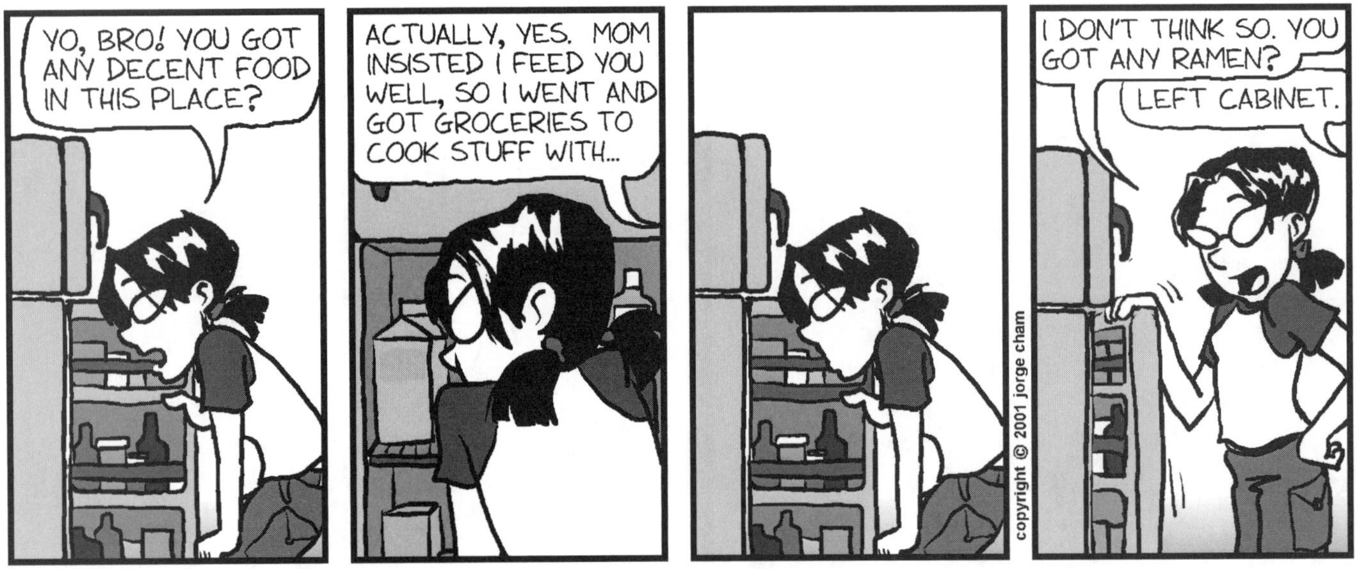
YO, BRO! YOU GOT ANY DECENT FOOD IN THIS PLACE?
ACTUALLY, YES. MOM INSISTED I FEED YOU WELL, SO I WENT AND GOT GROCERIES TO COOK STUFF WITH...
I DON'T THINK SO. YOU GOT ANY RAMEN?
LEFT CABINET.
copyright © 2001 jorge cham

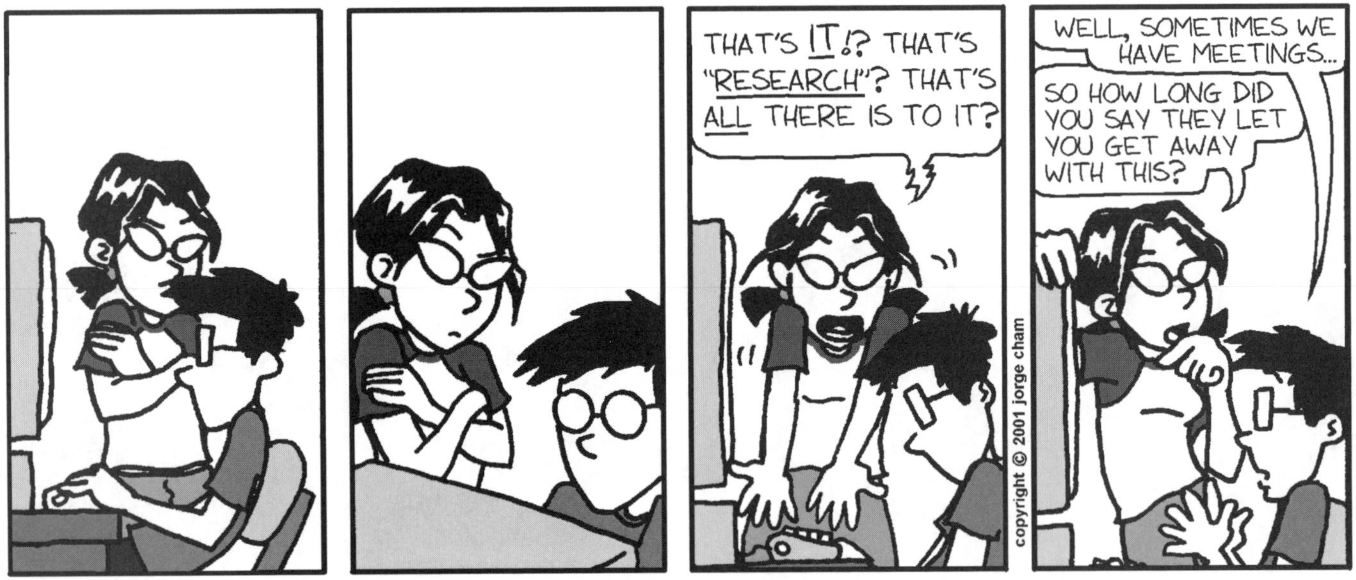
THAT'S IT!? THAT'S "RESEARCH"? THAT'S ALL THERE IS TO IT?
WELL, SOMETIMES WE HAVE MEETINGS...
SO HOW LONG DID YOU SAY THEY LET YOU GET AWAY WITH THIS?
copyright © 2001 jorge cham

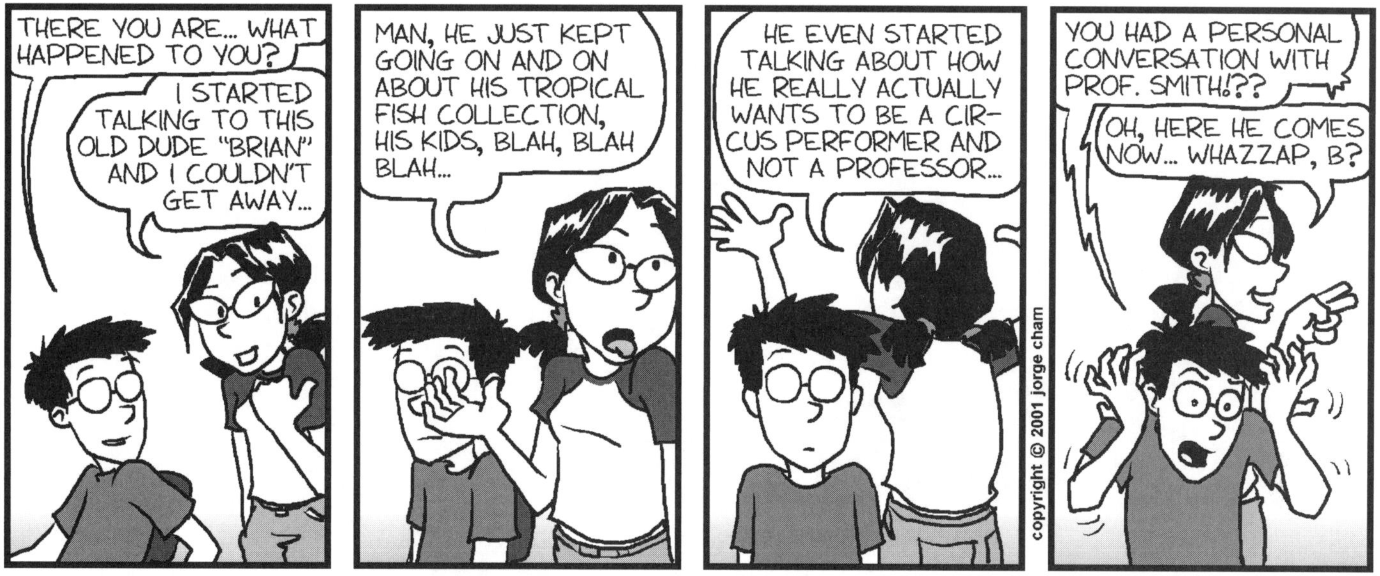
THERE YOU ARE... WHAT HAPPENED TO YOU?
I STARTED TALKING TO THIS OLD DUDE "BRIAN" AND I COULDN'T GET AWAY...
MAN, HE JUST KEPT GOING ON AND ON ABOUT HIS TROPICAL FISH COLLECTION, HIS KIDS, BLAH, BLAH BLAH...
HE EVEN STARTED TALKING ABOUT HOW HE REALLY ACTUALLY WANTS TO BE A CIR-CUS PERFORMER AND NOT A PROFESSOR...
copyright © 2001 jorge cham
YOU HAD A PERSONAL CONVERSATION WITH PROF. SMITH!??
OH, HERE HE COMES NOW... WHAZZAP, B?

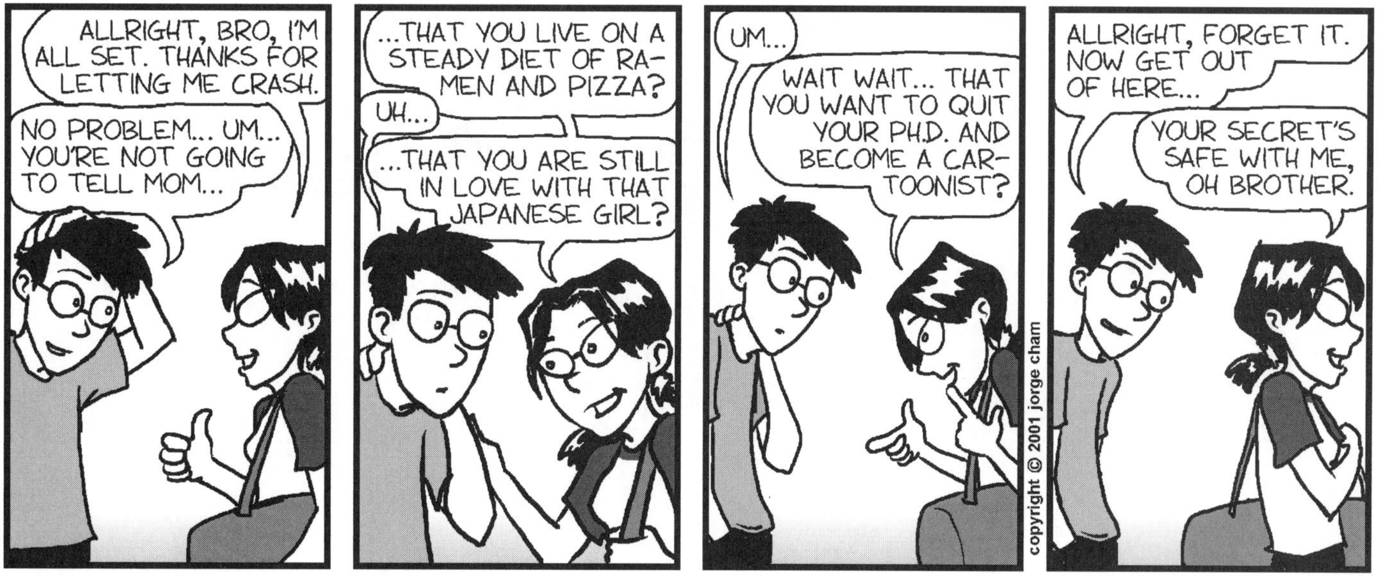
ALLRIGHT, BRO, I'M ALL SET. THANKS FOR LETTING ME CRASH.
NO PROBLEM... UM... YOU'RE NOT GOING TO TELL MOM...
...THAT YOU LIVE ON A STEADY DIET OF RA-MEN AND PIZZA?
UH...
...THAT YOU ARE STILL IN LOVE WITH THAT JAPANESE GIRL?
UM...
WAIT WAIT... THAT YOU WANT TO QUIT YOUR PH.D. AND BECOME A CAR-TOONIST?
copyright © 2001 jorge cham
ALLRIGHT, FORGET IT. NOW GET OUT OF HERE...
YOUR SECRET'S SAFE WITH ME, OH BROTHER.

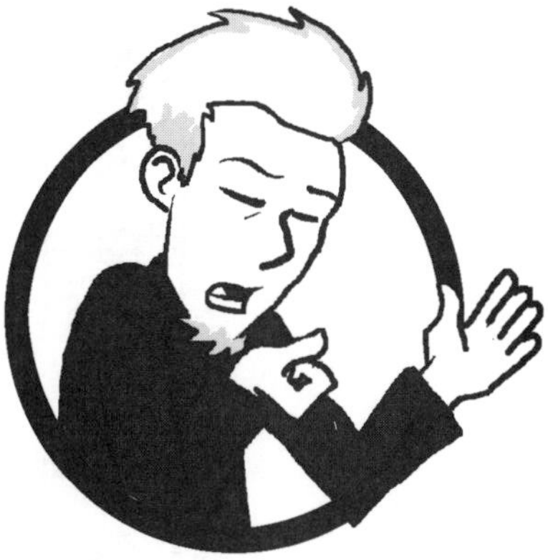

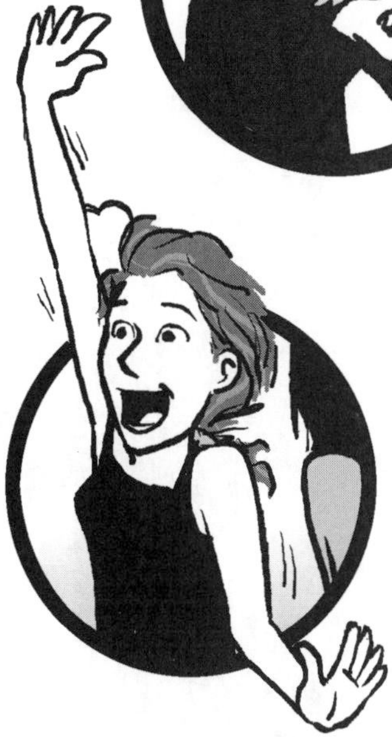

YEAR FIVE
2001-2002

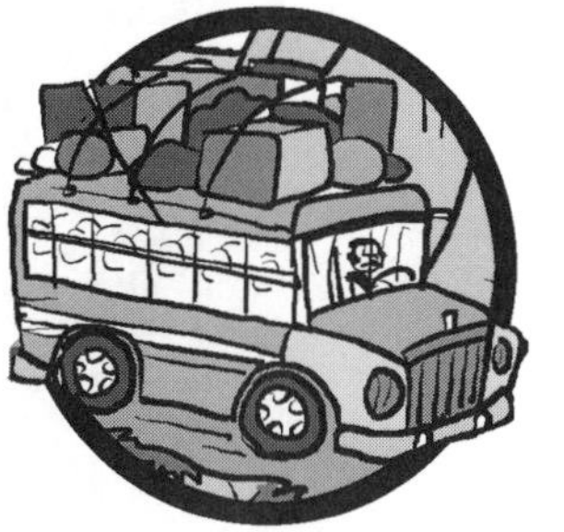

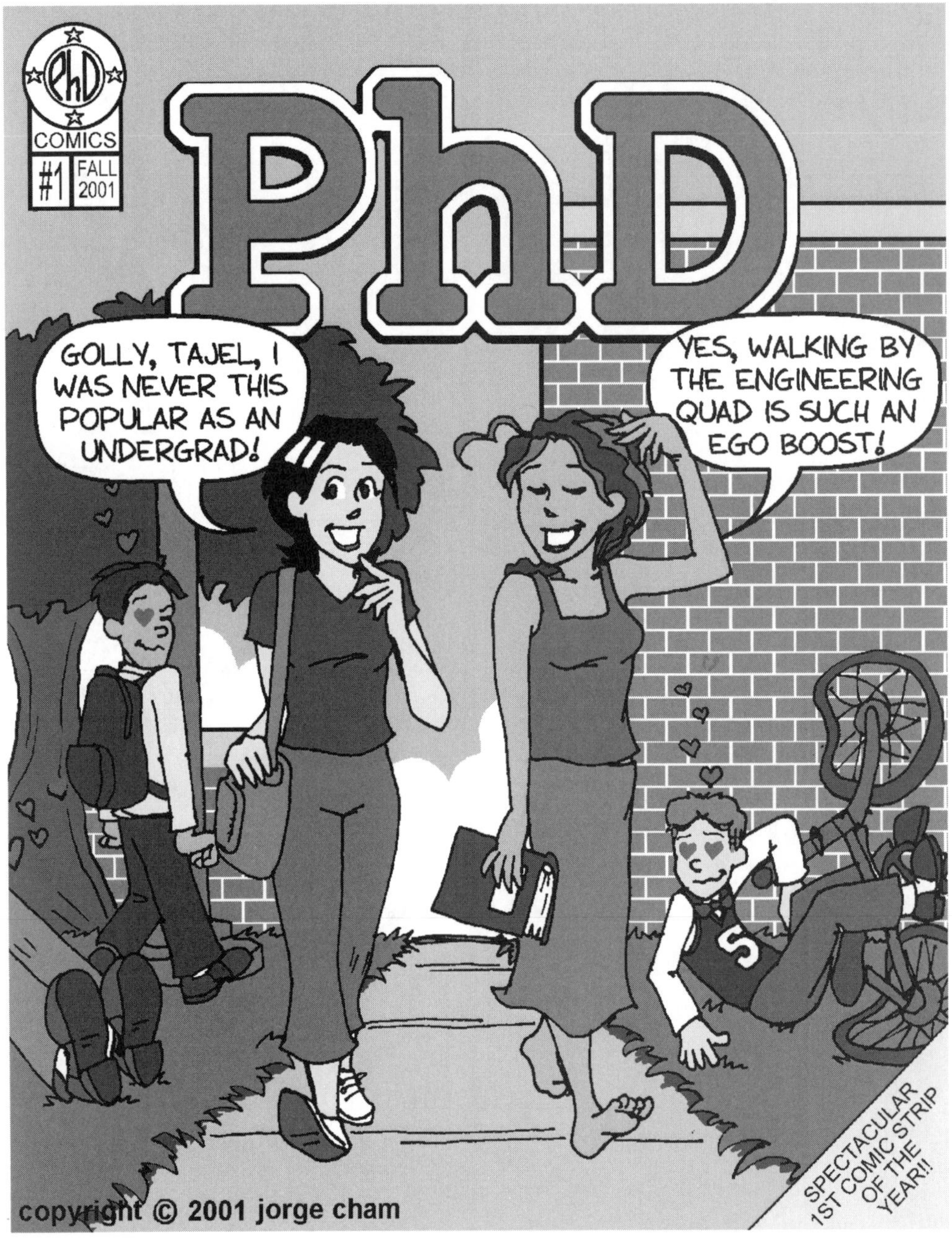
COMICS
#1 FALL 2001
PhD
GOLLY, TAJEL, I WAS NEVER THIS POPULAR AS AN UNDERGRAD!
YES, WALKING BY THE ENGINEERING QUAD IS SUCH AN EGO BOOST!
SPECTACULAR 1ST COMIC STRIP OF THE YEAR!!
copyright © 2001 jorge cham

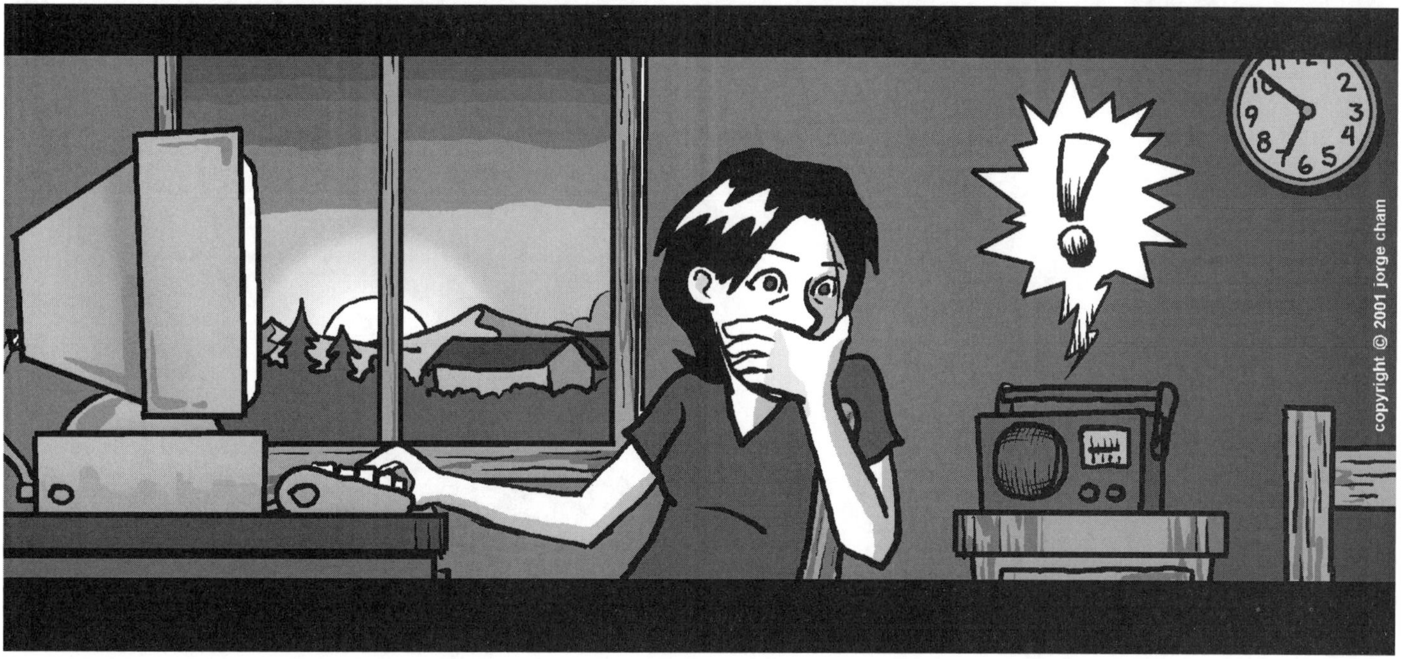
!
copyright © 2001 jorge cham

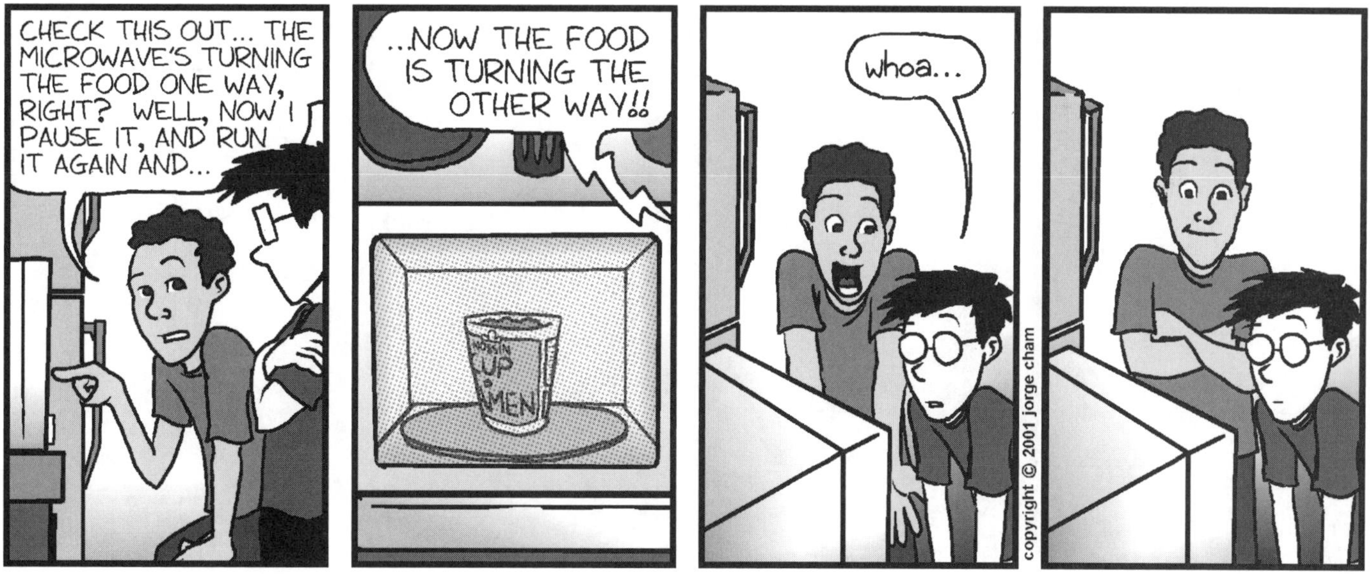
CHECK THIS OUT... THE MICROWAVE'S TURNING THE FOOD ONE WAY, RIGHT? WELL, NOW I PAUSE IT, AND RUN IT AGAIN AND...
...NOW THE FOOD IS TURNING THE OTHER WAY!!
whoa...
copyright © 2001 jorge cham

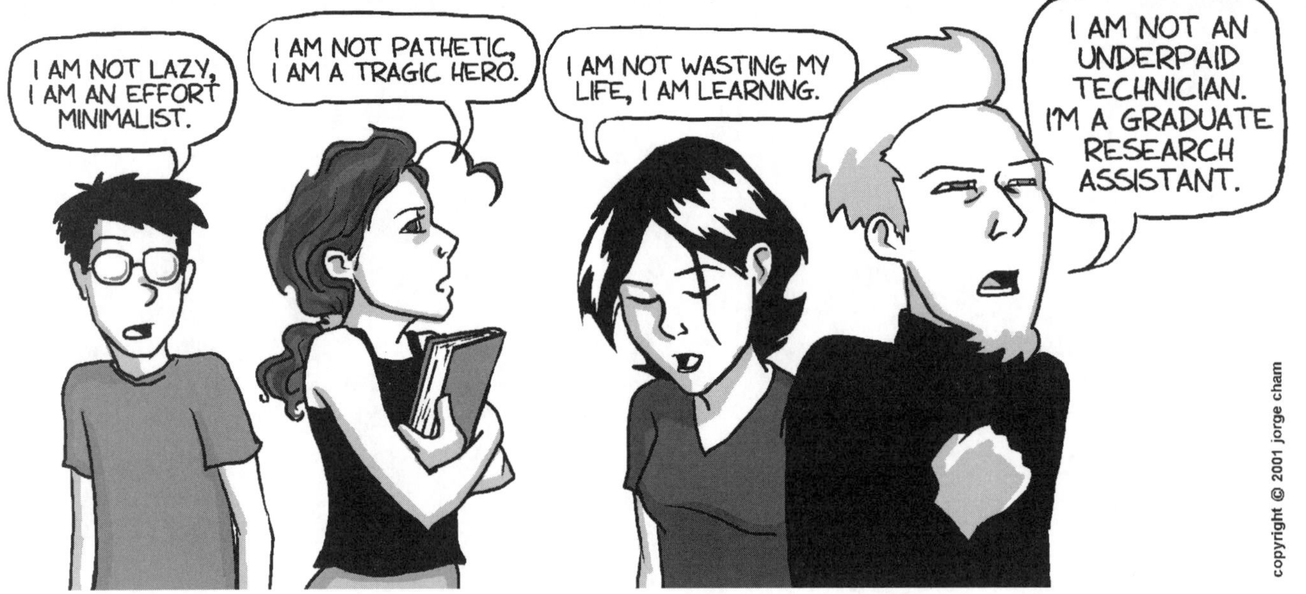
I AM NOT LAZY, I AM AN EFFORT MINIMALIST.
I AM NOT PATHETIC, I AM A TRAGIC HERO.
I AM NOT WASTING MY LIFE, I AM LEARNING.
I AM NOT AN UNDERPAID TECHNICIAN. I'M A GRADUATE RESEARCH ASSISTANT.
copyright © 2001 jorge cham

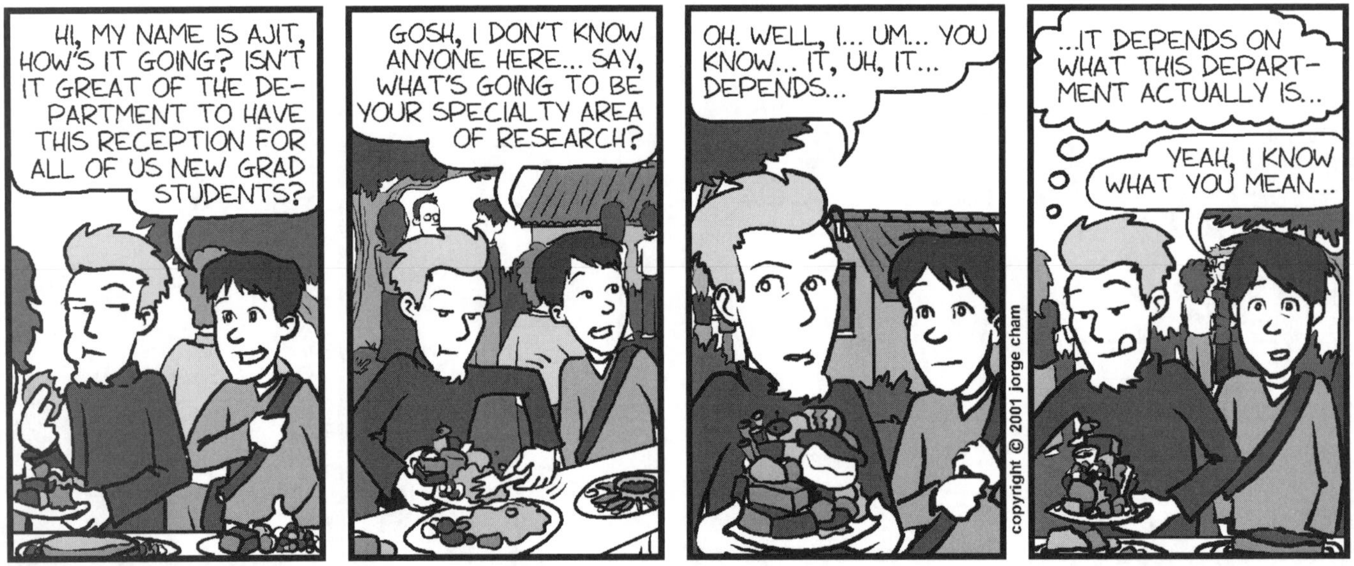
HI, MY NAME IS AJIT, HOW'S IT GOING? ISN'T IT GREAT OF THE DE-PARTMENT TO HAVE THIS RECEPTION FOR ALL OF US NEW GRAD STUDENTS?
GOSH, I DON'T KNOW ANYONE HERE... SAY, WHAT'S GOING TO BE YOUR SPECIALTY AREA OF RESEARCH?
OH. WELL, I... UM... YOU KNOW... IT, UH, IT... DEPENDS...
copyright © 2001 jorge cham
...IT DEPENDS ON WHAT THIS DEPART-MENT ACTUALLY IS...
YEAH, I KNOW WHAT YOU MEAN...

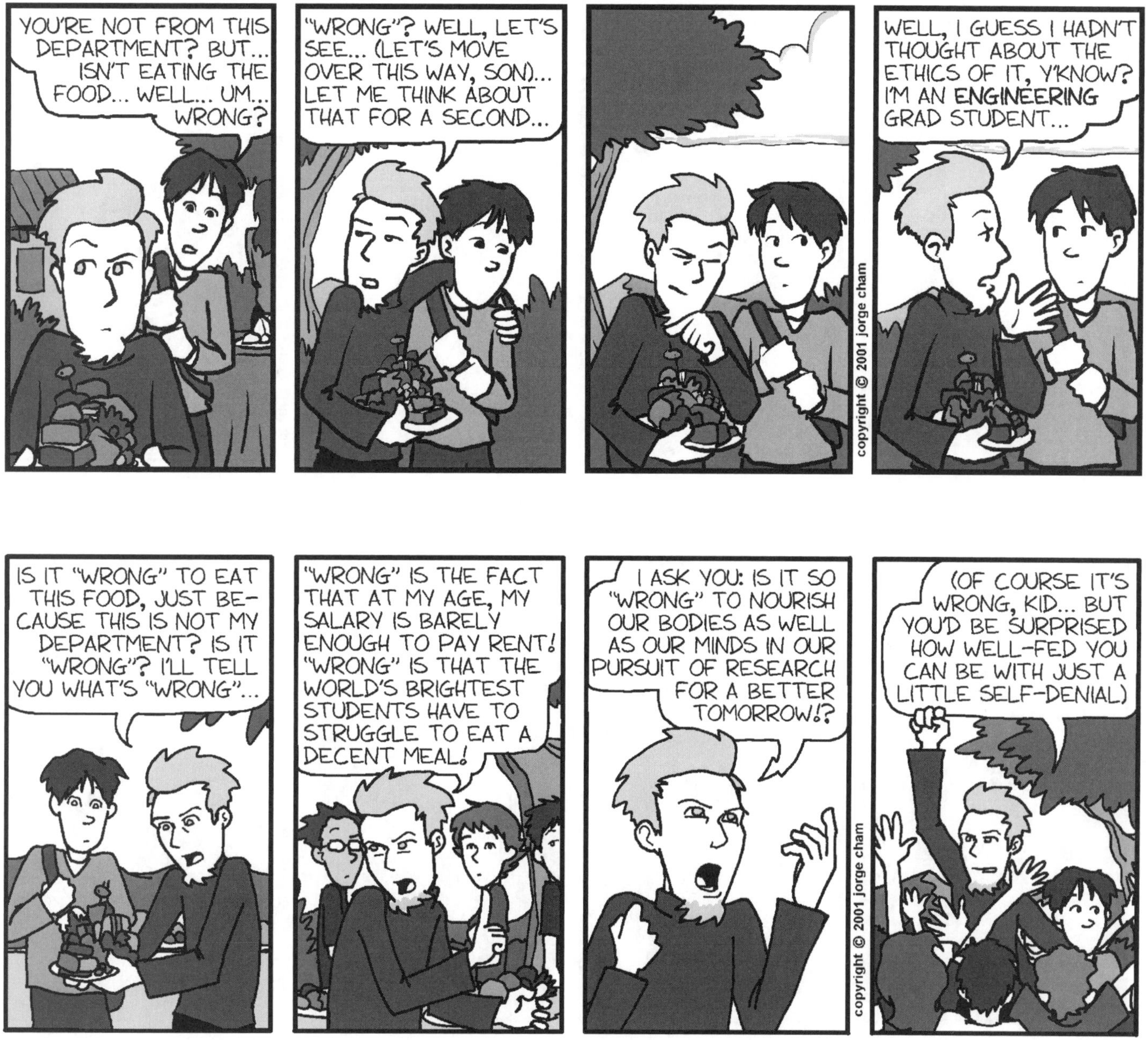
YOU'RE NOT FROM THIS DEPARTMENT? BUT... ISN'T EATING THE FOOD... WELL... UM... WRONG?
"WRONG"? WELL, LET'S SEE... (LET'S MOVE OVER THIS WAY, SON)... LET ME THINK ABOUT THAT FOR A SECOND...
WELL, I GUESS I HADN'T THOUGHT ABOUT THE ETHICS OF IT, Y'KNOW? I'M AN ENGINEERING GRAD STUDENT...
copyright © 2001 jorge cham
IS IT "WRONG" TO EAT THIS FOOD, JUST BECAUSE THIS IS NOT MY DEPARTMENT? IS IT "WRONG"? I'LL TELL YOU WHAT'S "WRONG"...
"WRONG" IS THE FACT THAT AT MY AGE, MY SALARY IS BARELY ENOUGH TO PAY RENT! "WRONG" IS THAT THE WORLD'S BRIGHTEST STUDENTS HAVE TO STRUGGLE TO EAT A DECENT MEAL!
I ASK YOU: IS IT SO "WRONG" TO NOURISH OUR BODIES AS WELL AS OUR MINDS IN OUR PURSUIT OF RESEARCH FOR A BETTER TOMORROW!?
(OF COURSE IT'S WRONG, KID... BUT YOU'D BE SURPRISED HOW WELL-FED YOU CAN BE WITH JUST A LITTLE SELF-DENIAL)
copyright © 2001 jorge cham

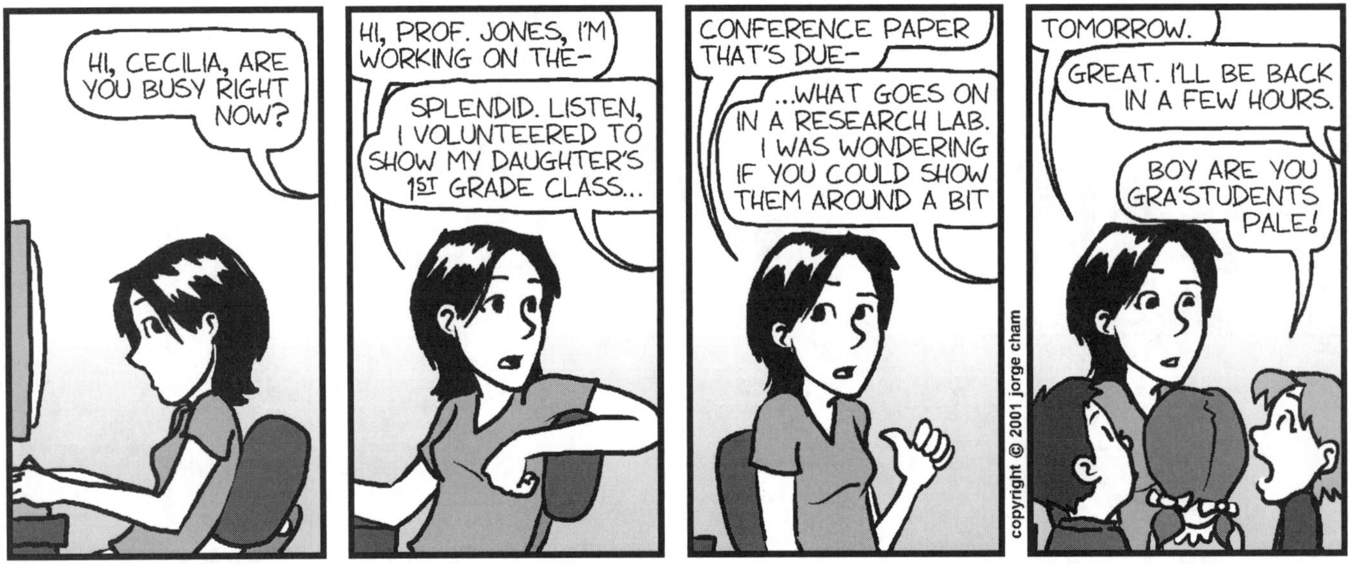
HI, CECILIA, ARE YOU BUSY RIGHT NOW?
HI, PROF. JONES, I'M WORKING ON THE-
SPLENDID. LISTEN, I VOLUNTEERED TO SHOW MY DAUGHTER'S 1ST GRADE CLASS...
CONFERENCE PAPER THAT'S DUE-
...WHAT GOES ON IN A RESEARCH LAB. I WAS WONDERING IF YOU COULD SHOW THEM AROUND A BIT
copyright © 2001 jorge cham
TOMORROW.
GREAT. I'LL BE BACK IN A FEW HOURS.
BOY ARE YOU GRA'STUDENTS PALE!

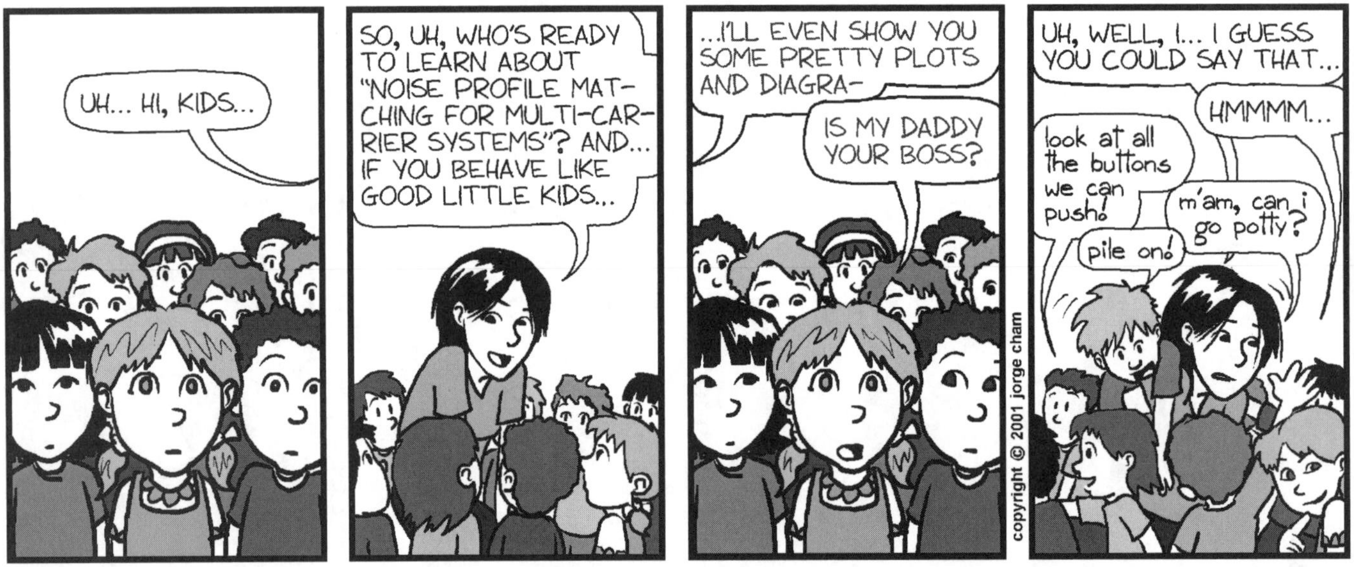
UH... HI, KIDS...
SO, UH, WHO'S READY TO LEARN ABOUT "NOISE PROFILE MATCHING FOR MULTI-CARRIER SYSTEMS"? AND... IF YOU BEHAVE LIKE GOOD LITTLE KIDS...
...I'LL EVEN SHOW YOU SOME PRETTY PLOTS AND DIAGRA-
IS MY DADDY YOUR BOSS?
copyright © 2001 jorge cham
UH, WELL, I... I GUESS YOU COULD SAY THAT...
HMMMM...
look at all the buttons we can push!
m'am, can i go potty?
pile on!

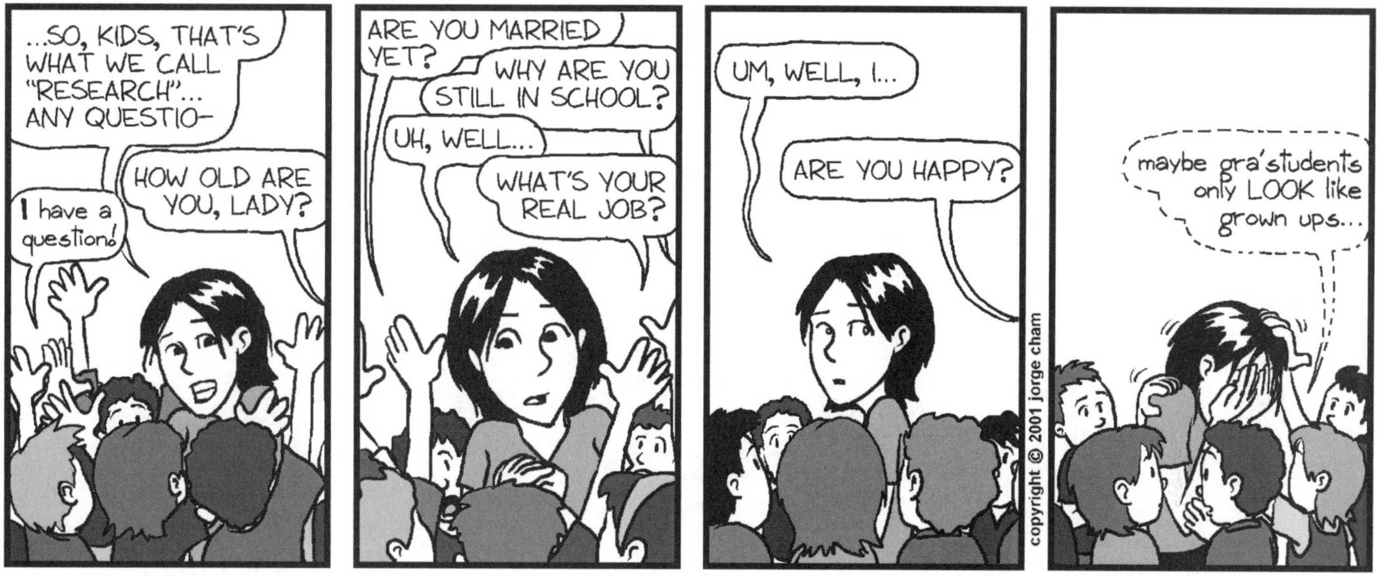
...SO, KIDS, THAT'S WHAT WE CALL "RESEARCH"... ANY QUESTIO-
I have a question!
HOW OLD ARE YOU, LADY?
ARE YOU MARRIED YET?
WHY ARE YOU STILL IN SCHOOL?
UH, WELL...
WHAT'S YOUR REAL JOB?
UM, WELL, I...
ARE YOU HAPPY?
copyright © 2001 jorge cham
maybe gra'students only LOOK like grown ups...

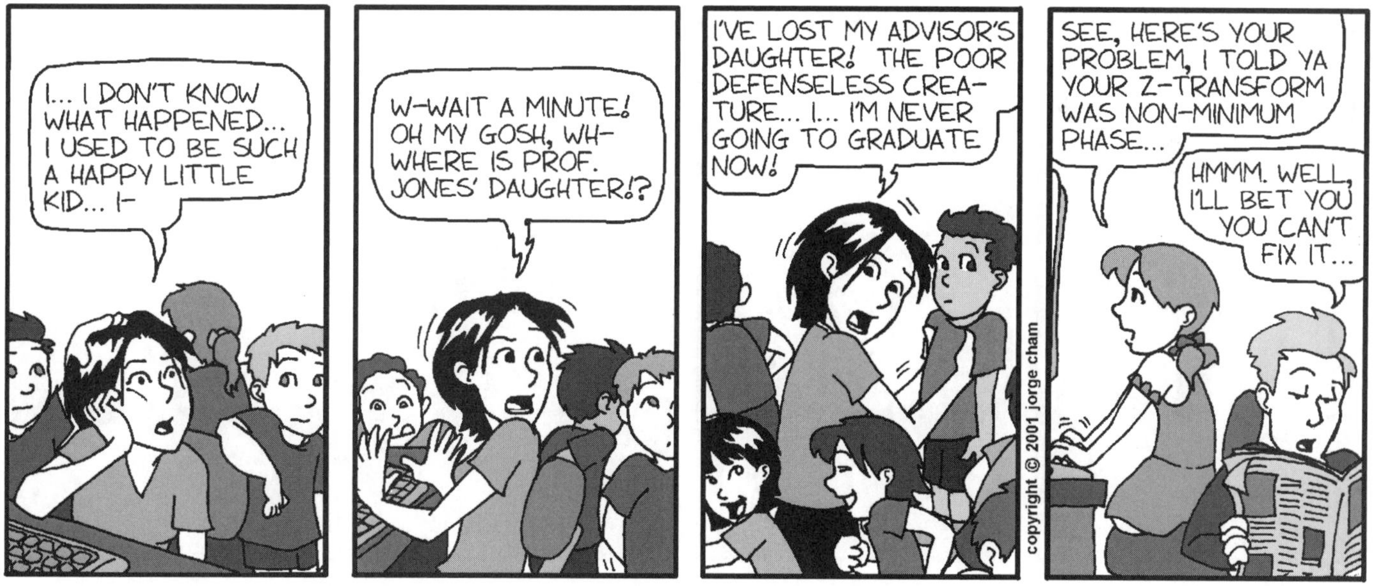
I... I DON'T KNOW WHAT HAPPENED... I USED TO BE SUCH A HAPPY LITTLE KID... I-
W-WAIT A MINUTE! OH MY GOSH, WH- WHERE IS PROF. JONES' DAUGHTER!?
I'VE LOST MY ADVISOR'S DAUGHTER! THE POOR DEFENSELESS CREA-TURE... I... I'M NEVER GOING TO GRADUATE NOW!
copyright © 2001 jorge cham
SEE, HERE'S YOUR PROBLEM, I TOLD YA YOUR Z-TRANSFORM WAS NON-MINIMUM PHASE...
HMMM. WELL, I'LL BET YOU YOU CAN'T FIX IT...

FUN with STATISTICS!

IF THE SAMPLE POPULATION IS LARGE ENOUGH, THEN IT'S TRUE! (SOURCE: U.S. CENSUS BUREAU)

13,154,000
Number of undergrads
currently enrolled

1,747,000
Number of grad students
currently enrolled

44,000
Number of PhD's conferred
this year (projected)

3.28
% of Bachelor degrees earned
by International Students (1997)

24.9
% of PhD's earned by
International Students (1997)

TOP 2 HIGHEST NUMBER OF PhD's CONFERRED IN 1997

	# PhD	% FEMALE
1. EDUCATION	6751	62.8
2. ENGINEERING	6210	12.3

MEAN EARNINGS (1999)

	MALE	FEMALE
MASTER'S	$64,533	$40,429
PhD	$82,619	$54,552

wait a minute!

28.7
% of general population
that has never married,
is separated or divorced

24.7
% of population with a
post-Bachelor's degree
that has never married,
is separated or divorced

(Finally, a reason
to hang in there!)

(all data refer to U.S. population)
phd.stanford.edu

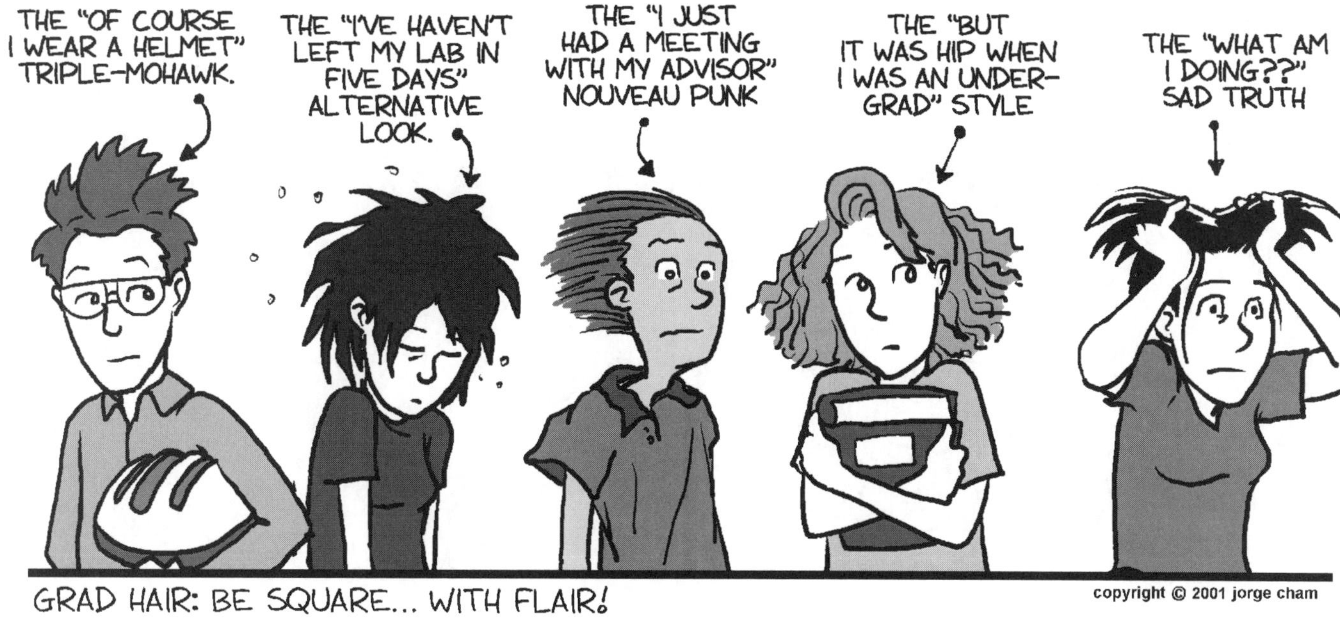
THE "OF COURSE I WEAR A HELMET" TRIPLE-MOHAWK.
THE "I'VE HAVEN'T LEFT MY LAB IN FIVE DAYS" ALTERNATIVE LOOK.
THE "I JUST HAD A MEETING WITH MY ADVISOR" NOUVEAU PUNK
THE "BUT IT WAS HIP WHEN I WAS AN UNDER-GRAD" STYLE
THE "WHAT AM I DOING??" SAD TRUTH
GRAD HAIR: BE SQUARE... WITH FLAIR!
copyright © 2001 jorge cham

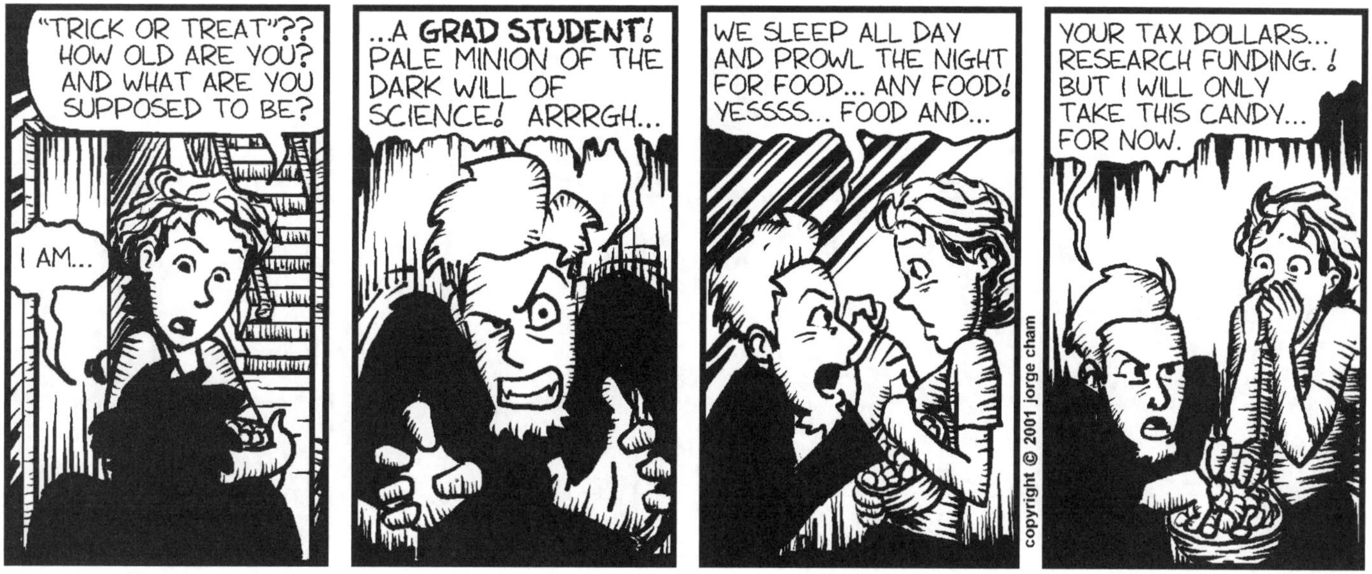
"TRICK OR TREAT"?? HOW OLD ARE YOU? AND WHAT ARE YOU SUPPOSED TO BE?
I AM...
...A **GRAD STUDENT**! PALE MINION OF THE DARK WILL OF SCIENCE! ARRRGH...
WE SLEEP ALL DAY AND PROWL THE NIGHT FOR FOOD... ANY FOOD! YESSSS... FOOD AND...
copyright © 2001 jorge cham
YOUR TAX DOLLARS... RESEARCH FUNDING. ! BUT I WILL ONLY TAKE THIS CANDY... FOR NOW.

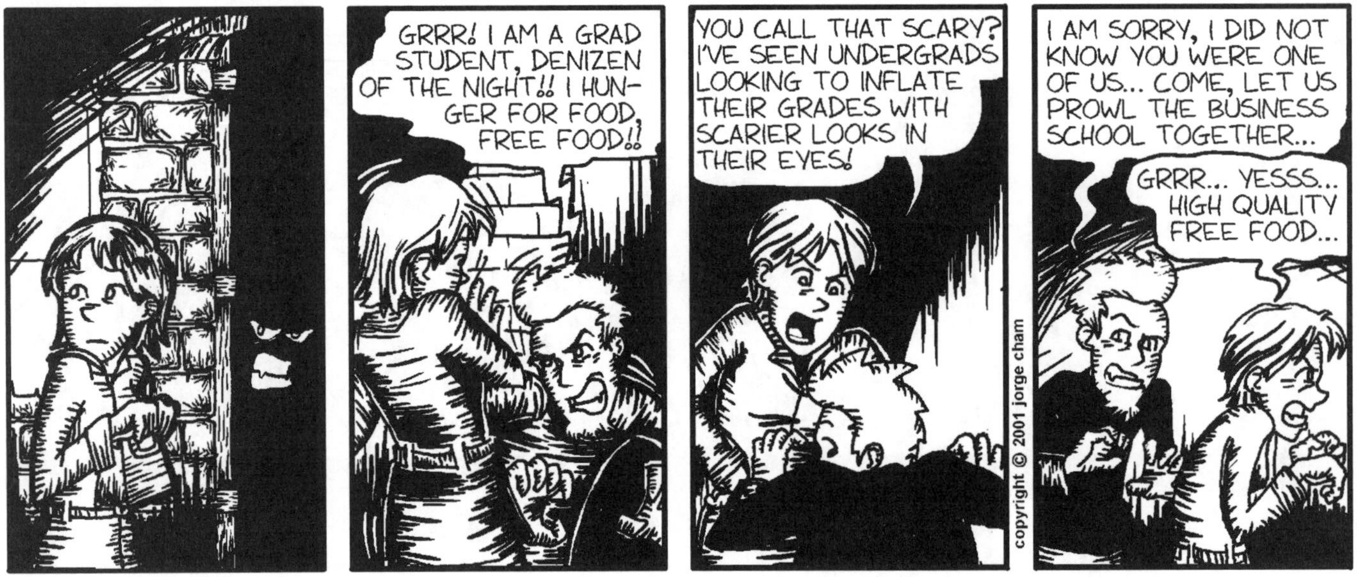
GRRR! I AM A GRAD STUDENT, DENIZEN OF THE NIGHT!! I HUNGER FOR FOOD, FREE FOOD!!
YOU CALL THAT SCARY? I'VE SEEN UNDERGRADS LOOKING TO INFLATE THEIR GRADES WITH SCARIER LOOKS IN THEIR EYES!
copyright © 2001 jorge cham
I AM SORRY, I DID NOT KNOW YOU WERE ONE OF US... COME, LET US PROWL THE BUSINESS SCHOOL TOGETHER...
GRRR... YESSS... HIGH QUALITY FREE FOOD...

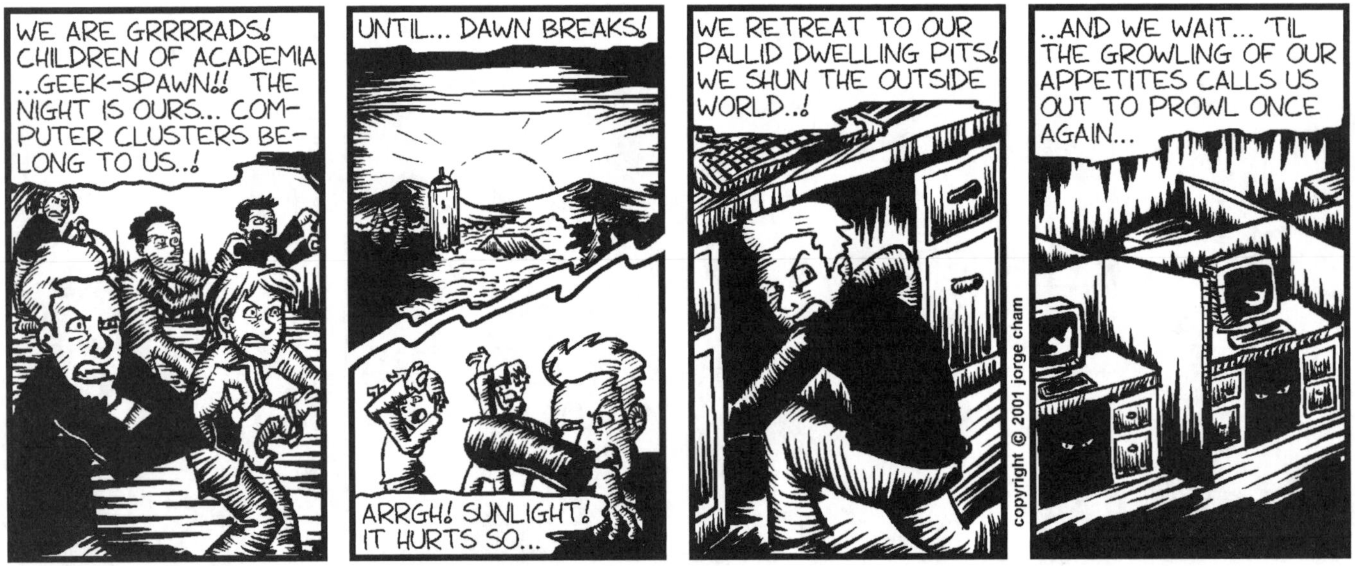
WE ARE GRRRRADS! CHILDREN OF ACADEMIA ...GEEK-SPAWN!! THE NIGHT IS OURS... COMPUTER CLUSTERS BELONG TO US..!
UNTIL... DAWN BREAKS!
ARRGH! SUNLIGHT! IT HURTS SO...
WE RETREAT TO OUR PALLID DWELLING PITS! WE SHUN THE OUTSIDE WORLD..!
copyright © 2001 jorge cham
...AND WE WAIT... 'TIL THE GROWLING OF OUR APPETITES CALLS US OUT TO PROWL ONCE AGAIN...

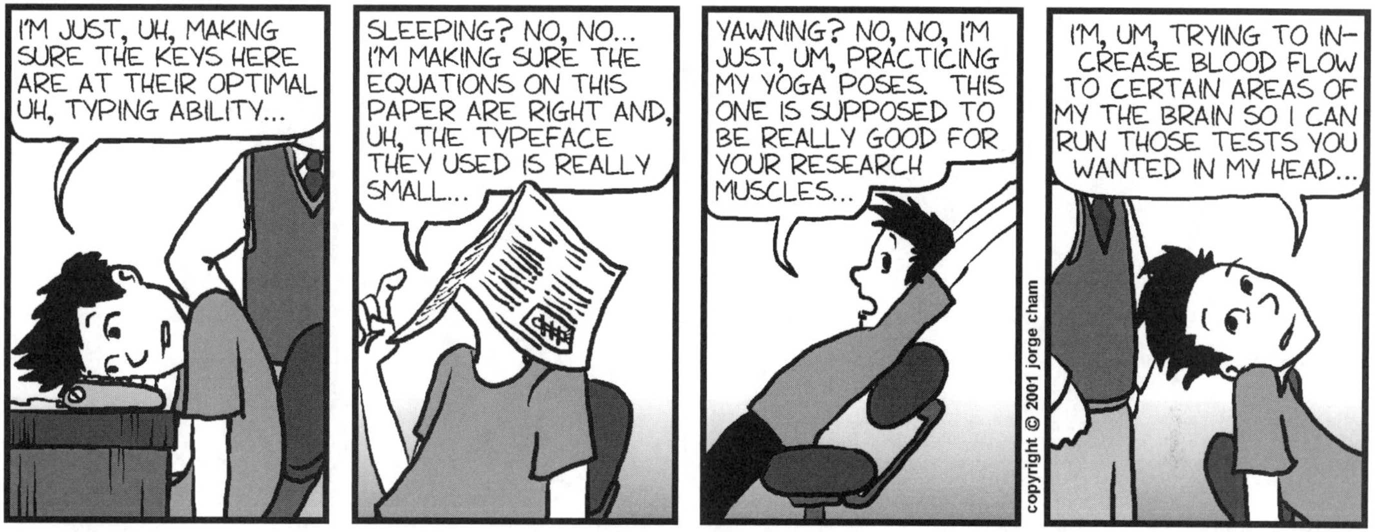
I'M JUST, UH, MAKING SURE THE KEYS HERE ARE AT THEIR OPTIMAL UH, TYPING ABILITY...
SLEEPING? NO, NO... I'M MAKING SURE THE EQUATIONS ON THIS PAPER ARE RIGHT AND, UH, THE TYPEFACE THEY USED IS REALLY SMALL...
YAWNING? NO, NO, I'M JUST, UM, PRACTICING MY YOGA POSES. THIS ONE IS SUPPOSED TO BE REALLY GOOD FOR YOUR RESEARCH MUSCLES...
copyright © 2001 jorge cham
I'M, UM, TRYING TO IN-CREASE BLOOD FLOW TO CERTAIN AREAS OF MY THE BRAIN SO I CAN RUN THOSE TESTS YOU WANTED IN MY HEAD...

WHAT ARE YOU THANKFUL FOR?

phd.stanford.edu

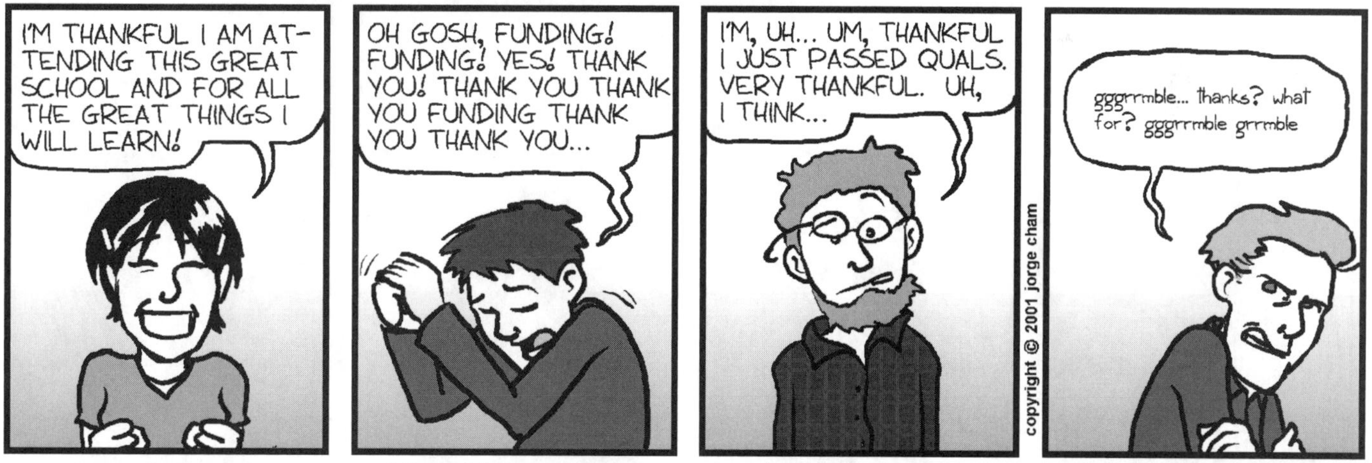
I'M THANKFUL I AM AT-TENDING THIS GREAT SCHOOL AND FOR ALL THE GREAT THINGS I WILL LEARN!
OH GOSH, FUNDING! FUNDING! YES! THANK YOU! THANK YOU THANK YOU FUNDING THANK YOU THANK YOU...
I'M, UH... UM, THANKFUL I JUST PASSED QUALS. VERY THANKFUL. UH, I THINK...
copyright © 2001 jorge cham
gggrrmble... thanks? what for? gggrrmble grrmble

Lily, 1st year graduate student

Hiroshi, 2nd year graduate student

John, 3rd year graduate student

Preston, 7th year graduate student

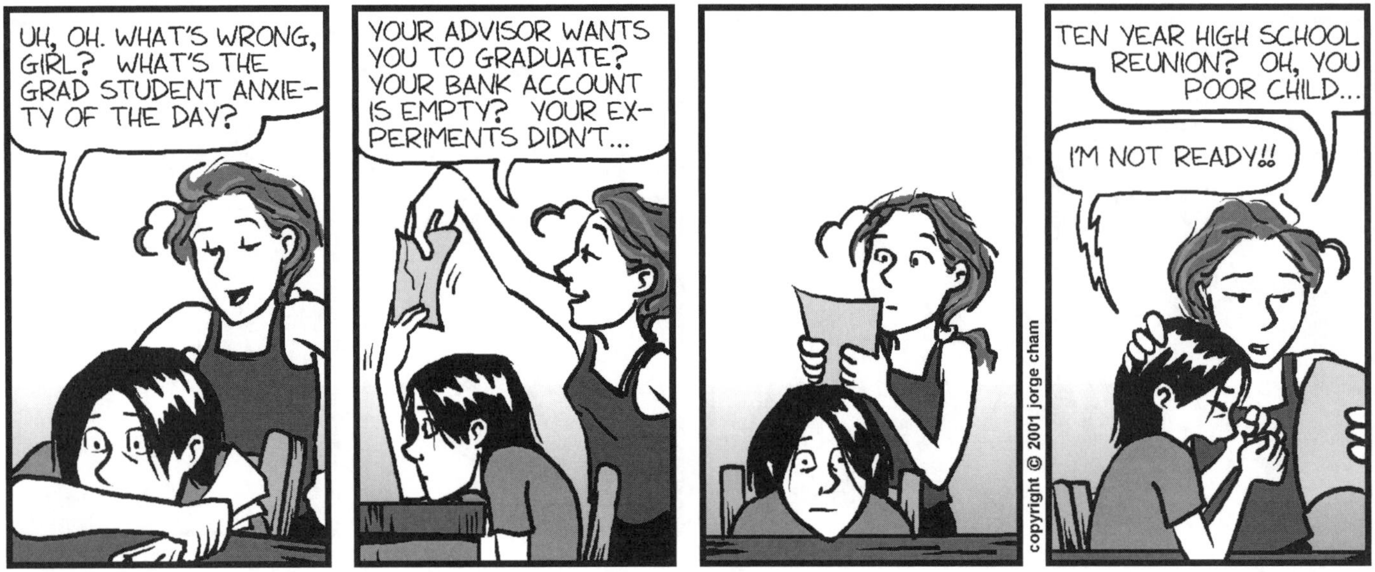
UH, OH. WHAT'S WRONG, GIRL? WHAT'S THE GRAD STUDENT ANXIETY OF THE DAY?
YOUR ADVISOR WANTS YOU TO GRADUATE? YOUR BANK ACCOUNT IS EMPTY? YOUR EXPERIMENTS DIDN'T...
TEN YEAR HIGH SCHOOL REUNION? OH, YOU POOR CHILD...
I'M NOT READY!!
copyright © 2001 jorge cham

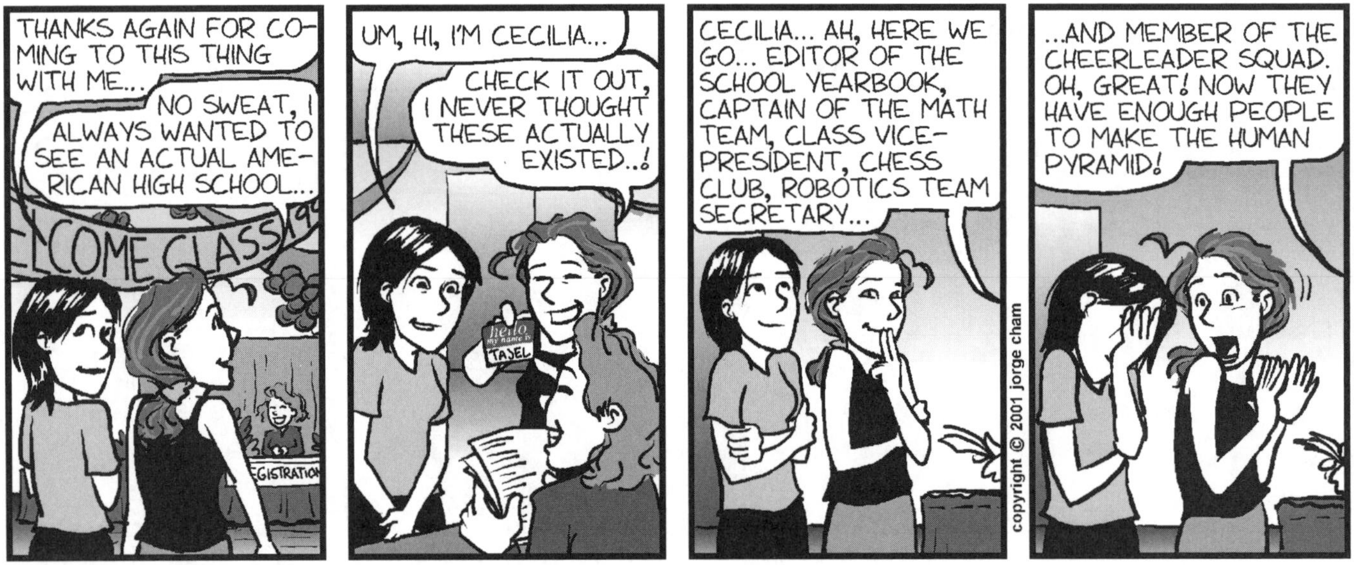
THANKS AGAIN FOR COMING TO THIS THING WITH ME...
NO SWEAT, I ALWAYS WANTED TO SEE AN ACTUAL AMERICAN HIGH SCHOOL...
UM, HI, I'M CECILIA...
CHECK IT OUT, I NEVER THOUGHT THESE ACTUALLY EXISTED..!
CECILIA... AH, HERE WE GO... EDITOR OF THE SCHOOL YEARBOOK, CAPTAIN OF THE MATH TEAM, CLASS VICE-PRESIDENT, CHESS CLUB, ROBOTICS TEAM SECRETARY...
...AND MEMBER OF THE CHEERLEADER SQUAD. OH, GREAT! NOW THEY HAVE ENOUGH PEOPLE TO MAKE THE HUMAN PYRAMID!
copyright © 2001 jorge cham

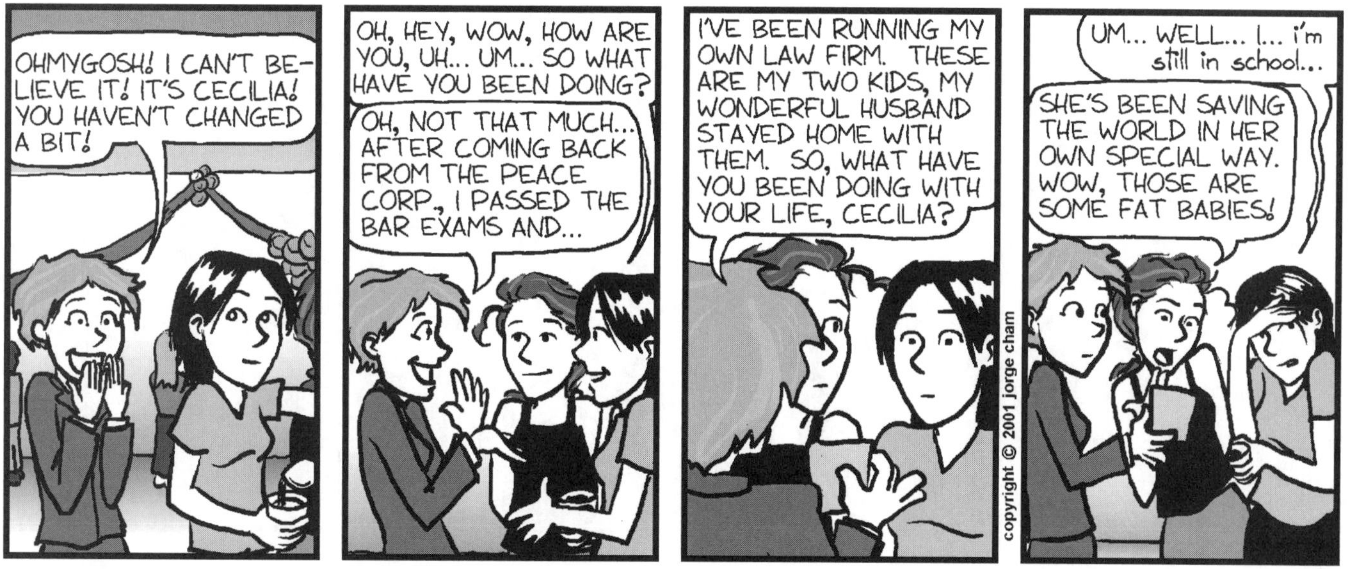
OHMYGOSH! I CAN'T BE-LIEVE IT! IT'S CECILIA! YOU HAVEN'T CHANGED A BIT!
OH, HEY, WOW, HOW ARE YOU, UH... UM... SO WHAT HAVE YOU BEEN DOING?
OH, NOT THAT MUCH... AFTER COMING BACK FROM THE PEACE CORP., I PASSED THE BAR EXAMS AND...
I'VE BEEN RUNNING MY OWN LAW FIRM. THESE ARE MY TWO KIDS, MY WONDERFUL HUSBAND STAYED HOME WITH THEM. SO, WHAT HAVE YOU BEEN DOING WITH YOUR LIFE, CECILIA?
copyright © 2001 jorge cham
UM... WELL... I... i'm still in school...
SHE'S BEEN SAVING THE WORLD IN HER OWN SPECIAL WAY. WOW, THOSE ARE SOME FAT BABIES!

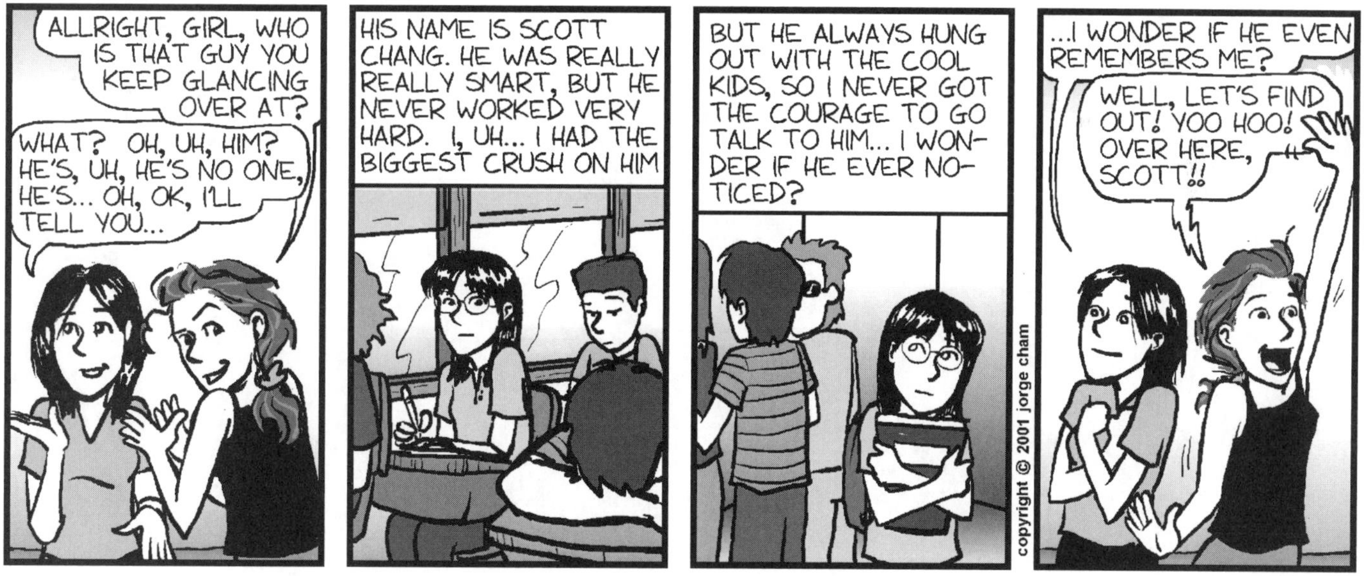
ALLRIGHT, GIRL, WHO IS THAT GUY YOU KEEP GLANCING OVER AT?
WHAT? OH, UH, HIM? HE'S, UH, HE'S NO ONE, HE'S... OH, OK, I'LL TELL YOU...
HIS NAME IS SCOTT CHANG. HE WAS REALLY REALLY SMART, BUT HE NEVER WORKED VERY HARD. I, UH... I HAD THE BIGGEST CRUSH ON HIM
BUT HE ALWAYS HUNG OUT WITH THE COOL KIDS, SO I NEVER GOT THE COURAGE TO GO TALK TO HIM... I WONDER IF HE EVER NOTICED?
copyright © 2001 jorge cham
...I WONDER IF HE EVEN REMEMBERS ME?
WELL, LET'S FIND OUT! YOO HOO! OVER HERE, SCOTT!!

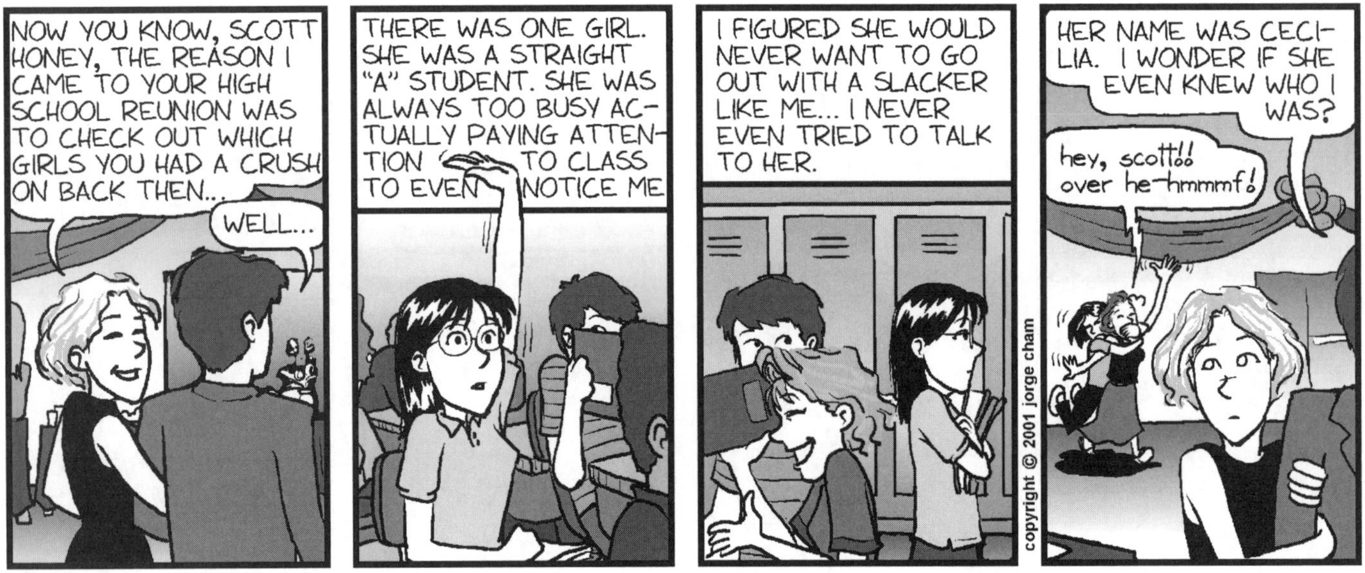
NOW YOU KNOW, SCOTT HONEY, THE REASON I CAME TO YOUR HIGH SCHOOL REUNION WAS TO CHECK OUT WHICH GIRLS YOU HAD A CRUSH ON BACK THEN...
WELL...
THERE WAS ONE GIRL. SHE WAS A STRAIGHT "A" STUDENT. SHE WAS ALWAYS TOO BUSY ACTUALLY PAYING ATTENTION TO CLASS TO EVEN NOTICE ME
I FIGURED SHE WOULD NEVER WANT TO GO OUT WITH A SLACKER LIKE ME... I NEVER EVEN TRIED TO TALK TO HER.
copyright © 2001 jorge cham
HER NAME WAS CECILIA. I WONDER IF SHE EVEN KNEW WHO I WAS?
hey, scott!! over he-hmmmf!

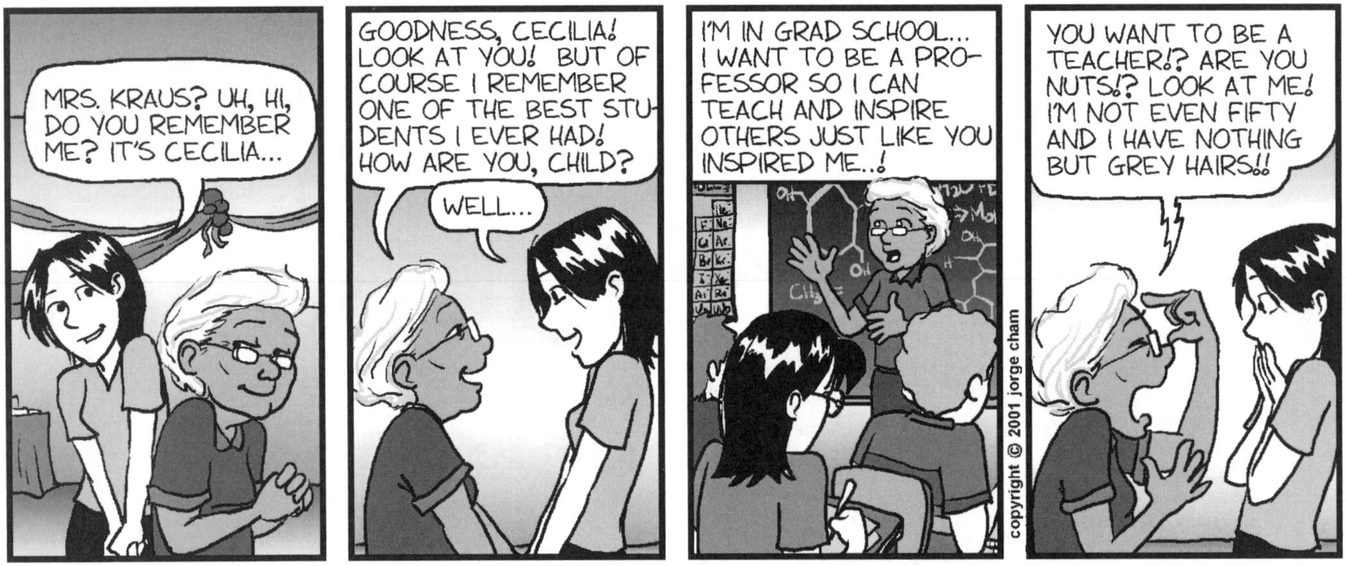
MRS. KRAUS? UH, HI, DO YOU REMEMBER ME? IT'S CECILIA...
GOODNESS, CECILIA! LOOK AT YOU! BUT OF COURSE I REMEMBER ONE OF THE BEST STUDENTS I EVER HAD! HOW ARE YOU, CHILD?
WELL...
I'M IN GRAD SCHOOL... I WANT TO BE A PROFESSOR SO I CAN TEACH AND INSPIRE OTHERS JUST LIKE YOU INSPIRED ME...!
copyright © 2001 jorge cham
YOU WANT TO BE A TEACHER!? ARE YOU NUTS!? LOOK AT ME! I'M NOT EVEN FIFTY AND I HAVE NOTHING BUT GREY HAIRS!!

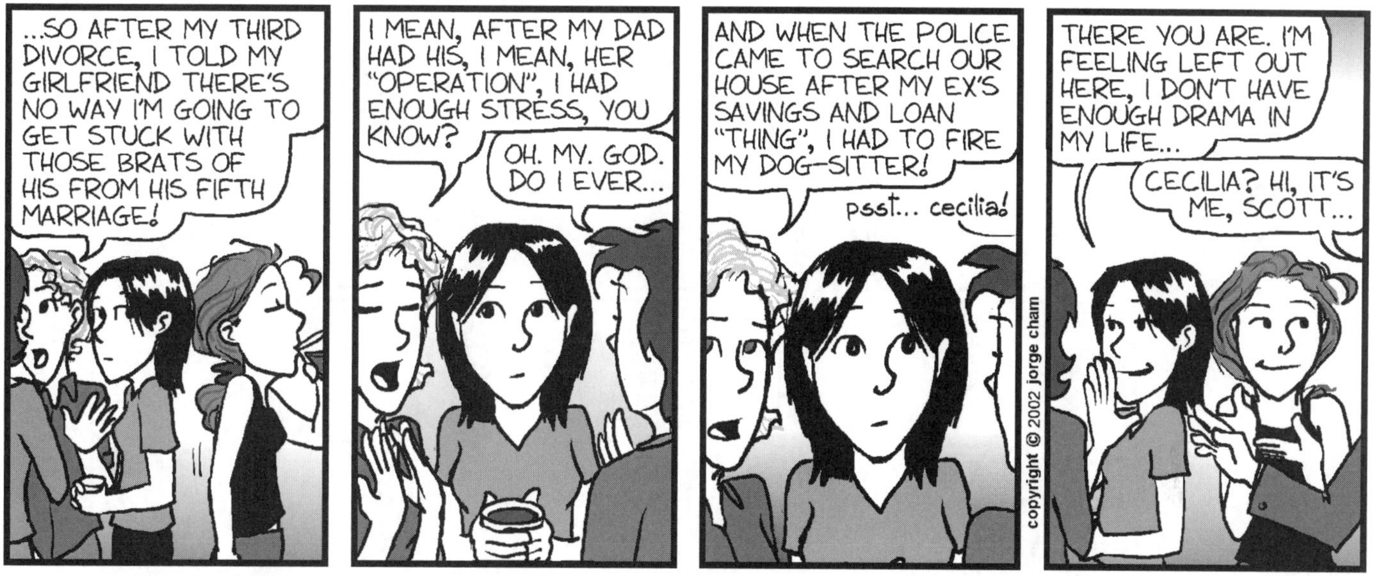
...SO AFTER MY THIRD DIVORCE, I TOLD MY GIRLFRIEND THERE'S NO WAY I'M GOING TO GET STUCK WITH THOSE BRATS OF HIS FROM HIS FIFTH MARRIAGE!
I MEAN, AFTER MY DAD HAD HIS, I MEAN, HER "OPERATION", I HAD ENOUGH STRESS, YOU KNOW?
OH. MY. GOD. DO I EVER...
AND WHEN THE POLICE CAME TO SEARCH OUR HOUSE AFTER MY EX'S SAVINGS AND LOAN "THING", I HAD TO FIRE MY DOG-SITTER!
psst... cecilia!
copyright © 2002 jorge cham
THERE YOU ARE. I'M FEELING LEFT OUT HERE, I DON'T HAVE ENOUGH DRAMA IN MY LIFE...
CECILIA? HI, IT'S ME, SCOTT...

GEEK LOVE COMICS

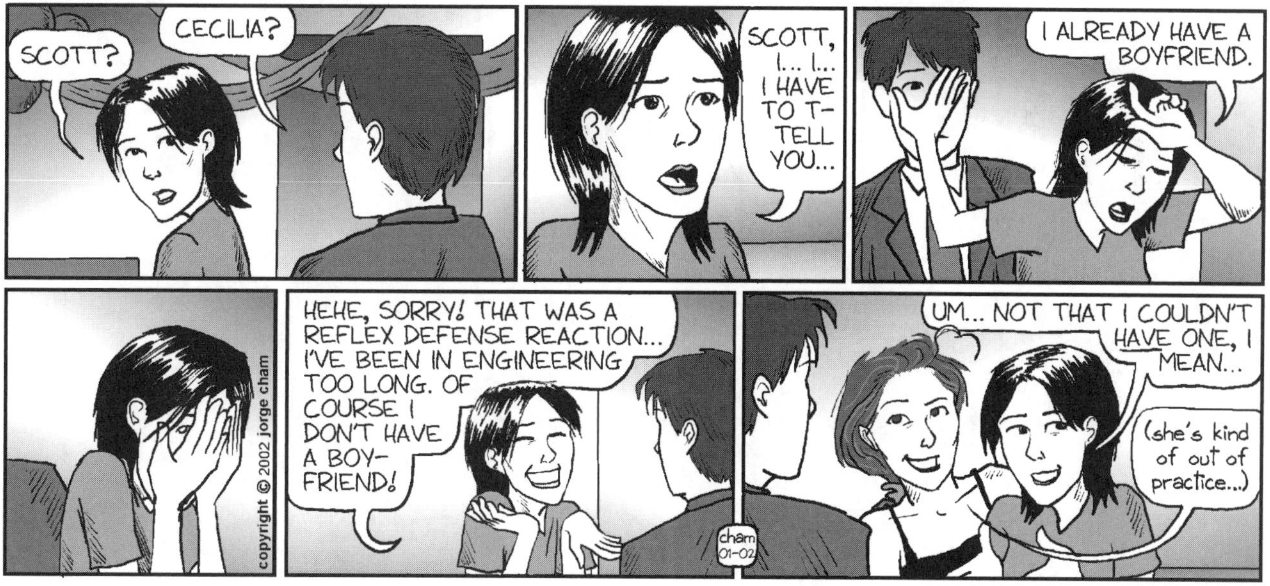
SCOTT?
CECILIA?
SCOTT, I... I... I HAVE TO T-TELL YOU...
I ALREADY HAVE A BOYFRIEND.
copyright © 2002 jorge cham
HEHE, SORRY! THAT WAS A REFLEX DEFENSE REACTION... I'VE BEEN IN ENGINEERING TOO LONG. OF COURSE I DON'T HAVE A BOY-FRIEND!
cham 01-02
UM... NOT THAT I COULDN'T HAVE ONE, I MEAN...
(she's kind of out of practice...)

GEEK LOVE COMICS

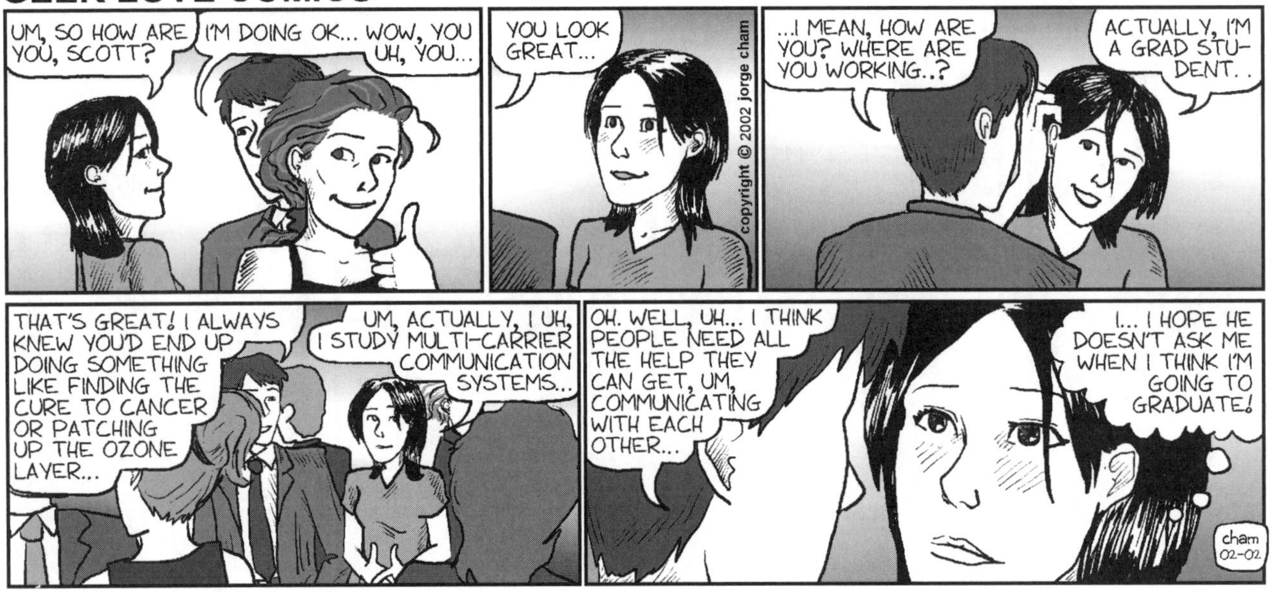
UM, SO HOW ARE YOU, SCOTT?
I'M DOING OK... WOW, YOU UH, YOU...
YOU LOOK GREAT...
copyright © 2002 jorge cham
...I MEAN, HOW ARE YOU? WHERE ARE YOU WORKING..?
ACTUALLY, I'M A GRAD STU-DENT..
THAT'S GREAT! I ALWAYS KNEW YOU'D END UP DOING SOMETHING LIKE FINDING THE CURE TO CANCER OR PATCHING UP THE OZONE LAYER...
UM, ACTUALLY, I UH, I STUDY MULTI-CARRIER COMMUNICATION SYSTEMS...
OH. WELL, UH... I THINK PEOPLE NEED ALL THE HELP THEY CAN GET, UM, COMMUNICATING WITH EACH OTHER...
I... I HOPE HE DOESN'T ASK ME WHEN I THINK I'M GOING TO GRADUATE!
cham 02-02

GEEK LOVE COMICS

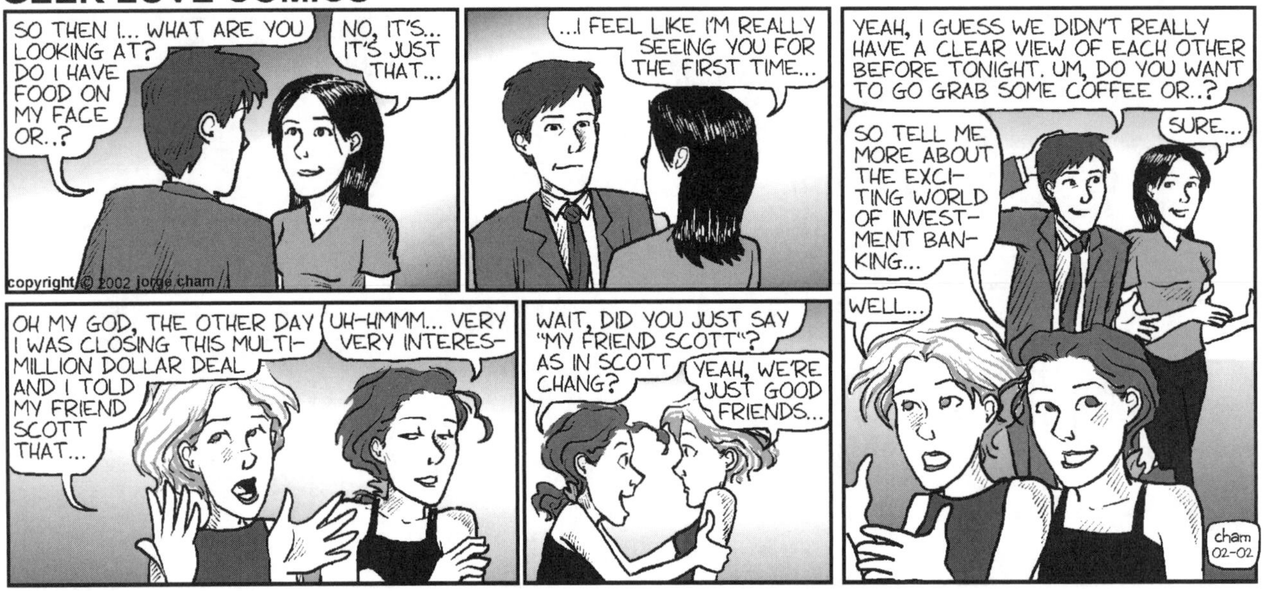
SO THEN I... WHAT ARE YOU LOOKING AT? DO I HAVE FOOD ON MY FACE OR..?
NO, IT'S... IT'S JUST THAT...
copyright © 2002 jorge cham
...I FEEL LIKE I'M REALLY SEEING YOU FOR THE FIRST TIME...
YEAH, I GUESS WE DIDN'T REALLY HAVE A CLEAR VIEW OF EACH OTHER BEFORE TONIGHT. UM, DO YOU WANT TO GO GRAB SOME COFFEE OR..?
SURE...
OH MY GOD, THE OTHER DAY I WAS CLOSING THIS MULTI-MILLION DOLLAR DEAL AND I TOLD MY FRIEND SCOTT THAT...
UH-HMMM... VERY VERY INTERES-
WAIT, DID YOU JUST SAY "MY FRIEND SCOTT"? AS IN SCOTT CHANG?
YEAH, WE'RE JUST GOOD FRIENDS...
SO TELL ME MORE ABOUT THE EXCI-TING WORLD OF INVEST-MENT BAN-KING...
WELL...
cham 02-02

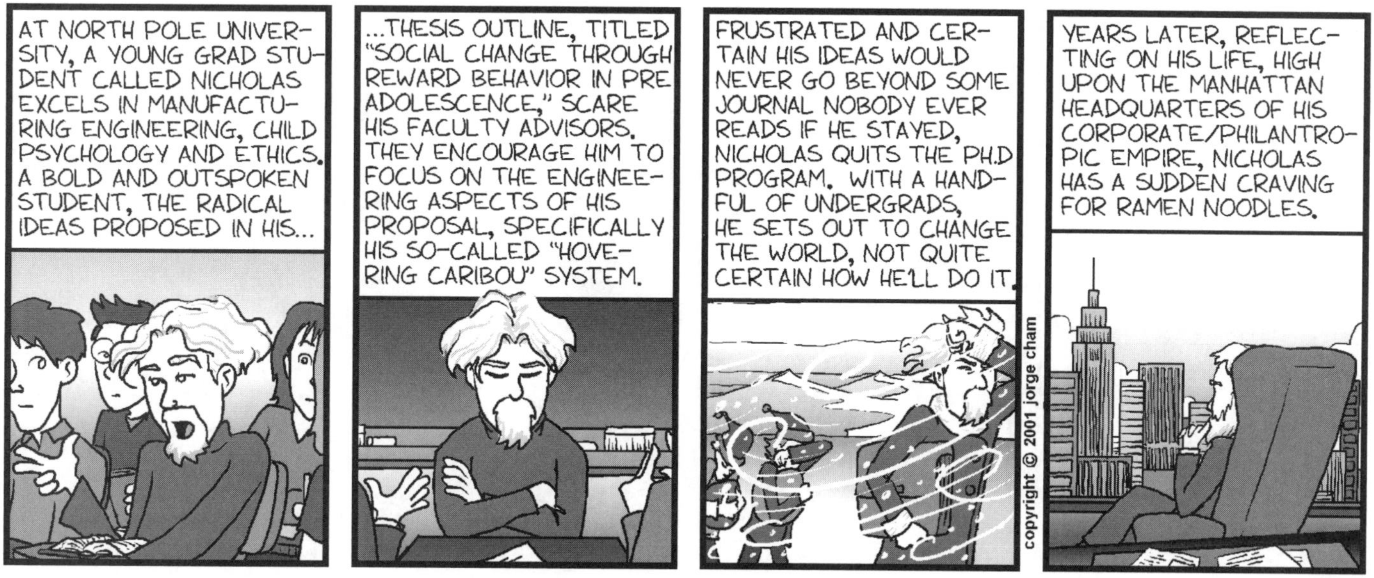

AT NORTH POLE UNIVERSITY, A YOUNG GRAD STUDENT CALLED NICHOLAS EXCELS IN MANUFACTURING ENGINEERING, CHILD PSYCHOLOGY AND ETHICS. A BOLD AND OUTSPOKEN STUDENT, THE RADICAL IDEAS PROPOSED IN HIS...
...THESIS OUTLINE, TITLED "SOCIAL CHANGE THROUGH REWARD BEHAVIOR IN PRE ADOLESCENCE," SCARE HIS FACULTY ADVISORS. THEY ENCOURAGE HIM TO FOCUS ON THE ENGINEERING ASPECTS OF HIS PROPOSAL, SPECIFICALLY HIS SO-CALLED "HOVERING CARIBOU" SYSTEM.
FRUSTRATED AND CERTAIN HIS IDEAS WOULD NEVER GO BEYOND SOME JOURNAL NOBODY EVER READS IF HE STAYED, NICHOLAS QUITS THE PH.D PROGRAM. WITH A HANDFUL OF UNDERGRADS, HE SETS OUT TO CHANGE THE WORLD, NOT QUITE CERTAIN HOW HE'LL DO IT.
copyright © 2001 jorge cham
YEARS LATER, REFLECTING ON HIS LIFE, HIGH UPON THE MANHATTAN HEADQUARTERS OF HIS CORPORATE/PHILANTROPIC EMPIRE, NICHOLAS HAS A SUDDEN CRAVING FOR RAMEN NOODLES.

NEW YEAR'S RESOLUTIONS

phd.stanford.edu

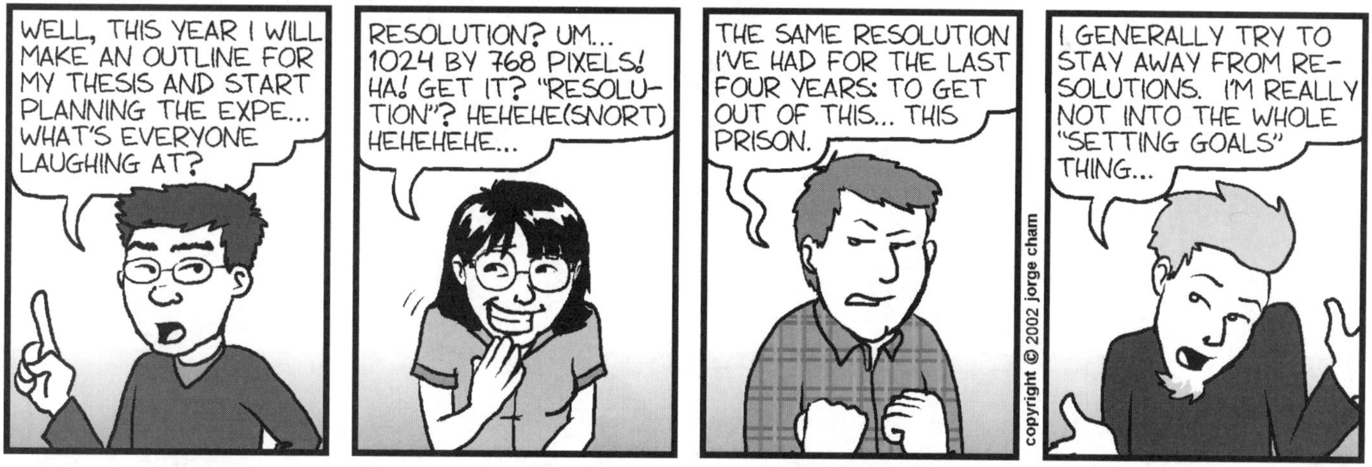

WELL, THIS YEAR I WILL MAKE AN OUTLINE FOR MY THESIS AND START PLANNING THE EXPE... WHAT'S EVERYONE LAUGHING AT?
RESOLUTION? UM... 1024 BY 768 PIXELS! HA! GET IT? "RESOLUTION"? HEHEHE(SNORT) HEHEHEHE...
THE SAME RESOLUTION I'VE HAD FOR THE LAST FOUR YEARS: TO GET OUT OF THIS... THIS PRISON.
copyright © 2002 jorge cham
I GENERALLY TRY TO STAY AWAY FROM RESOLUTIONS. I'M REALLY NOT INTO THE WHOLE "SETTING GOALS" THING...

Louis, 1st year graduate student

Gwendolyn, 2nd year (Computer Science)

Bill, 8th year graduate student

Mike, (unknown) year graduate student

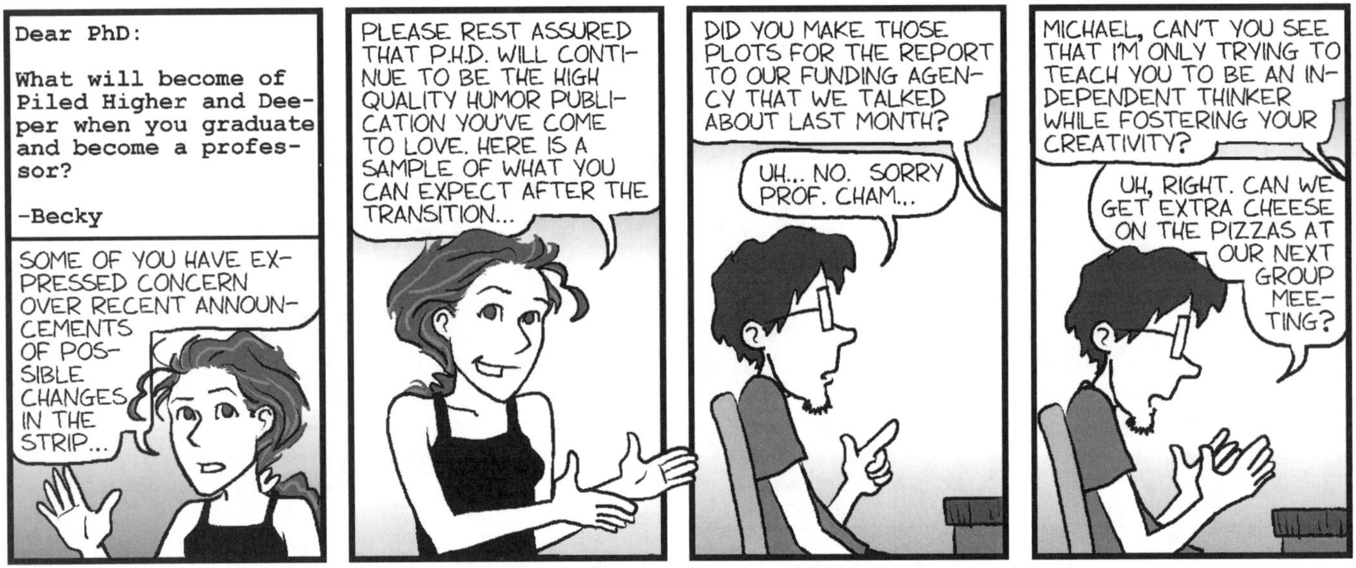
Dear PhD:
What will become of Piled Higher and Deeper when you graduate and become a professor?
-Becky
SOME OF YOU HAVE EXPRESSED CONCERN OVER RECENT ANNOUNCEMENTS OF POSSIBLE CHANGES IN THE STRIP...
PLEASE REST ASSURED THAT P.H.D. WILL CONTINUE TO BE THE HIGH QUALITY HUMOR PUBLICATION YOU'VE COME TO LOVE. HERE IS A SAMPLE OF WHAT YOU CAN EXPECT AFTER THE TRANSITION...
DID YOU MAKE THOSE PLOTS FOR THE REPORT TO OUR FUNDING AGENCY THAT WE TALKED ABOUT LAST MONTH?
UH... NO. SORRY PROF. CHAM...
MICHAEL, CAN'T YOU SEE THAT I'M ONLY TRYING TO TEACH YOU TO BE AN INDEPENDENT THINKER WHILE FOSTERING YOUR CREATIVITY?
UH, RIGHT. CAN WE GET EXTRA CHEESE ON THE PIZZAS AT OUR NEXT GROUP MEETING?

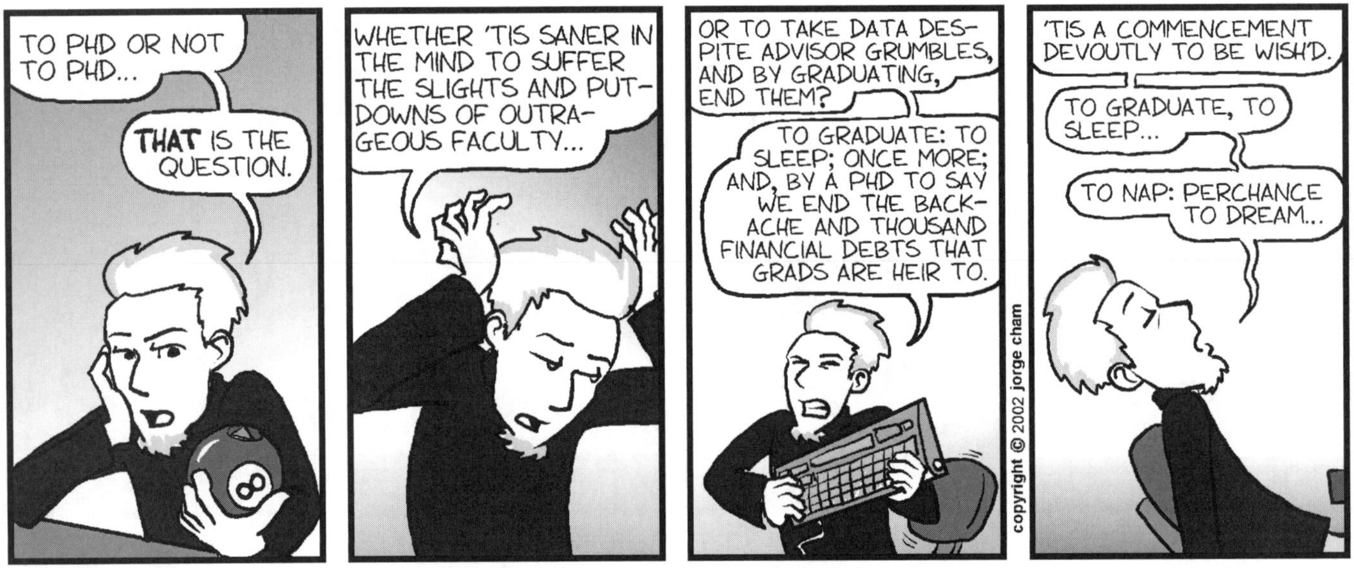
TO PHD OR NOT TO PHD...
THAT IS THE QUESTION.
WHETHER 'TIS SANER IN THE MIND TO SUFFER THE SLIGHTS AND PUT-DOWNS OF OUTRAGEOUS FACULTY...
OR TO TAKE DATA DESPITE ADVISOR GRUMBLES, AND BY GRADUATING, END THEM?
TO GRADUATE: TO SLEEP; ONCE MORE; AND, BY A PHD TO SAY WE END THE BACKACHE AND THOUSAND FINANCIAL DEBTS THAT GRADS ARE HEIR TO.
copyright © 2002 jorge cham
'TIS A COMMENCEMENT DEVOUTLY TO BE WISH'D.
TO GRADUATE, TO SLEEP...
TO NAP: PERCHANCE TO DREAM...

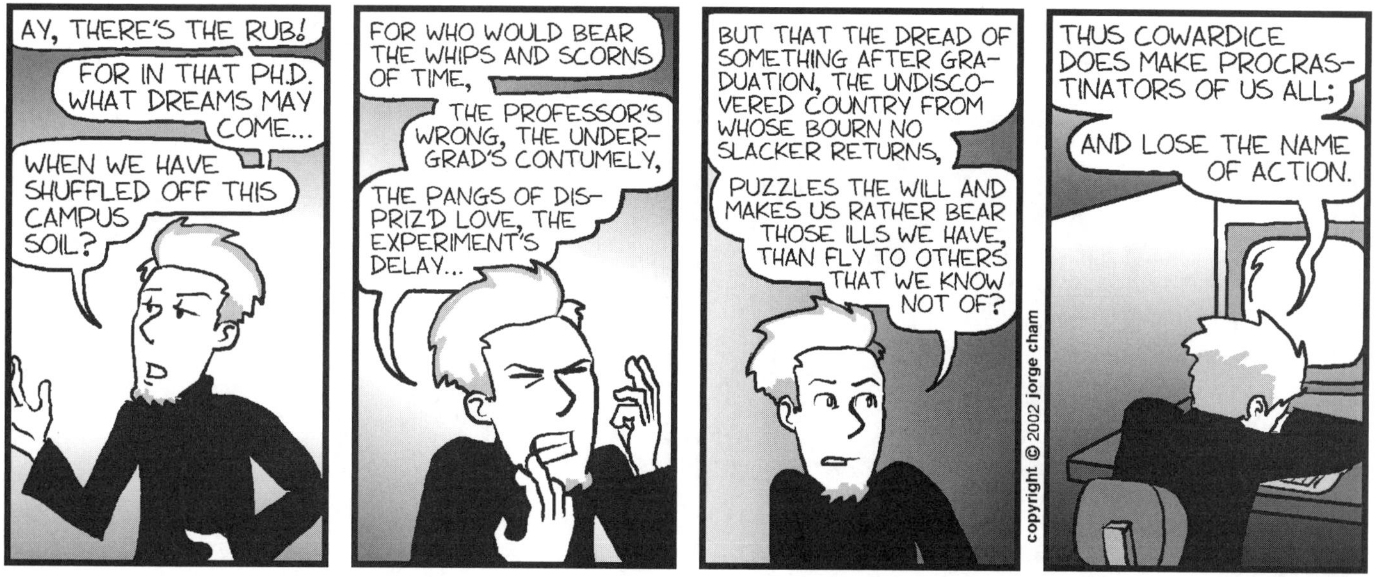
AY, THERE'S THE RUB!
FOR IN THAT PH.D. WHAT DREAMS MAY COME...
WHEN WE HAVE SHUFFLED OFF THIS CAMPUS SOIL?
FOR WHO WOULD BEAR THE WHIPS AND SCORNS OF TIME,
THE PROFESSOR'S WRONG, THE UNDERGRAD'S CONTUMELY,
THE PANGS OF DISPRIZ'D LOVE, THE EXPERIMENT'S DELAY...
BUT THAT THE DREAD OF SOMETHING AFTER GRADUATION, THE UNDISCOVERED COUNTRY FROM WHOSE BOURN NO SLACKER RETURNS,
PUZZLES THE WILL AND MAKES US RATHER BEAR THOSE ILLS WE HAVE, THAN FLY TO OTHERS THAT WE KNOW NOT OF?
copyright © 2002 jorge cham
THUS COWARDICE DOES MAKE PROCRASTINATORS OF US ALL;
AND LOSE THE NAME OF ACTION.

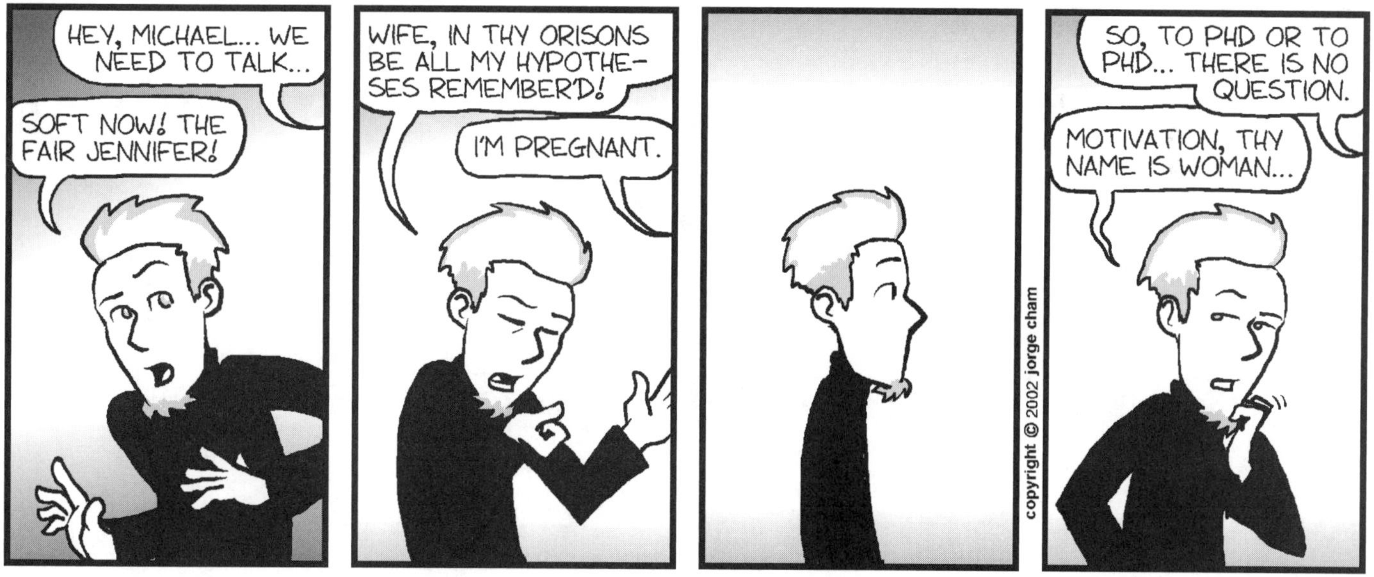
HEY, MICHAEL... WE NEED TO TALK...
SOFT NOW! THE FAIR JENNIFER!
WIFE, IN THY ORISONS BE ALL MY HYPOTHESES REMEMBER'D!
I'M PREGNANT.
copyright © 2002 jorge cham
SO, TO PHD OR TO PHD... THERE IS NO QUESTION.
MOTIVATION, THY NAME IS WOMAN...

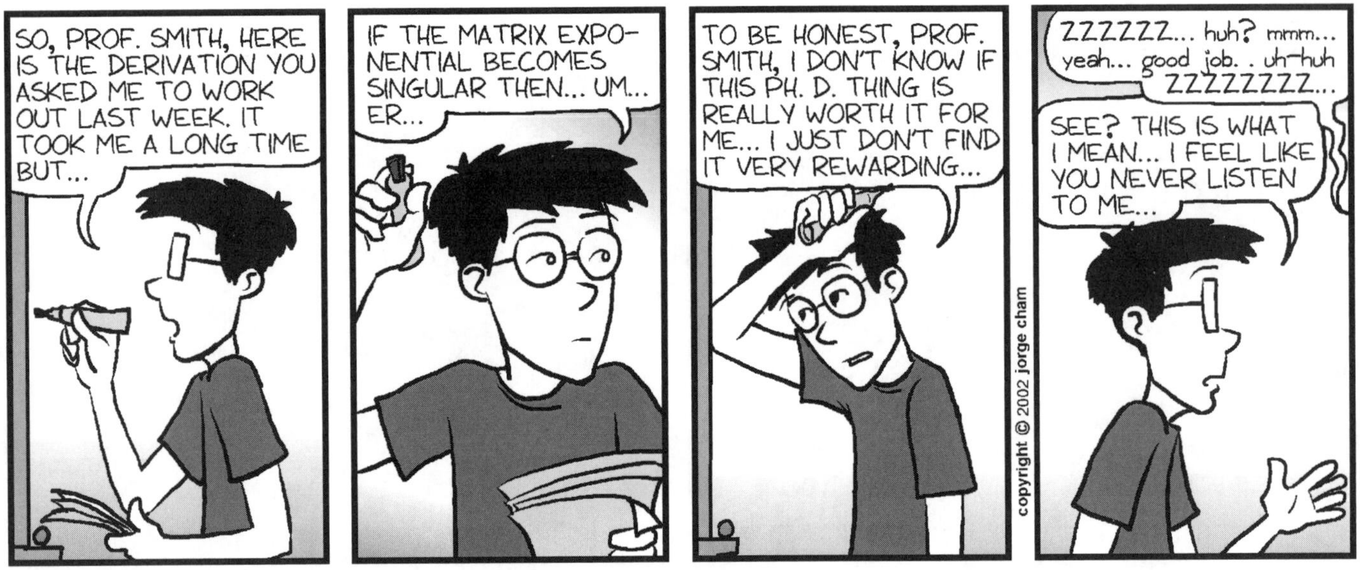
SO, PROF. SMITH, HERE IS THE DERIVATION YOU ASKED ME TO WORK OUT LAST WEEK. IT TOOK ME A LONG TIME BUT...
IF THE MATRIX EXPONENTIAL BECOMES SINGULAR THEN... UM... ER...
TO BE HONEST, PROF. SMITH, I DON'T KNOW IF THIS PH. D. THING IS REALLY WORTH IT FOR ME... I JUST DON'T FIND IT VERY REWARDING...
ZZZZZZ... huh? mmm... yeah... good job.. uh-huh ZZZZZZZZ...
SEE? THIS IS WHAT I MEAN... I FEEL LIKE YOU NEVER LISTEN TO ME...
copyright © 2002 jorge cham

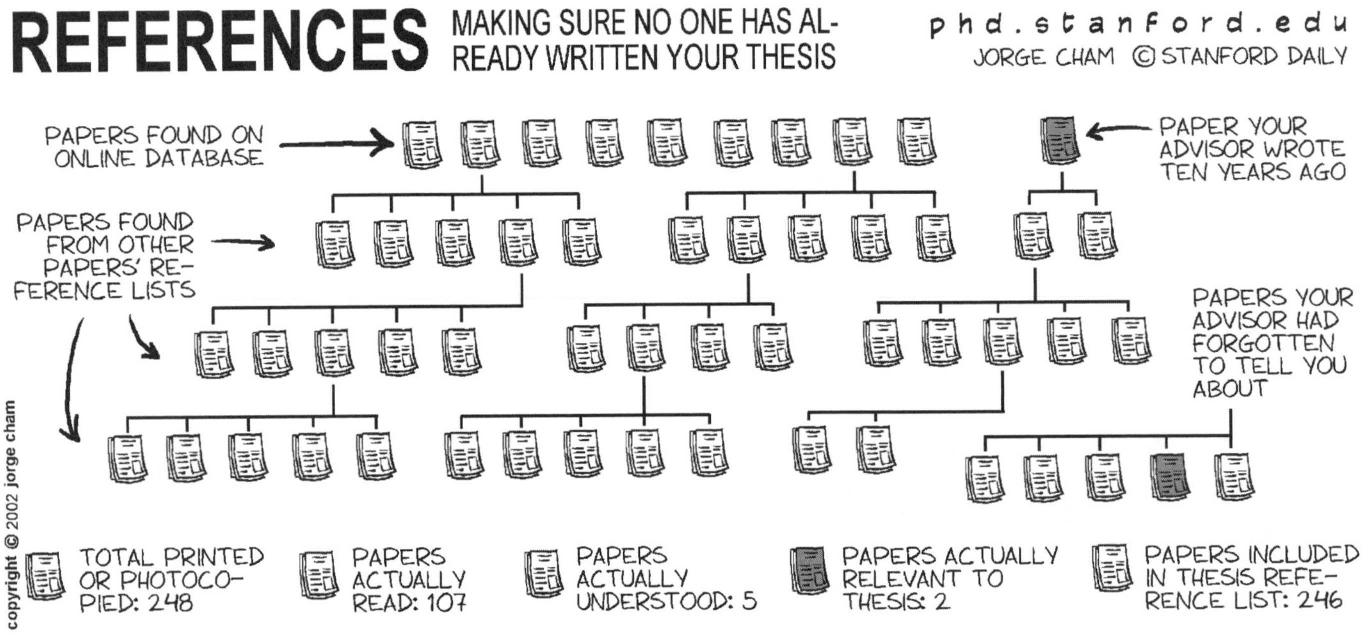
REFERENCES
MAKING SURE NO ONE HAS ALREADY WRITTEN YOUR THESIS
phd.stanford.edu
JORGE CHAM © STANFORD DAILY
PAPERS FOUND ON ONLINE DATABASE
PAPER YOUR ADVISOR WROTE TEN YEARS AGO
PAPERS FOUND FROM OTHER PAPERS' REFERENCE LISTS
PAPERS YOUR ADVISOR HAD FORGOTTEN TO TELL YOU ABOUT
TOTAL PRINTED OR PHOTOCOPIED: 248
PAPERS ACTUALLY READ: 107
PAPERS ACTUALLY UNDERSTOOD: 5
PAPERS ACTUALLY RELEVANT TO THESIS: 2
PAPERS INCLUDED IN THESIS REFERENCE LIST: 246
copyright © 2002 jorge cham

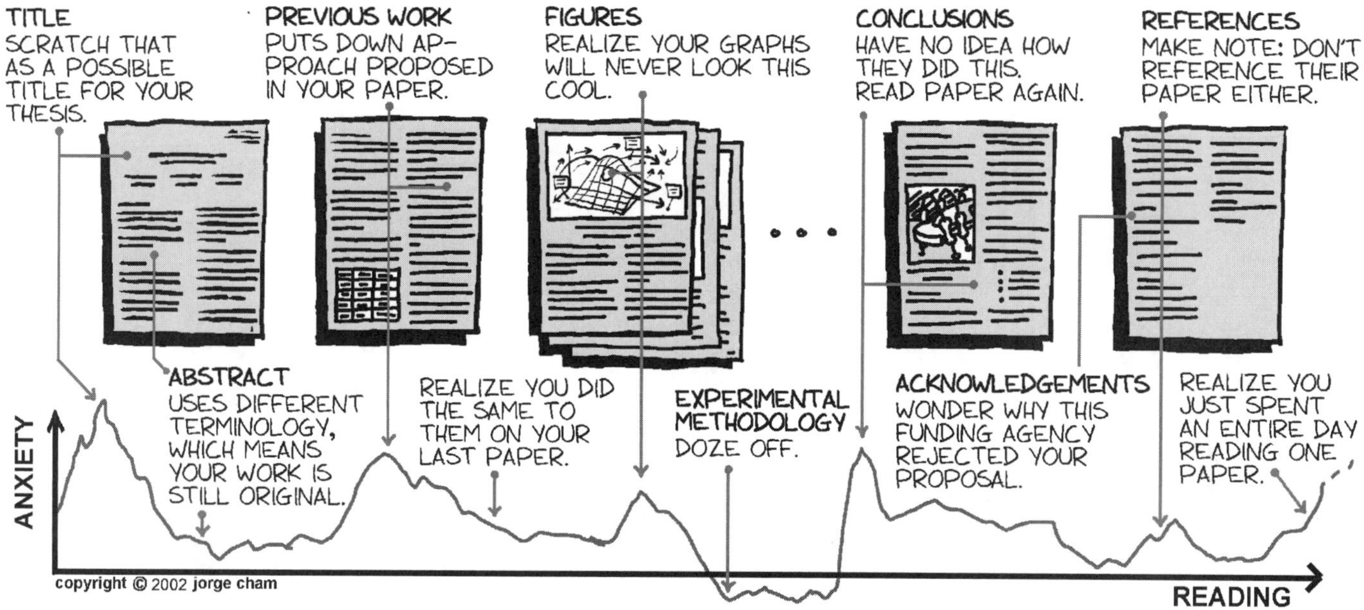
TITLE
SCRATCH THAT AS A POSSIBLE TITLE FOR YOUR THESIS.
PREVIOUS WORK
PUTS DOWN APPROACH PROPOSED IN YOUR PAPER.
FIGURES
REALIZE YOUR GRAPHS WILL NEVER LOOK THIS COOL.
CONCLUSIONS
HAVE NO IDEA HOW THEY DID THIS. READ PAPER AGAIN.
REFERENCES
MAKE NOTE: DON'T REFERENCE THEIR PAPER EITHER.
ABSTRACT
USES DIFFERENT TERMINOLOGY, WHICH MEANS YOUR WORK IS STILL ORIGINAL.
REALIZE YOU DID THE SAME TO THEM ON YOUR LAST PAPER.
EXPERIMENTAL METHODOLOGY
DOZE OFF.
ACKNOWLEDGEMENTS
WONDER WHY THIS FUNDING AGENCY REJECTED YOUR PROPOSAL.
REALIZE YOU JUST SPENT AN ENTIRE DAY READING ONE PAPER.
ANXIETY
READING
copyright © 2002 jorge cham

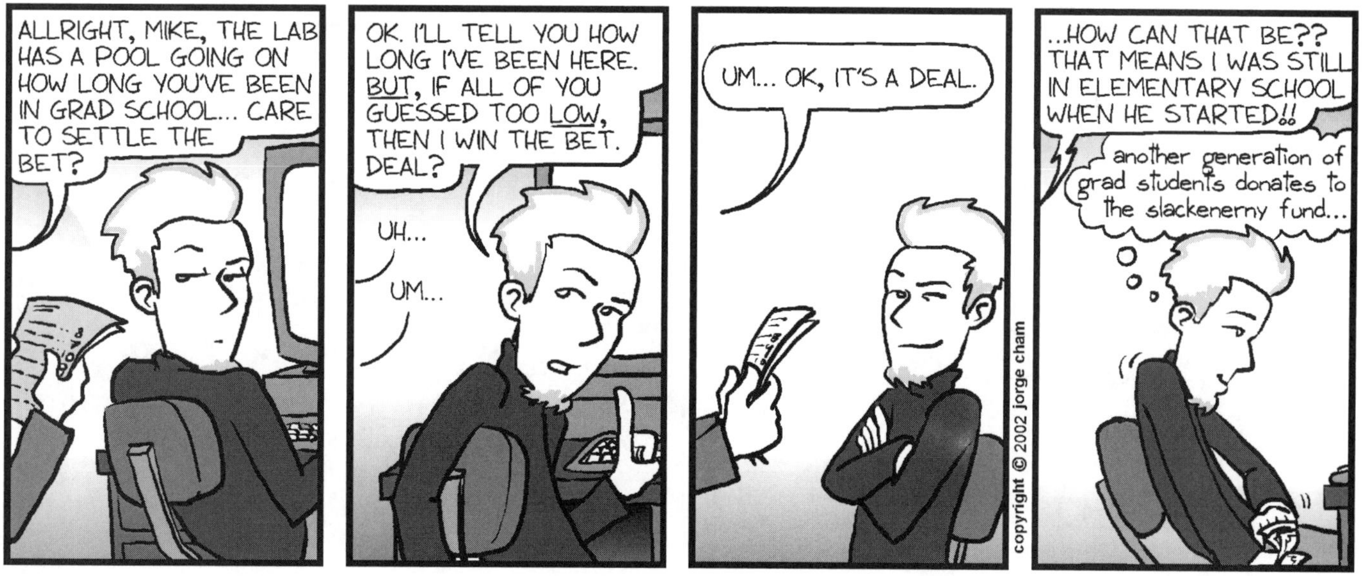
ALLRIGHT, MIKE, THE LAB HAS A POOL GOING ON HOW LONG YOU'VE BEEN IN GRAD SCHOOL... CARE TO SETTLE THE BET?
OK. I'LL TELL YOU HOW LONG I'VE BEEN HERE. BUT, IF ALL OF YOU GUESSED TOO LOW, THEN I WIN THE BET. DEAL?
UH...
UM...
UM... OK, IT'S A DEAL.
...HOW CAN THAT BE?? THAT MEANS I WAS STILL IN ELEMENTARY SCHOOL WHEN HE STARTED!!
another generation of grad students donates to the slackenerny fund...
copyright © 2002 jorge cham

SIGNS YOU'RE CLOSE TO GRADUATING

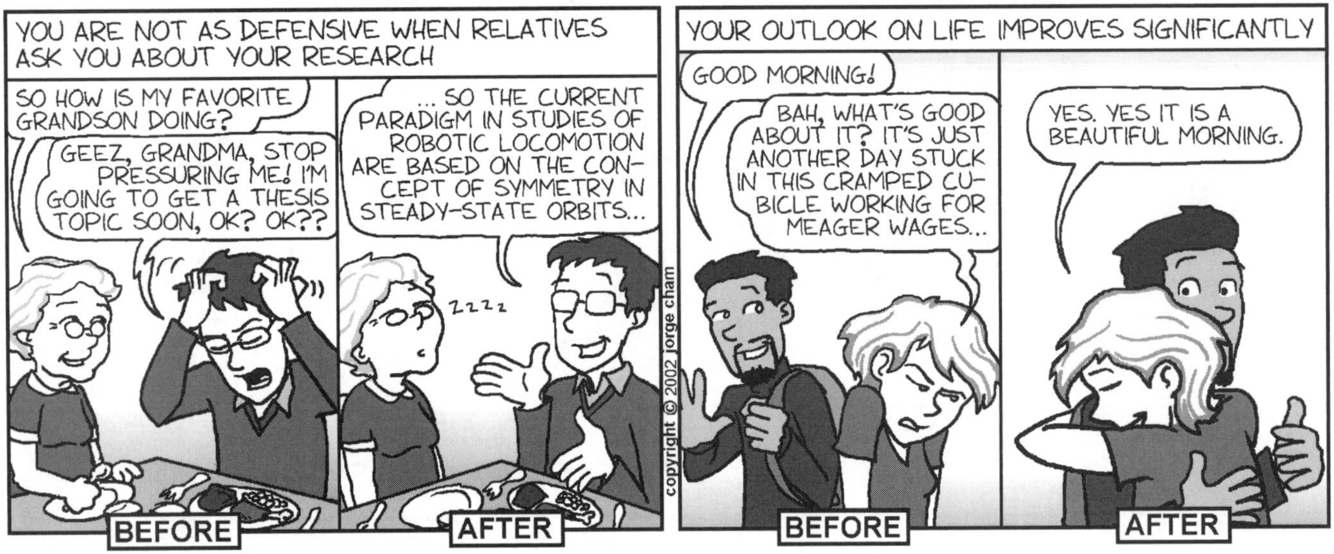
YOU ARE NOT AS DEFENSIVE WHEN RELATIVES ASK YOU ABOUT YOUR RESEARCH
SO HOW IS MY FAVORITE GRANDSON DOING?
GEEZ, GRANDMA, STOP PRESSURING ME! I'M GOING TO GET A THESIS TOPIC SOON, OK? OK??
BEFORE
... SO THE CURRENT PARADIGM IN STUDIES OF ROBOTIC LOCOMOTION ARE BASED ON THE CONCEPT OF SYMMETRY IN STEADY-STATE ORBITS...
ZZZZ
AFTER
copyright © 2002 jorge cham
YOUR OUTLOOK ON LIFE IMPROVES SIGNIFICANTLY
GOOD MORNING!
BAH, WHAT'S GOOD ABOUT IT? IT'S JUST ANOTHER DAY STUCK IN THIS CRAMPED CUBICLE WORKING FOR MEAGER WAGES...
BEFORE
YES. YES IT IS A BEAUTIFUL MORNING.
AFTER

SIGNS YOU'RE CLOSE TO GRADUATING 2

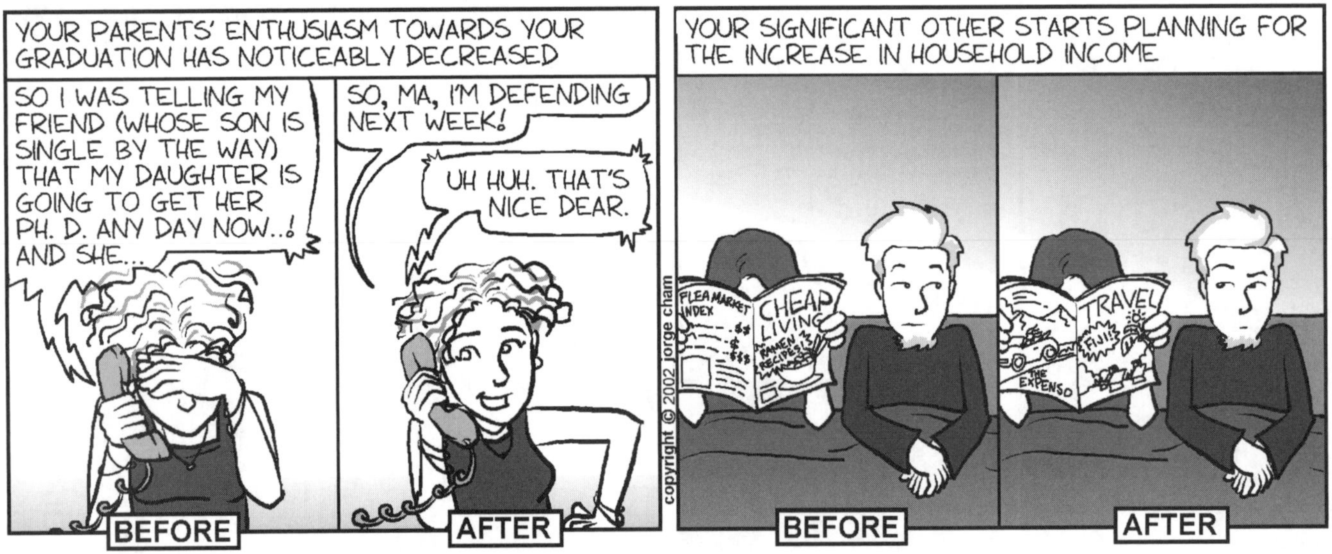
YOUR PARENTS' ENTHUSIASM TOWARDS YOUR GRADUATION HAS NOTICEABLY DECREASED
SO I WAS TELLING MY FRIEND (WHOSE SON IS SINGLE BY THE WAY) THAT MY DAUGHTER IS GOING TO GET HER PH. D. ANY DAY NOW...! AND SHE...
BEFORE
SO, MA, I'M DEFENDING NEXT WEEK!
UH HUH. THAT'S NICE DEAR.
AFTER
copyright © 2002 jorge cham
YOUR SIGNIFICANT OTHER STARTS PLANNING FOR THE INCREASE IN HOUSEHOLD INCOME
FLEA MARKET INDEX
CHEAP LIVING
RAMEN RECIPES
BEFORE
TRAVEL
FIJI!
THE EXPENSO
AFTER

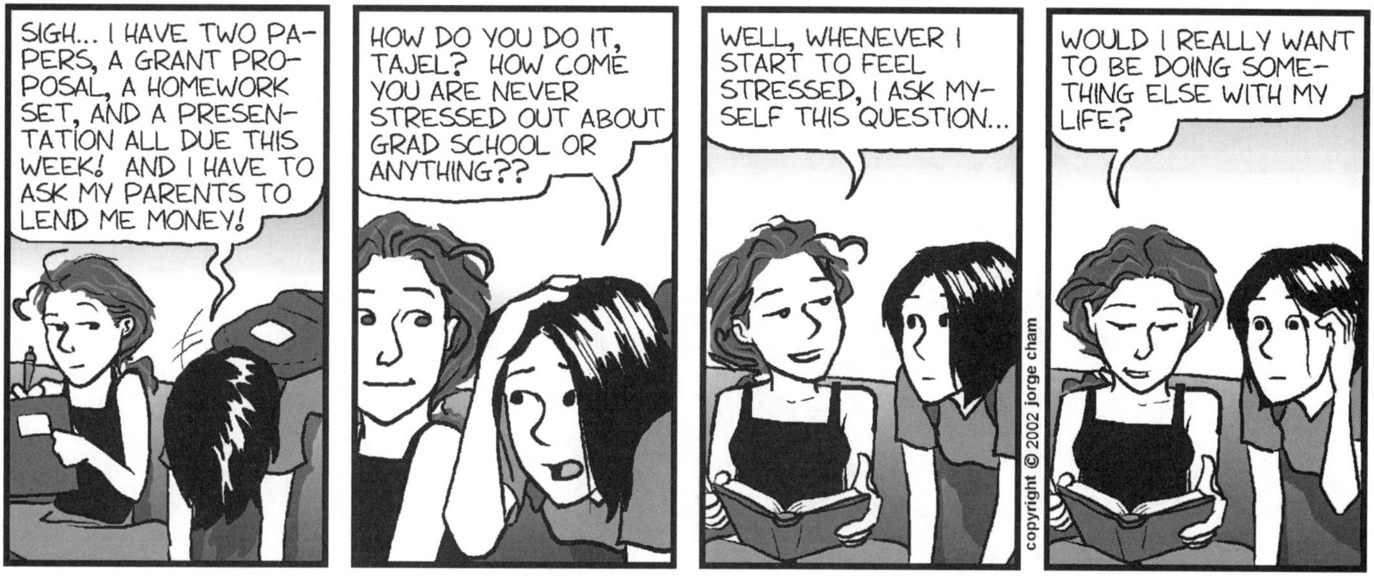
SIGH... I HAVE TWO PAPERS, A GRANT PROPOSAL, A HOMEWORK SET, AND A PRESENTATION ALL DUE THIS WEEK! AND I HAVE TO ASK MY PARENTS TO LEND ME MONEY!
HOW DO YOU DO IT, TAJEL? HOW COME YOU ARE NEVER STRESSED OUT ABOUT GRAD SCHOOL OR ANYTHING??
WELL, WHENEVER I START TO FEEL STRESSED, I ASK MYSELF THIS QUESTION...
WOULD I REALLY WANT TO BE DOING SOMETHING ELSE WITH MY LIFE?
copyright © 2002 jorge cham

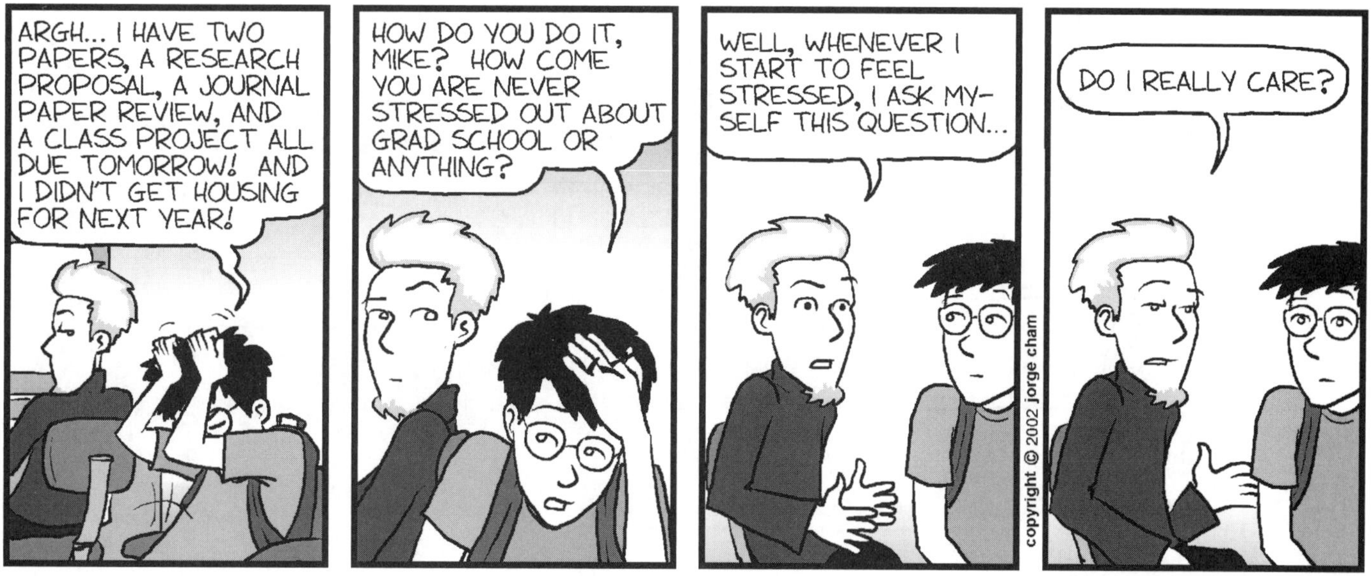
ARGH... I HAVE TWO PAPERS, A RESEARCH PROPOSAL, A JOURNAL PAPER REVIEW, AND A CLASS PROJECT ALL DUE TOMORROW! AND I DIDN'T GET HOUSING FOR NEXT YEAR!
HOW DO YOU DO IT, MIKE? HOW COME YOU ARE NEVER STRESSED OUT ABOUT GRAD SCHOOL OR ANYTHING?
WELL, WHENEVER I START TO FEEL STRESSED, I ASK MYSELF THIS QUESTION...
DO I REALLY CARE?
copyright © 2002 jorge cham

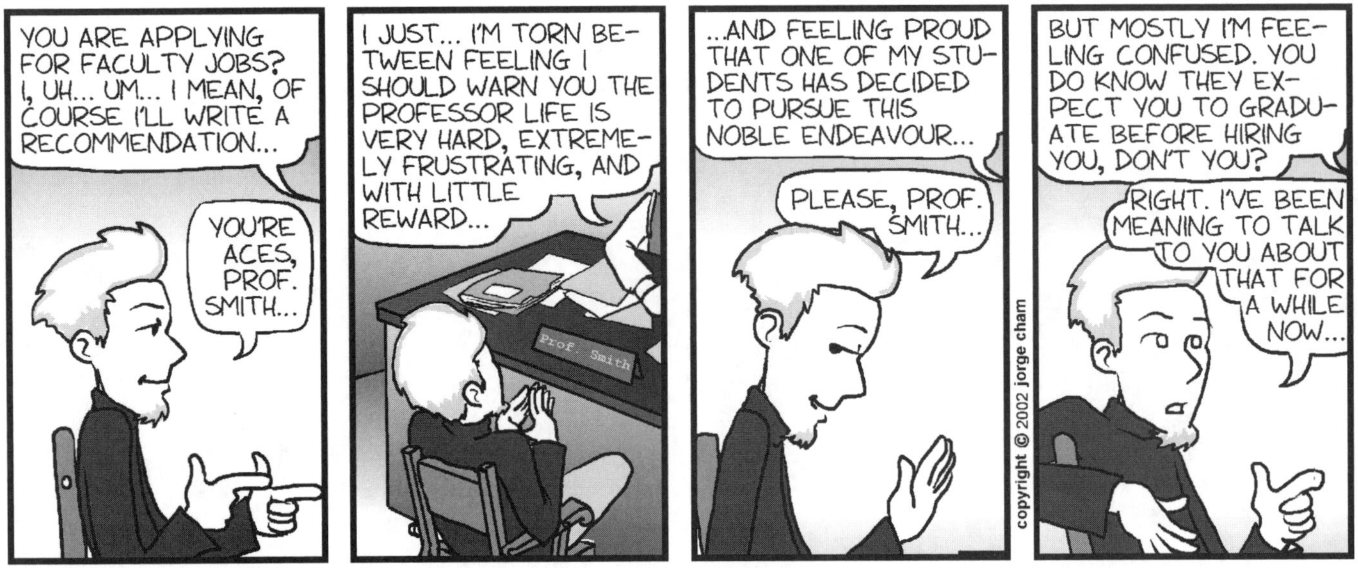
YOU ARE APPLYING FOR FACULTY JOBS? I, UH... UM... I MEAN, OF COURSE I'LL WRITE A RECOMMENDATION...
YOU'RE ACES, PROF. SMITH...
I JUST... I'M TORN BETWEEN FEELING I SHOULD WARN YOU THE PROFESSOR LIFE IS VERY HARD, EXTREMELY FRUSTRATING, AND WITH LITTLE REWARD...
Prof. Smith
...AND FEELING PROUD THAT ONE OF MY STUDENTS HAS DECIDED TO PURSUE THIS NOBLE ENDEAVOUR...
PLEASE, PROF. SMITH...
BUT MOSTLY I'M FEELING CONFUSED. YOU DO KNOW THEY EXPECT YOU TO GRADUATE BEFORE HIRING YOU, DON'T YOU?
RIGHT. I'VE BEEN MEANING TO TALK TO YOU ABOUT THAT FOR A WHILE NOW...
copyright © 2002 jorge cham

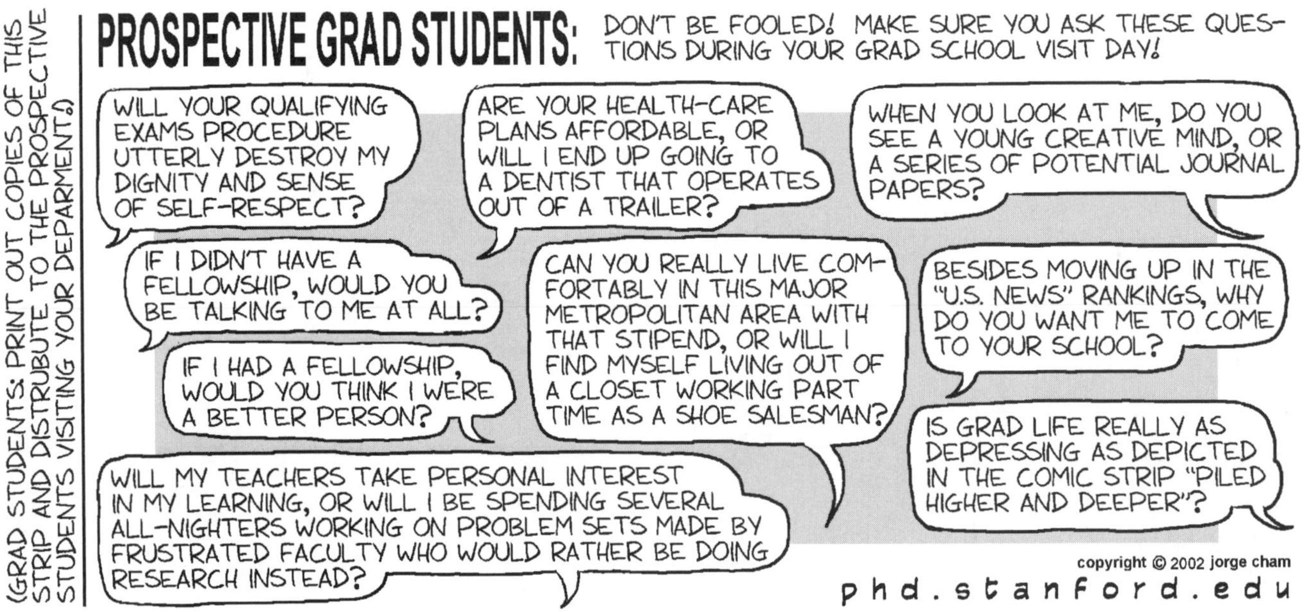
(GRAD STUDENTS: PRINT OUT COPIES OF THIS STRIP AND DISTRUBUTE TO THE PROSPECTIVE STUDENTS VISITING YOUR DEPARMENT.)
PROSPECTIVE GRAD STUDENTS:
DON'T BE FOOLED! MAKE SURE YOU ASK THESE QUESTIONS DURING YOUR GRAD SCHOOL VISIT DAY!
WILL YOUR QUALIFYING EXAMS PROCEDURE UTTERLY DESTROY MY DIGNITY AND SENSE OF SELF-RESPECT?
ARE YOUR HEALTH-CARE PLANS AFFORDABLE, OR WILL I END UP GOING TO A DENTIST THAT OPERATES OUT OF A TRAILER?
WHEN YOU LOOK AT ME, DO YOU SEE A YOUNG CREATIVE MIND, OR A SERIES OF POTENTIAL JOURNAL PAPERS?
IF I DIDN'T HAVE A FELLOWSHIP, WOULD YOU BE TALKING TO ME AT ALL?
IF I HAD A FELLOWSHIP, WOULD YOU THINK I WERE A BETTER PERSON?
CAN YOU REALLY LIVE COMFORTABLY IN THIS MAJOR METROPOLITAN AREA WITH THAT STIPEND, OR WILL I FIND MYSELF LIVING OUT OF A CLOSET WORKING PART TIME AS A SHOE SALESMAN?
BESIDES MOVING UP IN THE "U.S. NEWS" RANKINGS, WHY DO YOU WANT ME TO COME TO YOUR SCHOOL?
IS GRAD LIFE REALLY AS DEPRESSING AS DEPICTED IN THE COMIC STRIP "PILED HIGHER AND DEEPER"?
WILL MY TEACHERS TAKE PERSONAL INTEREST IN MY LEARNING, OR WILL I BE SPENDING SEVERAL ALL-NIGHTERS WORKING ON PROBLEM SETS MADE BY FRUSTRATED FACULTY WHO WOULD RATHER BE DOING RESEARCH INSTEAD?
copyright © 2002 jorge cham
phd.stanford.edu

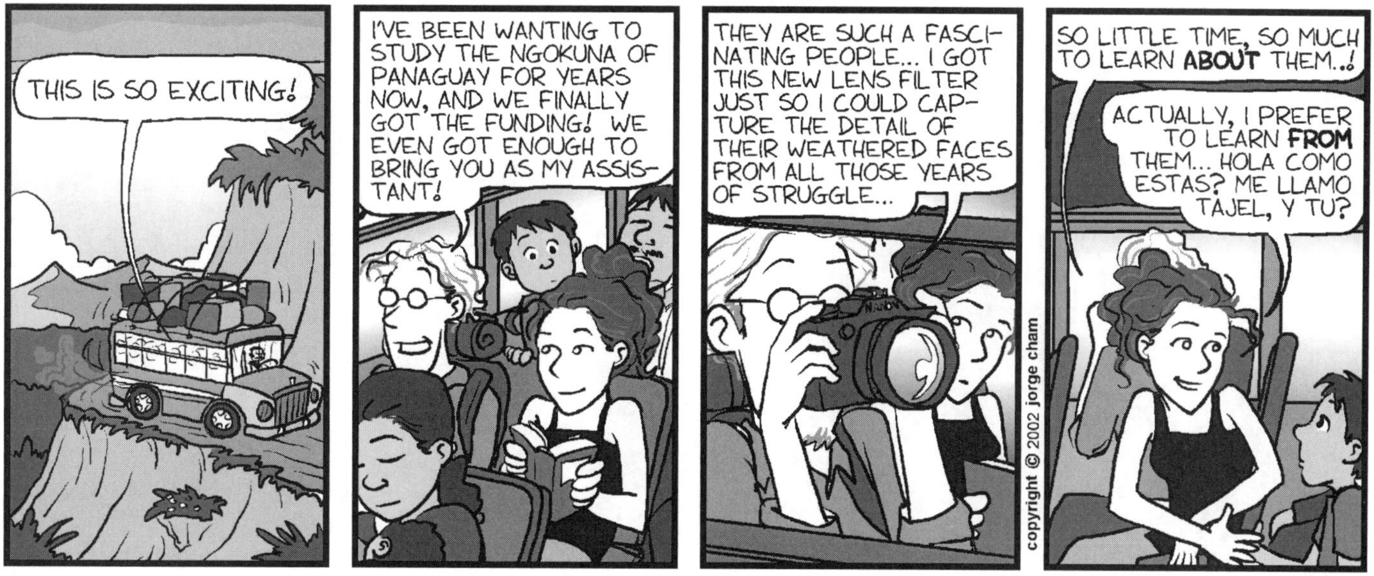
THIS IS SO EXCITING!
I'VE BEEN WANTING TO STUDY THE NGOKUNA OF PANAGUAY FOR YEARS NOW, AND WE FINALLY GOT THE FUNDING! WE EVEN GOT ENOUGH TO BRING YOU AS MY ASSISTANT!
THEY ARE SUCH A FASCINATING PEOPLE... I GOT THIS NEW LENS FILTER JUST SO I COULD CAPTURE THE DETAIL OF THEIR WEATHERED FACES FROM ALL THOSE YEARS OF STRUGGLE...
copyright © 2002 jorge cham
SO LITTLE TIME, SO MUCH TO LEARN ABOUT THEM..!
ACTUALLY, I PREFER TO LEARN FROM THEM... HOLA COMO ESTAS? ME LLAMO TAJEL, Y TU?

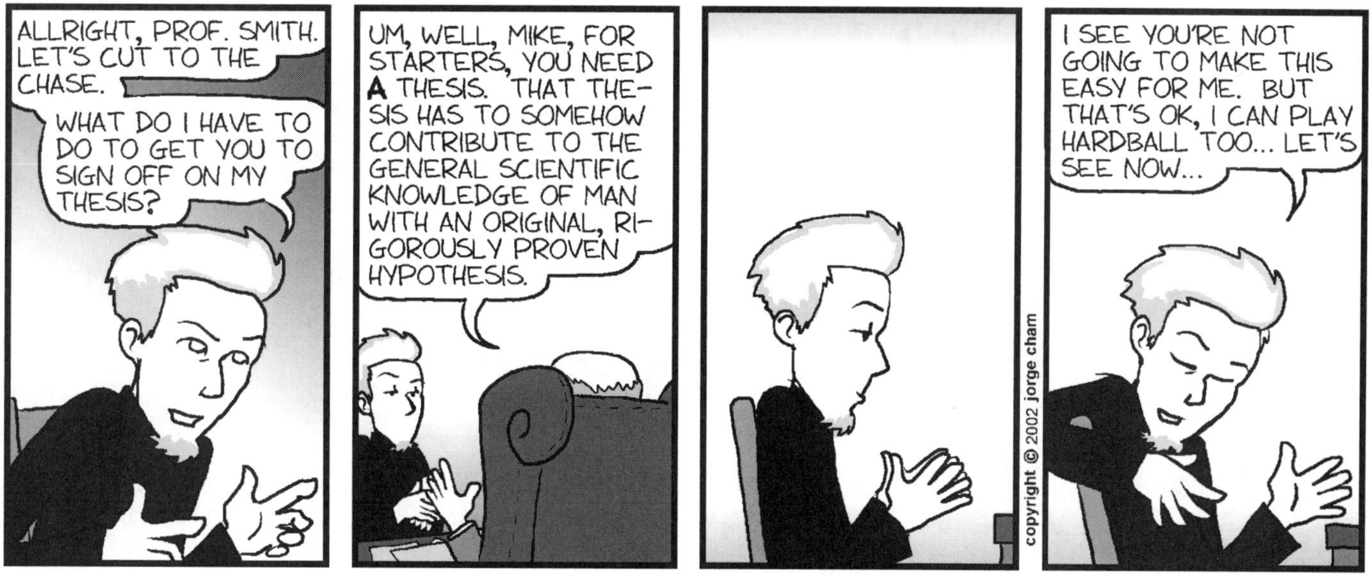
ALLRIGHT, PROF. SMITH. LET'S CUT TO THE CHASE.
WHAT DO I HAVE TO DO TO GET YOU TO SIGN OFF ON MY THESIS?
UM, WELL, MIKE, FOR STARTERS, YOU NEED A THESIS. THAT THESIS HAS TO SOMEHOW CONTRIBUTE TO THE GENERAL SCIENTIFIC KNOWLEDGE OF MAN WITH AN ORIGINAL, RIGOROUSLY PROVEN HYPOTHESIS.
copyright © 2002 jorge cham
I SEE YOU'RE NOT GOING TO MAKE THIS EASY FOR ME. BUT THAT'S OK, I CAN PLAY HARDBALL TOO... LET'S SEE NOW...

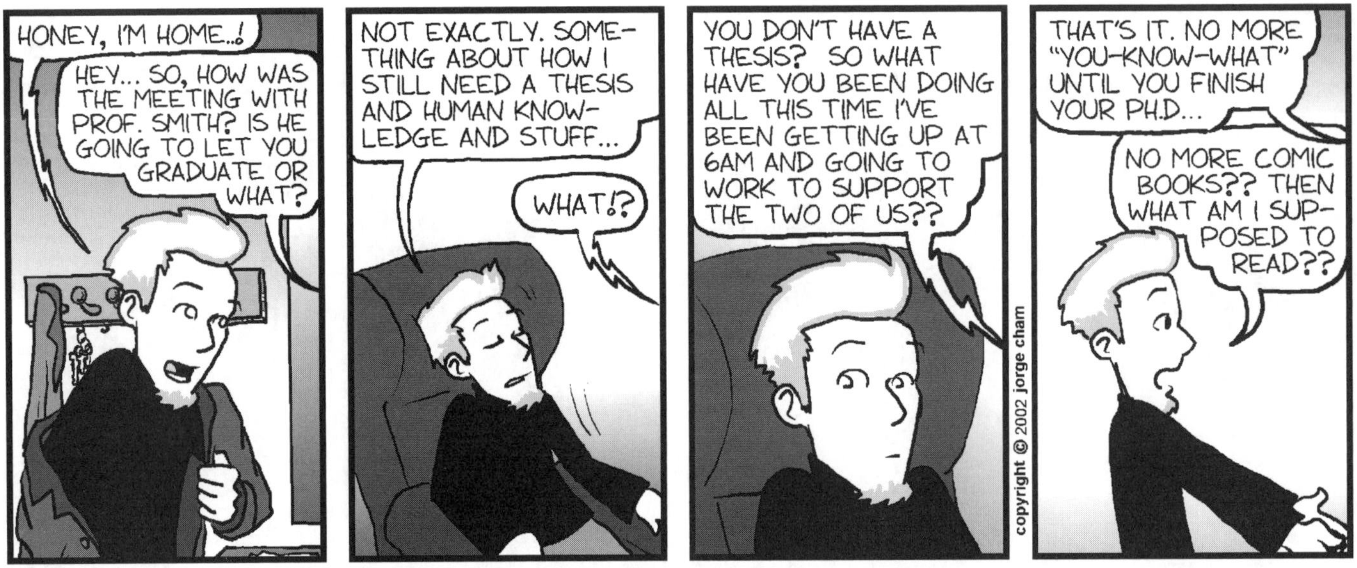
HONEY, I'M HOME..!
HEY... SO, HOW WAS THE MEETING WITH PROF. SMITH? IS HE GOING TO LET YOU GRADUATE OR WHAT?
NOT EXACTLY. SOME-THING ABOUT HOW I STILL NEED A THESIS AND HUMAN KNOW-LEDGE AND STUFF...
WHAT!?
YOU DON'T HAVE A THESIS? SO WHAT HAVE YOU BEEN DOING ALL THIS TIME I'VE BEEN GETTING UP AT 6AM AND GOING TO WORK TO SUPPORT THE TWO OF US??
copyright © 2002 jorge cham
THAT'S IT. NO MORE "YOU-KNOW-WHAT" UNTIL YOU FINISH YOUR PH.D...
NO MORE COMIC BOOKS?? THEN WHAT AM I SUP-POSED TO READ??

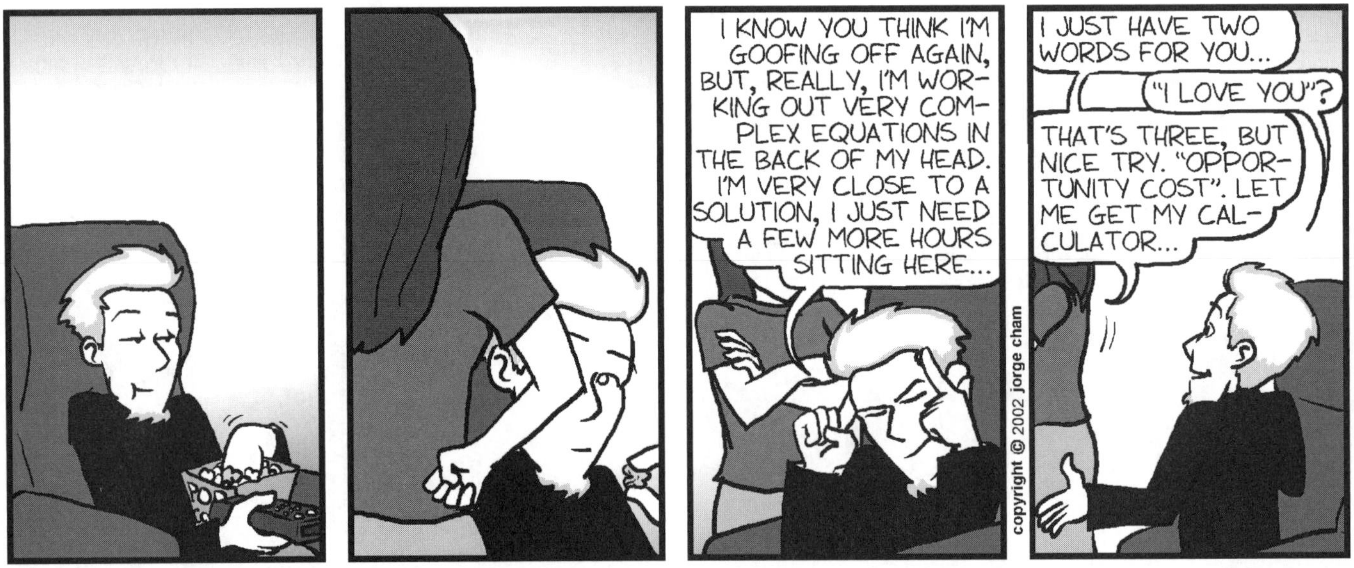
I KNOW YOU THINK I'M GOOFING OFF AGAIN, BUT, REALLY, I'M WOR-KING OUT VERY COM-PLEX EQUATIONS IN THE BACK OF MY HEAD. I'M VERY CLOSE TO A SOLUTION, I JUST NEED A FEW MORE HOURS SITTING HERE...
copyright © 2002 jorge cham
I JUST HAVE TWO WORDS FOR YOU...
"I LOVE YOU"?
THAT'S THREE, BUT NICE TRY. "OPPOR-TUNITY COST". LET ME GET MY CAL-CULATOR...

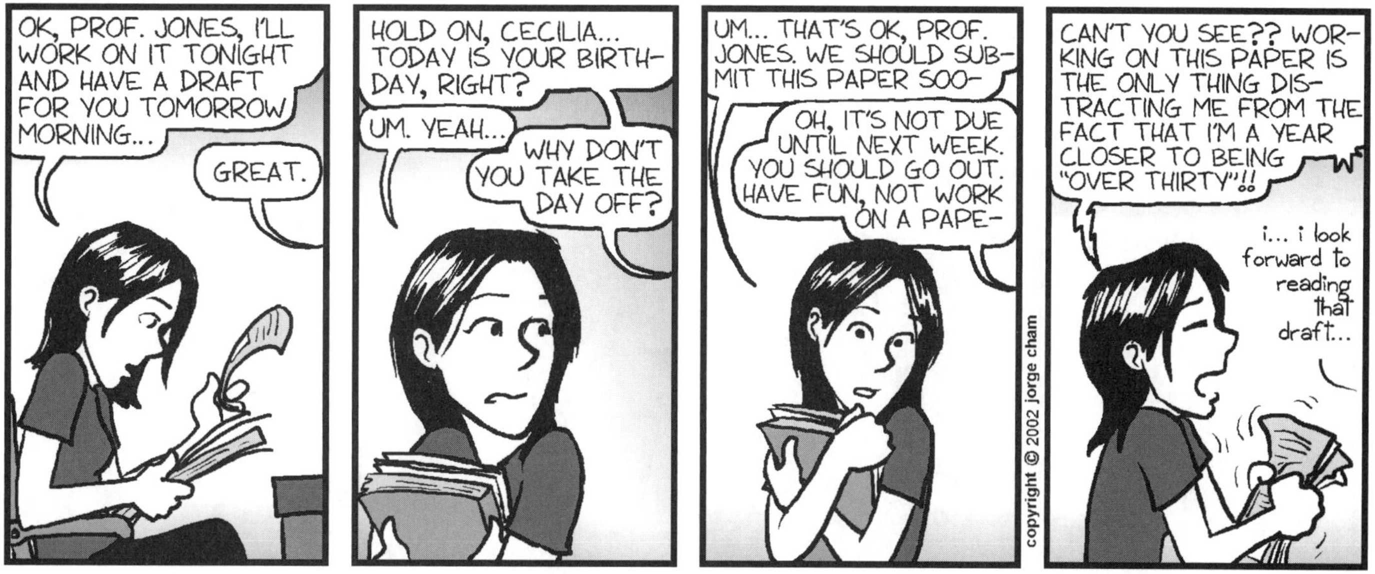
OK, PROF. JONES, I'LL WORK ON IT TONIGHT AND HAVE A DRAFT FOR YOU TOMORROW MORNING...
GREAT.
HOLD ON, CECILIA... TODAY IS YOUR BIRTHDAY, RIGHT?
UM. YEAH...
WHY DON'T YOU TAKE THE DAY OFF?
UM... THAT'S OK, PROF. JONES. WE SHOULD SUBMIT THIS PAPER SOO-
OH, IT'S NOT DUE UNTIL NEXT WEEK. YOU SHOULD GO OUT. HAVE FUN, NOT WORK ON A PAPE-
copyright © 2002 jorge cham
CAN'T YOU SEE?? WORKING ON THIS PAPER IS THE ONLY THING DISTRACTING ME FROM THE FACT THAT I'M A YEAR CLOSER TO BEING "OVER THIRTY"!!
i... i look forward to reading that draft...

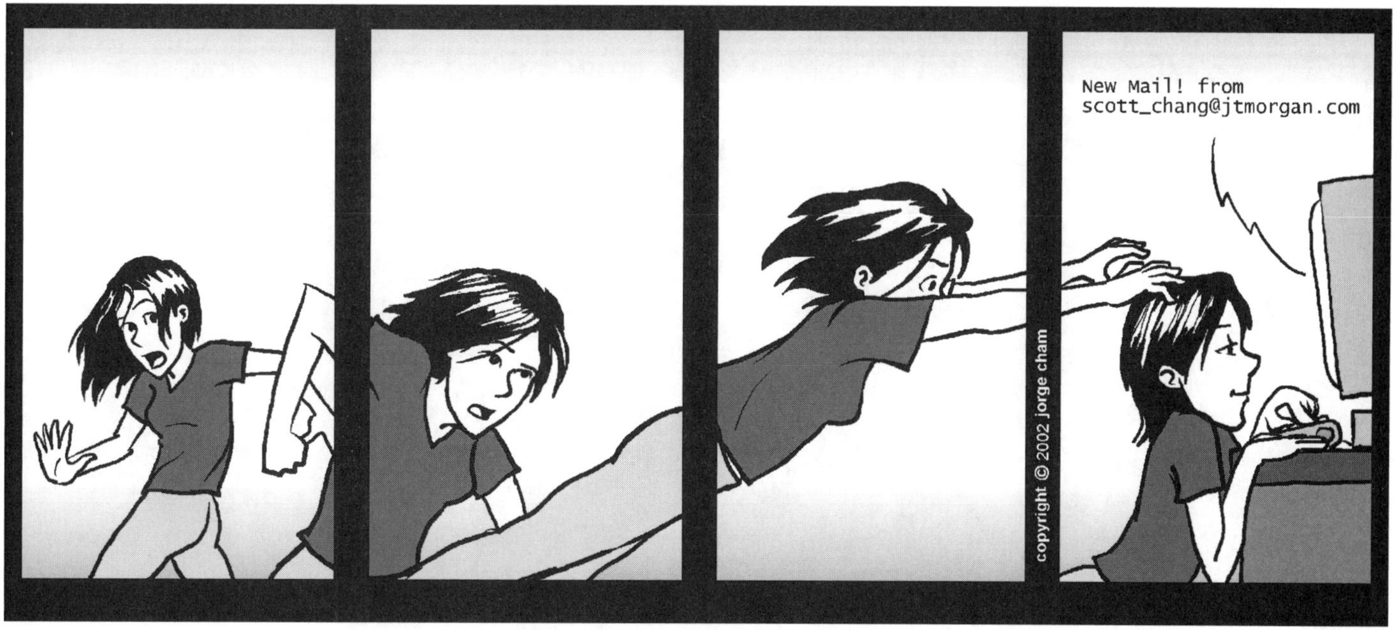
copyright © 2002 jorge cham
New Mail! from
scott_chang@jtmorgan.com

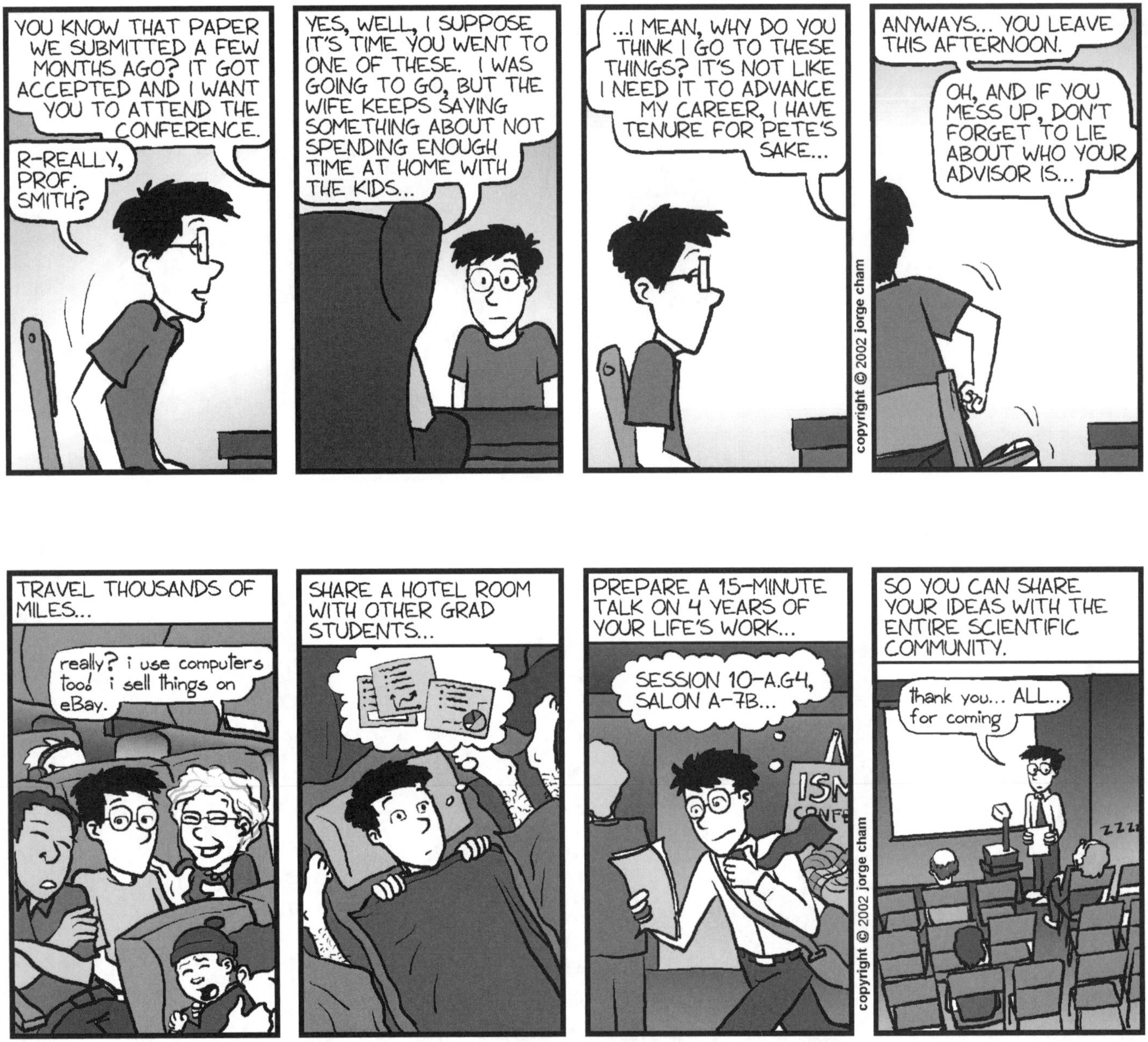
YOU KNOW THAT PAPER WE SUBMITTED A FEW MONTHS AGO? IT GOT ACCEPTED AND I WANT YOU TO ATTEND THE CONFERENCE.
R-REALLY, PROF. SMITH?
YES, WELL, I SUPPOSE IT'S TIME YOU WENT TO ONE OF THESE. I WAS GOING TO GO, BUT THE WIFE KEEPS SAYING SOMETHING ABOUT NOT SPENDING ENOUGH TIME AT HOME WITH THE KIDS...
...I MEAN, WHY DO YOU THINK I GO TO THESE THINGS? IT'S NOT LIKE I NEED IT TO ADVANCE MY CAREER, I HAVE TENURE FOR PETE'S SAKE...
copyright © 2002 jorge cham
ANYWAYS... YOU LEAVE THIS AFTERNOON.
OH, AND IF YOU MESS UP, DON'T FORGET TO LIE ABOUT WHO YOUR ADVISOR IS...
TRAVEL THOUSANDS OF MILES...
really? i use computers too! i sell things on eBay.
SHARE A HOTEL ROOM WITH OTHER GRAD STUDENTS...
PREPARE A 15-MINUTE TALK ON 4 YEARS OF YOUR LIFE'S WORK...
SESSION 10-A.G4, SALON A-7B...
copyright © 2002 jorge cham
SO YOU CAN SHARE YOUR IDEAS WITH THE ENTIRE SCIENTIFIC COMMUNITY.
thank you... ALL... for coming
ZZZZ

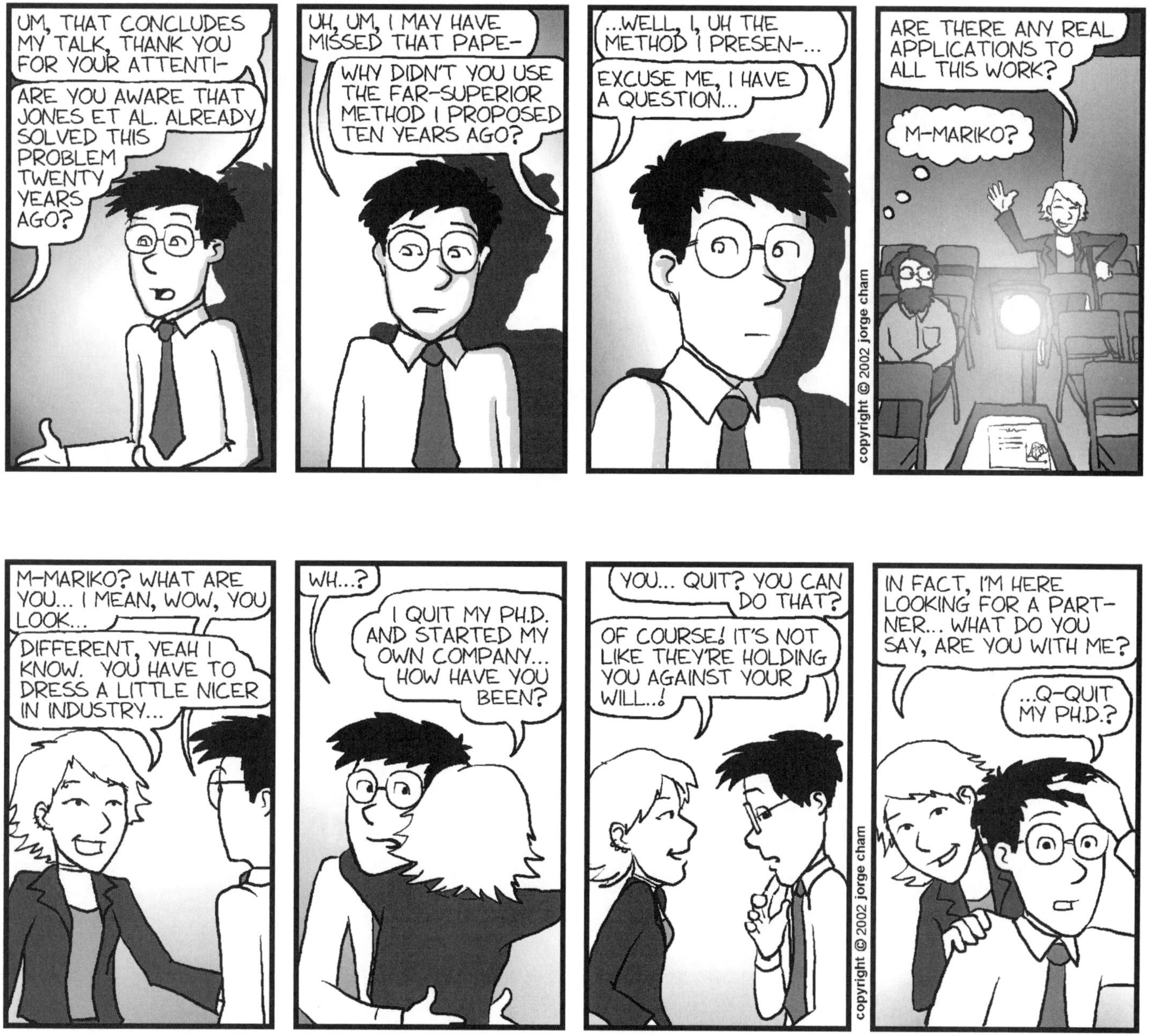
UM, THAT CONCLUDES MY TALK, THANK YOU FOR YOUR ATTENTI-
ARE YOU AWARE THAT JONES ET AL. ALREADY SOLVED THIS PROBLEM TWENTY YEARS AGO?
UH, UM, I MAY HAVE MISSED THAT PAPE-
WHY DIDN'T YOU USE THE FAR-SUPERIOR METHOD I PROPOSED TEN YEARS AGO?
...WELL, I, UH THE METHOD I PRESEN-...
EXCUSE ME, I HAVE A QUESTION...
ARE THERE ANY REAL APPLICATIONS TO ALL THIS WORK?
M-MARIKO?
copyright © 2002 jorge cham
M-MARIKO? WHAT ARE YOU... I MEAN, WOW, YOU LOOK...
DIFFERENT, YEAH I KNOW. YOU HAVE TO DRESS A LITTLE NICER IN INDUSTRY...
WH...?
I QUIT MY PH.D. AND STARTED MY OWN COMPANY... HOW HAVE YOU BEEN?
YOU... QUIT? YOU CAN DO THAT?
OF COURSE! IT'S NOT LIKE THEY'RE HOLDING YOU AGAINST YOUR WILL...!
copyright © 2002 jorge cham
IN FACT, I'M HERE LOOKING FOR A PARTNER... WHAT DO YOU SAY, ARE YOU WITH ME?
...Q-QUIT MY PH.D.?

OH, HI MOM... UH-HUH... YES... I DON'T KNOW... UH-HUH... EVERYTHING'S FINE... UH-HUH...
...UH-WHAT? WHAT AM I DOING AFTER GRADUATION? UH... I GUESS I HAVEN'T THOUGHT ABOUT IT TOO MUCH...
UM...
ACTUALLY, MOM, I'VE BEEN THINKING ABOUT GOING TO GRAD SCHOOL...
copyright © 2002 jorge cham

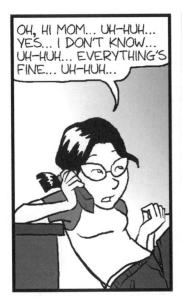

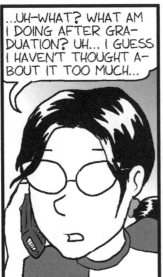

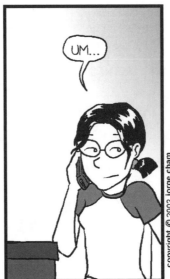

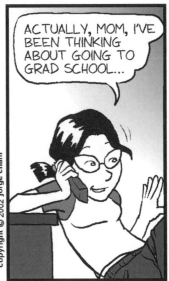

Afterword
by Prof. Smith

When the publishers of this book approached me to write the afterword for a compilation of work by one of the most brilliant researchers of our time, I told them I would be honored. When they explained that it was a collection of some comic strip by some unknown grad student, I called campus security. But by then it was too late. My secretary had already rearranged my schedule and I found myself only double-booked for this time slot, which is not enough to maintain my significant intellect occupied, and so here we are. (Plus, I am told I can list this as a "mentoring" activity in my year-end review to the department chair).

In any case, flipping through the pages of this book while pretending to listen to a student (he's sitting in front of me, yammering away, probably under the impression I'm taking notes as I write this), I can't help but feel a small shiver of nostalgia for my graduate years.

Yes, that's right, professors were once students too. Many students forget this fact. The cyclical nature of teaching and learning is one of the most enduring and rewarding aspects of academia (here's something to keep you awake in class: which came first, the advisor or the student?). Of course, the quality of grad students has dropped significantly since my time. Grad students today are soft. Case in point: this comic strip.

All this complaining about housing, stipends, quals, a social life... You'd think grad school was this horrible, torturous experience made inadvertently by universities. In fact, that's the whole point. You've got to suffer for your science. Misery breeds discontent, and discontent breeds good thesis topics. Some may argue that you don't have to fail to succeed or feel pain to learn, but without the fear of failure, what else will keep you motivated? Without humiliation, how will you gain the necessary humility to become great faculty such as myself?

Anyways, it looks like the student in front of me is nearly done. Time for me to give him some signal that I was actually paying attention. I'll give him a long, thoughtful "Hmm…" and then say something standard like, "Have you looked at the second order correlation equations?" That should keep him busy for a while.

-Prof. B. Smith, Ph.D.

Author Notes

Page 10, bottom: I started at Stanford the same year as President Clinton's daughter, which is what this strip refers to. A common game around that time was "Can you spot the Secret Service agents?" My fourth year there, she attended a poster session put up by my department and I gave her the 5 minute spiel of my research. I think she nodded politely and moved on to the next poster.

Page 28, top: My first year in California was an El Niño year. That winter it rained non-stop for three straight months (I kid you not). Weather played a big part in my decision to go to Stanford (re: page 35, bottom), so it seemed like a bad omen.

Page 32, bottom: This is still one of the most popular PHD strips ever.

Page 41, bottom: Housing was a big issue in those days. The dot com boom drove off-campus housing prices through the roof, so students were really struggling. Even today, I still hear horror stories from people who lived in The Manzanita Park plastic trailers or the Cro-Mem dorm (page 51, top). The Grad Student Council organized protests (page 63) and staged a huge camp-out in the main quad (page 42, top) that drew the attention of the local media.

Page 46, top: That Thursday was the last episode of Seinfeld.

Page 58: When you become a grad student, undergrad issues and traditions suddenly seem silly.

Page 89, top: Kurt Vonnegut didn't actually write this. At the time, a popular e-mail forwarded around was the "Wear Sunscreen" essay (look it up in Wikipedia) that was actually written by a Chicago Tribune columnist.

Page 111: These are the graphic placeholders for two songs recorded by "Tajel". If you go to the website www.phdcomics.com, you can download the .mp3's.

Page 124, top: The last photo is actually of Manuel Amador Guerrero, the first President of Panama (my home country).

Page 127: The seed for Newton's Laws of Graduation I attribute to my roommate, Wes, who made a comment once about the ratio of flexibility and motivation. I still find it hard to believe that is actually works out to be $F=mA$.

Page 142: This is a take on classic covers for Archie Comics, which had a big influence on me growing up.

Page 143, top: This was my response to 9/11. News reached the West Coast as the sun was coming up.

Page 143, bottom: I re-created this scene exactly as it happened with my roomate. Try it, it's true.

Sketches

Illustration for
Summer Break
2001 place-
holder